Inside Writing

A Writer's Workbook
With Readings

Form B

Fourth Edition

English 50
a class that everyone
should take, it is a must
to become a good writer

William Salomone
Palomar College

Stephen McDonald
Palomar College

Harcourt College Publishers

Fort Worth   Philadelphia   San Diego   New York   Orlando   Austin   San Antonio
Toronto   Montreal   London   Sydney   Tokyo

Publisher   Earl McPeek
Acquisitions Editor   Stephen Dalphin
Marketing Strategist   John Meyers
Developmental Editor   Jill Johnson
Project Manager   Angela Williams Urquhart

Cover image © PhotoDisc, Inc.
Cover design by Jane Tenenbaum Design.

ISBN: 0-15-506330-8
Library of Congress Catalog Card Number: 00-134555

Address for Domestic Orders
Harcourt College Publishers, 6277 Sea Harbor Drive, Orlando, FL 32887-6777
800-782-4479

Address for International Orders
International Customer Service
Harcourt College Publishers, 6277 Sea Harbor Drive, Orlando, FL 32887-6777
407-345-3800
(fax) 407-345-4060
(e-mail) hbintl@harcourtbrace.com

Address for Editorial Correspondence
Harcourt College Publishers, 301 Commerce Street, Suite 3700, Fort Worth, TX 76102

Web Site Address
http://www.harcourtcollege.com

Harcourt College Publishers will provide complimentary supplements or supplement packages to those adopters qualified under our adoption policy. Please contact your sales representative to learn how you qualify. If as an adopter or potential user you receive supplements you do not need, please return them to your sales representative or send them to:
Attn: Returns Department, Troy Warehouse, 465 South Lincoln Drive, Troy, MO 63379.

Printed in the United States of America

0 1 2 3 4 5 6 7 8 9   048   9 8 7 6 5 4 3 2 1

Harcourt College Publishers

check this out 5/14/01 —
SAN D library on Euclie. Av —

College
Credit
with out Classes - by James L
Carroll
Central Michigan
University
3-1336-05 012 62 76

To Rosemary and Marlyle

Contents

Chapter Five Using Punctuation and Capitalization 255

Chapter Six   Choosing the Right Words and Spelling Them Correctly 317

Chapter Seven Readings for Writers 377

Preface

Inside Writing was constructed on the premise that there is really only one reason for learning the essential rules of English grammar—to become better writers. In this text, we constantly stress that all college students are writers and that the aim of any college writing course—developmental or otherwise—is to improve writing. To this purpose, *Inside Writing* has been created with clear and simple organization, a friendly, nonthreatening tone, thorough integration of grammar sections with writing sections, and unique thematic exercises.

The Reason for This Text

We are all aware of widespread disagreement about what should be presented in a first-semester developmental writing course. *Inside Writing* was written to address the resulting diversity of course content with a union of grammar and writing instruction. In it, we teach basic grammar and sentence structure, yet we also provide extensive practice in sentence combining and paragraph writing.

Moving Beyond a Traditional Approach. The traditional approach to developmental writing has been to review the rules of grammar, punctuation, and usage and then to test the students' understanding of those rules through a series of chapter tests. However, as research and experience have demonstrated, there is no necessary correlation between the study of grammar and the development of competent writers. As a result, many English departments have restructured their developmental courses to focus on the process of writing, developing courses that have very little in common with each other from one campus to the next. Today, some developmental writing instructors teach the traditional exercises in grammar, others focus on journal and expressive writing, others emphasize sentence combining, and still others teach the writing of paragraphs and short essays.

Using an Integrated Approach. Inside Writing responds to this spectrum of course content by integrating grammar instruction and writing practice. Certainly the practice of writing is important in a first-semester developmental class. Yet the study of traditional grammar, punctuation, and usage is also important because it provides a fundamental knowledge of sentence structure—knowledge that writers need not only to revise their own writing but also to discuss their writing with others. The writing practices in this text are specifically designed to support, not merely to supplement, the grammar instruction. As soon as students have mastered a particular grammatical principle, they are asked to put their knowledge into practice in the writing sections of each chapter. This immediate reinforcement makes it more likely that students will improve their writing as well as retain the rules of grammar, usage, and mechanics.

Text Organization and Features

Inside Writing, Form B, is presented in seven chapters and an appendix. Each of the first six chapters consists of five sections that cover major principles of basic grammar, sentence construction, and paragraph writing. The text keeps this instruction as simple as possible, giving the students only the information that is absolutely essential. The seventh chapter includes eighteen reading selections to accompany the writing instruction in the first six chapters.

- Each chapter's grammar instruction is broken into three sections so that the students are not presented with too much at once.

- Each of the three grammar sections includes various practices and ends with three exercises that give the students an opportunity to apply the concepts and rules they have learned.

- Each chapter is followed by a practice test covering the material presented in the first three sections of the chapter, and the text closes with a practice final examination.

- The fourth section of each chapter presents both instruction and exercises in sentence combining, based on the specific concepts and rules covered in the three grammar sections. For example, in the chapter covering participial phrases and adjective clauses, the sentence-combining section instructs the students to combine sentences by using participial phrases and adjective clauses.

- The fifth section of each chapter includes instruction in writing and a choice of several writing assignments, again designed to reinforce the grammar sections of the chapter by leading students to employ in their own writing the rules for sentence structure they have studied.

- The seventh chapter, "Readings for Writers," offers eighteen reading selections that parallel the writing instruction in each of the first six chapters.

- The appendix, "Moving from Paragraph to Essay," allows instructors to include essay writing in their courses if they wish.

- At the end of the text, answers to the practices—but not to the exercises—are provided. These answers allow the students to check their understanding of the material as they read the text. The extensive exercises without answers permit the instructor to determine where more explanation or study is needed.

- Many of the practices and exercises develop thematic ideas or contain a variety of cultural, mythological, and historical allusions. Some exercises, for example, explain the body's flight-or-fight reaction, tell the story of Rosa Parks, or examine modern versions of *Romeo and Juliet* and *Cyrano de Bergerac.* In addition, individual sentences within practices and exercises often provoke questions and discussion when they refer to characters and events from history, mythology, or contemporary culture. This feature of *Inside Writing* encourages developmental writing students to look beyond grammar, mechanics, and punctuation. It reminds them—or it allows us as instructors to remind them—that the educated writer has command of much more than the correct use of the comma.

Connecting Concepts and Writing Practice. To emphasize further the connection between the writing assignments and the grammar exercises, the writing assignment in each chapter is modeled by three thematic exercises within the grammar sections of the chapter. For instance, in Chapter 3, Exercises 1C, 2C, and 3C are paragraphs that use examples to support a statement made in a topic sentence. The writing practice section then extends this groundwork by presenting instruction in the writing of a similar expository paragraph.

As each paragraph is assigned, the students are introduced gradually to the writing process and encouraged to improve their writing through prewriting and careful revision. They are also introduced to the basic concepts of paragraph writing—topic sentences, unity, specificity, completeness, order, and coherence. However, the main purpose of the writing instruction is to give the students an opportunity to use their new knowledge of grammar and sentence structure to communicate their own thoughts and ideas. If the instructor wishes to go beyond paragraph writing, he or she can use the appendix, entitled "Moving from Paragraph to Essay," which presents a brief discussion of essay form. In this appendix, some of the thematic paragraphs are rewritten as short essays.

Changes to This Edition

We have improved this Fourth Edition of *Inside Writing, Form B*, in several areas.

- We have added eighteen reading selections in a new chapter entitled "Readings for Writers." The selections are divided into six rhetorical modes to match the assignments in each of the six writing sections of the text. These reading selections reflect the diversity of students as well as introduce students to several of the wide-ranging social and cultural issues of today.

- We have made substantial changes to strengthen the paragraph-writing section of each chapter (Section 5). Each writing section now includes a sample student paragraph and several "applications" designed to guide the student through the writing process. Chapter 1, for example, now includes the following material: "Prewriting Application: Finding Your Topic" (ten suggestions); "Prewriting Application: Talking to Others" (an exercise in generating ideas); "Prewriting Application: Working with Topic Sentences" (five sentences); "Prewriting Application: Evaluating Topic Sentences" (ten sentences); "Writing Application: Producing Your First Draft"; "Rewriting Application: Responding to Writing" (an evaluation of a sample paragraph); "Rewriting Application: Revising and Editing Your Own Draft."

- We have moved the topic sentence instruction from Chapter 2 (Section 5) to Chapter 1 (Section 5).

- We have added more thematically related practices and exercises throughout the text. In Chapter 1 we have included material about Pyramus and Thisbe, the African American holiday of Juneteenth, Poon Lim's 133 days in a life raft, and Nicholas Alkamade's 18,000-foot fall. In Chapter 2 we have included practices and exercises about London Bridge, the Minotaur, Shakespeare's theater, and Mount Rushmore.

- In addition to the thematically related material, we have added more single-sentence allusions within the practices and exercises throughout the text. For example, in Section 1 of Chapter 1 are references to all of the following: Hester Prynne, Alice in Wonderland, the Loch Ness monster, Gulliver, the Cyclops, Pinnochio, General Burnside, Scrooge, Amelia Earhart, Satchmo, Freud, the Trojan War, Utopia, Galileo, Jesse Owens, Ichabod Crane, Mark Antony, the Wizard of Oz, the Montagues and Capulets, the Hatfields and McCoys, Don Quixote, and Julius Caesar.

  Many instructors use these allusions as part of their classes, asking students if they know what they refer to, or, if a joke is involved, whether or not they get the joke. Here's an example from page 4: "Gulliver was horrified when he discovered the Web site for *Yahoo!* on his new computer." Instructors can use this sentence as they would any other sentence in the practice (underlining nouns), or they can stop for a moment and ask if anyone knows who Gulliver was. A few students at this class level will have heard of him, but not many. An interesting follow-up question is to ask those who recognized Gulliver why he would be horrified by the *Yahoo!* Web site. Many allusions, of course, are more serious: "Amelia Earhart disappeared over the Pacific Ocean in 1937." The point is that such allusions provide a depth of content and often a lighthearted tone that go beyond the rote recitation of practices and exercises.

- We have rewritten more than 50 percent of all practices, exercises, and practice tests.

- We have simplified the spelling section in Chapter 6, Section 3, to make the basic rules of spelling more accessible to the student.

An Exceptional Support Package

The Instructor's Manual provides suggestions for how to use the text, answers to the exercises, diagnostic and achievement tests, a series of six chapter tests and six alternate chapter tests, a final examination, answers to the tests and final examination, additional writing assignments, and model paragraphs. With this material, the instructor can use a traditional lecture approach, working through each chapter and then testing the students together, or the instructor can allow the students to work through the book at their own pace, dealing with the students' questions individually and giving students tests as they complete each chapter.

This text is available in an alternate version, "Form A," for added teaching flexibility.

Acknowledgments

We thank our friends and colleagues in the English Department at Palomar College. As usual, we owe a particular debt of gratitude to Jack Quintero, whose observations, gentle criticism, and encouragement have made *Inside Writing* a better text with each edition.

We also wish to thank Stephen Dalphin of Harcourt College Publishers, who helped to make what could have been an awkward move from one publisher to another a painless—even a pleasant—experience. We extend our thanks also to Kim Johnson, who tirelessly helped us track down missing permission requests, and to Kate Thompson, who was not surprised at all that we were late with our work one more time. Finally, of course, we thank our families for their patience and support as we once again worked late into the night.

Naming the Parts

Let's face it. Few people find grammar a fascinating subject, and few study it of their own free will. Most people study grammar only when they are absolutely required to do so. Many seem to feel that grammar is either endlessly complicated or not important to their daily lives.

The problem is not that people fail to appreciate the importance of writing. The ability to express oneself clearly on paper is generally recognized as an important advantage. Those who can communicate their ideas and feelings effectively have a much greater chance to develop themselves, not only professionally but personally as well.

Perhaps the negative attitude toward grammar is due in part to the suspicion that studying grammar has little to do with learning how to write. This suspicion is not at all unreasonable—a knowledge of grammar by itself will not make anyone a better writer. To become a better writer, a person should study *writing* and practice it frequently.

However, the study of writing is much easier if one understands grammar. Certainly a person can learn to write well without knowing exactly how sentences are put together or what the various parts are called. But most competent writers do know these things because such knowledge enables them not only to develop their skills more easily but also to analyze their writing and discuss it with others.

Doctors, for example, don't necessarily have to know the names of the tools they use (stethoscope, scalpel, sutures), nor do mechanics have to know the names of their tools (wrench, screwdriver, ratchet). But it would be hard to find competent doctors or mechanics who were not thoroughly familiar with the tools of their trades, for it is much more difficult to master any important skill and also more difficult to discuss that skill without such knowledge.

The terms and concepts you encounter in this chapter are familiar to most of you but probably not familiar enough. It is not good enough to have a vague idea of what a linking verb is or a general notion of what a prepositional phrase is. You should know *precisely* what these terms mean. This chapter and subsequent chapters present only what is basic and necessary to the study of grammar, but it is essential that you learn *all* of what is presented.

A sound understanding of grammar, like a brick wall, must be built one level at a time. You cannot miss a level and go on to the next. If you master each level as it is presented, you will find that grammar is neither as difficult nor as complicated as you may have thought. You will also find, as you work through the writing sections of the text, that by applying your knowledge of grammar you can greatly improve your writing skills.

Subjects and Verbs

Of all the terms presented in this chapter, perhaps the most important are **SUBJECT** and **VERB**, for subjects and verbs are the foundation of every sentence. Sentences come in many forms, and the structures may become quite complex, but they all have one thing in common: Every sentence must contain a SUBJECT and a VERB. Like most grammatical rules, this one is based on simple logic. After all, without a subject you have nothing to write about, and without a verb you have nothing to say about your subject.

Subjects: Nouns and Pronouns

noun

A noun names a person, place, thing, or idea.

Before you can find the subject of a sentence, you need to be able to identify nouns and pronouns because the subjects of sentences will always be nouns or pronouns (or, occasionally, other words or groups of words that function as subjects). You probably know the definition of a noun: **A noun names a person, place, thing, or idea.**

This definition works perfectly well for most nouns, especially for those that name concrete things we can *see, hear, smell, taste,* or *touch.* Using this definition, most people can identify words such as *door, road,* or *tulip* as nouns.

► **EXAMPLES**

    N   N   N
Paula reads her favorite **book** whenever she goes to the **beach.**

       N   N   N
My **brother** likes to watch **football** on **television.**

Unfortunately, when it comes to identifying ideas as nouns, many people have trouble. Part of this problem is that nouns name even more than ideas. They name **emotions, qualities, conditions,** and many other **abstractions.** Abstract nouns such as *fear, courage, happiness,* and *trouble* do not name persons, places, or things, but they are nouns.

Below are a few examples of nouns, arranged by category. Add nouns of your own to each category.

Persons	*Places*	*Things*	*Ideas*
Paula	New York	spaghetti	sincerity
engineer	beach	book	anger
woman	India	sun	democracy
artist	town	bicycle	intelligence
_____	_____	_____	_____
_____	_____	_____	_____
_____	_____	_____	_____

■ **PRACTICE**   Place an "N" above all the nouns in the following sentences.

       N   N   N

1. Jane was playing my favorite song on my stereo.

2. Hester stared at the bright red letter on her dress.

3. Alice had not expected the Queen to be such a poor loser.

4. Many Scots think of Nessie with warmth and affection.

5. The questions that Leda asked the swan were of historical importance.

To help you identify <u>all</u> nouns, remember these points:

1. Nouns can be classified as **proper nouns** and **common nouns**. **Proper nouns** name specific persons, places, things, and ideas. The first letter in each of these nouns is capitalized (Manuelita, Missouri, Mazda, Marxism). **Common nouns** name more general categories. The first letter of a common noun is not capitalized (man, mansion, moss, marriage).

2. <u>**A, an,** and **the** are noun markers.</u> A noun will always follow one of these words.

▶ **EXAMPLES**

                        N   N

The young **policeman** was given a new **car.**

          N   N   N   N

The final **point** of **the lecture** concerned **an inconsistency** in **the** last **report.**

3. <u>If you are unsure whether or not a word is a noun, ask yourself if it **could** be introduced with **a, an,** or **the.**</u>

▶ **EXAMPLE**

                N   N   N

My **granddaughter** asked for my **opinion** of her new **outfit.**

4. Words that end in **ment, ism, ness, ence, ance,** and **tion** are usually nouns.

► **EXAMPLE**

               N   N

Her **criticism** of my **performance** made me very unhappy.

■ **PRACTICE**   Place an "N" above all the nouns in the following sentences.

                            N   N   N   N

1. The guide led the class on a tour of the caverns.

2. Aeneas and his crew left Carthage without even an apology or a thank-you note.

3. Homer licked his lips at the thought of a huge plate of Spam.

4. Gulliver was horrified when he discovered the Web site for *Yahoo!* on his new computer.

5. Some governments will never allow freedom of the press.

6. A deep depression and a sense of meaninglessness settled on the wounded king.

7. Hypocrites give other people a false impression of themselves.

8. His philosophy of life had never included ideas like acceptance and willingness.

9. In the United States, Christmas is celebrated in December with such traditions as decorated trees, bright lights, and wrapped gifts.

10. Darby anticipated every thought of her enemy.

---

pronoun

A pronoun takes the place of a noun.

    A pronoun takes the place of a noun. The "pro" in *pronoun* comes from the Latin word meaning "for." Thus, a <u>pro</u>noun is a word that in some way stands "for a noun." Pronouns perform this task in a variety of ways. Often, a pronoun will allow you to refer to a noun without having to repeat the noun. For instance, notice how the word *John* is awkwardly repeated in the following sentence:

<u>John</u> put on <u>John's</u> coat before <u>John</u> left for <u>John's</u> job.

Pronouns allow you to avoid the repetition:

John put on <u>his</u> coat before <u>he</u> left for <u>his</u> job.

In later chapters we will discuss the use of pronouns and the differences among the various types. For now, you simply need to be able to recognize pronouns in a sentence. The following list includes the most common pronouns. Read over this list several times until you are familiar with these words.

Personal Pronouns

I	we	you	he	she	they	it
me	us	your	him	her	them	its
my	our	yours	his	hers	their	
mine	ours				theirs	

Indefinite Pronouns

some	everyone	anyone	someone	no one
all	everything	anything	something	nothing
many	everybody	anybody	somebody	nobody
each				
one				
none				

Reflexive/Intensive Pronouns

myself	ourselves
yourself	yourselves
himself	themselves
herself	
itself	

Relative Pronouns   *Demonstrative Pronouns*

who, whom, whose	that this
which	those these
that	

Interrogative Pronouns

who, whom, whose
which
what

■   **PRACTICE**   Place an "N" above all nouns and a "Pro" above all pronouns in the following sentences.

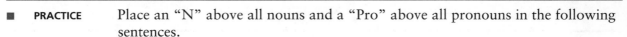

1. We enjoyed the ride on the river, but everyone kept falling out of

N

the raft.

2. Nobody wanted the cyclops to find the men under the sheep.

3. Homer ordered Spam and cheese for himself and a plate of grits for me.

4. What did the second little pig use to build his house?

5. Hortense bought one of the used saddles and gave it to her mother.

6. Pinocchio knew that something was wrong when everyone pointed at his nose.

7. General Burnside did not care if they laughed at the way he wore his hair.

8. Each of the children received a brand-new penny from Mr. Scrooge.

9. This is their favorite time of day.

10. Someone whom the host chooses will travel with him to the Super Bowl.

■ **PRACTICE**   In the following sentences, write nouns and pronouns of your own choice as indicated.

       N   N   Pro   N

1. A __*dog*__ at the __*picnic*__ ate __*our*__ __*lunch*__.

       N   Pro   N

2. The _____ might persuade _____ to play a _____ .

   Pro   N   N

3. _____ in the _____ applauded for the _____ on

     N

the _____ .

   Pro   Pro   N   N

4. _____ told _____ _____ about the _____?

     N   Pro   N   Pro

5. After _____ cooked _____ _____ , _____ asked

   Pro   N   N   Pro

_____ _____ to watch the _____ with _____ .

Verbs

verb
A verb either shows action or links the subject to another word.

Once you can identify nouns and pronouns, the next step is to learn to identify verbs. Although some people have trouble recognizing these words, you should be able to identify them if you learn the following definition and the few points after it: **A verb either shows action or links the subject to another word.**

As you can see, this definition identifies two types of verbs. Some are "action" verbs (they tell what the subject is <u>doing</u>), and others are "linking" verbs (they tell what the subject is <u>being</u>). This distinction leads to the first point that will help you recognize verbs.

Action Verbs and Linking Verbs

<u>One way to recognize verbs is to know that some verbs can do more than simply express an action.</u> Some verbs are action verbs; others are linking verbs.

ACTION VERBS

Action verbs are usually easy to identify. Consider the following sentence:

The deer leaped gracefully over the stone wall.

If you ask yourself what the **action** of the sentence is, the answer is obviously *leaped*. Therefore, *leaped* is the verb.

▶ **EXAMPLES OF ACTION VERBS** *run, read, go, write, think, forgive, wait, laugh*

■ **PRACTICE**   Underline the action verbs in the following sentences.

1. Hans <u>ran</u> all the way home after the game.

2. Amelia Earhart disappeared over the Pacific Ocean in 1937.

3. Homer and Hortense play kazoo duets every Sunday.

4. At the front of the brightly lit stage, Satchmo raised the trumpet to his lips.

5. Billie sang with a white flower in her hair.

LINKING VERBS

Linking verbs are sometimes more difficult to recognize than action verbs. Look for the verb in the following sentence:

Helen is a woman of integrity.

Notice that the sentence expresses no real action. The verb *is* simply links the word *woman* to the word *Helen*.

▶ **EXAMPLES OF LINKING VERBS**   forms of *be:* am, is, are, was, were, be, being, been

forms of *become, seem, look, appear, smell, taste, feel, sound, grow, remain*

Linking verbs can link three types of words to a subject.

1. They can link nouns to the subject:

Hank <u>became</u> a hero to his team. (*Hero* is linked to *Hank.*)

2. They can link pronouns to the subject:

Cheryl <u>was</u> someone from another planet. (*Someone* is linked to *Cheryl.*)

3. They can link adjectives (descriptive words) to the subject:

The sky <u>was</u> cloudy all day. (*Cloudy* is linked to *sky.*)

■ **PRACTICE**   Underline the linking verbs in the following sentences.

1. My father <u>was</u> a pilot during World War II.

2. Desdemona is fond of Othello.

3. Carl's dream seemed strange to Dr. Freud.

4. Priscilla's favorite tea tastes quite bitter.

5. I am anxious about the okra crop.

Verb Tense

Another way to identify verbs is to know that they appear in different forms to show the time when the action or linking takes place. These forms are called *tenses.* The simplest tenses are present, past, and future.

Present		*Past*	
I walk	we walk	I walked	we walked
you walk	you walk	you walked	you walked
he, she, it walks	they walk	he, she, it walked	they walked

Future	
I will walk	we will walk
you will walk	you will walk
he, she, it will walk	they will walk

Note that the verb *walk* can be written as *walked* to show past tense and as *will walk* to show future tense. When a verb adds "d" or "ed" to form the past tense, it is called a **regular verb.**

Other verbs change their forms more drastically to show past tense. For example, the verb *eat* becomes *ate,* and *fly* becomes *flew.* Verbs like these, which do not add "d" or "ed" to form the past tense, are called **irregular verbs.** Irregular verbs will be discussed in Chapter Six. For now, to help you identify verbs, remember this point: Verbs change their forms to show tense.

■ **PRACTICE**

In the following sentences, first underline the verb and then write the tense (present, past, or future) in the space provided.

present **1.** Fay <u>writes</u> her aunt in Washington once a month.

_____ **2.** The wabbit laughed at Elmer.

_____ **3.** We will visit the Movieland Wax Museum on Monday.

_____ **4.** The Trojans stared at the huge horse before the gates of the city.

_____ **5.** Brent likes his laptop computer.

Helping Verbs and Main Verbs

A third way to identify verbs is to know that the verb of a sentence is often more than one word. The **MAIN VERB** of a sentence may be preceded by one or more **HELPING VERBS** to show time, condition, or circumstances. The helping verbs allow us the flexibility to communicate a wide variety of ideas and attitudes. For example, note how adding a helping verb changes the following sentences:

I run indicates that an action is happening or happens repeatedly.

I will run indicates that an action is not now occurring but will occur in the future.

I should run indicates an attitude toward the action.

The **COMPLETE VERB** of a sentence, then, includes a **MAIN VERB** and any **HELPING VERBS.** The complete verb can contain as many as three helping verbs.

     MV
He *writes.*

    HV   MV
He *has written.*

    HV HV   MV
He *has been writing.*

     HV   HV   HV   MV
He *might have been writing.*

You can be sure that you have identified all of the helping verbs in a complete verb simply by learning the helping verbs. There are not very many of them. These words are **always** helping verbs:

can	may	could
will	must	would
shall	might	should

These words are sometimes helping verbs and sometimes main verbs:

Forms of *have*	Forms of *do*	Forms of *be*		
have	do	am	was	be
has	does	is	were	being
had	did	are		been

In the following examples, note that the same word can be a helping verb in one sentence and a main verb in another:

        MV
Anna **had** thirty pairs of shoes.

        HV   MV
Thomas **had** thought about the problem for years.

        MV
She **did** well on her chemistry quiz.

        HV MV
Bob **did** go to the game after all.

        MV
The bus **was** never on time.

        HV   MV
He **was** planning to leave in the morning.

When you are trying to identify the complete verb of a sentence, remember that any helping verbs will always come before the main verb; however, other words may occur between the helping verb(s) and the main verb. For instance, you will often find words like *not, never, ever, already,* or *just* between the helping verb and the main verb. Also, in questions you will often find the subject between the helping verb and the main verb.

▶   **EXAMPLES**   HV   S   MV
Will the telephone company raise its prices?

              S   HV   MV
Nobody has **ever** proved the existence of the Loch Ness Monster.

■ **PRACTICE** In the spaces provided, identify the underlined words as main verbs (MV) or helping verbs (HV).

_MV_ 1. Juneteenth <u>is</u> one of the most important days in African American history.

_____ 2. It <u>is</u> celebrated to commemorate the end of slavery.

_____ 3. Supposedly, the Emancipation Proclamation <u>was</u> not read to slaves in Houston until June 19, 1863.

_____ 4. That <u>was</u> more than five months after the Proclamation was supposed to have taken effect.

_____ 5. Why the news of the Proclamation <u>did</u> not spread faster is unclear.

_____ 6. Because slaves <u>did</u> the field work, perhaps they were kept ignorant of their freedom until the crops were in.

_____ 7. It <u>has</u> also been said that the person bearing the news of the Proclamation was murdered before he could deliver the message.

_____ 8. Juneteenth (June 19) <u>has</u> a special significance to the citizens of Texas, where it is called Emancipation Day.

_____ 9. It has <u>been</u> a state holiday in Texas since 1980.

_____ 10. For years, people in many states have <u>been</u> celebrating Juneteenth as the date when slavery ended in the United States.

■ **PRACTICE** A. In the following sentences, place "HV" over all helping verbs and "MV" over all main verbs.

          HV MV
1. The space shuttle has landed safely in Florida.

2. The Whippets have lost all of their games.

3. The Internet will change the lives of all of us.

4. Does anyone want a free root canal?

5. Gertrude could have given Ophelia a life preserver.

B. In the following sentences, write helping verbs and main verbs of your own choice as indicated.

               MV
6. Christie _sat_ with her best friend at the movie.

                   MV   MV

7. The ostrich _____ to the fence and _____ at the tub of water.

                MV   MV

8. The glass _____ to the floor and _____ into hundreds of small

pieces.

               HV   MV

9. A spider _____ slowly _____ along the wall behind my sister.

             HV   MV

10. One _____ never _____ his or her head in a lion's mouth

        MV

when it _____ hungry.

Verbals

A fourth way to identify verbs is to recognize what they are not. Some verb forms do not actually function as verbs. These are called **VERBALS.** One of the most important verbals is the **INFINITIVE**, which usually begins with the word *to* (*to write, to be, to see*). The infinitive cannot serve as the verb of a sentence because it cannot express the time of the action or linking. *I wrote* communicates a clear idea, but *I to write* does not.

    Another common verbal is the "-ing" form of the verb when it occurs without a helping verb (*running, flying, being*). When an "-ing" form without a helping verb is used as an adjective, it is called a **PRESENT PARTICIPLE.** When it is used as a noun, it is called a **GERUND.**

▶   **EXAMPLES**   MV   Verbal

I **hope to pass** this test.

       HV   MV

I **should pass** this test.

          Verbal   MV

The birds **flying** from tree to tree **chased** the cat from their nest.

        HV   MV

The birds **were flying** from tree to tree.

     Verbal MV

Jogging is good cardiovascular exercise.

     MV

I **jog** for the cardiovascular benefits of the exercise.

■ **PRACTICE**   In the following sentences, write "HV" above all helping verbs, "MV" above all main verbs, and "Verbal" above all verbals.

       HV MV Verbal

1. Anne would like to eat some chocolate with her popcorn.

2. Leaning against the stall, the mule would not move.

3. To please Homer, Hortense had prepared his favorite dessert, a Spam sundae delight.

4. The little mermaid did not see the great white shark swimming closely behind her.

5. The group waiting in the lobby asked Conchita for a guitar string.

■ **PRACTICE**   Place "HV" above all helping verbs and "MV" above all main verbs in the following sentences. Draw a line through any verbals.

       HV   MV

1. Engineers will attempt ~~to complete~~ work on the dam by November.

2. The student had tried to understand Homer's definition of Spamness.

3. Did you enjoy your recent trip to Utopia?

4. Dalila has decided to become the best rattlesnake bagger in Curwensville, Pennsylvania.

5. The driverless Ford has been spotted going across the border.

6. Young Galileo refused to keep his eyes on the ground.

7. Jesse Owens's performance in the 1936 Olympics certainly must have irritated Adolf Hitler.

8. Trembling fearfully, Ichabod Crane could not force himself to forget the legend of Sleepy Hollow.

9. The newspapers had refused to print the story.

10. Has Leonardo painted the smile yet?

Identifying Subjects and Verbs

Finding the Subject

Most sentences contain several nouns and pronouns used in a variety of ways. One of the most important ways is as the subject of a verb. To identify which of the nouns or pronouns in a sentence is the subject, you need to identify the complete verb first. After identifying the verb, it is easy to find the subject by asking yourself "Who or what _(verb)_?"

▶ **EXAMPLE**

           S   HV   MV

The **man** in the green hat **was following** a suspicious-looking stranger.

The complete verb in this sentence is _was following,_ and when you ask yourself "Who or what was following?" the answer is "the man." Therefore, _man_ is the subject.

Remember, most sentences contain several nouns and pronouns, but not all nouns and pronouns are subjects.

▶ **EXAMPLE**

           S   MV

The **people** from the **house** down the **street** often borrow our **tools**.

This sentence contains four nouns, but only _people_ is the subject. The other nouns in this sentence are different types of **objects**. The noun _tools_ is called a **direct object** because it receives the action of the verb _borrow_. The nouns _house_ and _street_ are called **objects of prepositions**. Direct objects will be discussed in Chapter Four. Objects of prepositions will be discussed later in this chapter. For now, just remember that not all nouns and pronouns are subjects.

■ **PRACTICE**

In the following sentences, place an "HV" above any helping verbs, an "MV" above the main verbs, and an "S" above the subjects.

1. The bobcat can leap over the fence easily.

2. Cleopatra desires to visit the reptile house.

3. Marc Antony has advised Cleopatra to stay away from snakes.

4. A poisonous asp does not make a good companion.

5. Hortense was proud of her new Spam license-plate holder.

Subject Modifiers

Words that modify or describe nouns or pronouns should not be included when you identify the subject.

▶ **EXAMPLE**

                    S   MV

The red **wheelbarrow is** in the yard.

The subject is *wheelbarrow*, not *the red wheelbarrow*.

    Remember that the possessive forms of nouns and pronouns are also used to describe or modify nouns, so do not include them in the subject either.

▶ **EXAMPLES**

                           S   MV

My brother's **suitcase is** very worn.

              S   MV

His **textbook was** expensive.

The subjects are simply *suitcase* and *textbook*, not *my brother's suitcase* or *his textbook*.

Verb Modifiers

Just as words that describe or modify the subject are not considered part of the subject, words that describe or modify the verb are not considered part of the verb. Watch for such modifiers because they will often occur between helping verbs and main verbs and may be easily mistaken for helping verbs. Notice that in the following sentence the words *not* and *unfairly* are modifiers and, therefore, not part of the complete verb.

▶ **EXAMPLE**

     S   HV

Parents should **not unfairly** criticize their children.

Some common verb modifiers are *not, never, almost, just, completely, sometimes, always, often,* and *certainly.*

■ **PRACTICE**

Place "HV" over helping verbs, "MV" over main verbs, and "S" over the subjects of the following sentences.

            S   *HV*   *MV*

1. My mother's tulips have not come up yet.

2. The last football game of the season had finally ended.

3. A hot summer night will sometimes prevent Carla from sleeping.

4. During the loud thunderstorm, my new umbrella would not open.

5. Surging over the barricades, the fans eagerly grabbed the Spam T-shirts.

Multiple Subjects and Verbs

Sentences may contain more than one subject and more than one verb.

▶ **EXAMPLES**

    S   MV
Fred petted the dog.

    S   S   MV
Fred and Mary petted the dog.

    S   S   MV   MV
Fred and Mary petted the dog and scratched its ears.

    S   MV   S   MV
Fred petted the dog, and Mary scratched its ears.

    S   S   MV   S   MV
Fred and Mary petted the dog before they fed it.

■ **PRACTICE**

Place "HV" over helping verbs, "MV" over main verbs, and "S" over subjects in the following sentences.

          S   MV
1. Mr. Caldron wanted to go on the scariest ride in the park.

2. The wind and rain were endless.

3. Dorothy and Toto opened the door and stared at the singing Munchkins.

4. The Montagues hated the Capulets, and the McCoys despised the Hatfields.

5. When the guide arrived, Homer and Hortense toured the Spam plant.

Special Situations

SUBJECT UNDERSTOOD

When a sentence is a command (or a request worded as a polite command), the pronoun *you* is understood as the subject. *You* is the only understood subject.

▶ **EXAMPLES**

   MV
Shut the door. (Subject *you* is understood.)

MV

Please **give** this book to your sister. (Subject is *you* understood.)

VERB BEFORE SUBJECT

In some sentences, such as in questions, the verb comes before the subject.

► **EXAMPLE**

MV   S

Is your **mother** home?

The verb also comes before the subject in sentences beginning with *there* or *here,* as well as in some other constructions.

► **EXAMPLES**

    MV   S

There **is** a **bug** in my soup.

    MV   S

Here **is** another **bowl** of soup.

        MV   S

Over the hill **rode** the **cavalry.**

            MV   S

On the front porch **was** a **basket** with a baby in it.

■ **PRACTICE**

Place "HV" over helping verbs, "MV" over main verbs, and "S" over subjects in the following sentences. Verbals and verb modifiers should not be included in the complete verb.

   MV

1. Spend all of this money on yourself.

2. Near the ship was a pile of harpoons.

3. Is he still waiting for Godot?

4. There are two unicorns hiding in Billy's closet.

5. Close that application.

■ **PRACTICE**

Underline all subjects once and complete verbs twice in the following sentences. Remember that the complete verb contains the main verb and all helping verbs and that verbals and verb modifiers should not be included in the complete verb.

1. Her new <u>novel</u> <u>will</u> certainly <u>be</u> a success.

2. Usher could have repaired his house.

3. Don Quixote will never forget the beautiful Dulcinea.

4. Hamlet's uncle had always wanted to rule a kingdom.

5. Does Wynton want me to play the drums?

6. The young knight could not remove the sword from the stone.

7. Ask the waiter to remove this bug from my soup.

8. The groundhog did not see its shadow, so spring is on its way.

9. Here is the recipe for turtle soup.

10. The Hellcat dove from the sky and destroyed the aircraft carrier.

■ **PRACTICE**   Write sentences of your own that follow the suggested patterns. Identify each subject (S), helping verb (HV), and main verb (MV).

1. A statement with two subjects and one main verb (S-S-MV):

   S   S   MV
   Sarah and Mireya met for lunch.
   _____

2. A statement with one subject and two main verbs (S-MV-MV):

   _____

   _____

3. A statement with one subject, one helping verb, and one main verb (S-HV-MV):

   _____

   _____

4. A question with one main verb and one subject (MV-S):

   _____

   _____

5. A command that begins with a main verb (MV):

_____

_____

6. A statement that starts with *there* and is followed by a main verb and a subject ("There" MV-S).

_____

_____

7. A statement with two subjects and two main verbs (S-S-MV-MV):

_____

_____

8. A statement with one subject, one helping verb, and one main verb followed by *after* and another subject and another main verb (S-HV-MV "after" S-MV):

_____

_____

9. A statement with a subject, a helping verb, and a main verb followed by *or* and another subject, helping verb, and main verb (S-HV-MV, "or" S-HV-MV).

_____

_____

10. A statement with a subject, a helping verb, and a main verb followed by *because* and another subject and a main verb (S-HV-MV "because" S-MV).

_____

_____

Section One Review

1. A **noun** names a person, place, thing, or idea.

    a. **Proper nouns** name specific persons, places, things, or ideas. They begin with a capital letter. **Common nouns** name more general categories and are not capitalized.

    b. **A, an,** and **the** are noun markers. A noun always follows one of these words.

    c. If you are unsure whether or not a word is a noun, ask yourself if it **could** be introduced with **a, an,** or **the.**

    d. Words that end in **ment, ism, ness, ence, ance,** and **tion** are usually nouns.

2. A **pronoun** takes the place of a noun.

3. A **verb** either shows **action** or **links** the subject to another word.

4. Verbs appear in different **tenses** to show the time when the action or linking takes place.

5. The **complete verb** includes a **main verb** and any **helping verbs.**

6. **Verbals** are verb forms that do not function as verbs.

    a. The **infinitive** is a verbal that begins with the word *to.* ———

    b. The "-ing" form of the verb without a helping verb is called a **present participle** if it is used as an adjective.

    c. The "-ing" form of the verb without a helping verb is called a **gerund** if it is used as a noun.

7. To identify the **subject** of any sentence, first find the verb. Then ask "Who or what (verb)?"

8. **Subject modifiers** describe or modify the subject. They should not be included when you identify the subject.

9. **Verb modifiers** describe or modify verbs. They are not considered part of the verb.

10. Sentences may contain **multiple subjects** and **multiple verbs.**

11. When a sentence is a command (or a request worded as a polite command), the pronoun *you* is understood as the subject. *You* is the only understood subject.

12. In some sentences the verb comes before the subject.

Exercise 1A

In the spaces provided, indicate whether the underlined word is a subject (write "S"), a helping verb (write "HV"), or a main verb (write "MV"). If it is none of these, leave the space blank.

_MV_ **1.** The heavy rains <u>caused</u> severe flooding in the Midwest.

_____ **2.** Thelonius waved to the <u>crowd</u> and played an encore.

_____ **3.** The <u>guest</u> apologized profusely for his lateness.

_____ **4.** The Mars probe <u>crashed</u> onto the surface of the planet.

_____ **5.** The lavishly decorated <u>float</u> broke down in the middle of the Rose Parade.

_____ **6.** From the <u>kitchen</u> floated the aroma of Homer's Spam and tuna casserole.

_____ **7.** Do you know if Julius Caesar <u>was</u> one of the emperors of Rome?

_____ **8.** Two tasty chocolate eclairs <u>will</u> make me a happy camper.

_____ **9.** Although the storm <u>had</u> damaged it, the ship managed to reach the port safely.

_____ **10.** Orlando watched in awe as the full moon slowly <u>turned</u> bright red.

_____ **11.** Picking up his hammer, Thor decided that <u>it</u> was time to rumble.

_____ **12.** Carefully hiding them, Daedalus <u>saved</u> wax and feathers.

_____ **13.** <u>Everyone</u> was worried when only six dwarves returned from the mine.

_____ **14.** Has anyone <u>seen</u> King Midas?

_____ **15.** Suzanne <u>was</u> searching for the Chinese tea and oranges.

Exercise 1B

A. Underline all subjects once and complete verbs twice in the following sentences. Remember that a sentence may have more than one subject and more than one verb.

1. A stranger in a gray suit was leaving the building.

2. Has Homer seen the Hillbilly Hall of Fame?

3. The victim should have said nothing at all.

4. Out of the fog glided a huge battleship.

5. Mr. Capp and his wife liked the boy but did not want him as a son-in-law.

6. The dragon roared loudly yet scared no one.

7. Arlo has been playing guitar in Alice's restaurant for many years.

8. The chocolate eclairs were expensive, but they were delicious.

9. Pierce insisted that he would make a better CIA agent than Sean.

10. Luckily, Mr. Tell's aim has always been quite accurate.

B. Write sentences of your own that follow the suggested patterns. Identify each subject (S), helping verb (HV), and main verb (MV).

11. A statement with one subject and two main verbs (S-MV-MV).

      S   MV   MV
     Sharon took the case and won it. _____

    _____

12. A statement with two subjects, one helping verb, and one main verb (S-S-HV-MV).

    _____

    _____

13. A question that begins with a helping verb followed by the subject and a main verb (HV-S-MV?).

    _____

    _____

Exercise 1B

continued

14. A statement with a subject, two helping verbs, and one main verb (S-HV-HV-MV).

_____

_____

15. A statement with a subject and main verb followed by a comma and *yet* and another subject and main verb (S-MV, "yet" S-MV):

_____

_____

Exercise 1C

In the following paragraph, underline all subjects once and complete verbs twice.

1. During World War II, a Chinese seaman experienced one of the most amazing survival adventures of the war. **2.** He survived alone for 133 days aboard a small life raft in the South Atlantic. **3.** On November 23, 1942, Poon Lim's ordeal began when his ship was torpedoed by a German submarine 565 miles off the coast of Africa. **4.** After he was thrown overboard, Poon Lim watched as his ship and its passengers disappeared into the sea. **5.** He had been swimming for two hours when he saw a wooden raft bobbing in the wreckage. **6.** He crawled into the raft. **7.** It was eight feet square and held a few tins of biscuits, a container of water, a flashlight, and a rope. **8.** These few rations lasted only sixty days before he was forced to improvise. **9.** To catch small fish, he made a hook from a wire spring from the flashlight, and then he attached some hemp from a rope to the hook. **10.** Sometimes he used bits of fish to lure seagulls, which he caught and killed with his bare hands. **11.** His life jacket provided him with material to make a receptacle to catch rain water. **12.** To keep physically fit, Poon swam in the ocean daily. **13.** On April 5, 1943, after Poon Lim had survived by his own ingenuity for 133 days, a fishing boat off Brazil picked him up. **14.** His rescuers could hardly believe that he had lost only twenty pounds from his five-foot-five frame and could walk without aid. **15.** Because his survival was such a feat, Poon Lim was awarded the British Empire Medal. **16.** Poon Lim's record of 133 days alone on a raft still stands today.

Modifiers

Although subjects and verbs form the basis of any sentence, most sentences also contain many other words that serve a variety of purposes. One such group of words includes the modifiers, which limit, describe, intensify, or otherwise alter the meaning of other words. The word *modify* simply means "change." Notice how the modifiers change the meaning in each of the following sentences.

The dictator had **total** power.

The dictator had **great** power.

The dictator had **little** power.

The dictator had **no** power.

As you can see, the word *power* is significantly changed by the different modifiers in these sentences.

Although modifiers can change the meaning of words in many different ways, there are basically only two types of modifiers, **ADJECTIVES** and **ADVERBS**. You will be able to identify both types of modifiers more easily if you remember these three points:

1. Sentences often contain more than one modifier.

▶ **EXAMPLE**   The **new** moon rose **slowly** over the desert.

In this example, the word *new* modifies *moon;* it describes the specific phase of the moon. The word *slowly* modifies *rose;* it describes the speed with which the moon rose.

2. Two or more modifiers can be used to modify the same word.

▶ **EXAMPLE**   The moon rose **slowly** and **dramatically** over the desert.

In this example the words *slowly* and *dramatically* both modify *rose*. *Slowly* describes the speed, and *dramatically* describes the manner in which the moon rose.

3. All modifiers must modify *something*. You should be able to identify the specific word that is being modified as well as the modifier itself.

▶ **EXAMPLE**   **Slowly** the **new** moon rose over the desert.

In this example, notice that the word *slowly* still modifies *rose,* though the two words are not close to each other. The arrows point from the modifiers to the words being modified.

■ **PRACTICE**   Draw an arrow from the underlined modifier to the word it modifies.

1. Stephanie wore <u>purple</u> hair to the party.

2. The day was <u>cold</u> and <u>rainy</u>.

3. The student walked <u>steadily</u> but <u>reluctantly</u> to the front of the room.

4. The <u>powerful</u> goddesss was <u>eager</u> to hear the story.

5. <u>Two</u> customers and a mechanic argued <u>angrily</u> about the price of the car

   repairs.

> **adjective**
> An adjective modifies a noun or a pronoun.

Adjectives

An adjective modifies a noun or a pronoun. In English most adjectives precede the noun they modify.

▶ **EXAMPLE**

The **young** eagle perched on the **rocky** cliff.

In this example, the word *young* **modifies** *eagle,* and the word *rocky* **modifies** *cliff.*

Although most adjectives precede the noun or pronoun they modify, they may also follow the noun or pronoun and be connected to it by a linking verb.

▶ **EXAMPLE**

Poisonous plants are **dangerous**.

In this example, the word *poisonous* describes the noun *plants*. Notice that it **precedes** the noun. However, the word *dangerous* also describes the noun *plants*. It is **linked** to the noun by the linking verb *are*. Both *poisonous* and *dangerous* are adjectives that modify the noun *plants*.

Many different types of words can be adjectives, as long as they **modify** a noun or pronoun. Most adjectives answer the questions **which? what kind?** or **how many?** Here are the most common types of adjectives.

1. Descriptive words

▶ **EXAMPLES**

I own a **blue** suit.

That is an **ugly** wound.

2. Possessive nouns and pronouns

▶ **EXAMPLE**

I parked **my** motorcycle next to **John's** car.

3. Limiting words and numbers

▶ **EXAMPLES**

Some people see **every** movie that comes out.

Two accidents have happened on **this** street.

4. Nouns that modify other nouns

▶ **EXAMPLE**

The **basketball** game was held in the **neighborhood** gym.

■ **PRACTICE**

A. In the following sentences, circle all adjectives and draw an arrow to the noun or pronoun each adjective modifies.

1. A severe rash covered his left arm.

2. The April dance will be held on Saturday night.

3. Five gray pelicans glided above the busy beach.

4. After their morning paper had been stolen for the third time, Sharon and her husband decided to cancel their subscription.

5. Next October Homer will spend his vacation time in his redecorated barn making a new Spam costume for the Halloween party.

B. Add two adjectives of your own to each of the following sentences.

6. The door of the *old* shed in the backyard hung by one *rusty* hinge.

7. Snow fell from the sky and covered our lawn.

8. Lamont found some items for his collection in the store.

9. The operator looked at the street full of cars.

10. The water flowed over the sandbags and into the town.

adverb
An adverb modifies a verb, adjective, or another adverb

Adverbs

An adverb modifies a verb, adjective, or another adverb. Adverbs are sometimes more difficult to recognize than adjectives because they can be used to modify three different types of words—verbs, adjectives, and other adverbs. They can either precede or follow the words they modify and are sometimes placed farther away from the words they modify than are adjectives.

► **EXAMPLES**

V   Adv
The president walked across the room **quickly**.
(adverb modifying a verb)

Adv   Adj
The president seemed **unusually** nervous.
(adverb modifying an adjective)

Adv   Adv
The president left **very** quickly after the press conference.
(adverb modifying an adverb)

Because adverbs are often formed by adding "ly" to adjectives such as *quick* or *usual*, many adverbs end in "ly" (*quickly* and *usually*). However, you cannot always use this ending as a way of identifying adverbs because some words that end in "ly" are *not* adverbs and because some adverbs do not end in "ly," as the following list of common adverbs illustrates:

already	now	still
also	often	then
always	quite	too
never	seldom	very
not	soon	well

Here are two ways to help you identify adverbs:

1. <u>Find the word that is being modified.</u> If it is a verb, adjective, or adverb, then the modifier is an adverb.

► **EXAMPLES**

V
Thelma **seriously** injured her finger during the tennis match.

Adj
My brother and I have **completely** different attitudes toward Spam.

Adv
Tuan **almost** always arrives on time for work.

2. <u>Look for words that answer the questions **when? where? how?** or **to what extent?**</u>

▶ **EXAMPLES**   My grandparents **often** bring gifts when they visit. (**when?**)

The turnips were grown **locally**. (**where?**)

Rachel **carefully** removed the paint from the antique desk. (**how?**)

Homer is **widely** known as a trainer in a flea circus. (**to what extent?**)

NOTE: Adverbs are **not** considered part of the complete verb, even if they come between the helping verb and the main verb. (See page 15 for a list of common adverbs that come between the helping verb and the main verb.)

▶ **EXAMPLE**
HV Adv   MV
He has **not** failed to do his duty.

■ **PRACTICE**   **A.** In the following sentences, circle all adverbs and draw an arrow to the word that each adverb modifies.

1. The (nearly) exhausted soldier ran (relentlessly) toward the fort.

2. When the hare finally awoke, the tortoise had already crossed the finish line.

3. Puff the Magic Dragon usually lived by the sea, but sometimes he missed his old home in the mountains.

4. The boxer slowly rose from the canvas and carefully adjusted his teeth.

5. Aeneas sadly remembered his lately departed friend, Dido.

B. Add one adverb of your own to each of the following sentences.

6. The dark limousine rolled to the curb and *abruptly* stopped.

7. Esteban toured many cities in Europe and studied the old cathedrals.

8. Medusa combed her hair before she jumped into the carriage.

9. Anna visits her father on Sundays.

10. Hortense gazed into Homer's bloodshot eyes.

Section Two Review

1. **Modifiers** limit, describe, intensify, or otherwise alter the meaning of other words.

   a. Sentences often contain more than one modifier.

   b. Two or more modifiers can be used to modify the same word.

   c. All modifiers must modify *something*.

2. An **adjective** modifies a noun or a pronoun.

3. Most adjectives answer the questions which? what kind? or how many?

4. Common types of adjectives are the following:

   a. <u>Descriptive words</u>

   b. <u>Possessive nouns and pronouns</u>

   c. <u>Limiting words and numbers</u>

   d. <u>Nouns that modify other nouns</u>

5. An **adverb** modifies a verb, adjective, or another adverb.

6. There are two ways to identify adverbs:

   a. <u>Find the word that is being modified. If it is a verb, an adjective, or an adverb, then the modifier is an adverb.</u>

   b. <u>Look for words that answer the questions when? where? how? or to what extent?</u>

Exercise 2A

A. In the following sentences, identify all adjectives by writing "Adj" above them.

1. The *Adj* cloudy skies did not bother the *Adj* professional sailors.

2. Bianca spent her entire savings on the new business.

3. Oliver reluctantly approached the stingy old man.

4. Our company was quite successful this year.

5. Bill's father wished his son would spend less time on the Internet.

B. In the following sentences, identify all adverbs by writing "Adv" above them.

6. Time passed *Adv* swiftly yet *Adv* silently on Dylan's brief vacation.

7. Rodrigo would sometimes watch football, but he usually preferred soccer.

8. When Tessie saw the black dot, she protested angrily, but no one really listened.

9. Fergal smiled triumphantly because he had finally captured a leprechaun.

10. Tory often watched the pelicans as they splashed noisily into the sea.

C. Add one adjective and one adverb to each of the following sentences. Do not use the same adjective or adverb more than once.

11. The heron *gracefully* landed on the *tall* pine tree.

12. The pioneers tried to cross the mountains before the snow closed the passes.

13. The band talked next to the table at the end of the auditorium.

14. Along the banks of the river, people waited for fishing season to begin.

15. The supervisor told the workers that the factory was closing.

Exercise 2B

In the following sentences, write "Adj" above all adjectives and "Adv" above all adverbs. Underline all subjects once and all verbs twice.

1. *Adj* The enraged <u>bull</u> *Adv* suddenly <u><u>turned</u></u> and <u><u>charged</u></u> toward the *Adj* unsuspecting matador.

2. Sheila nearly fell on the wet platform.

3. Our company was quite successful this year.

4. The dirty snow covered Oscar's new Honda.

5. Three police officers on yellow inline skates glided easily among the crowd.

6. Monica was unhappy with the judge's decision and protested angrily.

7. Tiger Woods could hardly believe that he had just missed a simple one-foot putt.

8. The usually shy panda moved boldly toward her surprised trainer.

9. A hundred noisy children charged through the door.

10. The Democratic candidate walked confidently onto the platform and began her speech.

11. Consuelo was very happy when she saw the new drawings of her plans for the clinic.

12. Maynard Krebs waited eagerly in line to meet Allen Ginsberg, who was signing copies of his most recent collection of poetry.

13. The curtain slowly rose, and the young actress graciously accepted the bouquet of beautiful red roses.

14. The salesperson spoke rapidly and enthusiastically about her new product.

15. Your brilliant victory will be handsomely rewarded by a gold medallion.

Exercise 2C

In the following sentences, identify each of the underlined words as noun (N), pronoun (Pro), verb (V), adjective (Adj), or adverb (Adv).

1. One of the most *Adj* <u>poignant</u> stories of all time is the *N* <u>myth</u> of Pyramus and Thisbe. **2.** It has been <u>used</u> by <u>many</u> writers throughout the years. **3.** <u>It</u> is the source of the story of Romeo and Juliet, and Shakespeare <u>also</u> used it in *Midsummer Night's Dream.* **4.** The Broadway musical *West Side Story* was also based on this <u>ancient</u> <u>tale</u>. **5.** Pyramus and Thisbe <u>were</u> a young man and woman <u>who</u> were in love. **6.** However, <u>their</u> families <u>refused</u> to let them see each other. **7.** Their homes adjoined each other, so they were able to speak <u>secretly</u> to each other through a hole in the common wall between their <u>two</u> houses. **8.** They became <u>desperate</u> and planned to sneak out to meet in the <u>woods</u>. **9.** <u>They</u> <u>agreed</u> to meet by a mulberry tree. **10.** Thisbe arrived first and waited <u>eagerly</u> for Pyramus, but she was scared away by a lioness <u>that</u> was hunting in the woods. **11.** When Thisbe ran, she <u>dropped</u> her veil, which the lioness tore to pieces with <u>jaws</u> stained by the blood of an ox. **12.** Pyramus <u>soon</u> arrived, and, seeing Thisbe's bloody veil, believed that she had been killed by a <u>wild</u> beast. **13.** In his <u>grief</u>, Pyramus stabbed <u>himself</u>. **14.** When Thisbe <u>returned</u> and saw her <u>lover</u> mortally wounded near the mulberry tree, she killed herself. **15.** According to legend, from that <u>time</u> on, the fruit of the mulberry, previously white, was <u>always</u> black. **16.** This <u>sad</u> story has always moved people and through time has been the <u>basis</u> of many other works.

Connectors

The final group of words consists of the connectors. These are signals that indicate the relationship of one part of a sentence to another. The two types of connectors are **conjunctions** and **prepositions**.

Conjunctions

conjunction

A conjunction joins two parts of a sentence.

A conjunction joins two parts of a sentence. The word *conjunction* is derived from two Latin words meaning "to join with." The definition is easy to remember if you know that the word *junction* in English refers to the place where two roads come together.

The two types of conjunctions are **coordinating** and **subordinating**. In Chapter Two we will discuss the subordinating conjunctions. You will find it much easier to distinguish between the two types if you memorize the coordinating conjunctions now.

The **coordinating conjunctions** are *and, but, or, nor, for, yet,* and *so.*

NOTE: An easy way to learn the coordinating conjunctions is to remember that their first letters can spell **BOYSFAN**: (<u>B</u>ut <u>O</u>r <u>Y</u>et <u>S</u>o <u>F</u>or <u>A</u>nd <u>N</u>or).

Coordinating conjunctions join elements of the sentence that are <u>equal</u> or <u>parallel</u>. For instance, they may join two subjects, two verbs, two adjectives, or two parallel groups of words.

► **EXAMPLE**

   S   Conj S   MV   Conj   MV
Ernie **and** Bert often disagree **but** never fight.

In this example the first conjunction joins two subjects and the second joins two verbs.

► **EXAMPLE**

   S   MV   Adj Conj   Adj   Conj   MV
Susan often felt awkward **or** uncomfortable **yet** never showed it.

In this example the first conjunction joins two adjectives, and the second joins two verbs.

Coordinating conjunctions may even be used to join two entire sentences, each with its own subject and verb.

► **EXAMPLES**

   S HV MV   S MV
The rain had fallen steadily all week long. The river was close to overflowing.

   S HV MV   Conj   S   MV
The rain had fallen steadily all week long, **so** the river was close to overflowing.

good ✓

Notice that the coordinating conjunctions have different meanings and that changing the conjunction can significantly change the meaning of a sentence. *A person should never drink **and** drive* communicates a very different idea from *A person should never drink **or** drive*.

■ The conjunction *and* indicates **addition.**

▶ **EXAMPLE**   Jules **and** Jim loved the same woman.

■ The conjunctions *but* and *yet* indicate **contrast.**

▶ **EXAMPLES**   She wanted to go **but** didn't have the money.

I liked Brian, **yet** I didn't really trust him.

■ The conjunctions *or* and *nor* indicate **alternatives.**

▶ **EXAMPLES**   You can borrow the record **or** the tape.

He felt that he could neither go **nor** stay.

■ The conjunctions *for* and *so* indicate **cause** or **result.**

▶ **EXAMPLES**   The plants died, **for** they had not been watered.

Her brother lost his job, **so** he had to find another.

■ **PRACTICE**   **A.** In the following sentences, circle all coordinating conjunctions. Underline all subjects once and all complete verbs twice.

1. My mother (or) my father will give you a ride home.

2. The rhinoceros charged Salvatore, (so) he jumped behind a tree.

3. Homer sometimes burned the okra or the Spam, yet Hortense still admired him.

4. The musicians in the band could not play in tune, but the audience did not seem to mind.

5. The weather has been warm yet not hot, so we could hike every day.

B. In the following sentences, add coordinating conjunctions that show the relationship indicated in parentheses.

6. Paul could warn the minutemen, ___*or*___ he could work on his

copper pan, but he could not do both. (alternatives)

7. Fortunato looked forward to a fine glass of sherry, _but_

    Montresor had other plans. (contrast)

8. His eulogy was "First in war, first in peace, _and_ first in the hearts

    of his countrymen." (addition)

9. Harriet Tubman was one of the heroes of the Underground Railroad,

    and she helped over three hundred slaves escape to freedom. (cause)

10. Business is improving, _and_ we might buy a new car. (result)

Prepositions

> ### preposition
> A preposition relates a noun or pronoun to some other word in the sentence.

A preposition relates a noun or a pronoun to some other word in the sentence. Prepositions usually indicate a relationship of **place** (in, near), **direction** (toward, from), **time** (after, until), or **condition** (of, without).

▶ **EXAMPLE**

          Prep
The boy ran **to** the store.

Notice how the preposition *to* shows the relationship (direction) between *ran* and *store*. If you change prepositions, you change the relationship.

▶ **EXAMPLES**

          Prep
The boy ran **from** the store.

          Prep
The boy ran **into** the store.

          Prep
The boy ran **by** the store.

Here are some of the most common prepositions:

above	before	except	of	toward
across	behind	for	on	under
after	beneath	from	onto	until
among	below	in	over	up
around	beside	in spite of	past	upon
as	between	into	through	with
at	by	like	till	without
because of	during	near	to	

NOTE: *For* can be used as a coordinating conjunction, but it is most commonly used as a preposition. *To* can also be used as part of an infinitive, in which case it is not a preposition.

■ **PRACTICE**   Write "Prep" above the prepositions in the following sentences.

1. Mr. Sanders took the will from the file cabinet and put it into his briefcase.

2. The ship sank because of the unseen log near the surface.

3. During the thunderstorm, Benjamin's kite was struck by lightning.

4. No one should walk through that park without an escort.

5. The Trojans behind the walls looked at the huge wooden horse.

Prepositional Phrases

The word *preposition* is derived from two Latin words meaning "to put in front." The two parts of the word (pre + position) indicate how prepositions usually function. They are almost always used as the first words in **prepositional phrases.**

> ### prepositional phrase
> Preposition + Object (noun or pronoun) = Prepositional Phrase.

A prepositional phrase consists of a preposition plus a noun or a pronoun, called the object of the preposition. This object is almost always the last word of the prepositional phrase. Between the preposition and its object, the prepositional phrase may also contain adjectives, adverbs, or conjunctions. A preposition may have more than one object.

▶   **EXAMPLES**

Prep   Obj
after a short **lunch**

Prep   Obj   Obj
with his very good **friend** and his **brother**

Prep Obj   Obj
to you and **her**

Prep   Obj
through the long and dismal **night**

Although prepositions themselves are considered connectors, prepositional <u>phrases</u> actually act as modifiers. They may function as adjectives, modifying a noun or pronoun, or they may function as adverbs, modifying a verb.

▶   **EXAMPLES**   The cat (**from next door**) caught a gopher.

The burglar jumped (**from the window**).

In the first example, the prepositional phrase functions as an adjective, modifying the noun *cat,* and in the second example, the prepositional phrase functions as an adverb, modifying the verb *jumped.*

NOTE: If you can recognize prepositional phrases, you will be able to identify subjects and verbs more easily **because neither the subject nor the verb of a sentence can be part of a prepositional phrase.**

In the following sentence it is difficult at first glance to determine which of the many nouns is the subject.

In a cave near the village, a member of the archaeological team found a stone ax from an ancient civilization.

If you first eliminate the prepositional phrases, however, the true subject becomes apparent.

S
(In a cave) (near the village), a member (of the archaeological team)

MV
found a stone ax (from an ancient civilization).

■   **PRACTICE**   Place parentheses around the prepositional phrases and write "Prep" above all prepositions and "Obj" above the objects of the prepositions.

　　　　　　Prep　　　　　　Obj　　　　Prep　　　Obj
1. (From the earliest years) (of our country), overeager reporters have pursued our presidents.

2. Anne Royall, who was one of the first female journalists in the United States, was determined to interview John Quincy Adams, our sixth president.

3. She had been trying for weeks to get an interview with him.

4. President Adams would often bathe naked in the Potomac River, and Anne Royall learned of this habit.

5. One morning she followed him to the riverbank, where he undressed and stepped into the cold water.

6. She crept near the shore and positioned herself on his clothes.

7. When President Adams began to move toward the bank, she introduced herself and asked for an interview.

8. In spite of his pleas, she refused to give him his clothes unless he agreed to talk to her.

9. Remaining decently submerged in the water, Adams answered the questions posed by the determined reporter.

10. After this incident, John Quincy Adams became one of Anne Royall's close friends.

Section Three Review

1. A **conjunction** joins two parts of a sentence.

2. The **coordinating conjunctions** are *and, but, or, nor, for, yet,* and *so.*

3. A **preposition** relates a noun or pronoun to some other word in the sentence.

4. A **prepositional phrase** consists of a **preposition** plus a noun or a pronoun, called the **object of the preposition.**

5. Neither the subject nor the verb of a sentence can be part of a prepositional phrase.

Exercise 3A

A. Combine each pair of sentences into one sentence. Use the coordinating conjunction indicated in the parentheses.

1. (contrast)
Elvis Presley was born in Tupelo, Mississippi.
He grew up in Memphis, Tennessee.

Elvis Presley was born in Tupelo, Mississippi, but he grew up in Memphis, Tennessee.

2. (addition)
Ernest Hemingway wrote *The Sun Also Rises*.
William Faulkner wrote *The Sound and the Fury*.

Ernest Hemingway wrote The Sun Also Rises, and William Faulkner wrote " ".

3. (cause)
Gary was not sure how he would get home.
His bike had been stolen from his office.   *For*

4. (alternative)
The Padres and the Chargers may have great seasons next year.   *So* — *7/19/07*
They may end up last in their respective leagues.   *but*

continued

5. (alternative)
Homer did not want to eat his plate of fat-free Spam.
He did not like the looks of his organic tofu shake.

_____

_____

6. (result)
Prosecutors could not convict Al Capone of most of his organized crime activities.
They sent him to jail for income tax evasion.

_____

_____

B. In each of the following sentences, change the underlined *and* to a coordinating conjunction that expresses the relationship between the ideas in the sentence. If the *and* does not need to be changed, do nothing to it.

7. Jenna loves her cockatiels, <u>and</u> she buys only the best birdseed for them.

Jenna loves her cockatiels, so she buys only the best birdseed for them.

_____

8. Some people think the monkey wrench is named after monkeys, <u>and</u> it really is named after its inventor, Charles Moncky.

_____

_____

9. You can have that tooth extracted, <u>and</u> you can have a root canal to try to save it.

_____

_____

Exercise 3A

continued

10. Miss Emily could not believe that her father was dead, <u>and</u> she refused to release his body.

_____

_____

11. Chelsea exercised every day, <u>and</u> she wanted to become a stronger gymnast.

_____

_____

12. Marilyn Monroe's original name was Norma Jean Baker, <u>and</u> Judy Garland's name was Frances Gumm.

_____

_____

13. Rocco was not excited about visiting the Liberace Museum, <u>and</u> he was not looking forward to seeing the tallest thermometer in the world.

_____

_____

14. Katie was not sure what it would be like to work with her father, <u>and</u> she took the job anyway.

_____

_____

15. Wal-Mart and Home Depot are good investments, <u>and</u> the price of their stock keeps going higher.

_____

_____

Exercise 3B

Place all prepositional phrases in parentheses and circle all conjunctions. For additional practice, underline all subjects once and all complete verbs twice.

1. The soldiers (and) the captain stood (at attention.)

2. The doctor had not been in practice for many years.

3. The leaves of maple trees turn red and yellow in the fall.

4. Popeye and one of his nephews have bought flowers for Olive.

5. On the daffodil was a butterfly with orange and black wings.

6. Holmes took the hair from the table and placed it in an envelope.

7. In the field behind our house landed a glowing, saucer-shaped aircraft.

8. The film must have been a foreign one, for there were subtitles at the bottom of the screen.

9. A nasty billy goat had lived under the bridge for years, but now he was missing.

10. A crowd of 20,000 people watched the fireworks from the banks of the river.

11. The sales representative tried to show the slides to us, but the projector would not work for her.

12. Luis wanted to redecorate his apartment, but the owner would not even pay for the paint.

13. The address book in his desk drawer must have contained the names of many important and influential people.

14. Because of a virus in the computer program, no one was able to apply for a license on Monday.

15. The Troglodytes had argued with the Luddites for years, but neither group had agreed on anything except the benefit of analog clocks.

Exercise 3C

In the following sentences, identify each of the underlined words as noun (N), pronoun (Pro), verb (V), adjective (Adj), adverb (Adv), conjunction (Conj), or preposition (Prep).

1. On March 25, 1944, Nicholas Alkemade reserved a place for <u>himself</u> ^{Pro} in <u>aviation</u> ^{Adj} history. 2. He was <u>in</u> the tail of a plane flying at 18,000 feet when the plane was hit by anti-aircraft fire. 3. Alkemade <u>looked</u> for his parachute only to find that he could <u>not</u> reach it because the plane was on fire. 4. He knew that he had <u>two</u> choices: burn alive in the tail of the plane <u>or</u> jump out without his parachute. 5. Believing <u>he</u> would be unconscious before he hit the ground, he <u>decided</u> to jump out. 6. As he plummeted <u>toward</u> the ground, he <u>had</u> no sensation of falling. 7. In fact, he <u>later</u> said that he felt as if he were floating on a soft cloud up to the <u>point</u> when he passed out. 8. Moments after he had jumped from the plane, Alkemade's <u>unconscious</u> body was falling <u>to</u> the earth at a speed of 120 m.p.h. 9. However, before he hit the ground, Alkemade crashed into a forest of <u>fir</u> trees where thick branches broke <u>his</u> fall. 10. Then, below the trees, he came to rest in eighteen inches of soft snow, which <u>acted</u> <u>as</u> a cushion. 11. When he <u>finally</u> regained <u>consciousness</u> several hours later, Alkemade was being cared for by a German patrol. 12. He told <u>them</u> his incredible story, <u>but</u> they did not believe that he had fallen from a plane without a parachute. 13. After all, Alkemade had <u>very</u> little to show as a <u>result</u> of his 18,000-foot fall. 14. He had a burned hand, a strained back, a <u>scalp</u> wound, <u>and</u> a twisted knee. 15. Nicholas Alkemade's story was later verified, and his fall <u>became</u> part of the folklore <u>of</u> aviation history.

Sentence Practice: Embedding Adjectives, Adverbs, and Prepositional Phrases

You have now learned to identify the basic parts of a sentence, but this skill it-self is not very useful unless you can use it to compose clear and effective sentences. Obviously, you have some flexibility when you compose sentences, but that flexibility is far from unlimited. The following sentence has a subject, a verb, five modifiers, one conjunction, and two prepositional phrases, but it makes no sense at all.

> Architect the quickly president for the drew up building new and plans the them to showed company.

With the parts arranged in a more effective order, the sentence, of course, makes sense.

> The architect quickly drew up plans for the new building and showed them to the company president.

There is no single correct pattern for the English sentence. The patterns you choose will be determined by the facts and ideas you wish to convey. For any given set of facts and ideas, there will be a relatively limited number of effective sentence patterns and an enormous number of ineffective ones. Knowing the parts of the sentence and how they function will help you choose the most ef-fective patterns to communicate your thoughts.

Assume, for example, that you have four facts to communicate:

1. *Moby Dick* was written by Herman Melville.

2. *Moby Dick* is a famous novel.

3. *Moby Dick* is about a whale.

4. The whale is white.

You could combine all these facts into a single sentence:

> *Moby Dick* was written by Herman Melville, and *Moby Dick* is a famous novel, and *Moby Dick* is about a whale, and the whale is white.

Although this sentence is grammatically correct, it is repetitious and sounds foolish.

If you choose the key fact from each sentence and combine the facts in the order in which they are presented, the result is not much better:

> *Moby Dick* was written by Herman Melville, a famous novel about a whale white.

A much more effective approach is to choose the sentence that expresses the fact or idea you think is most important and to use that as your **base sentence.** Of course, the sentence you choose as the base sentence may vary depending on the fact or idea you think is most important, but, whichever sentence you choose, it should contain the essential fact or idea that the other sentences somehow modify or explain. Once you have found the base sentence, you can **embed** the other facts or ideas into it as **adjectives, adverbs,** and **prepositional phrases.**

For example, let's use "*Moby Dick* is a famous novel" as the base sentence since it states an essential fact about *Moby Dick*—that it is a famous novel. The idea in sentence number one can be embedded into the base sentence as a **prepositional phrase:**

　　　　by Herman Melville
Moby Dick ˄is a famous novel.

The idea in sentence three can now be embedded into the expanded base sentence as another **prepositional phrase:**

　　　　　　　　　　　　　　　　　　about a whale
Moby Dick by Herman Melville is a famous novel˄.

Sentence number four contains an **adjective** that modifies the noun *whale,* so it can be embedded into the sentence by placing it before *whale:*

Moby Dick by Herman Melville is a famous novel

　　　　　white
about a ˄whale.

Thus, your final sentence will read:

Moby Dick by Herman Melville is a famous novel about a white whale.

The same facts could be embedded in a number of other ways. Two of them are:

Moby Dick, a famous novel by Herman Melville, is about a white whale.

Herman Melville's *Moby Dick* is a famous novel about a white whale.

This process of embedding is called **sentence combining.** The purpose of practicing sentence combining is to give you an opportunity to apply the grammatical concepts you have learned in the chapter. For instance, in the above example the base sentence was expanded into a more interesting sentence by means of prepositional phrases and an adjective. Practicing this process will also help you develop greater flexibility in your sentence structure and will show you how to enrich your sentences through the addition of significant details. After all, the use of specific details is one of the most important ways of making writing interesting and effective.

■   **PRACTICE**

a. The dalmatian was faithful.
b. The dalmatian was near the fire hydrant.
c. The dalmatian watched the firefighters.
d. The dalmatian was eager.
e. The firefighters were on the truck.

1. In the space below, write the base sentence, the one with the main idea.

   _____

2. Embed the **adjective** in sentence A into the base sentence by placing it before the noun that it modifies.

   _____

3. Embed the **prepositional phrase** in sentence B into the sentence by placing it after the word that it modifies.

   _____

4. Change the **adjective** in sentence D into an **adverb** (add "ly") and place it before the verb that it modifies.

   _____

   _____

5. Embed the **prepositional phrase** in sentence E by placing it after the word that it modifies.

   _____

   _____

Sentence Combining: Exercise A

In each of the following sets of sentences, use the first sentence as the base sentence. Embed into the base sentence the adjectives, adverbs, and prepositional phrases underlined in the sentences below it.

▶ **EXAMPLE**   a. The tiger paced its cage.
b. The tiger was <u>rare</u>.
c. The tiger was <u>black and white</u>.
d. The tiger paced <u>impatiently.</u>
e. The tiger paced <u>during the entire night</u>.

The rare black and white tiger impatiently

paced its cage during the entire night.

1. a. The mother found her child.
b. The child was <u>lost</u>.
c. The mother was <u>grateful</u>.
d. The child was lost <u>in the mall</u>.

2. a. The blacksnake was coiled.
b. The blacksnake was <u>huge</u>.
c. The blacksnake was <u>in the path</u>.
d. The path was <u>to the mailbox</u>.

3. a. The ocean liner was launched.
b. The ocean liner was <u>new</u>.
c. The ocean liner was <u>Australian</u>.
d. The ocean liner was launched <u>at the shipyard</u>.
e. The shipyard was <u>in the harbor</u>.
f. The harbor was <u>in San Francisco</u>.

continued

4. a. The singer sang the national anthem.
   b. The singer sang <u>before the baseball game</u>.
   c. The singer was <u>plump</u>.
   d. The baseball game was <u>in San Diego</u>.
   e. The singer sang <u>in a harsh voice</u>.

   _____

   _____

5. a. The city council members voted for a pay raise.
   b. The city council members were <u>recently elected</u>.
   c. The members were <u>from Grafton</u>.
   d. They voted <u>quickly</u>.
   e. The pay raise was <u>for themselves</u>.

   _____

   _____

Sentence Combining: Exercise B

First, choose a base sentence and circle the letter next to it. Then, using adjectives, adverbs, and prepositional phrases, embed the other facts and ideas into the base sentence.

▶ **EXAMPLE**
    a. The mountains were tall.
    b. The mountains were snow-covered.
    ⓒ The mountains towered over the hikers.
    d. There were three hikers.
    e. The hikers were from France.
    f. The hikers were lost.
    g. The mountains towered menacingly.

The tall, snow-covered mountains towered menacingly over the three lost hikers from France.

1. a. The trial was long.
    b. The trial was scandalous.
    c. The trial excited the journalists and spectators.
    d. The journalists and spectators were in the courtroom.
    e. The courtroom was crowded.

2. a. The shark was long.
    b. The shark attacked its prey.
    c. The shark was white.
    d. It attacked with deadly speed.
    e. It devoured its prey.

3. a. It was on a Friday night.
    b. It was rainy.
    c. The musicians held a concert.
    d. It was a jazz concert.
    e. It was for the benefit of homeless people.

Sentence Combining: Exercise B

continued

4. a. The storm was loud.
   b. The storm was fierce.
   c. The storm frightened the sailors.
   d. The sailors were on the ship.
   e. The sailors were inexperienced.

   _____

   _____

5. a. The players went on a trip.
   b. There were five players.
   c. They played guitar.
   d. They went to Memphis.
   e. They went to Elvis Presley's home.

   _____

   _____

6. a. It was in 1903.
   b. It was at Kitty Hawk.
   c. Kitty Hawk is in North Carolina.
   d. The Wright brothers did not make the first successful flying machine.

   _____

   _____

7. a. It was in 1889.
   b. It was at the Potomac River.
   c. Samuel Langley is generally given credit for building the first flying machine.
   d. It was a heavier-than-air flying machine.
   e. It was unmanned.

   _____

   _____

Sentence Combining: Exercise B

continued

8. a. It was on December 8, 1903.
   b. It was just nine days before the Wright brothers' flight.
   c. Langley tried a manned flight, but it failed.
   d. It failed due to a catapult problem.

   _____

   _____

9. a. The Wright brothers' flight was famous.
   b. It was historical.
   c. The Wright brothers' flight was considered the first manned flight.
   d. It was considered the first powered flight.
   e. It was considered the first controlled flight.
   f. It was considered the first sustained flight in a heavier-than-air craft.

   _____

   _____

10. a. Langley was discouraged.
    b. He was discouraged about his failed flight.
    c. He was discouraged about the Wright brothers' successful flight.
    d. He gave up aviation.
    e. He gave it up forever.

    _____

    _____

Paragraph Practice:
Narrating an Event

If you have ever sat for hours before a blank sheet of paper or stared for what seemed like forever at a blank computer screen, you know how difficult and frustrating it can be to write a paper. In fact, some people have such trouble simply <u>starting</u> their papers that for them writing becomes a truly agonizing experience.

Fortunately, writing does not have to be so difficult. If you learn how to use the steps involved in the process of writing, you can avoid much of the frustration and enjoy more of the satisfaction that comes from writing a successful paper. In this section, you will practice using the three general activities that make up the writing process—**prewriting, writing**, and **rewriting**—to produce a paragraph based on the following assignment.

Writing Assignment

Exercises 1C (page 24), 2C (page 33), and 3C (page 45) of Chapter One are about three memorable events: Poon Lim's record-setting ordeal in a life raft, a tragic love story, and Nicholas Alkemade's 18,000-foot fall from an airplane. Although few of us have had experiences as dramatic as these, we all have had things happen to us that we remember either with warm, positive feelings or with uncomfortable, negative ones.

For this writing assignment, use the writing process explained below to describe an event that has happened to you. Ask yourself, "What events—either from the distant past or from more recent times—have happened to me that I remember well?" Perhaps you remember your first date, your first traffic ticket, or even the birth of your first child. Or perhaps you remember the day you won a race in a track meet, performed alone on a stage, or attended your first college class. Often the <u>best</u> event to write about will not be the first one you think of.

Reading Assignment

The reading selections in the "Narrating an Event" section of Chapter Seven can help you see how professional writers tell their stories. Read one or more of the selections, as assigned by your instructor, and use the questions that follow them to develop ideas for your own paper.

Prewriting

Prewriting is the part of the writing process that will help you get past "writer's block" and into writing. It consists of <u>anything</u> you do to generate ideas and get started, but three of the most successful prewriting techniques are **freewriting**, **brainstorming**, and **clustering**.

Freewriting

Freewriting is based on one simple but essential idea: When you sit down to write, you write. You don't stare at your paper or look out the window, wondering what in the world you could write about. Instead, you <u>write down</u> your thoughts and questions even if you have no idea what topic you should focus on. In addition, as you freewrite, you do not stop to correct spelling, grammar, or punctuation errors. After all, the purpose of freewriting is to generate ideas, not to write the final draft of your paper.

Here is how some freewriting might look for the assignment described above.

> To describe an event? What could I write about that? I don't have a lot of "events" that I can think of—but I suppose I must have some. What do I remember? How about recently? Have I gone anywhere or has anything happened to me? I went skiing last month and took a bad fall—but so what? That wouldn't be very interesting. How about something I remember that I didn't like—like what? Death? Too depressing. Besides, I have never been closely involved in death. I was in a car accident once, but that was too long ago, and it doesn't really interest me. How about—what? I'm stuck. How about events I have good memories about—wait—I remember almost drowning when I was practicing for water polo in high school. <u>That</u> was a wild event. I could do it. Any other possibilities? How about good memories—like the time I made that lucky catch in Little League. That would be good. Or the fish I caught with my dad when I was a kid. Lots of good memories there. Any others? Yeah—I joined a softball league recently—that was a real experience, especially because it'd been so long since I'd played baseball. But I can't think of any particular thing I'd write about it.—Of all these, I think I like the drowning one best. I <u>really</u> remember that one and all the feelings that went with it.

You can tell that the above writer was not trying to produce a clean, well-written copy of his paper. Instead, he wrote down his thoughts as they occurred to him, and the result was a very informal rush of ideas that eventually led him to a topic, a near-drowning that occurred when he was in high school. Now that he has his topic, he can continue to freewrite to generate details about the event that he can use in his paper.

Brainstorming

Brainstorming is another prewriting technique that you can use to generate ideas. Brainstorming is similar to freewriting in that you write down your thoughts without censoring or editing them, but it differs in that the thoughts usually appear as a list of ideas rather than as separate sentences. Here is an example of how the above freewriting might have looked as brainstorming.

An event I remember well—what could I use?

    recently?

        fall while skiing—no

    things I didn't like

        death? too depressing

        car accident I was in? too long ago

        almost drowned at practice—<u>good one</u>

    good memories?

        lucky catch in Little League

        fishing with Dad

    <u>Use the one about almost drowning.</u>

Clustering is a third prewriting technique that many people find helpful. It differs from brainstorming and freewriting in that it is written almost like an informal map. To "cluster" your ideas, start out with an idea or question and draw a circle around it. Then connect related ideas to the circle and continue in that way. Here is how the brainstorming material might have looked if it were "clustered."

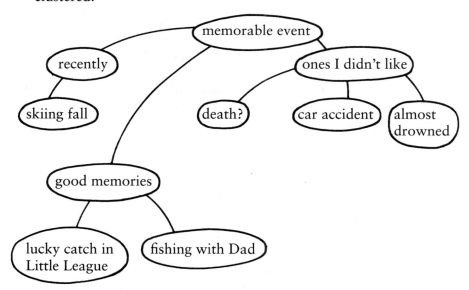

As you can see, clustering provides a mental picture of the ideas you generate. As such, it can help you organize your material <u>as</u> you think of it.

Freewriting, brainstorming, and clustering are only three of many techniques to help you get started writing. When you use them, you should feel free to move from one to the other at any time. And, of course, your instructor may suggest other ways to help you get started. Whatever technique you use, the point is to <u>start writing</u>. Do your thinking on paper (or at a computer), not while you are staring out a window. Here's a good motto that you should try to follow whenever you have a writing assignment due: **Think in ink**.

Prewriting Application: Finding Your Topic

Use freewriting, brainstorming, or clustering (or a combination of the three) to find a topic idea that you can use for the assignment to describe an event. Once you have decided on your topic, continue to prewrite to decide what details you will include in your paper. Remember that you should not correct spelling or sentence errors as you prewrite. Use the following questions to think of possible topics.

1. What experiences of yours have been particularly exciting, happy, or pleasant?

2. What experiences are you most proud of?

3. What events bring you disappointing, unpleasant, or fearful memories?

4. What are your most embarrassing memories?

5. What strange or unusual things have happened to you?

6. What dangerous or frightening experiences have you had?

7. What are the "firsts" in your life? Consider your first day in high school, your first day on a team or as part of a group, your first performance, your first date, your first camping trip, your first traffic ticket.

8. What experiences have inspired you, changed the way you think about life, or made you into a different person?

9. What events do you remember from your early childhood?

10. What events do you remember from elementary school or high school, from vacations or trips?

Prewriting Application: Talking to Others

Once you have your topic, form groups of two, three, or four and tell your experiences to each other. Telling others about an event is a good way to decide what details to include and how much to say. And listening to someone else's story will help you learn what will keep an audience interested in your own story.

As you describe your event to others, make it as interesting as you can by describing what happened, how you felt, and what you thought. As you listen to the stories of others and as you describe your own experience, consider these questions:

1. What are the time and place of the event? How old were you? What time of day did it occur? What time of year? What was the weather like?

2. Can you visualize the scene? What is the name of the place where the event occurred? What physical features are in the area—trees? buildings? furniture? cars? other people?

3. How did you feel as the event progressed? What were you thinking each step of the way?

4. Did your thoughts and feelings change as the event occurred?

5. What parts of the event would be clearer if they were explained more?

The Topic Sentence

When you have worked through the prewriting stage of the writing process, read over what you have so far. At this point you should be ready to focus your paper by limiting your event to details that illustrate one **central point**.

Focusing your writing on one **central point** is important, for the more you limit your topic to one point, the more likely you will be to describe your topic in a detailed and thorough manner. To limit your description, reread your prewriting. Look for related details that seem to focus on *one particular reaction* to the event. These are the details that you should emphasize in your paragraph. Once you have identified that particular reaction, you are ready to write a preliminary **topic sentence**.

The topic sentence is the one sentence in your paragraph that states both your **topic** and the **central point** that you intend to make about that topic. Although it can appear in a variety of places within the paragraph, for college writing you should write it as the first sentence of the paragraph so that the point you intend to make is clear from the start.

Even paragraphs about events, such as the one you are writing for this assignment, have some *point*. In a psychology text, for example, an airplane crash might be described in detail to help the reader understand how such an event can affect the relatives of those involved. And a history text might describe what happened at the Battle of Gettysburg to help the reader understand why it was a major turning point in the Civil War. Certainly in your own college papers, you will often be expected to use examples of events to illustrate the points you are trying to make.

Here are some examples of topic sentences drawn from the exercises in Chapter One. Note that each topic sentence contains a topic and a central point.

▶ **EXAMPLES**

topic

During World War II, **a Chinese seaman** experienced one of

central point

the most amazing survival adventures of the war.

central point   topic

One of the most poignant stories of all time is the myth of Pyramus

and Thisbe.

topic

On March 25, 1944, Nicholas Alkemade reserved a place

central point

for himself in aviation history.

As you write your topic sentence, be sure that it contains both a **topic** and a **central point**. Not all sentences make good topic sentences, as the following examples illustrate:

1. A sentence that has no central point.

► **EXAMPLE**   My paragraph is about my youngest sister's wedding.

In this sentence the topic (my youngest sister's wedding) is clear, but no central point about that wedding is expressed. An improved topic sentence might be:

► **EXAMPLE**   My youngest sister's wedding last July was one of the most hilarious events I have ever experienced.

In this sentence, a central point—that the wedding was hilarious—has been clearly expressed.

2. A sentence that merely states a fact.

► **EXAMPLE**   A few months ago I saw a major car accident.

This sentence simply states a fact. There is no central point to be explained after the fact is stated. An improved topic sentence might be:

► **EXAMPLE**   I will never forget how horrified I was a few months ago when I was an unwilling witness to a major car accident.

This sentence now makes a statement about the accident that causes the reader to want more explanation.

3. A sentence that is too general for the topic of a single paragraph.

► **EXAMPLE**   My spring break this year was really something.

Both the topic (spring break) and the central point (it was "something") are far too general to describe in detail in one paragraph. Here is a more focused topic sentence:

► **EXAMPLE**   On the last day of spring break this year, my vacation in Palm Springs, California, turned from wonderful to absolutely miserable in just one hour.

This sentence now focuses on a specific event—the last day of spring break in Palm Springs—and on a precise central point—it changed from wonderful to miserable.

Prewriting Application: Working with Topic Sentences

In each sentence below, underline the topic once and the central point twice.

1. While driving to Arrowhead Stadium last night, I had a terrifying experience.

2. I don't think I have ever been as embarrassed as I was on the night that I first met my future husband.

3. When I stepped out on the stage at Rancho Buena Vista High School, I had no idea that what was about to happen would change my life.

4. My first scuba diving experience was as exhilarating as it was nerve-wracking.

5. I feel a great sense of pride and satisfaction whenever I think of the day when I decided to take the biggest risk of my life.

Prewriting Application: Evaluating Topic Sentences

Write "No" before each sentence that would not make a good topic sentence and "Yes" before each sentence that would make a good one. Be prepared to explain your answers.

_____ 1. Last August I visited Lake Ponset, South Dakota.

_____ 2. Giving birth to my first child made me wonder if I would ever want to have children again.

_____ 3. My heart nearly broke the day I decided it was time to take my dog, Jasper, on his last ride to the veterinarian's office.

_____ 4. My first year in college was definitely interesting.

_____ 5. One of my earliest memories of my father and me spending time together is also one of my most disappointing ones.

_____ 6. It all happened when I decided to go skiing in Aspen, Colorado.

_____ 7. My paragraph will be about the time I was in the Rose Parade.

_____ **8.** I was amazed at everything that happened to us while driving from Amarillo, Texas, to Atlanta, Georgia.

_____ **9.** Spooky, strange, weird—these words don't even begin to describe what happened to me that night in the abandoned house on Elm Street.

_____ **10.** A simple ride on the roller coaster in Belmont Park turned out to be one of the most thrilling experiences of my life.

Writing

Writing a full draft of your paper is the next step in the writing process. The trick to writing your first draft without getting stuck is to remember that what you write now is not your final copy, so you can allow yourself to make mistakes and to write awkward sentences. Don't worry about how "correct" your writing is. Instead, just describe your experience as thoroughly as you can.

Here is a sample first draft of the paper on drowning. As you read it, notice that the writer has not yet corrected any errors it may contain.

The Challenge Set (First Draft)

I almost drowned when I was sixteen. It all happened one day at practice for water polo. I was a sophomore on the Kearney High School water polo team. One day I volunteered for the dreaded "Challenge Set." I had just finished the first lap underwater. I still felt good. As I come to the wall, I make the decison to go for another lap, I keep swimming, but my lungs collapse. I took a few more strokes, and then it happened. I blacked out. All I remember was seeing black. I felt completely relaxed. Then I remember hearing voices. Suddenly, starting to cough violently. When I opened my eyes, the first person I saw was my coach. He told me what had happened, I was a little shaken. I couldn't believe that I almost died. This was really a frightening experience that I remember whenever I go for a swim.

The above first draft is far from perfect. It contains writing errors and could use more descriptive details. However, it has accomplished its purpose: <u>It has given the writer a draft to work with and to improve with revision.</u>

Writing Application: Producing Your First Draft

Now write the first draft of your paragraph. Remember that your goal is <u>not</u> to write an error-free draft. Rather, it is to write a <u>first</u> draft that opens with a preliminary topic sentence, a draft that you can then continue to work on and improve.

Rewriting

Rewriting consists of two stages: **revising** and **editing**. In the **revising** stage of the writing process, you work on the "larger" areas of your paper—its content, organization, and sentence structure. Here are some suggestions.

1. Improve your preliminary topic sentence.

   You can often improve your topic sentence <u>after</u> you have written your first draft because now you really have something to introduce. In fact, if you look at the <u>concluding</u> sentences of your first draft, you may find a clearer statement of the central point of your paragraph than the one you have in your opening sentence. If that is the case, rewrite your opening sentence to include that statement.

2. Add more details.

   After you have written the first draft, add any further details that might improve your paper. Look especially for those that will emphasize the central point of your topic sentence.

3. Reorganize the details in the first draft.

   There are many ways to organize a paper, but one of the most common ones is to save the most important details for last. Another way to organize details, especially if you are describing an event, is to list the details in chronological order. Whichever way you choose, now is the time to make any changes in the order of your material.

4. Combine related sentences and ideas.

   Combine sentences that are obviously related. Where possible, use sentence combining techniques to embed material from one sentence into another.

Editing is the final stage of the writing process. When you edit, you correct the spelling, grammar, and punctuation errors that you find. Careful editing is an important step whenever you write, but remember not to edit too soon. As you can see, <u>most</u> of the writing process is spent on prewriting, writing, and revising.

Rewriting Application: Responding to Writing

Reread the first draft of "The Challenge Set" on page 63. Then respond to the following questions:

1. What is the writer's central feeling about his experience? Where is it stated? How would you reword the opening sentence to express that central feeling?

2. Where should the writer add more details? What kind of details would make his paragraph more colorful and descriptive?

3. Should any of the details be reorganized or presented in a different order?

4. What sentences would you combine because they contain related ideas?

5. What changes should the writer make in spelling, grammar, or punctuation?

Here is how the student who nearly drowned revised and edited his first draft. Compare it to his first draft

The Challenge Set

Revised opening sentence includes writer's reaction to the event.

When I was sixteen, I had a frightening experience that I still remember whenever I go for a swim. This event took place when I was a sophomore on the Kearney High School water polo team. One day at practice, I volunteered to try the dreaded "Challenge Set." **It consisted**

Added details.

of about three to four players attempting to swim fifty yards, two laps of the pool, on a single breath. I started out full of confidence, but I had

Combined sentences.

no idea what was about to happen. When I came to the wall at the end of the first lap, I still felt good, so I made the decision to go for another lap. I made the flip turn and pushed off the wall. I still felt okay, but

Added details.

without my knowing it, my lungs had started to collapse. **I remember beginning to worry when I saw the blue hash marks, the halfway markers. I had just a little way to go, but my head was whirling and my chest felt like it was about to explode.** I took a few more strokes, but

Combined sentences.

then it happened. I blacked out. **All I remember was seeing black and feeling completely relaxed. Then, just as I began to hear voices, I started to cough violently. Every time I tried to take a breath, a searing pain shot through me. I was terrified.** When I opened my eyes, the first

Added details.

person I saw was my coach, **a state beach lifeguard. I was lying in his arms, not knowing where I was or what had happened to me.** When he

Added details.

told me what had happened, I was really shaken. I couldn't believe I had almost died. **I got out of the pool, got dressed, and sat in the stands waiting for practice to end.** I don't think I'll ever forget the day I nearly drowned.

Rewriting Application: Revising and Editing Your Own Draft

Now revise and edit your first draft. As you do so, remember to <u>revise</u> first:

1. Improve your topic sentence.

2. Add more details, especially those that emphasize the central point.

3. Reorganize the details.

4. Combine related sentences and ideas.

Once you have revised, then <u>edit</u> for spelling, grammar, and punctuation errors. As you can tell, thorough revising and editing will involve several new drafts, not just one. Once you have a draft with which you are satisfied, prepare a clean final draft, following the format your instructor has requested.

Chapter One Practice Test

A. In the spaces provided, indicate whether the underlined word is a subject (S), a helping verb (HV), or a main verb (MV). If it is none of these, leave the space blank.

_____ **1.** The air traffic controllers <u>closed</u> the airport because of the dense fog.

_____ **2.** Then the lieutenant <u>tells</u> the general about Desdemona.

_____ **3.** The duck <u>waddling</u> up the driveway looked as if it had lost its best friend.

_____ **4.** I have <u>never</u> played golf, and I don't think that I ever will.

_____ **5.** Sherman was <u>making</u> plans for his trip to Georgia.

_____ **6.** Did <u>anyone</u> notice Ariel's bright purple hair?

_____ **7.** Although Karl had <u>been</u> diligent in his training, he was not very confident about the race.

_____ **8.** Onto the <u>stage</u> stepped a sinister man in a black cloak.

_____ **9.** <u>Give</u> this $150,000,000 to the first person you meet.

_____ **10.** Gertrude <u>might</u> have known about Dad's plan to take a nap in the garden.

B. Underline all subjects once and all complete verbs twice in the following sentences.

11. Are Robert and Enid coming with us?

12. The members of the band must have been delayed in Washington.

13. Some of the people at the concert wore spiked hair and nose rings.

14. Henry should not have eaten that moldy peach.

15. Somebody had left a book on the floor, and Darby had found it.

16. Sometimes politicians and advertisers do not make themselves clear.

17. A white toy poodle barked loudly at the intruder and then ran into the back room.

18. Did Ernest leave with Gertrude, or are they still angry at each other?

19. Cesar Chavez organized many boycotts but always insisted on nonviolent action.

20. As the wolf was blowing on the house, the pigs were running out the back door.

Chapter One Practice Test

continued

C. Write sentences of your own that follow the suggested patterns.

21. A statement with one subject, one helping verb, and one main verb (S-HV-MV):

_____

_____

22. A question with one helping verb, one subject, and one main verb (HV-S-MV?):

_____

_____

23. A statement with two subjects joined by *and,* one helping verb, and one main verb (S "and" S HV-MV):

_____

_____

24. A statement with one subject, two helping verbs, and a main verb (S-HV-HV-MV):

_____

_____

25. A statement with a subject and a main verb followed by *although* and another subject and main verb (S-MV "although" S-MV):

_____

_____

D. In the following sentences, identify all adjectives by writing "Adj" above them, and identify all adverbs by writing "Adv" above them.

26. Roy sometimes wondered if Trigger was a happy horse.

27. The groom suddenly fell to the marble floor and began to cry.

28. The pilot did not see the UFO near the wing of the company plane.

29. Queequeg's harpoon sailed swiftly through the air toward the whale.

30. Homer was dreaming about a Spam sandwich when he was rudely awakened.

Chapter One Practice Test

continued

E. In the following sentences, place all prepositional phrases in parentheses.

31. When he left for New Orleans, the doctor placed a single pink rose on his wife's plate.

32. During a long winter night, Victor persuaded Helen to accompany him to South America.

33. Because of the cold weather, Rodrigo wore his wet suit into the water.

34. After dark, Cecil played his saxophone under the bridge.

35. The man with the stolen money is standing between the two pillars.

F. In the following sentences, add coordinating conjunctions that show the relationship indicated in the parentheses.

36. My father ordered the bug zapper, _____ I zapped all of the bugs in the house. (addition)

37. Jelly beans are Jack's favorite candy, _____ he bought ten pounds of them. (result)

38. The Bermuda Triangle lay directly ahead, _____ the pilot did not change course. (contrast)

39. You may keep everything you have won so far, _____ you can trade it all for whatever is behind door number three. (alternative)

40. The sailors were frustrated, _____ they could not choose between that vicious dog and that treacherous whirlpool. (cause)

G. In the following sentences, identify the underlined words by writing one of the following abbreviations above each word: noun (N), pronoun (Pro), verb (V), adjective (Adj), adverb (Adv), conjunction (Conj), preposition (Prep).

41. The time <u>capsule</u> must <u>have</u> contained many interesting items.

42. The recent rains have turned Alisha's backyard <u>into</u> a <u>swamp</u>.

43. Edgar wondered if that <u>infernal</u> raven <u>would</u> ever stop saying "Nevermore."

continued

44. Either the fried okra <u>or</u> the shrimp gumbo was responsible for making Ralph <u>severely</u> ill.

45. Wearing his special Spam chef's hat, Homer <u>cooked</u> the catfish <u>over</u> the coals.

46. Mark McGwire signed the ball and handed <u>it</u> to a <u>young</u> fan.

47. While on a backpacking trip, the veterinarian <u>skillfully</u> sewed up a <u>gash</u> in her son's leg with a bit of fishing line.

48. *The Haunting* <u>was</u> a remake of *The Haunting of Hill House,* <u>but</u> it was not nearly as good.

49. Hillary is willing to trade <u>five</u> Frankie Avalon recordings <u>for</u> anything sung by Nancy Sinatra.

50. Until Mr. Coltrane had <u>completely</u> cleaned his saxophone, he would not allow <u>himself</u> to play "After the Rain."

Understanding Sentence Patterns

In Chapter One you learned the terms that describe how words function in a sentence. These terms will help you understand how the various word groups operate in a sentence. Understanding these word groups will help you see not only how sentences are put together but also how to revise your writing effectively and systematically. Without some knowledge of these word groups, you really can't even define what a sentence is.

Consider, for example, two common definitions of a sentence:

1. A sentence is a group of words that expresses a complete thought.

2. A sentence is a group of words that contains a subject and a verb.

These definitions may seem adequate, but, if you consider them carefully, you will see that neither of them is really accurate. For example, some sentences do not seem to express "a complete thought." Consider the sentence "*It fell.*" Do these two words really convey a complete thought? In one sense they do: A specific action is communicated, and a subject, though an indefinite one, is identified. However, the sentence raises more questions than it answers. What fell? Why did it fall? Where did it fall to? The sentence could refer to an apple, a star, the sky, or the Roman empire. If someone walked up to you in the street and said, "*It fell,*" you certainly would not feel that a complete thought had been communicated to you, and yet the two words do form a sentence.

The second definition is no more satisfactory. The words "*Because his father was sleeping*" do <u>not</u> make up a sentence even though they contain both a subject (*father*) and a verb (*was sleeping*). Although it is true that all sentences must contain a subject and a verb, it does not necessarily follow that every group of words with a subject and a verb is a sentence.

The only definition of a sentence that is <u>always</u> correct is the following one: A sentence is a group of words that contains at least one main clause.

> **sentence**
> A sentence is a group of words that contains at least one main clause.

You will understand this definition easily if you know what a **main clause** is, but it will be incomprehensible if you do not. Thus, it is critical that you be able to identify this word group, for, if you cannot identify a main clause, you cannot be certain that you are using complete sentences in your writing.

Clauses

Main Clauses and Subordinate Clauses

A clause is a group of words that contains at least one subject and at least one verb.

> **clause**
>
> A clause is a group of words that contains at least one subject and at least one verb.

The two types of clauses are **main clause** and **subordinate clause**.

1. A **main clause** is a group of words that contains at least one subject and one verb and that <u>expresses a complete idea</u>.

2. A **subordinate clause** is a group of words that contains at least one subject and one verb but that <u>does not express a complete idea</u>. All subordinate clauses begin with **subordinators**.

▶ **EXAMPLE**

                        sub. clause   main clause
[Although he seldom plays,] [Raymond is an excellent golfer.]

This example contains two clauses, each with a subject and a verb. As you can see, the clause *Raymond is an excellent golfer* could stand by itself as a sentence. But the clause *Although he seldom plays* cannot stand by itself (even though it has a subject and a verb) because it needs the main clause to complete its thought and because it begins with the subordinator *although*.

Subordinators

Subordinators indicate the relationship between the subordinate clause and the main clause. Learning to recognize the two types of subordinators—subordinating conjunctions and relative pronouns—will help you identify subordinate clauses.

Subordinating Conjunctions		Relative Pronouns	
after	so that	that	who(ever)
although	than	which	whom(ever)
as	though		whose
as if	unless		
as long as	until		
because	when		
before	whenever		
even though	where		
if	wherever		
since	while		

NOTE: Some of the words in the above list of subordinators are underlined (*after, as, before, since, until*). These words are used as prepositions when they do not introduce a subordinate clause.

► **EXAMPLES**   prepositional phrase: *after dinner*

subordinate clause: *after I eat dinner*

The following are examples of sentences containing subordinate clauses. (Note that each subordinate clause begins with a subordinator.)

► **EXAMPLES**

                    sub. clause   main clause

[**Before** his horse had crossed the finish line,] [the jockey suddenly stood up in his saddle.]

        main clause   sub. clause

[Fried Spam is a dish] [**that** few people love.]

        main clause   sub. clause

[Antonio won the spelling bee] [**because** he spelled *penicillin* correctly.]

■ **PRACTICE**   Identify the following word groups as main clauses (MC) or subordinate clauses (SC) or neither (N).

1. When Tico bought his new car.   *SC*

2. He repainted it.   *MC*

3. Then he bought new tires.   *MC*

4. In the summer.   *N*

5. When his sister borrowed the car.   *SC*

6. She painted it a new color.   _____

7. That he disliked.   _____

8. He was angry about the paint job.   _____

9. Which he hated.   _____

10. At first sight.   _____

■   **PRACTICE**   Identify the following word groups as subordinate clauses (SC) or prepositional phrases (PP).

    1. Until I see you again.   _SC_

    2. Until Monday's deadline.   _____

    3. Until next year.   _____

    4. As the Queen of Egypt.   _____

    5. As I was turning the corner.   _____

    6. Before we begin.   _____

    7. Before midnight.   _____

    8. After the final game.   _____

    9. After the dinner is finished.   _____

  10. After church.   _____

■   **PRACTICE**   Underline the subordinate clauses in the following sentences and circle the subordinators. Not all sentences contain subordinate clauses.

    1. An epicurean is a person (who) is rather fond of eating and drinking.

    2. When Fergal and Rory entered the room, everyone stood.

    3. Before the end of the movie, half of the audience had walked out.

    4. Good things happen to people who are generous.

    5. If the new software arrives, we will search the Internet.

6. On New Year's Eve, the station showed folk dances that were performed around the world.

7. The clock broke after one year because it was poorly made to begin with.

8. The teacher looked at the student whose poem she was reading.

9. Mr. Rojas decided not to leave the house until he had eaten dinner.

10. The officer looked at the house where the hostages were held.

Adverb and Adjective Subordinate Clauses

Subordinate clauses may function as adverbs, adjectives, or nouns in their sentences. Therefore, they are called **adverb clauses, adjective clauses,** or **noun clauses.** We will be discussing adverb and adjective clauses, but not noun clauses. Although we frequently use noun clauses in our writing, they seldom present problems in punctuation or clarity.

Adverb Clauses

Like single-word adverbs, adverb subordinate clauses can modify verbs. For example, in the sentence *Clare ate a big breakfast because she had a busy day ahead of her,* the adverb clause *because she had a busy day ahead of her* modifies the verb *ate.* It explains <u>why</u> Clare ate a big breakfast.

Another characteristic of adverb clauses is that they begin with a **subordinating conjunction,** not a relative pronoun. In addition, in most cases an adverb clause can be moved around in its sentence, and the sentence will still make sense.

► **EXAMPLES**   [**When** she ate the mushroom,] Alice grew taller.

Alice grew taller [**when** she ate the mushroom.]

Alice, [**when** she ate the mushroom,] grew taller.

NOTE: When the adverb clause begins the sentence, it is followed by a comma, as in the first example. When the adverb clause ends a sentence, no comma is needed. When the adverb clause interrupts the main clause, it is enclosed by commas.

■ **PRACTICE**   Underline the adverb clauses in the following sentences. Circle the subordinating conjunctions.

1. (Unless) you leave soon, you will miss your flight.

2. Whenever Calista sees a doughnut shop, she heads the other way.

3. The snow chains fell off because they had not been fastened correctly.

4. Admiral Nelson and Captain Aubrey always stand straight when the sea battle is raging around them.

5. Clyde Merdly waited until Homer had eaten the Spam cordon bleu.

■ **PRACTICE**   Add adverb clauses of your own to the following main clauses in the spaces indicated. Use commas where they are needed.

1. The train could not make it across the mountain _because snow was_ _blocking the tracks._

2. _____

   _____ King Richard asked for a horse.

3. The house seemed to shake for about two minutes _____

   _____

4. _____

   _____ Sherri checked her answering machine.

5. _____

   _____ they asked for the leftovers to take home to their dog.

Adjective Clauses

Adjective subordinate clauses modify nouns or pronouns just as single-word adjectives do. Adjective clauses follow the nouns or pronouns they modify, and they usually begin with a **relative pronoun**—*who, whom, whose, which, that* (and sometimes *when* or *where*). As you can see in the examples below, relative pronouns sometimes serve as subjects of their clauses. We will discuss the rules for punctuating adjective clauses in Chapter Three.

▶ **EXAMPLES** The horse [**that** Mr. Lee liked best] was named Traveller. (The adjective clause modifies *horse*.)

On the top shelf was the trophy [**that** Irma had won for her model of the Battle of Shiloh]. (The adjective clause modifies *trophy*.)

Hampton, [**which** is Michelle's hooded rat,] resides at the foot of her bed. (The adjective clause modifies *Hampton,* and the relative pronoun *which* is the subject of the clause.)

NOTE: As you can see in the example above, the adjective clause often appears between the subject and the verb of the main clause. In addition, as you can see in the following example, sometimes the relative pronoun is left out.

▶ **EXAMPLE** The man [I met yesterday] works for the CIA. (Here the adjective clause modifies the noun *man*, but the relative pronoun *whom* is left out.)

A note about relative pronouns:

1. Use *who* or *whom* to refer to people only.

2. Use *which* to refer to nonhuman things only, such as animals or objects.

3. Use *that* to refer to either people or nonhuman things.

■ **PRACTICE** Underline the adjective clauses in the following sentences and circle the relative pronouns.

1. Our newest movie theater, (which) appeals to a special audience, opened just last week.

2. Called Pardner, it is especially for people who like western movies.

3. It has a snack bar that sells beans and beef jerky.

4. The films, which are always westerns, feature stars like John Wayne, Clint Eastwood, Roy Rogers, and Gene Autry.

5. The street where the theater is located is next to the stockyards.

■ **PRACTICE**   Add adjective clauses of your own to the following main clauses.

1. Jason noticed a light go on in an upper floor of the building.

   Jason noticed a light go on in an upper floor

   of the building that he was passing.

2. The girl made her yo-yo do many tricks.

   _____

   _____

3. Ms. Than wore a new coat.

   _____

   _____

4. Euphegenia showed us a picture of her house.

   _____

   _____

5. A major battle of World War I took place at Gallipoli.

   _____

   _____

■ **PRACTICE**   In the following sentences, underline the subordinate clauses and identify them as adverb clauses (Adv) or Adjective clauses (Adj).

1. When the film ended, Tran stayed to watch the credits.   *Adv*

2. Desdemona looked for the handkerchief that she had given to

   her husband.   _____

3. One man pretended to bump into the tourist accidentally while

   the other man picked his pocket. _____

4. Tran stayed in his seat until the lights came on. _____

5. Darby, my Australian shepherd, liked the man who tossed popcorn

   to her. _____

■ **PRACTICE**   Add subordinate clauses of your own to the following main clauses and indicate whether you have added an adverb clause or an adjective clause.

1. Waldo enjoyed his new computer game.

   Waldo enjoyed his new computer game, which he had purchased

   at Best Buy. (Adj)

2. The game was called Flunk.

   _____

   _____

3. Each player enrolled in college and tried to fail.

   _____

   _____

4. For instance, Waldo stayed out late and didn't show up for classes.

   _____

   _____

5. Other players didn't study and never looked at their books.

   _____

   _____

Section One Review

1. A **clause** is a group of words <u>that contains at least one subject and at least one verb</u>.

2. A **main clause** is a group of words that contains at least one subject and one verb and that <u>expresses a complete idea</u>.

3. A **subordinate clause** is a group of words that contains at least one subject and one verb but that <u>does not express a complete idea</u>.

4. **Subordinate clauses** begin with <u>subordinators</u>.

5. **Adverb subordinate clauses** usually modify verbs and begin with <u>subordinating conjunctions</u>.

6. **Adjective subordinate clauses** modify nouns or pronouns and begin with <u>relative pronouns</u>.

Exercise 1A

Underline all subordinate clauses and circle the subordinators. In the spaces provided, indicate whether the subordinator is a subordinating conjunction (SC) or a relative pronoun (RP). If a sentence contains no subordinate clause, do nothing to it.

1. The violinist played the tune (that) he had composed.   *RP*

2. Elizabeth held on tightly as her horse jumped the creek.   _____

3. Because of the political situation in Chile, Anne decided not to visit there.   _____

4. Everyone was laughing at Homer's new Volkswagen, which had been painted like

    a Spam can.   _____

5. If I am late, I will search for all of the Spam pages on the World Wide Web.   _____

6. Because the sculpture was not finished, Rodin worked through the night.   _____

7. The runner who does stretching exercises before running is smart.   _____

8. The reporters asked questions after the president spoke.   _____

9. Whenever Michelle spoke, her accent caused her much embarrassment.   _____

10. Before the evening services, the minister worked on his talk.   _____

11. Homer knew Hortense was the woman whom he would marry.   _____

12. Around the table, the yellowish substance that surrounded the Spam in the can

    was the major topic of discussion.   _____

13. Although elephants are supposed to have long memories, their ability to

    remember has never been proven.   _____

14. If the weather is pleasant, the picnic will be a success.   _____

15. Even though it was just a joke, Bruce apologized for setting Deborah's sleeve

    on fire.   _____

Exercise 1B

A. Join the pairs of sentences below by making one of them either an adverb or an adjective subordinate clause. You may need to delete or change some words.

1. The Spectre showed us the okra and turnips.
   The okra and turnips had been destroyed by his disintegrator.

   The Spectre showed us the okra and turnips that

   had been destroyed by his disintegrator.

2. Katie wanted to visit Costa Rica.
   She would be able to practice her Spanish there.

3. Homer finished his hushpuppies.
   Homer started on the catfish.

4. Jack refused to sell the old catechism on the Internet.
   Someone offered him $100,000 for it.

5. Marlow was sitting by the fire.
   Marlow had told the woman in black a lie.

B. Write subordinate clauses (adjective or adverb) in the blanks as indicated in parentheses at the beginning of the sentence. Make sure your clauses have subjects and verbs.

6. (adverb clause) *After the ants carried the okra away,*

   Hortense decided to call an exterminator.

7. (adjective or adverb clause) The man decided to activate his burglar alarm _____

continued

8. (adjective clause) The Phantom is a new car _____

_____

9. (adverb clause) _____

_____ the students complained loudly.

10. (adverb clause) Sonia smiled at her brother _____

_____

C. To the main clauses below, add the types of subordinate clauses indicated in parentheses. Add your clause at any place in the sentence that you feel is appropriate. For instance, you may add an adjective clause to any noun in a sentence.

11. (Adv) Mr. Barth resumed reading his newspaper.

After he had eaten his dinner, Mr. Barth resumed

reading his newspaper.

12. (Adj) The cadet quickly picked up her rifle.

_____

_____

13. (Adj) Ruth was completely unaware of the grizzly bear.

_____

_____

14. (Adv or Adj) The spy secretly sent the message.

_____

_____

15. (Adv) The clown jumped into the barrel and floated toward the falls.

_____

_____

Exercise 1C

Underline all subordinate clauses and identify the type of clause (adjective or adverb) in the spaces provided.

1. A number of "London bridges" span the Thames River at London, England, but the bridge that is <u>the source of the famous nursery rhyme has an</u> especially interesting history.

adjective **2.** The song "London Bridge Is Falling Down" probably refers to an early wooden version of the bridge that was destroyed by King Olaf of Norway in the eleventh century.

_____ **3.** On the other hand, because the tolls to pay for the bridge's repair were rarely collected, the song might also refer to the general shabbiness of the bridge. _____ **4.** Between 1176 and 1209, the wooden bridge was rebuilt by Peter of Colechurch, who constructed nineteen stone arches to support the new bridge. _____ **5.** Because of an ancient superstition that the river gods had to be appeased, its cornerstones were spattered with the blood of little children.

_____ **6.** In the middle of the river on the largest pier stood a chapel where a visitor could stop and say a prayer. _____ **7.** All across the surface of the bridge were buildings that were used as residences and businesses. _____ **8.** Three years after it was completed, the bridge was severely damaged by a fire. _____ **9.** Despite such setbacks, for centuries the bridge remained a choice residential and business site for the people who owned the houses and shops on it. _____

10. During Shakespeare's time, people would cross the bridge to Southwark, where the theaters and other places of entertainment were. _____ **11.** Until the 1740s, it was the only bridge that crossed the Thames. _____ **12.** Although it was extensively rebuilt in the 1750s, it was demolished in the 1820s and replaced by New London Bridge. _____ **13.** New London Bridge, which was itself replaced in the 1960s, was dismantled and shipped across the Atlantic. _____ **14.** It was re-erected at Lake Havasu, Arizona, where it is now a tourist attraction. _____ **15.** The old bridge built by Peter of Colechurch stood for more than six hundred years, five hundred years more than the one that was built to replace it. _____

two

Simple, Compound, Complex, and Compound-Complex Sentences

Sentences are categorized according to the number and types of clauses they contain. The names of the four types of sentences are **simple, compound, complex**, and **compound-complex**. You need to be familiar with these sentence patterns for a number of reasons:

1. **Variety.** Varying your sentence patterns creates interest and avoids monotony. Repeating a sentence pattern endlessly will bore even your most interested reader.

2. **Emphasis.** You can use these sentence patterns to emphasize the ideas that you think are more important than others.

3. **Grammar.** A knowledge of the basic sentence patterns of English will help you avoid the major sentence structure errors discussed in Section Three.

Being able to recognize and use these sentence patterns will help you control your writing and thus express your ideas more effectively.

The Simple Sentence

The introduction to this chapter points out that a sentence must contain at least one main clause. A sentence that contains only one main clause and no other clauses is called a **simple sentence.** However, a simple sentence is not necessarily an uncomplicated or short sentence because, in addition to its one main clause, it may also contain a variety of phrases and modifiers.

The basic pattern for the simple sentence is subject–verb (SV). This pattern may vary in several ways:

▶ **EXAMPLES**

                               S   V

subject–verb (SV): The plane flew over the stadium.

                                    V   S

verb–subject (VS): Over the stadium flew the plane.

                               S   S   V

subject–subject–verb (SSV): The plane and the helicopter flew over the stadium.

                             S   V   V

subject–verb–verb (SVV): The plane flew over the stadium and turned north.

S   S V

subject–subject–verb–verb (SSVV): The plane and the helicopter flew

V

over the stadium and turned north.

S V

A simple sentence can be brief: *It rained.*

S

Or it can be rather long: *Enraged by the taunting of the boys, the huge gorilla*

V   V

leaped from his enclosure and chased them up a hill and down a pathway to the exit gates.

The important thing to remember about the simple sentence is that it has only one main clause and no other clauses.

■ **PRACTICE** Write your own simple sentences according to the instructions.

1. A simple sentence with the pattern subject–verb–verb:

The dog ran and jumped over the wall.

_____

2. A simple sentence that has the pattern subject–verb and ends with a prepositional phrase:

_____

_____

3. A simple sentence that begins with *Here* and has the pattern verb–subject:

_____

_____

4. A simple sentence that begins with a prepositional phrase and has the pattern subject–verb:

_____

_____

5. A simple sentence that begins with a prepositional phrase and has the pattern verb–subject:

_____

_____

_____

good

look → ## The Compound Sentence

Simply put, a **compound sentence** contains two or more main clauses but no subordinate clauses. The basic pattern of the clauses may be expressed subject–verb/subject–verb (SV/SV). The main clauses are always joined in one of three ways:

1. Two main clauses may be joined by a comma and one of the seven coordinating conjunctions (*and, or, nor, but, for, so, yet*).

▶ **EXAMPLE**

       S   V   S V

Maria registered for all of her classes by mail, **but** Brad was not able to do so.

Remember, the two main clauses must be joined by **both a comma and a** → **coordinating conjunction**, and the comma always comes before the coordinating conjunction.

2. Two main clauses may be joined by a semicolon (;).

▶ **EXAMPLE**

       S   V   S   V

Maria registered for all of her classes by mail; Brad was not able to do so.

3. Two main clauses may be joined by a semicolon and a transitional word or phrase. Such transitional words or phrases are followed by a comma.

▶ **EXAMPLE**

       S   V   S

Maria registered for all of her classes by mail; **however,** Brad

       V

was not able to do so.

Below is a list of the most commonly used transitional words and phrases. Do not confuse these words or phrases with coordinating conjunctions or subordinating conjunctions.

accordingly	hence	next	thus
also	however	nonetheless	undoubtedly
besides	instead	otherwise	for instance
consequently	meanwhile	similarly	for example
finally	moreover	still	on the other hand
further	namely	then	that is
furthermore	nevertheless	therefore	

■ **PRACTICE**   Write compound sentences of your own according to the instructions.

1. A compound sentence that uses a comma and *and* to join two main clauses:

   Myrtle likes to grow okra, and she likes to

   serve it to Vergil.

2. A compound sentence that joins two main clauses with a semicolon, followed by *however* and a comma:

   _____

   _____

3. A compound sentence that joins two main clauses with a semicolon and an appropriate transitional word or phrase followed by a comma:

   _____

   _____

4. A compound sentence that joins two main clauses with a comma and *yet:*

   _____

   _____

5. A compound sentence that joins two main clauses with a semicolon, followed by *therefore* and a comma:

_____

_____

■ **PRACTICE** In the following sentences, write S above each subject and V above each verb. Then, in the spaces provided, identify each sentence as either **simple** or **compound**.

1. Captain Bush flew airplanes during World War II.   *simple*

2. He was stationed in Burma and flew planes over the mountains into China.   _____

3. The mountains were very high, so the flights were dangerous.   _____

4. The mountains were the Himalayas; the pilots were called "hump" pilots.   _____

5. Flying over these mountains was treacherous yet exciting, too.   _____

6. In his hut in Burma, Captain Bush befriended a mongoose.   _____

7. The mongoose had made a nest in the roof of the hut; therefore, Captain Bush let it stay.   _____

8. Captain Bush's mother would send him food in packages, and he would share it with the mongoose.   _____

9. The mongoose had a litter of babies in her nest in the hut.   _____

10. A mongoose will kill a cobra, so the hut was safe from cobras.   _____

The Complex Sentence

The **complex sentence** has the same subject–verb pattern (SV/SV) as the compound sentence. However, the complex sentence features only one main clause and always contains at least one subordinate clause and sometimes more than one. The subordinate clauses in a complex sentence may occur at any place in the sentence.

▶ **EXAMPLES**

S   V   S   V

Before a main clause: <u>After he retired from the army,</u> Eisenhower ran for president.

S   V   S   V

After a main clause: Rugby is a sport <u>that I have played only once</u>.

S   S   V

Interrupting a main clause: Emilio's grandfather<u>, who fought in World</u>

V

<u>War II,</u> told him about his experiences during the war.

S   V

Before and after a main clause: <u>When the pianist sat down at the piano,</u>

S   V   S   V

she played a melody <u>that she had written recently</u>.

■ **PRACTICE**   Write complex sentences of your own according to the instructions.

1. A complex sentence with a main clause followed by an adverb clause beginning with *because:*

   Vergil burned the cornbread because he was

   on the telephone.

2. A complex sentence with an adverb clause beginning with *When* followed by a main clause:

   _____

   _____

3. A complex sentence that contains a noun modified by an adjective clause beginning with *who:*

_____

_____

4. A complex sentence that contains a main clause and an adverb clause beginning with *after:*

_____

_____

5. A complex sentence that contains one main clause and one adjective clause:

_____

_____

The Compound-Complex Sentence

The **compound-complex sentence** is a combination of the compound and the complex sentence patterns. It is made up of two or more main clauses and one or more subordinate clauses. Therefore, it must contain a minimum of three sets of subjects and verbs (<u>at least</u> two main clauses and <u>at least</u> one subordinate clause).

▶ **EXAMPLES**

               main clause   sub. clause
[On the day-long bicycle trip, Ophelia ate the food] [that she had packed,]

              main clause
[but Henry had forgotten to bring anything to eat.]

          sub. clause   main clause
[Although he was exhausted,] [Ernesto cooked dinner for his mother,]

              main clause
[and after dinner he cleaned the kitchen.]

         main clause   sub. clause
[The travelers were excited] [when they arrived in Paris;]

             main clause
[they wanted to go sightseeing immediately.]

look →

■ **PRACTICE**   Write compound-complex sentences of your own according to the instructions.

1. A sentence that contains two main clauses joined by *and* and one adjective clause beginning with *which:*

Cassandra went to the drugstore, and she found the

memory medicine, which was hidden behind the antacids.

2. A compound-complex sentence that contains a main clause and an adjective clause followed by a semicolon and another main clause:

_____

_____

3. A compound-complex sentence that contains two main clauses joined by a semicolon and a transitional word or phrase. Modify one of the nouns in either main clause with an adjective clause beginning with *who* or *that.*

_____

_____

4. A compound-complex sentence that contains two main clauses joined by *or* and one adverb subordinate clause beginning with *if, before,* or *because.*

_____

5. A compound-complex sentence about your family with a pattern of your own choice:

_____

_____

■   PRACTICE   In the following sentences, write S above each subject and V above each verb. Then, in the spaces provided, identify the sentences as simple, compound, complex, or compound-complex.

1. According to Greek mythology, the Minotaur, which was part
   $\overset{S}{} \overset{S}{} \overset{V}{}$

   bull and part man, lived deep within the labyrinth on Crete.   *complex*
   $\overset{V}{}$

2. The story about the Minotaur concerns Theseus and Ariadne.   _____

3. Each year King Minos of Crete ordered Athens to send seven boys

   and seven girls, who were to be devoured by the Minotaur.   _____

4. One year, however, the hero Theseus accompanied the children.   _____

5. Ariadne was the daughter of Minos, and she fell in love with

   Theseus.   _____

6. Ariadne gave Theseus a ball of string to take with him into the

   labyrinth of the Minotaur.   _____

7. Theseus took the string with him, and he unraveled it as he went

   into the maze.   _____

8. He would use the string when he wanted to leave the labyrinth;

   then he would follow it out to the opening.   _____

9. Theseus followed the sound of the bellowing of the Minotaur,

   and he found the beast at last.   _____

10. When he reached the Minotaur, he killed it and led the children

    to safety.   _____

Section Two Review

1. A **simple sentence** contains only one main clause and no other clauses.

2. A **compound sentence** contains two or more main clauses that are joined by a comma and a coordinating conjunction <u>or</u> a semicolon <u>or</u> a semicolon and a transitional word or phrase.

3. A **complex sentence** contains only one main clause and one or more subordinate clauses.

4. A **compound-complex sentence** contains two or more main clauses and one or more subordinate clauses.

Exercise 2A

In the spaces provided, identify the following sentences as simple, compound, complex, or compound-complex.

1. Writers come and go, but Shakespeare remains constantly popular.   *compound*

2. As the twenty-first century begins, several movies of Shakespeare's plays are being filmed.   _____

3. Even a new *Hamlet* is in production.   _____

4. In fact, *Hamlet* is an industry of its own; at any hour of any day, somewhere *Hamlet* is being put on.   _____

5. Hamlet is one of the top five most written about people in history even though he is only a character in a play.   _____

6. Many writers have tried to explain the popularity of Shakespeare, but there is not just one explanation.   _____

7. Among the reasons given are the vivid stories, the compelling characters, and the beautiful use of the language.   _____

8. Although there have been many great writers, not one has combined these elements so well.   _____

9. Even though Shakespeare borrowed almost all of his stories, he transformed them, and they came to life in his hands.   _____

10. *Hamlet*, for instance, contains as much killing and double-crossing as a Mafia movie.   _____

11. *Macbeth* has an ambitious husband-and-wife team; it could be the story of a modern businessman clawing his way to the top.   _____

12. The sad tale of the star-crossed lovers Romeo and Juliet is one that has been told over and over.   _____

continued

13. Characters like Othello, Brutus, and King Lear have enthralled people over the

    centuries.   _____

14. Even less major characters like Iago, Falstaff, and Lady Macbeth have captivated

    audiences, and actors still compete to play them.   _____

15. Because Shakespeare's use of language is so eloquent, authors use phrases from

    his works for their titles; we come across expressions like "Something is rotten

    in the State of Denmark" every day.   _____

A. Combine each pair of sentences according to the instructions. You may need to delete or change some words.

   1. A simple sentence with the pattern verb–subject:
   a. The stamp was in the drawer of the desk in the attic.
   b. The stamp was very rare and valuable.

   In the drawer of the desk in the attic was a very

   rare and valuable stamp.

   2. A compound sentence that uses a semicolon as the connector:
   a. First, Brutus stabbed Caesar.
   b. Then the rest of them joined in.

   3. A complex sentence that uses the subordinator *although:*
   a. I do not like beets.
   b. I do sometimes eat grits.

   4. A simple sentence in the form of a question:
   a. Has the living room been dusted?
   b. Has the living room been swept?

   5. A compound sentence that uses *so* as the connector:
   a. Hamlet was not pleased with his mother's activities.
   b. Hamlet told his mother about his concerns.

continued

B. Following the instructions, construct sentences of your own.

6. A compound-complex sentence that uses a semicolon:

_____

_____

7. A complex sentence that uses *who* to begin the subordinate clause:

_____

_____

8. A compound sentence that uses a semicolon and the transitional word *however:*

_____

_____

9. A simple sentence that uses the pattern SVV:

_____

_____

10. A complex sentence that uses the subordinator *while:*

_____

_____

11. A compound sentence that uses *but* as the connector:

_____

_____

12. A simple sentence that begins with a prepositional phrase:

_____

_____

continued

13. A complex sentence that uses *which* to begin the subordinate clause:

_____

_____

14. A compound sentence that uses a semicolon as the connector, followed by the transitional word *therefore:*

_____

_____

15. A compound-complex sentence that uses the subordinator *when, whenever,* or *while* to begin a subordinate clause. Do not use a semicolon.

_____

_____

Identify the sentences as simple, compound, complex, or compound-complex.

1. Most of the theaters where Shakespeare put on his plays were circular. _complex_ **2.** Some were made from bear-baiting pits. _____ **3.** In a bear-baiting pit, a bear was chained in the center, and dogs were sent to attack it. _____ **4.** Some people bet on the bear; some people bet on the dogs. _____ **5.** Because these theaters were renovated bear-baiting pits, they were open to the sky, and the floors were bare dirt. _____ **6.** Around the inside of the theater and extending to the roof were boxes for spectators. _____ **7.** These were the higher-priced seats; the lower-priced ones were on the floor around the stage, where the "groundlings" sat. _____ **8.** The stage was a platform that was about forty feet wide and twenty-five feet deep. _____ **9.** Most of the stage was covered by a projecting roof known as the shadow or the heavens. _____ **10.** It was called the heavens because the underside was decorated with pictures of the sun, the moon, the planets, and the constellations. _____ **11.** Near the middle of the stage was a door in the floor, which led below the stage; this space below the stage was called hell for obvious reasons. _____ **12.** Ghosts could appear from this door._____ **13.** In the back of the stage was the tiring-house, which, as the name (attiring-house) implies, contained the actors' dressing rooms. _____ **14.** Here also were the two doors where the actors entered and exited. _____**15.** These doors were important because there was no opening or closing of curtains in these theaters. _____**16.** The stage represented the world, with the heavens above and hell below. _____

Fragments, Fused Sentences, and Comma Splices

Now that you are combining main and subordinate clauses to write different types of sentences, we need to talk about a few of the writing problems you might encounter. Fortunately, the most serious of these problems—the **fragment**, the **fused sentence**, and the **comma splice**—are also the easiest to identify and correct.

Fragments

The easiest way to identify a **sentence fragment** is to remember that <u>every sentence must contain a main clause</u>. If you do not have a main clause, you do <u>not</u> have a sentence. You can define a fragment, then, like this: A sentence fragment occurs when a group of words that lacks a main clause is punctuated as a sentence.

> ### sentence fragment
> A sentence fragment occurs when a group of words that lacks a main clause is punctuated as a sentence.

Using this definition, you can identify almost any sentence fragment. However, you will find it easier to locate fragments in your own writing if you know that fragments can be divided into three basic types.

Three Types of Sentence Fragments

1. <u>Some fragments contain no clause at all.</u> This type of fragment is simple to spot. It usually does not even sound like a sentence because it lacks a subject or verb or both.

▶ EXAMPLE   The snow in the street.

2. <u>Some fragments contain a verbal but still no clause.</u> This fragment is a bit less obvious because a verbal can be mistaken for a verb. But remember, neither a participle nor an infinitive is a verb. (See Chapter One, page 12, if you need to review this point.)

look —→

▶ EXAMPLES   The snow **falling** on the street. (participle)

The **To slip** on the snow in the street. (infinitive)

3. Some fragments contain a **subordinate clause** but no **main clause**. This type of fragment is perhaps the most common because it does contain a subject and a verb. But remember, a group of words without a main clause is not a sentence.

▶ EXAMPLES **After** the snow had fallen on the street.

Because I had slipped on the snow in the street.

Repairing Sentence Fragments

Once you have identified a fragment, you can correct it in one of two ways.

1. Add words to give it a main clause.

good look

▶ EXAMPLES

	(fragment)	The snow in the street.
good	(sentence)	**I gazed** at the snow in the street.
	(sentence)	The snow **was** in the street.
	(fragment)	The snow falling in the street.
	(sentence)	The snow falling in the street **covered my car.**
Good	(sentence)	The snow **was** falling in the street.
	(fragment)	After the snow had fallen in the street.
Good	(sentence)	**I looked for a shovel** after the snow had fallen in the street.

2. Join the fragment to a main clause written before or after it.

▶ EXAMPLES

	(incorrect)	I love to see the ice on the lake. And the snow in the street.
good →	(correct)	I love to see the ice on the lake and the snow in the street.
	(incorrect)	My back was so sore that I could not stand straight. Because I had slipped on the snow in the street.
good	(correct)	My back was so sore that I could not stand straight because I had slipped on the snow in the street.

No cw

One final point might help you identify and correct sentence fragments. Remember that we all speak in fragments every day. (If a friend asks you how you are, you might respond with the fragment "Fine.") Because we speak in fragments, you may find that your writing seems acceptable even though it contains fragments. When you work on the exercises in this unit, do not rely on your "ear" alone. Look at the sentences. **If they do not contain main clauses, they are fragments, no matter how correct they may sound.**

■ **PRACTICE**   Underline any fragment you find. Then correct it either by adding new words to give it a main clause or by joining it to a main clause next to it.

1. The rain dripped slowly from the trees. <u>Falling quietly from the dark green leaves.</u>

   The rain dripped slowly from the trees as it fell quietly from the dark green leaves.

2. The bridge in London that fell down.

   _____

   _____

3. When Mr. Nguyen found his missing textbook. He returned the new one. Hoping that the bookstore would take it back.

   _____

   _____

4. The tea party was canceled. Because of the hatter's madness.

   _____

   _____

5. After Roberto had tried several times to start his car.

   _____

   _____

6. Gulliver found himself tied down by some little people. Probably because they were afraid of him.

_____

_____

7. The bus pulled away from the curb as Adrian raced down the sidewalk after it. Yelling for it to wait for him.

_____

_____

8. After he explained how big the fish was. The poor little fellow's nose began to grow.

_____

_____

9. To buy the car after saving enough money for a down payment.

_____

_____

10. While rowing across the Styx River.

_____

_____

Fused Sentences and Comma Splices

The **fused sentence** and **comma splice** are serious writing errors that you can correct with little effort. Either error can occur when you write a compound or compound-complex sentence. The fused sentence occurs when two or more main clauses are joined without a coordinating conjunction and without punctuation.

> ### fused sentence
> The fused sentence occurs when two or more main clauses are joined without a coordinating conjunction and without punctuation.

▶ **EXAMPLE**   (fused)   Raoul drove by his uncle's house he waved at his cousins.

As you can see, the two main clauses in the above example (*Raoul drove by his uncle's house* and *he waved at his cousins*) have been joined without a coordinating conjunction and without punctuation of any kind.

The comma splice is a similar error: The comma splice occurs when two or more main clauses are joined with a comma but without a coordinating conjunction.

> ### comma splice
> The comma splice occurs when two or more main clauses are joined with a comma but without a coordinating conjunction.

▶ **EXAMPLE**   (comma splice)   The hot sun beat down on the construction workers, they looked forward to the end of the day.

In this example, the two main clauses (*The hot sun beat down on the construction workers* and *they looked forward to the end of the day*) are joined by a comma, but a comma alone is not enough to join main clauses.

NOTE: One of the most frequent comma splices occurs when a writer joins two main clauses with a comma and a transitional word rather than with a semicolon and a transitional word.

▶ **EXAMPLE**   (comma splice)   I wanted a dog for Christmas, however, my parents gave me a cat.

Repairing Fused Sentences and Comma Splices

Because both fused sentences and comma splices occur when two main clauses are joined, you can correct either error using one of five methods. Consider these two errors:

► EXAMPLES

(fused)   Jack left for work early he arrived late.

(comma splice)   Jack left for work early, he arrived late. *[handwritten: wrong good — this good]*

Both of these errors can be corrected in one of five ways:

1. Use a comma and a coordinating conjunction.
   Jack left for work early, **but** he arrived late.

2. Use a semicolon.
   Jack left for work early; he arrived late.

3. Use a semicolon and a transitional word or phrase.
   Jack left for work early; **however,** he arrived late.

NOTE: Do <u>not</u> use a semicolon before a transitional word that does <u>not</u> begin a main clause. For example, in the following sentence, *however* does not need a semicolon. *[handwritten: I have not seen my father for ten year (good]*

I have not seen my father, **however,** for ten years.

4. Change one of the clauses to a subordinate clause by beginning it with a subordinator.
   [handwritten: Subordinate]
   Although Jack left for work early, he arrived late.

5. Punctuate the clauses as two separate sentences.
   [handwritten: good →]
   Jack left for work early. He arrived late.

NOTE: Sometimes the two main clauses in a fused sentence or comma splice are interrupted by a subordinate clause. When this sentence pattern occurs, the two main clauses must still be connected in one of the five ways.

► EXAMPLES

(fused)   Alma bought a new Mercedes even though she could not afford one she fell behind in her monthly payments.

(comma splice)   Alma bought a new Mercedes even though she could not afford one, she fell behind in her monthly payments.

These errors can be corrected in any of the five ways mentioned above.

► EXAMPLE

Alma bought a new Mercedes even though she could not afford one; consequently, she fell behind in her monthly payments.

■ **PRACTICE**   Identify the following sentences as fused (F), comma splice (CS), or correct (C). Then correct the incorrect sentences. Use a different method of correction each time.

_____CS_____ **1.** Pierre walked down the hall and insulted Erica, Erica forgave him later.

Pierre walked down the hall and insulted Erica;

however, Erica forgave him later.

_____ **2.** Homer picked up the cow chip and smelled it then he rejected it.

_____

_____

_____ **3.** When Ben was a very young boy, he used to watch the steam rise from the manhole covers on the street.

_____

_____

_____ **4.** One day Snow White went off to work in the mine, therefore, the dwarves had to clean the house and cook supper.

_____

_____

_____ **5.** Each morning Eustace works on his novel he sits down at his computer and writes for two hours.

_____

_____

_____ **6.** The doorbell rang five times, eventually, someone began to bang on the door.

_____

_____

_____ **7.** Melvin ate two packages of potato chips a day even though he knew they were not good for him he kept on eating them.

_____

_____

_____ **8.** The body snatchers and their pods, however, were taking over.

_____

_____

_____ **9.** Dr. Frankenstein searched all night he knew that he would find the body that he needed.

_____

_____

_____ **10.** The Count went to the Bloodmobile, he often had plenty of extra blood to donate.

_____

_____

Section Three Review

1. A **sentence fragment** occurs when a group of words that lacks a main clause is punctuated as a sentence.

2. There are three types of sentence fragments.

   a. Some contain no clause at all.

   b. Some contain a verbal but still no clause.

   c. Some contain a subordinate clause but no main clause.

3. You can correct a sentence fragment in one of two ways.

   a. Add words to give it a main clause.

   b. Join it to an already existing main clause.

4. The **fused sentence** occurs when two or more main clauses are joined without a coordinating conjunction and without punctuation.

5. The **comma splice** occurs when two or more main clauses are joined with a comma but without a coordinating conjunction.

6. You can correct fused sentences and comma splices in one of five ways.

   a. Use a comma and a coordinating conjunction.

   b. Use a semicolon.

   c. Use a semicolon and a transitional word or phrase.

   d. Change one of the clauses to a subordinate clause by adding a subordinator at the beginning of it.

   e. Punctuate the clauses as two separate sentences.

Exercise 3A

Identify each of the following as correct (C), fused (F), comma splice (CS), or sentence fragment (Frag). Then correct each error using any of the methods discussed in this unit.

Frag **1.** Although Aaron called as many people as he could think of to find where the computer had gone.

Although Aaron called as many people as he could think of to find where the computer had gone, he did not think to call his business partner.

_____ **2.** Odysseus was tied to the mast, therefore, the Sirens' songs caused no problem.

_____ **3.** Sit down.

_____ **4.** After my last class, I drove home then I realized I had left my backpack at school.

_____ **5.** The scientist explaining the fate of the dinosaurs.

_____ **6.** Computer technology has improved in the last five years, automotive technology has, too.

continued

_____ **7.** The car turning left at the intersection almost hit Naoko, but luckily she jumped out of the way in time.

_____

_____

_____ **8.** Lisa enjoyed watching *Frasier* however Kurt could not stand Frasier's brother, Niles.

_____

_____

_____ **9.** Adrian was very worried about his grades he studied all night.

_____

_____

_____ **10.** Fergal was so angry that he shouted ancient Irish oaths at the Shankill Butcher.

_____

_____

_____ **11.** At night Anthony cannot see very well, he asks others to drive him if he has to go somewhere.

_____

_____

_____ **12.** The concert was over, the audience rose to applaud.

_____

_____

Exercise 3A

continued

_____ **13.** Ramon will try to do almost anything, for example, last year he learned how to fly a hang glider and a hot air balloon.

_____

_____

_____ **14.** After Crazy Horse won the battle and headed back home as the sun was setting.

_____

_____

_____ **15.** The Australian shepherd was rounding up the cattle, even though they were bigger, they were afraid of her.

_____

_____

Exercise 3B

A. Correct the following sentence fragments by adding words to them to make them complete sentences.

1. Trinh, who had been studying for three hours.

Trinh, who had been studying for three hours, finally decided it was time for bed.

2. As the snails were frying.

3. The bell ringing in the middle of the night.

4. That I discovered on the back of my leg.

5. Near the Serbian village.

B. Join the following main clauses by using a comma and a coordinating conjunction, a semicolon, a semicolon and a transitional word or phrase, or by making one of the clauses a subordinate clause. Use each of these four methods at least once.

6. I once was famous for my Spam Bombay. Now all they ask for is okra spring rolls.

I once was famous for my Spam Bombay; now all they ask for is okra spring rolls.

continued

7. Sophia wanted to sit by the stream and read her book. Basra wanted to take a walk by the stream.

_____

_____

8. Count Tolstoy finished the long novel. He was quite pleased with it.

_____

_____

9. Sergio stared in amazement at the convertible. The convertible was parked in his driveway.

_____

_____

10. Chicken Little tried desperately to warn people. No one would listen.

_____

_____

C. Expand each of the following sentences by adding a **clause** to it. Identify the subject and verb of each clause you use and vary the placement of the clauses. (Don't place every clause at the end of its sentence.) When you add the clauses, use each of the following methods at least once: a) use a comma and a coordinating conjunction; b) use a semicolon; c) use a semicolon and a transitional word or phrase; d) make one clause a subordinate clause.

11. Near the corner of the yard, a toy poodle cowered in fear before a Siamese cat.

Near the corner of the yard, a toy poodle cowered in fear before

a Siamese cat; however, the cat only wanted to make a new friend.

12. The meal depicted in the movie looked delicious.

_____

_____

Exercise 3B

continued

13. Using a word processor can improve the appearance and quality of your writing.

_____

_____

14. I ride my mountain bike every day.

_____

_____

15. The two armies met in a valley between two mountains.

_____

_____

In the following paragraph, correct any fragments, fused sentences, or comma splices.

1. Mount Rushmore is sometimes described as one of the wonders of the world it is a memorial to four of our presidents. **2.** The story of Mount Rushmore began sixty million years ago pressures originating deep within the earth pushed up layers of rock. **3.** When the forces caused a granite and limestone dome to tower above the South Dakota prairie. **4.** Sculpted by wind and water. **5.** One especially prominent peak emerged. **6.** The peak was unnamed until 1885, it was eventually named for Charles E. Rushmore, who surveyed the mountain range on horseback that year. **7.** Then, in 1923, a South Dakota historian, Doane Robinson, presented to the state his plan he wanted to transform the gigantic mountaintop into a colossus of human figures. **8.** To immortalize Kit Carson, Jim Bridger, and John Colter, three Western heroes. **9.** A commission sought an artist with special skills, it called on sculptor John Gutzon de la Mothe Borglum. **10.** Opposed to the idea of the portrayal of Western heroes. **11.** Borglum proposed the faces of four influential American presidents. **12.** Beginning in 1927, Borglum worked fourteen years he sculpted the faces of George Washington, Abraham Lincoln, Thomas Jefferson, and Theodore Roosevelt into the mountain. **13.** Encountering numerous problems like bitter winters and lack of funds. **14.** The sculptor worked relentlessly. **15.** The monument was unveiled in 1941, then it became a new world wonder. **16.** Borglum often spoke about his work, he would say that a monument's size should be determined by the importance to civilization of the events commemorated by the monument.

SECTION four

Sentence Practice:
Combining Main and Subordinate Clauses

In this chapter you have learned the basic sentence patterns of English, and you have seen that you can combine the major word groups of a sentence—the clauses—in various ways. Of course, how you present your ideas in your sentences can affect the way a reader perceives your ideas. Take, for instance, the following sentences.

1. Sub-compact cars are economical.

2. Sub-compact cars are easy to handle.

3. Sub-compact cars are simple to park.

4. Full-size sedans are roomier.

5. Full-size sedans are safer.

6. Full-size sedans are quieter.

You can present these ideas in six simple sentences like those above, but doing so makes the writing choppy and simplistic. On the other hand, you can use the sentence patterns discussed in this chapter to combine these six ideas in several ways.

1. You can present these ideas as two simple sentences.

► EXAMPLE   Sub-compact cars are economical, easy to handle, and simple to park. Full-size sedans are roomier, safer, and quieter.

2. Or you can group the ideas into one compound sentence by using a comma and a coordinating conjunction.

► EXAMPLE   Sub-compact cars are economical, easy to handle, and simple to park, but full-size sedans are roomier, safer, and quieter.

Note that the coordinating conjunction *but* allows you to emphasize the contrast between the ideas in the two main clauses.

3. You can also group these ideas into a compound sentence by using a semi-colon as a connector.

► EXAMPLE   Sub-compact cars are economical, easy to handle, and simple to park; full-size sedans are roomier, safer, and quieter.

In this sentence the contrast in the ideas is implied rather than directly stated.

4. Of course, you can add a transitional word after the semicolon.

▶ **EXAMPLE**

Sub-compact cars are economical, easy to handle, and simple to park; however, full-size sedans are roomier, safer, and quieter.

Note that *however* now signals the contrast between the ideas in the two clauses.

5. Finally, you can group the ideas into a main clause and a subordinate clause by adding a subordinator. Now you have a complex sentence.

▶ **EXAMPLE**

Although sub-compact cars are economical, easy to handle, and simple to park, full-size sedans are roomier, safer, and quieter.

Like the other sentences, this sentence shows the reader the contrast between the ideas in the two clauses. However, it also shows the ideas the writer thinks are most important—the ones in the main clause.

Sentence Combining Exercises

Using the knowledge of sentence patterns that you have gained from this chapter, combine the following lists of sentences into longer sentences according to the directions. Be sure to punctuate carefully to avoid comma splices or fused sentences. Remember to look for a base sentence or a main idea to build on. The most important idea should be in a main clause.

▶   **EXAMPLE**   First, combine these ideas into a compound sentence, using one of the three methods presented in Section Two of this chapter. Then form a complex sentence, using a subordinator to make one clause subordinate.

1. Cooking can be enjoyable.
2. Cooking can be creative.
3. Cooking can be satisfying.
4. Someone has to shop for ingredients.
5. Someone has to chop onions.
6. Someone has to put everything away.
7. Someone has to wash the dishes.

A. Compound sentence:

Cooking can be enjoyable, creative, and satisfying, but someone has to shop for ingredients, chop onions, put everything away, and wash the dishes.

B. Complex sentence:

Although cooking can be enjoyable, creative, and satisfying, someone has to shop for ingredients, chop onions, put everything away, and wash the dishes.

Sentence Combining Exercises

continued

1. Combine these sentences into a compound-complex sentence. Use sentences b and c to form an adjective clause beginning with *who*.

   a. Albert Hartfelt was an author.
   b. He wrote long novels.
   c. He wrote complicated novels.
   d. Hardly anyone understood them.
   e. No publisher would publish them.

   _____

   _____

   _____

   _____

2. First combine these ideas into a compound sentence. Then combine them into a complex sentence. Begin each sentence with a prepositional phrase.

   a. It was morning.
   b. Luisa was jogging.
   c. She was at the Oakland waterfront.
   d. The waterfront was beautiful.
   e. Suddenly she slipped on a wet spot.
   f. She sprained her arm.
   g. The sprain was severe.

   _____

   _____

   _____

   _____

Sentence Combining Exercises

continued

3. Combine these sentences into a complex sentence. Form sentences d and e into a subordinate clause beginning with *because* or *when*.

   a. Rudolph, the Red-Nosed Reindeer, got his start at a Montgomery Ward department store.
   b. The store was in Chicago.
   c. The year was 1939.
   d. The store wanted to distribute something to parents and children.
   e. The store wanted it to be unique.

   _____

   _____

   _____

   _____

4. Combine these sentences into one complex sentence.

   a. An advertising copywriter suggested a poem.
   b. The poem would be illustrated.
   c. Families would want to save it.
   d. Families would want to reread it each year.

   _____

   _____

   _____

   _____

Sentence Combining Exercises

continued

5. Combine these sentences into one sentence. Use the most effective pattern you can find. At the end of your new sentence, indicate which type of sentence you have written.

  a. The copywriter got the idea of a reindeer.
  b. The reindeer was shiny-nosed.
  c. The reindeer was Santa's helper.
  d. An artist spent time at the zoo.
  e. The artist created sketches of reindeer.
  f. The sketches were whimsical.

_____

_____

_____

_____

6. Combine these sentences into one sentence. Use the most effective pattern you can find. At the end of your new sentence, indicate which type of sentence you have written.

  a. The copywriter considered names for the reindeer.
  b. His daughter preferred "Rudolph."
  c. The copywriter decided on "Rudolph."

_____

_____

_____

_____

continued

7. Combine these sentences into one sentence. Indicate which type of sentence you have written.

    a. "Rudolph, the Red-Nosed Reindeer" was reprinted until 1947.
    b. It was reprinted sporadically.
    c. In 1947 Johnny Marks decided to put the poem to music.

    _____

    _____

    _____

    _____

8. Combine these sentences into one sentence. Indicate which type of sentence you have written.

    a. At first no singer wanted to record the song.
    b. Gene Autry agreed to record the song.
    c. "Rudolph, the Red-Nosed Reindeer" became the second–best-selling record of all time.

    _____

    _____

    _____

    _____

continued

9. Combine these sentences into one sentence. Indicate which type of sentence you have written.

   a. It is an interesting fact.
   b. The fact is about "Rudolph, the Red-Nosed Reindeer."
   c. Sociologists have studied the song.
   d. Sociologists have called it the only new addition to the folklore of Santa Claus in the twentieth century.

   _____

   _____

   _____

   _____

10. Combine these sentences into one sentence. Indicate which type of sentence you have written.

    a. Reindeer may look like deer.
    b. Reindeer may have a deer-like name.
    c. Reindeer are actually the same as caribou.
    d. Caribou are found in the Western Hemisphere.
    e. They are referred to as reindeer in Northern Europe and Asia.

    _____

    _____

    _____

    _____

Paragraph Practice:
Describing a Person or a Place

Writing Assignment

In Chapter Two you have read paragraphs that discuss a variety of places. Exercise 1C (page 82) presents the history of London Bridge, Exercise 2C (page 98) describes a Shakespearean theater, and Exercise 3C (page 114) examines the background of Mount Rushmore. Your assignment in this writing section is to describe a place that you remember for one particular reason. As you do so, you will practice limiting your paragraph to one idea that is expressed in a topic sentence and developing your paragraph with details that are both specific and concrete.

Reading Assignment

The reading selections in the "Describing a Place" section of Chapter Seven can help you see how professional writers describe memorable places. Read one or more of the selections, as assigned by your instructor, and use the questions that follow them to develop ideas for your own paper.

Prewriting

To find a topic, use freewriting, brainstorming, or clustering (or all three) to generate ideas about places that you remember well. Try to develop a list of as many places as you can. Sometimes the most interesting place to describe will be buried deep in your memory, so give prewriting a chance to uncover that memory before you decide on a topic. As you prewrite, avoid topics that are too broad to cover in one paragraph. For example, a city or an amusement park would be too large of a topic to cover in detail in a brief piece of writing. However, one particular characteristic of a small town or one particular section of an amusement park might work very well.

Prewriting Application: Finding Your Topic

Consider the following questions as you prewrite:

1. What places have you visited in the past several years? Think about vacations you have taken or places you have traveled to.

2. Where have you been in the past two weeks? Make a list of everywhere you have gone.

3. What places from your childhood give you the most pleasant memories?

4. Where do you go to relax, meditate, or find peace of mind?

5. Have you ever been somewhere when you felt frightened or concerned for your safety?

6. What are the most beautiful places you have ever seen?

7. What are the most unpleasant ones? What are the strangest ones?

8. Have any places ever made you feel confused or lost?

9. Do you know any places that are particularly chaotic and noisy?

10. Where have you been today? Can you describe an ordinary, everyday place so that a reader sees it in a new way?

Once you have chosen the one place that is most interesting to you, keep prewriting about it. Try to remember as many details as you can about the place. Don't worry about writing well at this point—just brainstorm (make lists) or freewrite to get down as many of the details as you can remember. After you have written for a while, read over what you have so far. Look for related details that focus on <u>one particular impression</u> of the place. These details and others that give that same impression are the ones you should emphasize in your paragraph. Once you have identified that particular impression, you are ready to write a preliminary **topic sentence**.

Remember, a topic sentence contains both a **topic** and a **central point**. In this writing assignment, your topic will be the place you are describing, and your central point will be the particular impression about that place that your details emphasize and illustrate.

Prewriting Application: Working with Topic Sentences

In each sentence below, underline the topic once and the central point twice.

1. Mammoth Cave, in southwestern Kentucky, is full of eerie, unearthly

   sights.

2. One of the most confusing places I have ever visited was the Los Angeles

   International Airport.

3. Snow Summit, in Big Bear, California, is a popular ski resort because it has

   such a variety of ski runs to choose from.

4. My grandmother's kitchen was one of the few places where I always felt

   safe and welcome.

5. The fake, artificial decorations and dreary atmosphere were not at all what

   I had expected when I decided to visit the Excalibur casino in Las Vegas.

Prewriting Application: Evaluating Topic Sentences

Write "No" before each sentence that would not make a good topic sentence and "Yes" before each sentence that would make a good one. Be prepared to explain your answers.

_____ 1. Last year I spent three days hiking through Yellowstone National Park.

_____ 2. Balboa Island, near Newport Beach, California, is clearly a place designed for the rich and famous.

_____ 3. Whenever I look around my bedroom, I get thoroughly depressed.

_____ 4. One of my favorite places to visit is the beach.

_____ 5. The waiting area in Dr. Larson's dentist's office is one of the most welcoming, relaxing places that I have ever seen.

_____ 6. Last December 30, we had the opportunity to visit Stone Mountain in Atlanta, Georgia.

_____ 7. My paragraph will describe the Hearst Castle in San Simeon, California.

_____ 8. The undeveloped canyon behind my house is one place where I can feel free and unrestricted.

_____ 9. The most unusual restroom that I have ever seen was the one at the Bahia de Los Angeles Research Station in Baja California, Mexico.

_____ 10. The deep South is one of the most memorable places that I have ever seen.

Prewriting Application: Talking to Others

Before you write your first draft, form groups of two, three, or four and describe the place that you have decided to write about. Tell them what central point you are trying to emphasize, and then describe as many details as you can to make that point. As you tell others about the place you have chosen, describe all of the sights, sounds, and smells that contributed to your overall impression of the place. As you listen to the places described by others and as you describe your own place, consider these questions:

1. Where exactly is this place? Has its location been clearly identified? What time of year is it? What time of day? What is the weather like?

2. Can you visualize the place? What physical features are in the area? Trees? Buildings? Furniture? Cars? Other people? What colors should be included?

3. How did you feel about this place? Is the central point or impression of the place clear?

4. Were there sounds, smells, or physical sensations that should be included in the description of the place?

5. What parts of the scene should be described in more detail?

Writing

Once you have a preliminary topic sentence and a list of related details, it is time to write the first draft of your paragraph. Open your paragraph with your topic sentence and then write out the details that illustrate the central point of your topic sentence. Do <u>not</u> worry about writing a "perfect" first draft. You will have the chance to improve the draft when you revise it.

Rewriting

1. When you have completed the first draft, read it over to see if your preliminary topic sentence accurately states the central point of your paper. If you can improve the topic sentence, do so now.

2. As you read over your draft, see if you can add still more descriptive details that relate to your central point. Add those that come to mind.

3. Finally, check the words and phrases you have used in your first draft. You will find that many of them can be more descriptive if you make them more **specific** and **concrete**.

Specific and Concrete Details

A specific detail is limited in the number of things to which it [...]
ample, the word *poodle* is more specific than the word *dog*, and [...]
is more specific than *tree*. A **concrete** detail appeals to one of the f[...]
helps a reader to **see, hear, smell, taste,** or **feel** what you describe. Fo[...]
rather than writing that your grandmother's kitchen smelled "wonderfu[...]
might write that it was always "filled with the aromas of freshly baked br[...]
and my grandfather's cigar smoke."

Unfortunately, most writers—even most professional writers—do not write
specific and concrete details naturally. You need to *add* these details to your
draft. You do so by reading back through what you have written and changing
words from general to specific and from abstract to concrete. As you read, ask
yourself which of the five senses you have left out. You probably have included
sight, but have you also included sound? Were there any smells that you should
mention? Should you add the sensations of touch or taste? Not all senses need
to be included, especially if they don't emphasize your central point, but most
first drafts have too few concrete and specific details rather than too many.

Rewriting Application: Adding Specific and Concrete Details

Rewrite the following sentences to make the underlined words more concrete.

▶ **EXAMPLE**   The house was run down.

The three-bedroom tract house on the corner of Elm and Vine

had deteriorated into a ruin of broken windows, peeling

paint, and splintered, termite-infested walls.

1. The woman walked through the entrance.

_____

_____

_____

2. The food tasted terrible.

_____

_____

_____

can refer. For ex-
the word *elm*
e senses. It
instance,
," you
ead

_olorful.

5. The <u>trees</u> along the driveway smelled <u>wonderful</u>.

Rewriting Application: Responding to Writing

Read the following description of Breaks Interstate Park. Then respond to the questions following it.

Breaks Interstate Park

In my opinion there is no more beautiful place in the spring than the Breaks Interstate Park. Last year I spent part of the spring with my father and my grandmother in the Great Smoky Mountains of Virginia. Because the Smoky Mountains are a very remote area, there was not much to do during my vacation until some of my cousins wanted to go to a place called "The Breaks." We drove into the mountains for about an hour. When we got to the entrance, the first thing I noticed was the incredible number of flowers. There were flowers on the ground, flowers in the trees and on the rocks, and there were some on the log cabins and picnic tables. We pulled off the road to one of the campsites and got out of the car. The smell of spring was everywhere. We could smell honeysuckle, strawberry, and the heady scent of wildflowers. All we could hear were bees working the blossoms and birds bathing in the springs trickling out of the mountainside. My cousin Charon came up to me and told me to follow her. We went across the road and down a winding dirt path, past a sign that said "Twin Towers Overlook." I then beheld one of the most striking and magnificent views I have ever seen in my life. I was on an overlook, looking down at a gorge where the river flowing through it makes a horseshoe-shaped bend and the mountains on the other side look like twin towers. I ran back to the car to get my camera. While on my way back, I slipped on a moss-covered rock and skinned my knee. When I got back to the overlook, I sat down on some strawberry vines, ate wild strawberries, and took pictures. I finally ran out of film and deliciously sweet strawberries, not to mention daylight. We packed it up and went back home; however, I will never forget about the Breaks Interstate Park in the springtime.

1. Identify the topic sentence. State its topic and central idea. Is it an effective topic sentence? Why or why not?

2. Identify specific and concrete details. What words do you find particularly effective?

3. Which of the five senses does the writer employ in the description? Identify each of them in the paragraph.

4. What details would you make still more specific or concrete?

5. What sentences would you combine because they contain related ideas?

Rewriting Application: Working with Subordinate Clauses

In Chapter Two you have studied main and subordinate clauses and the four sentence types: simple, compound, complex, and compound-complex. As you rewrite papers, look for opportunities to change main clauses to subordinate clauses. Combine the following sentences by changing some of them to subordinate clauses.

1.
   a. We pulled off the road to one of the campsites and got out of the car.
   b. The smell of spring was everywhere.

2.
   a. My cousin Charon came up to me and told me to follow her.
   b. We went across the road and down a winding dirt path, past a sign that said "Twin Towers Overlook."
   c. I then beheld one of the most striking and magnificent views I have ever seen in my life.

3.

    a. Bright, warm sunlight filters through eucalyptus trees and presses against my shoulders.

    b. An old man greets me with a warm smile.

    c. The old man is raking leaves in the middle of the yard.

4.

    a. My grandfather sits on an old, rust-covered metal stool.

    b. The stool used to be painted yellow.

    c. He tells me stories about my father's boyhood.

5.

    a. I have visited my grandparents' house many times during my childhood.

    b. I have not fully appreciated it until recently.

Revise each of the following sentences by changing one of the main clauses to a subordinate clause.

1. I looked to the right, and I could see an astonishingly high water slide.

2. I visited the cemetery in Escondido, California, to attend the funeral of my friend Jake McDonnell, for he had died in a head-on motorcycle accident.

3. The brevity of life was impressed on me, and I read the short accounts of unknown people's lives on the hundreds of tombstones.

4. Each weekend our family visited the Waimanalo Beach Park, and it is surrounded by the evergreen mountain range that towers over the valley below.

5. We took off our jackets and sweaters, but we still felt uncomfortably warm.

Rewriting Application: Revising and Editing Your Own Draft

1. Examine your own draft before you do your final editing of it. Rework your topic sentence if it needs to be improved. Add specific and concrete details. Identify any main clauses that would work better as introductory subordinate clauses.

2. When you are finished, do the final **editing** of your paragraph. Check the spelling of words you are uncertain about. Examine each sentence closely to be sure it is not a **fragment**, **comma splice**, or **fused sentence**. If it is, repair the error using the techniques you have studied in this chapter.

3. Once you have a draft you are satisfied with, prepare a clean final draft, following the format your instructor prefers.

Chapter Two Practice Test

I. Review of Chapter One

A. In the following sentences, identify the underlined words by writing one of the following abbreviations above the words: noun (N), pronoun (Pro), verb (V), adjective (Adj), adverb (Adv), conjunction (Conj), or preposition (Prep).

1. The huge white <u>cross</u> had stood <u>at</u> the top of the mountain for fifty years.

2. The Yankees were <u>in</u> Boston for a <u>crucially</u> important game with the Red Sox.

3. After the war, Nelson <u>started</u> an electronics company with <u>his</u> savings.

4. Harly Bindlestiff <u>usually</u> rubs Bag Balm <u>or</u> coal tar on his baseball bat.

5. When Clyde and Hortense entered the cafe, <u>they</u> requested <u>three</u> tables.

6. It was past the <u>deadline</u> when Cinderella left the palace <u>and</u> started for home.

7. After observing the flooded city <u>from</u> a helicopter, the governor declared <u>it</u> a disaster area.

8. The <u>silly</u> man <u>challenged</u> Xena to a fight.

9. <u>During</u> the monsoon season, Elisa wore <u>green</u> rubber boots whenever she went out.

10. As the airliner flew <u>into</u> the black cloud, <u>everyone</u> could see the lightning flashes.

B. For the following sentences, underline all subjects once and all complete verbs twice. Place parentheses around all prepositional phrases.

11. Is there a fly in the ointment again?

12. The anteater in my backyard was searching for its dinner.

13. Actually, the mail should have been here before noon.

14. During the night someone broke into our kitchen and stole our Spam recipes.

15. There were four cars in the driveway, but none of them would start.

16. In the beginning, either Manuel or Antonio would wake us for breakfast.

17. Will Mr. Alvarez reach Seattle by morning, or will he stop somewhere in Oregon?

18. While Icarus and Daedalus lived in the labyrinth, they tried to develop a plan of escape.

continued

19. I have given money to charity many times and have never regretted my decision.

20. Ahab called for the first mate because he wanted some cappuccino.

II. Chapter Two

A. Underline the subordinate clauses and identify the type of clause (adjective or adverb) in the space provided.

21. The hummingbirds that visit my backyard are quite tame.   _____

22. Some of them will even sit on my shoulder if I am very still.   _____

23. There is a special one that has a bright, iridescent red throat and extra long

tail feathers.   _____

24. When several of the birds are at the feeder at the same time, it is a colorful

sight.   _____

25. Until the meeting resumes, we cannot speak.   _____

B. To the main clauses below, add the types of subordinate clauses indicated in parentheses. Add your clause at any place in the sentence that is appropriate.

26. (adverb clause) Jonah was swallowed by the whale.

_____

_____

27. (adjective clause) The veterinarian carefully examined my dog.

_____

_____

continued

28. (adjective clause) The car had been driven only two miles a day by a librarian from Milwaukee.

_____

_____

29. (adverb clause) Casey ate three cherry-rhubarb pies in a half hour.

_____

_____

30. (adverb clause) Woz insisted on paying for everyone.

_____

_____

C. In the spaces provided, identify the following sentences as simple, compound, complex, or compound-complex.

31. After growing orchids for years, Eloise suddenly switched to nasturtiums. _____

32. She liked the spelling of the word, and she liked the colors of the flowers. _____

33. Eloise also changed her name to Michael because she didn't want people to take her for granted. _____

34. Michael was the name of a woman who performed on a television series; she admired the actor in that role. _____

35. To notify her friends, Eloise posted the change on her Web site. _____

D. Compose sentences of your own according to the instructions.

36. Write a simple sentence. Begin it with a prepositional phrase.

_____

_____

continued

37. Write a compound sentence. Use the coordinating conjunction *but* and appropriate punctuation.

_____

_____

38. Write a complex sentence. Use *because* as the subordinator.

_____

_____

39. Write a compound sentence. Use *yet* as the conjunction.

_____

_____

40. Write a compound-complex sentence. Use the coordinating conjunction *or* and the subordinator *while*.

_____

_____

E. Identify each of the following sentences as correct (C), fused (F), comma splice (CS), or fragment (Frag). Then correct any errors by using the methods discussed in Chapter Two.

_____ **41.** Even though he got rid of all the old friends who had been a bad influence on him.

_____

_____

_____ **42.** Williametta boarded the plane, then she noticed her passport was missing.

_____

_____

continued

_____ **43.** Please read the directions carefully before using the chain saw.

_____

_____

_____ **44.** A bear approaching from upstream.

_____

_____

_____ **45.** In her bedroom Desdemona kept looking for her handkerchief she never could find it.

_____

_____

_____ **46.** The fight had ended, Ali had beaten Joe Frazier.

_____

_____

_____ **47.** Before leaving for Florida but not until he had checked on his dog, which was staying with neighbors.

_____

_____

_____ **48.** Charlie sat in the dentist's chair, he was worried.

_____

_____

continued

_____ **49.** After receiving a promotion and a raise, Cora sold her accordion to her sister and vowed never to play again.

_____

_____

_____ **50.** The emperor was disappointed in Brutus, therefore, he said something to him in Latin.

_____

_____

anything related to cause effect

Improving Sentence Patterns

Now you have a fundamental knowledge of the sentence patterns of English. Although sentences may fall into four broad categories according to the number and types of clauses, the ways to express any thought in a sentence are almost infinitely variable.

You may make a sentence short and to the point:

> Eniko sold her netsuke collection.

Or, through the addition of modifying words, phrases, and additional clauses, you can expand it.

> After much soul searching and after seeking the advice of her mother, her brother, and her best friend, Eniko, a person who always carefully considered important decisions, sold her netsuke collection, which was worth several thousand dollars, but she kept one special carving of a frog and a sacred bird.

The essential idea—*Eniko sold her netsuke collection*—is the same for both sentences. Sometimes you will want to be short and to the point, and a five-word sentence will serve your purpose best. But sometimes you will want to be more explanatory, and then you may need more words.

The difference between the five words of the first sentence and the fifty words of the second one is the addition of modifying words, phrases, and clauses. These modifiers can help you write more clearly and vividly. The second sentence, though admittedly a bit overdone, tells a story, paints a picture. Modifying words, phrases, and clauses can be overused and should never be substituted for strong verbs and nouns, but most writers err in the opposite direction, leaving their writing limp and colorless.

You need to follow certain guidelines when you use the various modifying phrases and clauses. First we will discuss the most effective ways to use phrases and clauses in your sentences, and then we will discuss how to avoid the typical errors that writers make in using these devices. We hope that by the end you will have gained an appreciation of the wonderful flexibility of the English sentence and that you will have acquired more tools for making your own writing more interesting and effective.

Modifying with Participial and Infinitive Phrases

You can use **participial and infinitive phrases** as modifiers in your sentences. These phrases can help you streamline your sentences and achieve sentence variety. In most cases, participial and infinitive phrases take the place of subordinate clauses.

▶ EXAMPLES   (subordinate clause)   **As he drove to work,** Harry saw a black cat run in front of his car.

                             (participial phrase)   **Driving to work,** Harry saw a black cat run in front of his car.

As you already know, **a clause is a word group that contains a subject and a verb. A phrase,** on the other hand, **is a word group that does not contain a subject and a verb.** You are already aware of prepositional phrases. Other phrases, generally called verbal phrases, include **present participial phrases, past participial phrases,** and **infinitive phrases.**

Present Participial Phrases

As we mentioned in Chapter One, the present participle is a verbal. It is the form of the verb that ends in "ing" (*running, typing, looking*). Without a helping verb it cannot be used as the verb of a sentence. Instead, it is used as an adjective. For example, you can use it as a one-word adjective.

▶ EXAMPLE   The **running** man stumbled as he rounded the corner.

In this sentence, the present participle *running* modifies the noun *man*.

You can also use the present participle as part of a phrase that functions as an adjective. Such a phrase is called a **participial phrase,** and it is often used to begin sentences.

▶ EXAMPLE   Rounding the corner, the running man stumbled.

In this sentence, the present participial phrase *Rounding the corner* is an adjective phrase modifying the noun *man*. The present participle is *Rounding*.

The present participial phrase, then, is an adjective phrase consisting of the present participle plus any other words attached to it. When a present participial phrase introduces a sentence, it is always followed by a comma.

Past Participial Phrases

The past participle is the form of the verb that you use with the helping verbs *have, has,* or *had* (*have eaten, has defeated, had bought*). Like the present participle, the past participle is a verbal when used without a helping verb. And, like the present participle, it is used as an adjective.

You can use a past participle as a single-word adjective.

► **EXAMPLE**   The defeated army retreated into the mountains.

In this sentence, the past participle *defeated* modifies the noun *army.*

Or you can use the past participle as part of a past participial phrase.

► **EXAMPLE**   **Pursued by the enemy,** the army retreated into the mountains.

In this sentence, the past participial phrase *Pursued by the enemy* modifies the noun *army.* Notice that it is followed by a comma. As with the present participial phrase, when the past participial phrase introduces a sentence, you should place a comma after it.

Participial phrases make good introductions to sentences, but you can use them anywhere. To avoid confusion, though, you should place them as closely as possible to the words they modify.

► **EXAMPLES**   All of the students **submitting essays for the contest** used word processors.

The man **bitten by the rattlesnake** walked ten miles to the hospital.

The present participial phrase *submitting essays for the contest* modifies the noun *students.* The past participial phrase *bitten by the rattlesnake* modifies the noun *man.*

■ **PRACTICE**   Underline the participial phrases in the following sentences and circle the words they modify.

   1. Frightened by his addiction, Kevin sought help.

   2. In the water, Achilles saw his mother holding him by one heel.

   3. Turning the corner, the ant saw a dead aardvark.

   4. Dancing across the stage, Bill gave his best performance ever.

   5. Taught by Aristotle, Alexander the Great was a wise ruler most of the time.

6. The (man) injured in the accident was taken to the hospital.
[handwritten: Sub, Verb]

7. Blaise wanted to meet the (woman) giving the lecture on South Africa.
[handwritten: Sub]

8. Hurt by her remark, (Chris) slowly turned red.
[handwritten: Verb, Sub]

9. Looking through an old locker in the attic, (Kent) found his high school sweater.
[handwritten: Sub, Verb, P. Phrase]

10. The harpoon (sharpened on Monday,) was in the white whale on Tuesday.
[handwritten: Sub, Verbal, Verb, modifier]

Infinitive Phrases

The infinitive is a verbal that you can use as a noun, an adjective, or an adverb. You form the infinitive by adding **to** to the present tense form of the verb (*to write, to run, to listen*).

You can use the infinitive by itself.

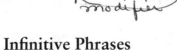
[handwritten: what is Fly doing =]

▶ **EXAMPLE**   To fly, you must first take lessons and get a license.
[handwritten: Sub, Ver]

Or you can use the infinitive to form an infinitive phrase.

▶ **EXAMPLE**   **To play the saxophone well,** you must practice often.

Notice that the infinitive phrase consists of the infinitive plus any words attached to it. Like the two participial phrases, it is followed by a comma when it introduces a sentence. However, when you use the infinitive as a noun, it can act as the subject of a sentence. In this case, you do not use a comma.

▶ **EXAMPLE**   **To be a good husband,** was Clint's ambition.
[handwritten: main verb, verb]

The infinitive phrase *To be a good husband* is the subject of the verb *was*.

Generally, like the two participial phrases, the infinitive phrase can appear in a variety of places in a sentence.

▶ **EXAMPLE**   Carla's motives were hard **to understand at first.**
[handwritten: Sub, Verb]

Here the infinitive phrase *to understand at first* acts as an adverb to modify the adjective *hard*.

▶ **EXAMPLE**   Eduardo liked having a sister **to talk to** even though she teased him constantly.

Here, the infinitive phrase *to talk to* acts as an adjective to modify the noun *sister*.

[handwritten at bottom: (To fly, lessons are Needed) wrong]

July 15

— Circumlocutionary Periphrasis —

■ **PRACTICE**   Underline the modifying participial and infinitive phrases in the following sentences and circle the words they modify.

1. Mrs. Tran bought a thesaurus to give to her son.

2. Beating around the bush, Polonius practiced circumlocution.
   Participial Fnce   modifier →

3. Most of the shoppers were glad to buy the Girl Scout Cookies from Tomasita.
   verb   Infinitive fnce
   adj

4. Bored by the tedious speech, the people in the audience drifted away.
   Past Parti   modifier →

5. Sherise finally bought a pink and purple tapestry to hang in her living room.
   Past   Infinitive Fnce

6. Sarafina looked for an outfit to wear to the graduation.
   Participial Fnce   INFINITIVE   prepositioP

7. Racing to the end of the rainbow, Alicia searched for the pot of gold.

8. Delighted by the success of his music, Carlos Santana accepted his award.

Pass Participin
9. Staring directly into the camera, the presidential candidate gave his best
   Participial Phrace
PrssenT
   imitation of a sincere smile.

10. Madame Lafarge had a very good reason to storm the Bastille.

One Review

present participle is a verbal that ends in "ing" and that is used as an ...ive. (When the "ing" form is used as a noun, it is called a **gerund.**)

...ent participial phrase consists of the present participle plus any ...attached to it.

...A comma follows a **present participial phrase** that introduces a sentence.

4. The **past participle** is the form of the verb used with the helping verbs *have, has,* and *had.*

5. The **past participle** is a verbal used as an adjective.

6. A **past participial phrase** consists of the past participle plus any words attached to it.

7. A comma follows a **past participial phrase** that introduces a sentence.

8. An **infinitive** is formed by adding *to* to the present tense of a verb.

9. The **infinitive** is a verbal that can be used as a noun, an adjective, or an adverb.

10. An **infinitive phrase** consists of the infinitive plus any words attached to it.

11. A comma follows an **infinitive phrase** that introduces a sentence and acts as a modifier.

Exercise 1A

Underline all participial and infinitive phrases. Circle the words that they modify. In the spaces, identify the phrase as present participle (Pres P), past participle (Past P), or infinitive (Inf).

Inf 1. Jose knew that Dr. Martinez was the best (person) to see about his sore ankle.

_____ 2. Besieged by Santa Anna's army, Davy Crockett and the Tennesseeans fought on.

_____ 3. The poem written by Dylan Thomas reminded me of my own father's death.

_____ 4. Scarlett could not stand the idea of all those Union soldiers marching through Atlanta.

_____ 5. Jumping into the ring, Ali looked at Joe Frazier and sneered.

_____ 6. The philatelist ordered some new stamps to add to his collection.

_____ 7. The grizzly bear is an animal to be wary of.

_____ 8. Frustrated by the emptiness in his heart, Jimmy Gatz stared at the green light across the water.

_____ 9. The cashier blamed for the theft did not steal the money.

_____ 10. Sitting in his cell in Birmingham, the Reverend King began to write a lengthy letter.

_____ 11. General Lee was looking for a strategy to break the blockade.

_____ 12. The firefighters raised a ladder to the people trapped by the fire.

_____ 13. Insulted by the rude comment, Beauregarde challenged his rival to a duel of honor.

_____ 14. Fishing near the jetty, Paul caught a moray eel.

_____ 15. Horatio thought that the American dream was something to write about.

Exercise 1B

In the places indicated by ^, add your own participial or infinitive phrases to the following sentences. Use the verbs in parentheses. Be sure to place a comma after any phrase that introduces a sentence.

1. ^ Francis turned on the lights, closed the draperies, and locked the doors. (leave)

   Leaving the house, Francis turned on the lights, closed the draperies, and locked the doors.

2. ^ You must travel to Italy. (see)

3. The boy ^ was taken to the hospital by helicopter. (injure)

4. ^ Ricardo hid his face. (embarrass)

5. After hearing her husband was dead, Mrs. Mallard was stunned to find him ^ . (walk)

6. ^ Do not drink coffee or watch television before going to bed. (sleep)

7. ^ The SWAT team was soon able to arrest the suspect. (surround)

Exercise 1B

continued

   8. ^ Arthur said goodbye to Queen Guinevere. (hope)

   _____

   _____

   9. The campers ^ were afraid that the roads would be closed by the snowstorm. (drive)

   _____

   _____

   10. ^ Roger found that he suffered from acrophobia. (climb)

   _____

   _____

   11. The ball ^ went over fifty yards in the air before it was caught. (throw)

   _____

   _____

   12. ^ Hercules cleaned out the Augean stables. (work)

   _____

   _____

   13. Alicia could not find the last Easter egg ^ . (hide)

   _____

   _____

   14. ^ The pilot arose long before dawn. (arrive)

   _____

   _____

Exercise 1B

continued

15.^ The ship reached the Andromeda galaxy in two days. (fly)

_____

_____

Exercise 1C

Underline all infinitive and participial phrases and circle the words that they modify.

1. Throughout history, the many cultures of the world have developed (mythologies) *modifier* expressing their own unique world views, yet almost all of these mythologies share similar characteristics.

2. One characteristic that is central to myths of every culture is that of a (hero) traveling on a lonely, dangerous journey. **3.** For instance, leaving his home and family in Ithaca, (Odysseus) sailed away and fought in the Trojan War. **4.** When the war ended and it was time (to return) to Ithaca, *modifies* Odysseus spent ten (years) journeying from one adventure to another before he finally arrived *modifies year — always* home. **5.** In addition, Kutoyis, a Native American Blackfoot hero, went on a (quest) during which *Preposition* he killed bears, wrestled a mysterious woman, and engaged in other (fights) (to prove himself.)

6. Also, Quetzalcoatl, an Aztec hero challenged by his own people, left on a (journey) to regain his youth. **7.** Encountering many hardships, (he) grew old but gained immortality. *P / P* **8.** Another element discovered in most myths is the divine origin or miraculous birth of the hero. **9.** Gilgamesh, a hero found in myths of the ancient Middle East, was two-thirds divine and one-third human.

10. Aeneas, a Trojan hero, was the son of the goddess Aphrodite, and the Greek hero Hercules was the son of the god Zeus. **11.** Of course, most people are aware of the stories relating the miraculous births of two of today's most influential figures, Jesus and Buddha. **12.** Finally, many mythic heroes travel to the underworld, where they gain knowledge to take back to the upper world. **13.** Descending into the underworld, the African maiden Wanjiru, the Greek Odysseus and Persephone, the Judaic Jesus, and the Roman Aeneas all returned with wisdom to share. **14.** The mythologies of the world have many other similar characteristics, reminding all people that, in spite of their diversity, they share a common humanity.

Modifying with Adjective Clauses and Appositives

by adding a comma endieater apostrreus thing
when no comma means - having more then on

Adjective Clauses

We discussed adjective clauses earlier in a section on subordinate clauses. An adjective clause is an important option when you want to modify a noun or pronoun in a sentence. Using an adjective clause instead of single-word adjectives or modifying phrases tends to place more emphasis on what you are saying about the noun or pronoun you are modifying. Consider the following sentences, for instance.

▶ **EXAMPLES**

(adjective)   My **insensitive** neighbor plays his trombone all night long.

(adjective clause)   My neighbor, **who is insensitive,** plays his trombone all night long.

Using the adjective clause *who is insensitive* places more importance on the neighbor's insensitivity. Sometimes you need only single-word modifiers, but it is good to be aware of all of your choices for modifying words.

Here is a brief review of adjective clauses.

1. Adjective clauses follow the noun or pronoun they modify.

2. Adjective clauses begin with the relative pronouns *who, whom, whose, which, that* (and sometimes *when* or *where*).

▶ **EXAMPLES**

We returned the money to the *person* **who had lost it.** (*Who* introduces an adjective clause that modifies the noun *person*.)

I remember the *time* **when Homer and Hortense were married at the Spam factory.** (*When* introduces an adjective clause that modifies the noun *time*.)

Sidney decided to move to *Colorado*, **where his family used to spend summer vacations.** (*Where* introduces an adjective clause that modifies the noun *Colorado*.)

3. If the adjective clause provides information that is necessary to identify the noun or pronoun, do not set it off with commas.

▶ **EXAMPLE**

The man **who was sitting next to my uncle at the banquet** is a famous sportswriter.

The information in this adjective clause is necessary to identify which man at the banquet is the famous sportswriter.

Restricted { *needs to*
Essential { *identify which one*
noun

4. If the adjective clause provides information that is merely descriptive and is not necessary to identify the noun or pronoun, then set the clause off with commas.

▶ **EXAMPLE**   Merlin Olsen, **who was an all-pro football player,** became a famous sportscaster.

Merlin Olsen's name already identifies him, so the adjective clause contains added but unnecessary information. Therefore, you need the commas.

We will discuss the rules for the use of commas with adjective clauses again in Chapter Five.

■ **PRACTICE**   Underline all adjective clauses and circle the words they modify. For further practice, try to determine which clauses need commas and add them where necessary.

1. The man who was chosen to succeed the governor was a political cartoonist.

2. Jason Groves told me about Gregor Mendel who discovered the basic laws of genetics.

3. None of the operators who answered the phone could speak Lithuanian.

4. Camelot which was the center of King Arthur's realm was usually crowded with knights who wanted to become members of the Round Table.

5. Caesarean section is a surgical procedure named after Julius Caesar who was supposedly born by that method.

6. The probe that was supposed to land on Mars never did send back any signals.

7. The reporter called the actress to find out a time when he could interview her.

8. Mark Twain who wrote *The Adventures of Huckleberry Finn* took his name from a river measurement.

9. The prize went to the runner who came in second because the one who came in first was disqualified.

10. Heather grew up in San Diego, where she spent her summers sailing and

surfing.

Appositives

Appositives give you another option for adding descriptive detail. An **appositive** is a noun or pronoun, along with any modifiers, that **renames** another noun or pronoun. The appositive almost always follows the word it refers to, and it is usually set off with commas.

Note how the following two sentences can be combined not only by adding an adjective clause but also by adding an appositive:

My neighbor plays the trombone all night long.

He is an insensitive man.

(adjective clause)   My neighbor, **who is insensitive,** plays his trombone all night long.

(appositive)   My neighbor, **an insensitive man,** plays his trombone all night long.

In the appositive, the noun *man* renames the noun *neighbor.*

▶ **EXAMPLES**   The wedding ring, **a symbol of eternal love,** dates back to 2800 B.C. in Egypt. (The noun *symbol* renames the noun *ring.*)

The huge trout, **the one still in the river,** would have made an impressive trophy on the wall of Harold's den. (The pronoun *one* renames the noun *trout.*)

The honeymoon, **a popular marriage custom,** comes from an ancient Northern European practice of stealing brides. (The noun *custom* renames the noun *honeymoon.*)

■ **PRACTICE**   Underline the appositives and circle the nouns or pronouns that the appositives rename.

1. The television, a central feature of most American households, has changed the way we view the world.

2. Mammoth Mountain, a ski resort in California, did not get much snow this year.

3. Homer and Hortense will be married at the Spam factory, the place of their first date.

4. For the reception, Hortense has prepared Spam artichoke, a favorite dish of Homer's.

5. E-Bay, a popular online auction site, allows people to buy and sell almost anything that one might think of.

6. My neighbor, one of the rudest persons I have ever met, did not know how to respond when Jonathan called him a yahoo.

7. *A Christmas Carol*, by Charles Dickens, tells the story of Ebenezer Scrooge, a rich but ungrateful man.

8. Athlete card collecting, once a hobby for boys, has become a popular hobby for people of both genders and all ages.

9. Mica, Jenna's friend from Argentina, will visit her this summer.

10. Shirley Jackson, who wrote *The Haunting of Hill House*, also wrote "The Lottery," an unsettling short story about a gruesome tradition in a small town.

■ **PRACTICE** Add an appositive or an adjective clause to each of the following sentences. Use commas when they are needed.

1. The bicycle was leaning against the tree.

   The bicycle that Josh had hit with his car was

   leaning against the tree.

2. The pyrotechnics began a small fire.

   _____

   _____

3. The siren woke up the firefighters, and they slid down the pole.

   _____

   _____

4. Ichabod Crane listened fearfully to the story about the strange rider.

_____

_____

5. Antigone knew her mother would not be hanging around for long.

_____

_____

6. The postal carrier stared at the fierce dog.

_____

_____

7. The people had been evacuated and were watching from a nearby store.

_____

_____

8. One member of the audience stood up on her chair and then kicked the usher.

_____

_____

9. One of the police officers helped the young boy find his mother and father.

_____

_____

10. Nero watched the fire, and his dog listened to the fiddling.

_____

_____

Section Two Review

1. **Adjective clauses** modify nouns and pronouns.

2. **Adjective clauses** follow the nouns or pronouns they modify.

3. **Adjective clauses** begin with *who, whom, whose, which, that* (and sometimes *when* or *where*).

4. **Adjective clauses** that contain information necessary to identify the words they modify are not set off with commas.

5. **Adjective clauses** that do not contain information necessary to identify the words they modify are set off with commas.

6. **Appositives** are words or word groups containing a noun or pronoun that renames another noun or pronoun in a sentence.

7. **Appositives** usually follow the nouns or pronouns they rename.

8. **Appositives** are usually set off with commas.

Exercise 2A

Underline all adjective clauses and appositives. Circle the words they modify or rename. Indicate whether the modifier is an appositive (AP) or an adjective clause (Adj). Add commas where necessary.

_AP_ **1.** _The Babe_ is a contemporary movie about (Babe Ruth,) the famous baseball player. *no verb*

add coma

_____ **2.** Babe Ruth whose pictures usually show him to be somewhat overweight was famous for his appetite.

no comma

_____ **3.** There are rumors that he could eat more than twenty hot dogs and drink several *add clause* beers before a game.

_____ **4.** The pin-striped uniforms a Yankee trademark were not adopted to make Ruth look thinner.

comm

_____ **5.** The Yankees began wearing pinstripes in 1912 which was eight years before Babe *adj clos* Ruth joined the team.

comm

_____ **6.** _The Babe Ruth Story_ an early black-and-white movie starred William Bendix.

comma

_____ **7.** Bendix who had been a batboy with the New York Giants knew Ruth well. *adjectue cla*

_____ **8.** Once, before a game, Bendix brought Ruth twelve hot dogs and two quarts of soda which made the Babe sick and sent him to the hospital.

_____ **9.** It was a (favor) that caused the batboy to be fired. *No Com* *adjective claus*

_____ **10.** In 1930 and 1931 his top years Ruth made $80,000 per year in salary. *Appositive*

_____ **11.** Today, it is not unusual to see players who make over several million dollars a year. *adjective*

_____ **12.** Some players make hundreds of thousands of dollars a year just to wear items of equipment that sports companies give them.

_____ **13.** For many years, Muhammed Ali a famous boxer had the record for career earnings among athletes.

Exercise 2A

continued

_____ **14.** Ali who was barred from boxing for several years earned $69 million between 1960 and 1981.

_____ **15.** Some people have come up with an estimate that Ruth's total earnings would be worth about $24 million today.

I broke the dish Simpl finished action
on the past

I have broken the dish finish action now

adjective Clauses = who
                    which

add comma Bendix, who

Rubens who no comma

Exercise 2B

A. Add adjective clauses of your own to each of the sentences below. Make sure you use commas where necessary.

1. My brother always enjoyed riding his bicycle in the mountains.

   My brother, who loves the outdoors, always enjoyed

   riding his bicycle in the mountains.

2. The television program was about a wedding in Argentina.

   _____

   _____

3. Abraham Lincoln was responsible for the Emancipation Proclamation.

   _____

   _____

4. Pamela Salazar usually waits until Saturday to wash her car.

   _____

   _____

5. Las Vegas is famous for its casinos.

   _____

   _____

6. A person performed balloon tricks for the children.

   _____

   _____

7. The toys for the Christmas party were delivered by the man late in the week.

   _____

   _____

continued

   8. The company sent Mr. Canisero tapes of classic books.

   _____

   _____

B. Add appositives of your own to the sentences below. Make sure you use commas where necessary.

   9. The car collided with the delivery van on the interstate freeway.

   The car, a late model Ford, collided with the

   delivery van on the interstate freeway.

   10. The prince did not know what the princess was doing, but the duke told the duchess.

   _____

   _____

   11. On the next day the inspector declared the airplane unsafe to fly.

   _____

   _____

   12. Nora bought her husband a tie with a picture of a doll house on it.

   _____

   _____

   13. In the summer, the Lees liked to camp in the Smoky Mountains of Tennessee.

   _____

   _____

   14. The astronomer discovered a new planet when he used the extremely powerful telescope in a remote part of Idaho.

   _____

   _____

continued

15. James cocked his pistol, jumped onto his horse, and rode toward Dallas.

Very important:

the AC is Fixel Simple present it is working

" AC was Fited Simple past it was working at some past time

4/23/01

the AC has been Fix Preseo Penfect
the Fixing is Finished so it should worn

the AC had been Fixed past perfec

The Fixed wor Finished in the Past at some time — but I can not say yit is working now

Very good information
Please = Review as often as you can it is good idea to master this information:

Exercise 2C

Underline all adjective clauses and circle the words they modify. Underline all appositives and circle the words they rename. Add commas where necessary.

1. Many (people) who are otherwise well informed are of the mistaken (opinion) that pigs are sloppy, greedy, and stupid. **2.** However, the pig, a rather clean and intelligent animal, does not deserve its reputation. **3.** For instance, since it does not perspire, the main (reason) that a pig rolls in mud is to cool itself off. **4.** In addition, the mud protects a pig's (skin) which is as tender as human skin from painful insect bites. **5.** Unfortunately, this activity has led to the (misconception) that pigs are sloppy. **6.** In fact, pigs prefer to bathe if they can find (water) that is clean. **7.** Pigs are also not greedy. **8.** In contrast to (humans) who are known to "pig out", pigs will seldom overeat. **9.** And even though pigs which are omnivorous animals will eat almost anything, including garbage, they prefer a diet that is cleaner and less smelly. **10.** My oldest brother a farmer in the Midwest feeds his pigs the family garbage, but his pigs will pass up the garbage if something better is offered. **11.** Finally, pigs are certainly not stupid. **12.** There are many studies that show pigs to be intelligent, and primates much more popular animals than pigs are only slightly more intelligent. **13.** Pigs which are the smartest of farm animals can actually be taught tricks. **14.** Certainly the pig a maligned animal deserves more respect than it gets from many people who are often more piggish than it is.

Misplaced and Dangling Modifiers

In Chapter Two, when you combined clauses to form various sentence types, you learned that joining clauses improperly can lead to comma splices and fused sentences. As you can probably guess, adding modifiers to sentences leads to an entirely new set of problems. In some cases, these problems are a bit more complicated than those caused by comma splices and fused sentences, but with a little practice, you should have no trouble at all handling them.

Misplaced Modifiers

Misplaced modifiers are exactly what their name says they are—modifiers that have been "misplaced" within a sentence. But how is a modifier "misplaced"? The answer is simple. If you remember that a modifier is nearly always placed just before or just after the word it modifies, then a misplaced modifier must be one that has been mistakenly placed so that it causes a reader to be confused about what it modifies. Consider the following sentence, for example:

▶ **EXAMPLE**   Albert said **quietly** to move away from the snake.

Does the modifier *quietly* tell us how Albert said what he said, or does it tell us how we should move away from the snake? Changing the placement of the modifier will clarify the meaning.

▶ **EXAMPLES**   Albert **quietly** said to move away from the snake. (Here, the word modifies the verb *said*.)

Albert said to move **quietly** away from the snake. (Here the word modifies the verbal *to move*.)

Sometimes finding the correct placement of a modifier can be a bit difficult. Let's look at a few other typical examples.

Misplaced Words

Any modifier can be misplaced, but one particular group of modifiers causes quite a bit of trouble for many people. These words are *only, almost, just, merely,* and *nearly.* Consider, for example, the following sentences:

▶ **EXAMPLES**   By buying her new computer on sale, Floretta **almost** saved $100.   *did not save*

By buying her new computer on sale, Floretta saved **almost** $100.

misplaced = modifier
two-way modifier

As you can see, these sentences actually make two different statements. In the first sentence, *almost* modifies *saved*. If you *almost* saved something, you did *not* save it. In the second sentence, *almost* modifies *$100*. If you saved *almost* $100, you saved $85, $90, $95, or some other amount close to $100.

Which statement does the writer want to make—that Floretta did *not* save any money or that she *did* save an amount close to $100? Because the point was that she bought her computer on sale, the second sentence makes more sense.

To avoid confusion, be sure that you place all of your modifiers carefully.

► **EXAMPLES**

(incorrect) Her piano teacher encouraged her **often** to practice.

(correct) Her piano teacher **often** encouraged her to practice.

(correct) Her piano teacher encouraged her to practice **often**.

good →

(incorrect) Sophia **nearly** drank a gallon of coffee yesterday.

(correct) Sophia drank **nearly** a gallon of coffee yesterday.

■ **PRACTICE**

Underline and correct any misplaced words in the following sentences. Some of the sentences may be correct.   *Stop*

when a modifier goes both ways

1. I have not finished all of my work because I ~~only~~ started it ^*only* an hour ago.

2. The band leader told her loudly to play her tuba. ——

3. Manuela arrived early just to meet the mayor.

4. The customer who barged into the office angrily demanded to speak to the manager.

5. After she had almost driven two hundred miles, Hillary was ready to stop.

6. The soldier nearly carried her friend for ten miles before she could find help.

7. Even though Alejandro had sat before his computer all day, he had <u>merely</u> *written* written three pages.

8. My doctor told me frequently to get some exercise.

9. Billie Bob was disappointed at the county fair because his prize pig only received a second-place ribbon.

10. Merilee nearly slept twenty hours the night after she ran the marathon.

Misplaced Phrases and Clauses

The phrases and clauses that you studied earlier in this chapter are as easily misplaced as individual words. Phrases and clauses often follow the words they modify.   *Follow words that modify)*

► **EXAMPLES**   (prepositional phrase)   The driver **in the blue sports car** struck an innocent pedestrian.

(present participial phrase)   The dog **chasing the car** barked at the bewildered driver.

(past participial phrase)   They gave the bicycle **donated by the shop** to the child.

(adjective clause)   Lucia gave the money **that she had borrowed from her sister** to the homeless woman.

In each of the above sentences, the modifier follows the word it modifies. Notice what happens when the modifier is misplaced so that it follows the wrong word.

► **EXAMPLES**   The driver struck an innocent pedestrian **in the blue sports car.**

The dog barked at the bewildered driver **chasing the car.**

They gave the bicycle to the child **donated by the shop.**

Lucia gave the money to the homeless woman **that she had borrowed from her sister.**

Obviously, misplaced phrases and clauses can create rather confusing and sometimes even humorous situations. Of course, not all phrases and clauses follow the words they modify. Many occur before the word they refer to.

► **EXAMPLES**   (past participial phrase)   **Angered by the umpire's poor call,** Dana threw her bat to the ground.

(present participial phrase)   **Hoping to win the debate,** Cyrus practiced three hours every day.

Regardless of whether the modifier appears before or after the word it modifies, the point is that you should place modifiers so that they clearly refer to a specific word in the sentence.

■   **PRACTICE**   Underline and correct any misplaced phrases and clauses in the following sentences. Some of the sentences may be correct.

1. The cat leaped at the canary <u>that had been hungrily eyeing it.</u>

   The cat that had been hungrily eyeing the

   canary leaped at it.

2. The boy showed the book to his mother that he had found in a thrift shop.

   The boy showed to his Mother the book that he had

   found in thrift shop.

3. Chuck avoided his teammates <u>worried</u> about the argument he had just had with his wife.

   Chuck, worried about the Argument he had just had

   with his wife ANd avoided his teamate

4. The ten-year-old boy showed the bug to his grandmother that had bitten him on his toe.

   _____

   _____

5. A thirsty vampire stared at the boy with sharp fangs.

   _____

   _____

6. Arthur sold a house to his brother that had leaky plumbing.

   _____

   _____

ur comma th
wich)

7. Basil caught some fish for his mother with worms.

_____

_____

8. I gave some treats to the dog near that little boy that sat up, begged, and rolled over.

_____

_____

9. The monkeys in the cage looked out at the people hanging from limbs by their tails.

The monkeys hanging from limb by them tails

in the cage looked out at the people

10. Mr. Wolfe showed the pig to his neighbor that he had boiled for dinner.

Mr wolfe —

_____

Dangling Modifiers

A **dangling modifier** is an introductory phrase (usually a verbal phrase) that lacks an appropriate word to modify. Since these modifiers usually represent some sort of action, they need a **doer** or **agent** of the action represented.

For example, in the following sentence the introductory participial phrase "dangles" because it is not followed by a noun or pronoun that could be the doer of the action represented by the phrase.

Driving madly down the boulevard, the horse just missed being hit and killed.

The present participial phrase *Driving madly down the boulevard* should be followed by a noun or pronoun that could logically do the action of the phrase. Instead, it is followed by the noun *horse,* which is the subject of the sentence. Was the horse "driving"? Probably not. Therefore, the modifying phrase "dangles" because it has no noun or pronoun to which it can logically refer. Here are some more sentences with dangling modifiers.

► **EXAMPLES**

Nearly exhausted, the game was almost over.
(Was the *game* exhausted?)

After studying all night, the test wasn't so difficult after all.
(Did the *test* study all night?)

To impress his new girlfriend, Dominic's Chevrolet was polished.
(Did the *Chevrolet* want to impress Dominic's girlfriend?)

As you can see, you should check for dangling modifiers when you use introductory phrases.

■ **PRACTICE**

In the following sentences, indicate whether the modifying phrases are correctly used by writing either C for correct or D for dangling modifier in the spaces provided.

_____D____ **1.** Walking up to receive his medal, Sal's zipper broke.

_____ **2.** Sitting on the table, the smile disappeared from the Cheshire cat.

____C____ **3.** Fascinated by the movements of the rattlesnake, Jake's dog stood and stared at it.

_____ **4.** To learn to play the piano well, daily lessons are needed.

_____ **5.** Prized by cooks, the truffles were uncovered by the French pigs.

Sentences ~~with~~ that start with infinitive force to you have to have a person to do Something

Correcting Dangling Modifiers

You can correct a dangling modifier in one of two ways.

1. Rewrite the sentence so that the introductory modifier logically refers to the subject of the sentence it introduces.

▶ **EXAMPLES**   Nearly exhausted, **I** hoped the game was almost over.
(*I* was nearly exhausted.)

After studying all night, **Lucilla** passed the test easily.
(*Lucilla* studied all night.)

To impress his new girlfriend, **Dominic** polished his Chevrolet.
(*Dominic* wanted to impress his girlfriend.)

2. Change the introductory phrase to a clause.

▶ **EXAMPLES**   **Because I was nearly exhausted,** I hoped the game was almost over.

After Lucilla had studied all night, she passed the test easily.

Dominic wanted to impress his girlfriend, so he polished his Chevrolet.

NOTE: Do not correct a dangling modifier by moving it to the end of the sentence or by adding a possessive noun or pronoun to a sentence. In either case, it will still "dangle" because it lacks a **doer** or **agent** that could perform the action of the modifier.

▶ **EXAMPLES**   (incorrect)   **After searching for three weeks,** the lost watch was finally found. (There is no doer for *searching*.)

(still incorrect)   The lost watch was finally found **after searching for three weeks.** (There still is no logical doer.)

(still incorrect)   **After searching for three weeks,** Alfredo's lost watch was finally found. (Adding the possesive form *Alfredo's* does not add a doer of the action.)

(correct)   ⟶ **After searching for three weeks,** Alfredo finally found his watch. (The noun *Alfredo* can logically perform the action—*searching*—of the modifying phrase.)

(correct)   **After Alfredo had searched for three weeks,** he finally found his watch. (Here again, the doer of the action is clear.)

■ **PRACTICE**   Underline and correct any dangling modifiers in the following sentences. Some of the sentences may be correct.

1. To pass the time, another movie was watched.

To pass the time, we watched another movie.

We watched

watched another movie to pass the time ?

2. Strolling through the museum, the paintings were enjoyed by Darby until she had to leave for lunch.

   Strolling throug the museum DARby enjoyed the painting until she had to leave for lunch

3. After running on a hot day, a long soak in the tub is enjoyable.

   after running on a hot day I enjoy a long soak in the tub

4. Worried about Tom's constant smoking, his mother bought him a case of chewing gum.

   ol

5. Shouting profanities, Lear's will was changed last night.

6. Talking nervously to the police officer, Tomás's nose began to itch.

   discovered that his nose began to itch

7. To watch the solar eclipse, sunglasses will protect your eyes.

   if you wont to watch the solar ecleipe, you will need —— to protect your eyes

8. Looking at the horizon, the sun could be seen reflected on the sea.

9. Disgusted by his behavior, an apology was written by Sid.

_____

_____

10. To become accurate, much practice with the longbow is needed.

_____

_____

4/23/01   (Simple Present)

the AC is Fited- = it is working

the AC was Fited ——Simple Past—— it was working at some past Time

The ac ~~was Fited~~ has been Fixed ——Present Perfect
the Fixing is finished so it should work
——

the AC had been Fixed - Past p.enfect = The
Fixed was finished in the past at some time, but F
can not say if it is working now

Yestardar   now Now
                                  Some one
Someone   working
working   Done
done
                                     It work

Section Three Review

1. A **misplaced modifier** is a modifier that has been mistakenly placed so that it causes the reader to be confused about what it modifies.

2. Commonly misplaced words are *only, almost, just, merely,* and *nearly.*

3. Place modifying phrases and clauses so that they clearly refer to a specific word in a sentence.

4. A **dangling modifier** is an introductory phrase (usually a verbal phrase) that lacks an appropriate word to modify. Since these modifiers usually represent some sort of action, they need a **doer** or **agent** of the action represented.

5. You can correct a dangling modifier in one of two ways.

   a. Rewrite the sentence so that the introductory modifier logically refers to the subject of the sentence it introduces.

   b. Change the introductory phrase to a clause.

6. Do not correct a dangling modifier by moving it to the end of the sentence or by adding a possessive noun or pronoun.

Exercise 3A

A. Underline and correct any misplaced words in the following sentences. Some sentences may be correct.

1. After <u>nearly</u> working for a week, I finally finished planting my garden.

almost

After working for nearly a week, I finally finished

planting my garden.

✓ **2.** The angry diner said that he had merely asked for a ham and cheese sandwich, not for a sirloin steak dinner.

The angry diner

✓ **3.** Henry thinks that the Seahawks will decide secretly to move from Seattle to Los Angeles.

will

Henry thinks that the Seahawks secretly ~~will~~ decide to

move from Seattle to Al

✓ **4.** When I went to the mountains, I only skied two times all weekend.

Skied only

I only skied two times all weekend

5. Porter was angry because the plumber said he just wanted five more days to fix the hot water heater.

0

B. Underline and correct any misplaced phrases or clauses in the following sentences. Some of the sentences may be correct.

6. Leon showed a chicken to his daughter <u>that had two heads</u>.

Leon showed a chicken that had two heads to

his daughter.

Exercise 3A

continued

7. The sailor's wife waved as her husband's ship left port, weeping quietly.

_____

_____

8. The tired monkey stared at the line of ants slowly peeling the banana.

_____

_____

9. Renata admired the butterflies on her wallpaper singing a lullaby to her baby.

_____

_____

10. The investigator searched for the weapon that belonged to the criminal that had been thrown out the car window.

_____

_____

C. Underline and correct any dangling modifiers in the following sentences. Some of the sentences may be correct.

11. Worried about the poor weather, a raincoat and an umbrella are advised.

     If you are worried about the poor weather, we advise you to take a

     raincoat and an umbrella.

12. To know more about the Civil War, a trip to the South might be necessary.

_____

_____

Exercise 3A

continued

13. Surprised by the party for his fiftieth birthday, a heart attack was suffered by Homer.

_____

_____

14. Swimming carefully to conserve strength, Conrad's chances for survival improved.

_____

_____

15. Looking for a special way to spend their summer, a cabin in the Mojave Desert was rented.

_____

_____

Exercise 3B

Underline and correct any misplaced or dangling modifiers in the following sentences. Some of the sentences may be correct.

1. <u>After driving for seven straight hours</u>, all of the towns began to look the same.

   After I drove for seven straight hours, all of the towns began to look the same.

2. The woman in the red and yellow Mustang eating the sushi collided with the fresh fish truck.

3. The computer only crashes when an important assignment is due.

4. Pushing wildly at the crowd, Cheryl tried to make room for her mother to breathe.

5. Bothered by the rudeness of the audience, Randall's bass drum was thrown from the stage.

6. The server set a bacon, lettuce, and tomato sandwich before the diner smeared with a generous helping of guacamole.

continued

7. Although at first I thought I had found a diamond in the sand, it merely turned out to be a piece of costume jewelry.

_____

_____

8. Before leaving the table, please ask to be excused.

_____

_____

9. The delegates paused to stare at the statue walking down the hall.

_____

_____

10. Hiding escaping slaves during the Civil War, Harriet Tubman's actions saved the lives of many men and women.

_____

_____

11. Enrique gave the flowers to his wife that had made him sneeze all the way home.

_____

_____

12. To prepare for his Thanksgiving dinner, Homer almost bought all of the Spam in the store.

_____

_____

continued

13. After jogging for two miles, my lungs began to ache.

_____

_____

14. I like escargots, but since last month I have only been eating green vegetables.

_____

_____

15. A man wielding a gun with green eyes threatened the bank teller.

_____

_____

Exercise 3C

Correct any dangling or misplaced modifiers in the following paragraph.

1. The human body's "flight or fight" reaction to stress is an ancient defense mechanism that can allow people to accomplish remarkable feats of strength or endurance. **2.** For example, struck by lightning in August, 1989, Mary O'Leary's life was saved by the "flight or fight" system. **3.** She had been hiking alone in Colorado's Roosevelt National Forest when a bolt of lightning struck her in the back, which can carry as much as 100 million volts of electricity. **4.** Afterward, barely conscious, she pulled herself across the ground to get to a trail that almost was two miles away. **5.** At one point, only using her hands, she had to climb over a fallen tree that was sixty feet long and three feet high. **6.** Another example of this defense mechanism at work is Lorraine Lengkeek's experience with a grizzly bear. **7.** While camping in Montana, a five-hundred-pound grizzly bear attacked her and her husband. **8.** When the bear started to maul her husband, feeling an intense anger, Lorraine rushed at the grizzly. **9.** Swinging her binoculars, the bear was struck four times and driven off by the sixty-two-year-old, five-foot-three-inch woman. **10.** Finally, a dramatic example of the body's ability to react to dangerous situations happened to John Thompson, a North Dakota farm boy. **11.** While working alone, his arms were severed by a tractor-powered auger. **12.** He staggered to his house, used his mouth to turn the doorknob, and dialed for help with a pencil held in his teeth. **13.** Then, to avoid getting blood on his parents' carpet, the bathtub was where he sat until help arrived. **14.** Doctors who reattached Thompson's arms say that his body's "flight or fight" system saved his life, which automatically clotted blood in his severed arteries. **15.** These examples and others like them are evidence of the human body's extraordinary ability to protect itself.

Sentence Practice: Using Participial and Infinitive Phrases, Appositives, and Adjective Clauses

In this chapter, you have become aware of the many choices you have when you want to modify words in your sentences. Your options range from single-word modifiers to modifying phrases to subordinate clauses. Let's explore some of the possibilities with the following sentence.

> The beautiful Dalmatian looked hungrily at the thick steaks cooking on the grill and quietly begged the chef for a bite.

By changing various modifiers, you can express the sentence in several other ways. For instance, *The beautiful Dalmatian,* with its single-word modifier *beautiful* describing *Dalmatian,* could be changed into an appositive.

> The dog, **a beautiful Dalmatian,** looked hungrily at the thick steaks cooking on the grill and quietly begged the chef for a bite.

This version tends to emphasize the beauty of the dog.

If you change the part of the sentence that contains the verb *looked* to a present participial phrase, you will get a different effect.

> **Looking hungrily at the thick steaks cooking on the grill,** the beautiful Dalmatian quietly begged the chef for a bite.

This version places a bit more emphasis on the dog's hungry look.

Another alternative is to change the present participial phrase *cooking on the grill* to an adjective clause.

> The beautiful Dalmatian looked hungrily at the thick steaks **that were cooking on the grill** and quietly begged the chef for a bite.

As you can see, the choices are many, and good writers often try several versions of a sentence before deciding on the one that best expresses their ideas. Experimenting with your sentences in this way is part of the fun and the challenge of writing.

The exercises in this section are designed to give you practice in using various types of modifiers when you compose your sentences.

Sentence Combining Exercises

Using your knowledge of modifying phrases and clauses, combine the following lists of sentences according to the directions. Avoid dangling and misplaced modifiers. Add commas where necessary.

▶ **EXAMPLE**   Combine these sentences into one sentence. Use sentence a as a present participial phrase. Use sentence b as an appositive.

   a. Lupe felt good about her promotion to manager.
   b. Lupe was a generous person.
   c. Lupe invited her co-workers to dinner.
   d. The dinner would be at their favorite Thai restaurant.

   Feeling good about her promotion to manager, Lupe, a

   generous person, invited her co-workers to dinner

   at their favorite Thai restaurant.

1. Combine the following sentences into one sentence. Combine sentences a and b into one adverb clause.

   a. A physician was from the ancient world.
   b. A physician wanted to relieve fever.
   c. The physician recommended the bark of the willow tree.

   _____

   _____

   _____

2. Combine the following sentences into one sentence. Use sentence b as an appositive. Use sentence e as an adjective clause.

   a. Aspirin is a variation of the old remedy.
   b. Aspirin is an acid.
   c. The remedy was rediscovered by a German chemist.
   d. It was rediscovered in 1853.
   e. He was looking for a cure for arthritis.

   _____

   _____

   _____

Sentence Combining Exercises

continued

3. Combine these sentences into one sentence. Use sentence a as an introductory past participial phrase. Use sentence d as an adjective clause.

   a. Aspirin was ignored for years.
   b. Aspirin is an extract from that ancient willow tree.
   c. It is also an extract from another plant.
   d. The other plant is a relative of the rose.

   _____

   _____

   _____

4. Combine these sentences into one sentence. Use sentence c as an appositive. Use sentence d as an adjective clause.

   a. It was 1893.
   b. Felix Hoffman was looking for a way to ease his father's arthritis pain.
   c. Felix Hoffman was a German chemist.
   d. Felix Hoffman worked for the Bayer Chemical Company.

   _____

   _____

   _____

5. Combine the following sentences into one sentence. Use sentence a as an introductory present participial phrase. Use sentence c as an adjective clause.

   a. Felix Hoffman remembered the formula for aspirin.
   b. Felix Hoffman prepared a batch of the drug.
   c. Remarkably it relieved his father's pain.

   _____

   _____

   _____

Sentence Combining Exercises

continued

6. Combine the following sentences into one sentence. Use sentence a as a past participial phrase. Use sentence d as an adjective clause.

   a. Aspirin was marketed in 1899 as powder.
   b. Aspirin became the world's most prescribed drug.
   c. In 1915 Bayer introduced aspirin tablets.
   d. The tablets mysteriously relieve pain, fever, and inflammation.

   _____

   _____

   _____

7. Combine the following sentences into one sentence. Use sentence b as an appositive phrase. Use sentence c as an adjective clause.

   a. The apple is never mentioned in the Bible.
   b. The apple is the forbidden fruit.
   c. Adam and Eve supposedly ate the apple.

   _____

   _____

   _____

8. Combine the following sentences into one sentence. Use sentence b as an appositive. Use sentence c as an appositive.

   a. The Baby Ruth was not named after Babe Ruth.
   b. The Baby Ruth is a popular candy bar.
   c. Babe Ruth was a famous baseball player.
   d. It was named after the first daughter of Grover Cleveland.

   _____

   _____

   _____

continued

9. Combine these sentences into one sentence. Use sentence a as an infinitive phrase. Use sentence c as an adjective clause. Use sentence e as an adjective clause.

   a. Brad surprised his parents.
   b. He replaced the windows.
   c. The windows had been broken.
   d. He replaced the carpet.
   e. The carpet had been ruined.
   f. It was while his parents were on vacation.

   _____

   _____

   _____

10. Combine the following sentences into one sentence. Use sentence a as an introductory prepositional phrase. Use sentence d as an adjective clause.

   a. It was morning.
   b. The Trojans saw the horse.
   c. The horse was wooden.
   d. The horse was in the middle of their city.
   e. The Trojans were afraid.

   _____

   _____

   _____

five

Paragraph Practice: Using Examples

Writing Assignment

In the first two chapters of this text, you have written paragraphs about an event and a place. Such writing is usually called "narrative" or "descriptive" because it either narrates (tells about) an event or describes a place. In this chapter you will write an **expository** paragraph. Expository writing **explains** a topic or idea to a reader, or it **informs** the reader about a topic or idea. The topic of an expository paragraph or essay can range from explaining how to conduct an experiment in chemistry to analyzing the causes of World War II. In fact, most of the writing you will do in college classes will be expository.

One common type of expository writing is the paragraph or essay that relies on **examples** to make its point. If you look at Exercises 1C, 2C, and 3C of Chapter Three, you will see that they all rely on examples to support the statements made in the topic sentences. Paragraph 1C gives examples of the similar characteristics of myths throughout the world. Paragraph 2C gives examples of false ideas about pigs. And Paragraph 3C gives examples of people whose "flight or fight" reaction allowed them to accomplish remarkable feats of strength or endurance.

Supporting your ideas with examples is a powerful way to help your readers understand your point. Examples allow your readers to see your topic at work in real-life situations, and they show your readers that your topic is based on reality. Of course, examples are also important when you take tests. Your ability to back up general answers with specific examples can show an instructor that you have understood and mastered the material you have been studying.

For this chapter, your assignment is to write a paragraph that uses *at least three specific examples* to support a statement made in a topic sentence. Develop your paragraph from one of the following prewriting suggestions or from an idea suggested by your instructor.

Reading Assignment

The reading selections in the "Using Examples" section of Chapter Seven can help you see how professional writers include examples to illustrate their ideas. Read one or more of the selections, as assigned by your instructor, and use the questions that follow them to develop ideas for your own paper.

Prewriting

Use the prewriting techniques of freewriting, brainstorming, and clustering to develop topic ideas from the list that follows. Look for topics that you can illustrate with specific, detailed examples of your own.

Prewriting Application: Finding Your Topic

Read the following topic suggestions before you begin to prewrite. Not all of them will apply to you. Find the suggestions that interest you the most and then spend five or ten minutes freewriting on each of them. Try not to settle for a topic that seems only mildly interesting. Instead, look for that "Aha!" experience, the emotional reaction that identifies a topic that really moves you.

1. Give examples of *one* particular personality characteristic of your own. Are you a hard-working, "Type A" personality? Do you overeat when you experience stress, anger, or boredom? Are you sometimes too outspoken? Are you overly impulsive? Choose *one* personality characteristic of your own and illustrate it with examples.

2. Give examples of *one* particular personality characteristic of someone you know. Choose someone close to you—a family member, a close friend, or someone you work with or have known for a while. Identify *one* of that person's personality characteristics, and then illustrate it with examples.

3. Have you ever found that at times telling a lie is the ethical, responsible thing to do? Have you ever told a lie to protect someone from danger or from unnecessary pain? Use specific examples to illustrate times when lying seemed to you to be the correct, responsible behavior.

4. Take any simple statement that you know to be true and illustrate it with specific examples. Consider ideas like these:

   • Last year's rains damaged many homes in my hometown.

   • The food served in some restaurants can have appalling things happen to it while it is still in the kitchen.

   • At last year's comic convention I was introduced to some of the weirdest people that I have ever seen.

   • The Sun City Senior Center is full of people who have led exciting, adventurous lives.

   • Some people treat their pets as if they were people.

5. Have you ever experienced intolerance or bigotry because of your race, gender, religious beliefs, or age? Write a paragraph in which you use specific examples to illustrate what has happened to you.

6. People sometimes say that the simplest things in life are the most valuable. If you agree, use specific examples to illustrate the truth of that statement in your own life.

7. Choose a sport, activity, or hobby with which you are familiar. Use specific examples to illustrate something that you know to be true about it.

8. Use examples to illustrate an idea about something that you own: your car, an animal, your computer, your clothing.

9. Choose a statement that people commonly believe to be true and use examples to show why it is or is not true in your life. Here are some examples:

    - Whatever can go wrong will go wrong.

    - Sometimes help can come from the most unlikely places.

    - If you try hard enough, you will succeed.

    - You can't tell who your real friends are until you need help.

10. Choose a technological device—the computer, cell phone, answering machine, fax machine, and so on—and use examples to illustrate your attitude toward it.

Once you have decided on a topic, write a preliminary topic sentence with a central point that your examples will illustrate. Your topic and central point should not be too general. For example, don't try to illustrate something like "The United States has many problems." Although the statement is obviously true, it could not be easily supported with only a few examples in one paragraph. A more manageable topic might be something like "My cousin's drinking problem has become quite serious in the past few months." With just a few detailed examples, you could support such a statement.

Prewriting Application: Working with Topic Sentences

Identify the topic sentences in Exercises 1C (page 147), 2C (page 159), and 3C (page 176). Then identify the topic and the central point in each topic sentence.

Prewriting Application: Evaluating Topic Sentences

Write "No" before each sentence that would not make a good topic sentence *for this assignment*. Write "Yes" before each sentence that would make a good one. Be prepared to explain your answers.

_____ 1. I have many different personality characteristics.

_____ 2. Computers are supposed to be convenient, time-saving machines, but mine has brought me nothing but trouble.

_____ 3. People who believe that money can't buy happiness have obviously never met my uncle.

_____ 4. Basketball has been my favorite sport for as long as I can remember.

_____ 5. After having owned a horse for ten years, I have decided that my particular horse has to be one of the stupidest animals alive.

_____ 6. Whenever I go to a garage sale or a swap meet, I end up buying some absolutely useless item.

_____ 7. My paragraph is about why Idaho holds such pleasant memories for so many people.

_____ **8.** My best friend's parties always seem to turn into near riots.

_____ **9.** Our country is a wonderful place to live, but it has many serious problems that need to be resolved.

_____ **10.** My father believes that we should never lie, but sometimes his honesty is so painful it is almost cruel.

Prewriting Application: Talking to Others

Once you have decided on a topic and a preliminary topic sentence, you need to develop your examples. A good way to do so is to tell three or four other members of your class why your topic sentence is true. Think of yourself as an attorney before a jury. You must provide the evidence—the examples—to support the central idea in your topic sentence.

For example, if your topic is that your father's honesty borders on cruelty, convince the other people in your group with brief, specific examples. Consider these questions as you discuss your topics.

1. Exactly where and when does each example occur? Has the place and time of each instance been clearly identified?

2. Can you visualize the examples? Are the people mentioned in the example identified by name or by relationship to the student? Are physical features specifically named or described?

3. What point do these examples reveal? Should the student's topic sentence be revised to express that point more clearly?

4. Are you convinced? Has the student provided enough examples to illustrate the topic idea? Should any of the examples be more convincing?

5. Which example should the student's paper open with? Which should it close with?

Writing

Write the first draft of your paragraph. Your first sentence should be your preliminary topic sentence. After writing the topic sentence, write the examples that illustrate your point. Devote several sentences to each example and be as specific and as detailed as you can in each of those sentences.

Using Transitions

Transitions are words, phrases, or clauses that let the reader know when you are moving from one idea or example to another. They are essential for clear writing because they help your readers follow your train of thought. Because you will be writing several examples in one paragraph for this assignment, you need to let your readers know when one example has ended and another is beginning. One of the clearest ways to do so is to write a **transitional sentence** to introduce each example.

The following transitional sentences introduce each example in Exercise 1C, page 147.

► **EXAMPLES**   **One characteristic** that is central to myths of every culture is that of a hero traveling on a lonely, dangerous journey.

For instance, leaving his home and family in Ithaca, Odysseus sailed away and fought in the Trojan War.

In addition, Kutoyis, a Native American Blackfoot hero, went on a quest during which he killed bears, wrestled a mysterious woman, and engaged in other fights to prove himself.

Also, Quetzalcoatl, an Aztec hero challenged by his own people, left on a journey to regain his youth.

Another element discovered in most myths is the divine origin or miraculous birth of the hero.

Finally, many mythic heroes travel to the underworld, where they gain knowledge to take back to the upper world.

Writing Application: Identifying Transitional Sentences

Examine Exercises 2C (page 159) and 3C (page 176). In each paragraph, identify the transitional sentences that introduce each example.

Rewriting

1. Once your first draft is complete, read it over to determine how you can improve the examples you have used. In particular, try to make the examples as specific and as concrete as you can. Use actual names of people and places, and refer to specific details whenever possible.

2. As you read your draft, make sure you can tell where each of your examples ends and the next begins. Revise your transitions as needed to make them clearer still.

3. If your preliminary topic sentence can be improved so that it more accurately states the central point of your paragraph, change it now.

4. Examine your draft for sentences that can be combined using participial phrases, appositives, infinitive phrases, or adjective clauses. Combine such sentences the way you did in the Sentence Combining Exercises.

Rewriting Application: Responding to Writing

Read the following paragraph. Then respond to the questions following it.

I Enjoy H_2O to Relax

Whenever I feel stressed, I find that I can relax best if I am near the water. For example, as a teenager living in San Bernardino, I would drive many miles into the local foothills of the mountains, where a small river or a large stream called Lytle Creek was located in the little town of Applewhite. I would walk down between the trees and then over all of the rocks to find a place where I would sit for hours. I enjoyed watching the water rush by because it made me become very relaxed. Then, in the late 1980s, I moved to San Diego County. My first apartment was in Escondido, and times were troubled and stressful nearly every day, yet I was able to find comfort by driving to Lake Dixon. After several weekend trips I began taking this drive at all different times of the week. Usually alone, but sometimes with my boys, I would go to the lake and feed the ducks or just fish from the shore. Now, living in San Marcos, I prefer the ultimate water experience by relaxing at the beach. During most of my quick trips, I drive down Del Dios Highway and across the railroad tracks into Solana Beach parking lot. I walk down the large ramp and sit on the sand or walk along the shoreline to the cave. Watching the water really washes away any troubles that I arrived with. It seems to clear my head and bring a warm feeling of contentment to my soul. In conclusion, no matter whether the water is a stream, lake, or ocean, its appearance and its soothing sounds take away all of my stress and troubles

1. Identify the topic sentence. State its topic and central idea. Is it an effective topic sentence? Why or why not?

2. Identify the transitional sentences that introduce each example.

3. Are the examples specific? Point out which words in each example identify specific places or things.

4. Which words in each example would you make still more specific?

5. Which example is the most effective? Why? Which one would you improve? How?

Rewriting Application: Revising and Editing Your Own Draft

Before you do the final editing of your paper, revise it one more time. If the topic sentence needs work, improve it now. Check the examples. Are they as specific and descriptive as they can be? Add transitional sentences between examples. Wherever you can, combine related sentences using subordinate clauses as well as participial and infinitive phrases.

Now edit the paper. Check your draft for any of the following errors:

- Sentence fragments
- Comma splices
- Fused sentences
- Misplaced modifiers
- Dangling modifiers
- Misspelled words

Prepare a clean final draft, following the format your instructor has asked for. Before you turn in your final draft, proofread it carefully and make any necessary corrections.

Chapter Three Practice Test

I. Review of Chapters One and Two

A. In the following sentences, identify the underlined words by writing one of the following abbreviations above the words: noun (N), pronoun (Pro), verb (V), adjective (Adj), adverb (Adv), conjunction (Conj), preposition (Prep).

1. The story was <u>sad</u>, <u>yet</u> the ending was hopeful.

2. Adrian had three mountain bikes, yet he <u>still</u> <u>wanted</u> another one.

3. <u>Everyone</u> who worked <u>at</u> the mint was eager to see what the new coins would look

   like.

4. Someone left an <u>envelope</u> containing $2,000 <u>under</u> my desk.

5. Beale Street <u>could</u> be one of the most <u>important</u> places for the blues.

B. In the following sentences, underline the subjects once and the complete verbs twice. Put parentheses around all prepositional phrases.

6. Neither Homer nor Hortense wants to prepare the okra in the usual way.

7. Did John Marcher ever meet that beast in the jungle?

8. After he saw the freak show at the fair, Melvin wanted to have two heads himself.

9. Felix had just vacuumed the carpet, but Oscar still threw peanut shells onto the floor.

10. Buffalo Bill hit all of the bull's-eyes and rode around the arena on his horse.

C. Compose sentences of your own according to the instructions.

11. Write a simple sentence with two subjects, one verb, and at least one prepositional phrase.

    _____

    _____

12. Write a compound sentence. Use a semicolon, a transitional word, and a comma to join the two clauses.

    _____

    _____

Chapter Three Practice Test

continued

13. Write a complex sentence that ends with a subordinate clause.

_____

_____

14. Write a complex sentence that uses the subordinator *which*.

_____

_____

15. Write a compound-complex sentence. Use a semicolon and a transitional word.

_____

_____

D. Identify the following items as being correct (C), fused (F), comma splice (CS), or fragment (Frag). Then correct the errors. If a sentence is correct, do nothing to it.

_____ **16.** Chelsea could not eat her food, it tasted like axle grease.

_____

_____

_____ **17.** Don't forget to take your Vitameatavegemines.

_____

_____

_____ **18.** The moon came up over the lake then the fish began biting.

_____

_____

Chapter Three Practice Test

continued

_____ **19.** Even though we don't get to see each other very often.

_____

_____

_____ **20.** Often young Ludwig enjoyed practicing, often he would rather be eating apple strudel.

_____

_____

II. Chapter Three

A. Underline all infinitive and participial phrases and circle the words they modify.

    21. Crossing the English Channel, the Normans conquered England in 1066.

    22. Ahab's plan to find the white whale worried some of his crew.

    23. Worried about the wolf, the third pig built a house of brick.

    24. Rachel forgot her promise to return home by midnight.

    25. We will no longer see Lucy holding the football for Charlie Brown.

B. Add infinitive or participial phrases to the following sentences at the places indicated. Use the verbs in parentheses.

    26. The roses ^ blossomed every year. (plant)

_____

_____

    27. After looking at both roads in the yellow wood, he decided ^ . (take)

_____

_____

Chapter Three Practice Test

continued

28. The photograph ^ was taken with a digital camera. (hang)

_____

_____

29. ^ Always check your equipment carefully and always dive with at least one other person. (be)

_____

_____

30. ^ Elvis moved in a way that shocked many people. (sing)

_____

_____

C. Underline the adjective clauses and appositives in the following sentences and circle the words they modify.

31. Mrs. Gutierrez, the chairperson of the school board, spoke to all of the first grade classes.

32. The lawyer who defended Dunlap was also his best friend.

33. *The Catcher in the Rye*, a novel by J. D. Salinger, is a classic tale of rebellious youth.

34. The Susan B. Anthony dollar, which was supposed to take the place of the dollar bill, was a confusing and unpopular coin.

35. The donut that I like the most is the one in my hand.

D. Add adjective clauses or appositives to the following sentences and punctuate them correctly.

36. Mr. Ramirez was worried about his neighbor's dog.

_____

_____

continued

37. The cotton candy was sticky, but Sara ate all of it.

_____

_____

38. The Marshalls played cards with the Smiths on Saturdays.

_____

_____

39. Pierce Brosnan ignored Sean Connery at the Academy Awards ceremony.

_____

_____

40. The new minister climbed up the steps and entered the church.

_____

_____

E. Underline and then correct any dangling or misplaced modifiers in the following sentences. Do nothing if a sentence is correct.

41. Running in the marathon, one of my contact lenses fell out.

_____

_____

42. Studying for examination after examination, the last week of finals is always the worst.

_____

_____

continued

43. Standing at the top of the hill, the view was magnificent.

_____

_____

44. Ignoring his father, Danny only ate one of the vegetables on his plate.

_____

_____

45. To see the parade, a tall ladder was leaned against the wall.

_____

_____

46. When he fell, Amos almost broke all of the bones in his right hand.

_____

_____

47. The man walking the dog reading a paperback novel nearly bumped into a lamppost.

_____

_____

48. Irritated by the pesky mosquitoes, Roger's hands slapped at his neck.

_____

_____

continued

49. After moving from Maple Street to Ivy Street, she started having nightmares.

_____

_____

50. Carving for three straight days, the statue was finished by Giuseppe in record time.

_____

_____

Always Singular
Everyone —
Someone
Anyone
Each
Every

Always Plural
Many
both
A few
Several

__Either__

ASHMAN
all
Some
half
MOST
AN
NONE

Some of the cake is missing
Some of the Boxes are late

both ___ and ___ = plural
not only ___ but also = plural

Singular   Either OR
           neither nor
           wheather or

Lining Up the Parts
of a Sentence

The Careful Writer

As you have probably already noticed, effective writing is less a matter of inspiration and more a matter of making innumerable choices and paying careful attention to detail. Strictly speaking, every word in each of your sentences represents a specific choice on your part. Good writers carefully choose words and their positions in sentences, not only to be grammatically correct but also to make their writing clear and concise.

Although close attention to detail alone will not ensure good writing, it does have a number of advantages. The most important reason for you to take care in your writing is to make certain that you communicate your ideas clearly. As you can see from having worked through the last chapter, if your sentences contain misplaced or dangling modifiers, your reader will sometimes be confused about what you mean. In addition, a clear and careful piece of writing in itself creates a good impression, just as a well-tended lawn does. You have probably already found that people are often judged by their writing. If your writing is carefully thought out and presented with an attention to correctness and detail, it will be taken seriously.

Making sure that your sentences are correctly constructed and checking to see that your modifiers clearly and logically modify the right words are two ways of taking care in your writing. In this chapter we will discuss a few others: paying attention to the special relationship between those two most important parts of your sentences, the subjects and verbs; making sure that the pronouns you use are in their correct forms; and checking the connection between your pronouns and the words they stand for.

When sentence have nor or or between two
subjects choose the one near the verb
and mach iT

John or the (grils are going) to call tonight

Subject–Verb Agreement

One reason you need to be able to identify subjects and verbs accurately is that the form of the verb often changes to match the form of its subject. If the subject of your sentence is singular, your verb must be singular. If the subject is plural, your verb must be plural. This matching of the verb and its subject is called **subject–verb agreement.**

You need to pay special attention to subject–verb agreement when you use present tense verbs. **Most present tense verbs that have singular subjects end in "s." Most present tense verbs that have plural subjects do not end in "s."** Here are some examples.

Singular	*Plural*
The dog bark**s**.	The dogs bark.
He walk**s**.	They walk.
It i**s**.	They are.
The man ha**s**.	The men have.
She doe**s**.	They do.

Notice that in each case the verb ends in "s" when the subject is singular. This rule can be confusing because an "s" at the end of a <u>noun</u> almost always means that the noun is plural, but **an "s" at the end of a <u>verb</u> almost always means it is singular.**

■ **PRACTICE**

Change the subjects and verbs in the following sentences from singular to plural or from plural to singular. You may need to add *a*, *an*, or *the* to some of the sentences.

1. After dark, the street lights turn on automatically.

   After dark, the street light turns on automatically.

2. The door was unlocked.

   The door were unlocked

3. Every Halloween, my daughters operate a neighborhood haunted house.

   Every Halloween, my daughter operates a neighborhood

4. Students in my class bring coffee each morning.

   A Student in my class brings coffee each morning.

5. The cottonwood tree in my back yard provides shade in the summer.

Identifying Subjects: A Review

1. <u>Make sure you accurately identify the subject.</u> Sentences usually contain several nouns and pronouns.

▶   EXAMPLE   The **boys** from the private **school** on the other **side** of **town** often use our **gymnasium**.

This sentence contains five nouns, but only *boys* is the subject.

2. <u>Remember that a noun or pronoun that is part of a prepositional phrase cannot be the subject.</u>

▶   EXAMPLE   Each of the children takes a vitamin with breakfast.

The subject is *Each*, not *children*, because *children* is part of a prepositional phrase.

3. <u>Indefinite pronouns can be subjects.</u> The indefinite pronouns are listed on page 5.

▶   EXAMPLE   Everyone sitting at the tables under the trees has a picnic lunch.

Subject–Verb Agreement: Points to Know

1. <u>Two subjects joined by *and* are plural.</u>

▶   EXAMPLES
        S   S   V
The **boy** <u>and</u> his **dog** **were** far from home.

        S   S   V
Ham <u>and</u> **rye** **make** a delicious combination.

2. <u>However, if a subject is modified by *each* or *every*, it is singular.</u>

▶   EXAMPLES
         S   S   V
<u>Every</u> **boy** and **girl** at the party <u>was</u> given a present to take home.

         S   S   V
<u>Each</u> **envelope** and **piece** of paper <u>has</u> the name of the company on it.

3. Indefinite pronouns are usually singular.

▶ **EXAMPLES**

     S   V

Each of the band members **has** a new uniform.

     S   V

Everyone sitting under the trees **is** part of my family.

4. A few nouns and indefinite pronouns, such as *none, some, all, most, more, half,* or *part* may sometimes be considered plural and sometimes singular, depending on the prepositional phrases that follow them. If the object of the preposition is singular, treat the subject and verb as singular. If the object of the preposition is plural, treat the subject and verb as plural.

▶ **EXAMPLES**

               S   V

(singular)   **None** of the cake **is** left.

               S   V *— plural*

(plural)   **None** of the people **are** here.

■ **PRACTICE**   Place an "S" above the subjects and underline the correct verb form in the parentheses.

                  S   S

1. A man and woman from the modeling agency (was <u>were</u>) interviewing

    the college student.

                    S

2. My new stereo with six speakers (<u>has</u> have) arrived.

3. Each mother and child (hopes hope) to be chosen to appear in the movie.

          S   S

4. Courtesy and timely service (improve improves) customer satisfaction.

                    S

5. Most of the rose bushes in the planter (was were) dying.

6. From the beginning of the game, each of the players (was were) playing

    with enthusiasm.

          S

7. <u>Everyone</u> in the church pews (seem seems) to be having a good time.

         S   S

8. The murder of a king and the appearance of his ghost (create creates)

    interest from the first scene of the play.

         S

9. None of the oil from the car (have has) dripped onto your driveway.

10. The Potomac, in addition to other famous American rivers, (is are) to be

   discussion in the program.

important

---

5. When *either/or, neither/nor,* or just *or* joins the subjects, the subject closer to the verb determines the form of the verb.

▶ EXAMPLE

Neither **Alberto** nor his **brothers want** to go fishing anymore.

Of course, if you reverse the order of the subjects above, you must change the verb form.

▶ EXAMPLE

Neither his **brothers** nor **Alberto wants** to go fishing anymore.

This rule applies to questions also.

▶ EXAMPLES

Does Alberto or his **brothers** want to go fishing?

OR

Do his **brothers** or **Alberto** want to go fishing?

NOTE: When you have helping verbs in a sentence, as in the example above, the helping verb—not the main verb—changes form.

6. Collective nouns usually take the singular form of the verb. Collective nouns represent groups of people or things, but they are considered singular. Here are some common collective nouns.

audience	crowd	herd
band	factory	jury
class	family	number
college	flock	school
committee	government	society
company	group	team

▶ EXAMPLES

The **audience was** delighted when the curtain slowly rose to reveal the orchestra already seated.

My **family goes** to Yellowstone National Park every summer.

7. The relative pronouns *that, which,* and *who* may be either singular or plural. When one of these pronouns is the subject of a verb, you will need to know which word it refers to before you decide whether it is singular or plural.

we don't have found for who

▶ **EXAMPLES**

(singular)	I bought the <u>peach</u> **that was** ripe.
(plural)	I bought the <u>peaches</u> **that were** ripe.
(plural)	Colleen is one of the <u>students</u> **who are** taking flying lessons.
(singular)	Colleen is the only <u>one</u> of the students **who is** taking flying lessons.

■ **PRACTICE**   Place an "S" above the subjects and underline the correct verb form in the parentheses.

1. Either pasta or potatoes (goes go) well with veal.

act   *look important*

2. A team of marine scientists (has have) discovered a white whale.

plural

3. Jason is one of the employees who (deserves deserve) a raise.   *if it say only is singular*

4. Either my roommate or some bold mice (was were) involved in the theft of my Nutrageous bar.

5. My daughter in Idaho or my two sisters in Maine (sends send) me some extra money every month.

you need to know who with that

6. In that society a jury of one's peers (makes make) the decision.

7. The only one of the cars that (interests interest) me so far is the Mazda.

8. (Has Have) Mr. Ed or Private Francis said anything to you?

ask

9. The team that makes the most points (loses lose) in that game.   *ask*

if it does not say only it is pronoun

10. Marcela saw one of the actors who (was were) being considered for the part in the film.

The boy who owns the bike was injured   *relative clause*

the boys who the dogs were searching all night

What is prepositional phrase

8. A few nouns that end in "s" are usually considered singular, so they take the singular form of the verb. These nouns include *economics, gymnastics, mathematics, measles, mumps, news, physics,* and *politics.*

► EXAMPLES

good intro for a Essay

S   V
World **economics** <u>has</u> been an important international issue for years.

S   V
Gymnastics <u>is</u> one of the most popular events in the Olympics.

important →

9. When units of measurement for distance, time, volume, height, weight, money, and so on are used as subjects, they take the singular verb form.

► EXAMPLES *look!*

time, volume, height, weight, money.

S   V
Two **teaspoons** of sugar **was** all that the cake recipe called for.

S   V
Five **dollars** **is** too much to pay for a hot dog.

10. In a question or in a sentence that begins with *there* or *here,* the order of the subject and verb is reversed.

► EXAMPLES

V   S
Was the **bus** on time?

V   S
Is there a squeaking **wheel** out there somewhere?

questions look over

V   S
There **is** an **abundance** of wildflowers in the desert this spring.

V   S
Here **are** the **keys** to your car.

11. The verb must agree only with the **subject.**

► EXAMPLE

S   V
Our biggest **problem is** termites in the attic.

The singular verb form *is* is correct here because the subject is the singular noun *problem.* The plural noun *termites* does not affect the form of the verb.

■ PRACTICE

Place an "S" above the subjects and underline the correct verb form in the parentheses.

S
1. Economics (<u>determines</u> determine) almost everything in our lives, even

marriage customs.

2. Five ounces of gold (weighs weigh) the same as the same amount of dirt.

3. Charles's best idea yesterday (was were) pizza for breakfast.

4. Carlos has found that gymnastics (helps help) him get into shape for the
   season.

5. (Has Have) the measles recently become a problem in your neighborhood?

6. Six thousand square feet of bare wall (inspires inspire) the muralist.

7. (Does Do) James always work so efficiently and serenely?

8. There (flies fly) the last geese to leave our lake for the winter.

9. The main problem of this neighborhood (is are) the planes flying over
   every half hour.

10. Here (lies lie) the last slice of one gigantic pizza.

Section One Review

1. In the present tense, when the subject is a singular noun or a singular pronoun, the verb form usually will end in "s."

2. Subject–verb agreement: points to know

   a. Two subjects joined by *and* are plural.

   b. If a subject is modified by *each* or *every,* it is singular.

   c. Indefinite pronouns are usually singular.

   d. Sometimes nouns and indefinite pronouns like *some, half,* or *part* are considered plural, depending on the prepositional phrases that follow them.

   e. When *either/or, neither/nor,* or just *or* joins two subjects, the subject closer to the verb determines the verb form.

   f. When a collective noun, such as *family* or *group,* is the subject, the singular form of the verb is used.

   g. The relative pronouns *that, which,* and *who* may be either singular or plural, depending upon the word the pronoun refers to.

   h. A few nouns, such as *economics* or *news,* end in "s" but are considered singular.

   i. When the subject is a unit of measurement, such as distance, weight, or money, the singular form of the verb is used.

   j. In a question or in a sentence that begins with *there* or *here,* the verb will often come before the subject.

   k. The verb must agree only with the **subject.**

Exercise 1A

Circle the subjects and underline the correct verb form in the parentheses.

1. (No one) without sunglasses (was were) able to look at the eclipse.

2. Neither high prices nor a poor salesman (is are) able to discourage Margaret when her mind is made up.

3. On the Fourth of July, the Optimists and the Rotary Club (has have) always presented a patriotic fireworks display.

4. Professor Sandoval's class on cultural anthropology (goes go) to Guadalajara each semester.

5. In the past five years, gymnastics (has have) become one of the most popular sports in my community.

6. A good book next to a roaring fire (makes make) life easier.

7. Six feet (is are) the average height in this basketball league.

8. A man with an Australian shepherd (walks walk) on that beach almost every day.

9. (Is Are) a rain storm and ants required for every picnic?

10. Each boulder and tree (was were) unique to John Muir and Ansel Adams.

11. For some children, measles (causes cause) an uncomfortable fever.

12. (Anyone) who stayed on the mountain (was were) snowed in last night.

13. Three hours (is are) a long time to sit and listen to a lecture about the Paris sewer system—or about anything, for that matter.

14. (Does Do) red wine or white wine go well with this dish?

15. Some of the snow from last month's storms (has have) finally begun to melt.

Exercise 1B

Correct any subject–verb agreement errors in the following sentences. If a sentence is correct, do nothing to it. To check your answers, circle the subjects.

1. For most people, either (Mozart) or (Beethoven) are *is* considered the greatest musical composer of all time.

2. (Anyone) eating at one of those places take a chance on being insulted.

3. Each horse and rider were eagerly waiting for the race to begin.

4. The politics of the United States interest Fidel.

5. The dark sky and the strong wind make me think that a storm is approaching.

6. Willy Loman, as well as his son Biff, are better suited to be a carpenter or rancher.

7. A large flock of pelicans *are* feed in this lagoon every evening.

8. *was* Were either Circe or the Sirens able to defeat Odysseus?

9. Mr. Savage and Mrs. Delgado from the recreation department always do more for the annual Christmas party than anyone else.

10. Every one of the crusaders *was* were informed about the dopey assassins.

11. Xavier and his family *go* goes rafting on a different river every summer.

12. In Fellini's film somebody on a motorcycle races around the town square each night.

13. Protection for all armadillos *has* have been Homer's crusade for the last three months.

14. The price of a room at both of the hotels were much too high.

15. Everything in this store except for the lawnmowers and television sets are on sale.

Correct all subject–verb agreement errors. Not all sentences will contain errors.

1. One of the world's greatest inventions ~~have~~ *has* to be our common alphabet, the one used in this book, but why it is so widespread and why the letters are shaped the way they are remain relatively unanswered questions. 2. Millions of these marks, a squiggle here, a line there, is used everyday. 3. But it is largely unknown why these symbols spread so rapidly. 4. Most historians of the alphabet believes that it was first used in the lands around present-day Syria. 5. This system of marks were spread by the Phoenicians to places as far away as the Spanish peninsula. 6. One of the Greek legends claim that the alphabet was brought to Greece by Cadmus, a famous hero. 7. In the Greek legend, this alphabet contain no vowels, so the Greeks add them. 8. When the Romans conquered Etruria, which were in the center of Italy, they found the alphabet in use there. 9. Neither the Roman alphabet nor the English alphabet have changed much since Roman times. 10. As intriguing as the rapid spread of the alphabet are the shape of many of its letters. 11. *D* is shaped like a door, especially the door of a tent that were commonly used three thousand years ago. 12. The letter *G* begins *gimel*, an ancient word which mean throwing stick. 13. The shape of the letters *C* and *G* are similar to the Australian boomerang if one use his imagination. 14. The shape of *M* supposedly imitate the movements of waves; *mem* is an ancient word for water. 15. The most appropriate name for all of the letters are *double u*, for *W*. 16. In the history of the alphabet, lowercase or "small" letters comes into use around the year 800 A.D., but that is another story.

the winner was I.

SECTION

two

Pronoun Case

singular →
Someone left their book here   wrong
Someone left a book here   or
Someone left his book here

5/8/01

Pronouns, like verbs, can appear in a variety of different forms, depending on how they function in a sentence. For example, the pronoun that refers to the speaker in a sentence may be written as *I, me, my,* or *mine.* These different spellings are the result of what is called **pronoun case.**

The three pronoun cases for English are the **subjective,** the **objective,** and the **possessive.**

Subjective Case

Singular	Plural
I	we
you	you
he, she, it	they
who	who

Objective Case

Singular	Plural
me	us
you	you
him, her, it	them
whom	whom

possesive adjectives

Possessive Case

possesive Pronouns.

Singular	Plural
my, mine	our, ours
your, yours	your, yours
his, her, hers, its	their, theirs
whose	whose

Subjective Pronouns

The subjective pronouns are *I, we, you, he, she, it, they,* and *who.* They are used in two situations.

1. Subjective pronouns are used as subjects of sentences.

► **EXAMPLES**

S
I will return the car on Monday.

S
They are trying to outwit me.

209

to be = linking verbs.

2. Subjective pronouns are used when they follow linking verbs. Because the linking verb <u>identifies</u> the pronoun after it with the subject, the pronoun must be in the same case as the subject.

► **EXAMPLES**

s
It was **she** who won the award for being the best-dressed mud wrestler. (The subjective pronoun *she* is <u>identified</u> with the subject *it* by the linking verb *was*.)

s
That was **I** you saw rowing across the lake yesterday.

s
It was **they** who caused the huge traffic jam.

Objective Pronouns

The **objective pronouns** are *me, us, you, him, her, it, them,* and *whom.* They are used in three situations.

1. <u>Objective pronouns are used as objects of prepositions.</u>

► **EXAMPLES**

Sally loved the chrysanthemums that Mr. Kim had given <u>to her</u>.

The difficulties <u>between Samantha and me</u> continued into the fall.

2. <u>Objective pronouns are used as direct objects of action verbs.</u> The noun or pronoun that receives the action of the action verb is called the **direct object.**

For example, in the simple sentence *Tuan visited Serena yesterday,* the verb is *visited,* an action verb. The direct object of *visited* is *Serena* because *Serena* receives the action of the verb *visited.* If you substitute a pronoun for *Serena,* it must be the objective pronoun *her—Tuan visited* **her** *yesterday.*

► **EXAMPLES**

Brenda married **him** on March 7, 1987.

Last summer Joan beat **me** at tennis every time we played.

Both classes helped clean up the park, and the city rewarded **them** with a picnic.

3. <u>Objective pronouns are used as indirect objects.</u> The **indirect object** indicates **to whom or for whom (or to what or for what) an action is directed,** but the prepositions *to* and *for* are left out.

► **EXAMPLES**

(prepositional phrase)   He threw the ball **to her.**

(indirect object)   He threw **her** the ball.

In the first sentence, *her* is the object of the preposition
ond sentence, the *to* is omitted and the pronoun is moved, m
indirect object. In both sentences, the direct object is *ball*. Her
examples.

► **EXAMPLES**   She had already given **me** two chances to make up for my mistakes.

The architect showed **them** a picture of how the new city hall would lo

---

■ **PRACTICE**   In the blanks, identify the underlined pronouns as subjective (sub) or objective
(obj).

Sub as the sentences

   sub   **1.** In the morning, <u>I</u> will begin a trip back to my home town.

sub   *object*
        2. Bill tried to give <u>her</u> his email address.

     sub)
        3. It was <u>she</u> who first taught me how to ride a bicycle.

        4. George was embarrassed because everyone was staring at <u>him</u>. —

Preposition / object

     object
        5. We were surprised to see <u>them</u> on television.

       subject
        6. As soon as the detective opened the door, <u>she</u> was suspicious.

        7. That was <u>he</u> they saw struggling to put the saddle on the horse.

        8. Homer called Hortense and asked <u>her</u> to pick up some Spam.

        9. Because <u>he</u> is left-handed, he has a hard time finding a school desk
that is comfortable.

      10. Michelle gave <u>me</u> $1,000 for my Jimi Hendrix records.

Possessive Pronouns

The **possessive pronouns** are *my, mine, our, ours, your, yours, his, her, hers, its,
their, theirs,* and *whose.* They are used in two situations.

  1. Possessive pronouns are used as adjectives to indicate possession.

► **EXAMPLES**   The old sailor had turned up **his** collar against the wind.

The weary travelers shuffled off to **their** rooms.

The polar bear constantly paced up and down **its** enclosure.

Some one left a book
Some one left his book

...traction *it's* means "it is." The word *its* is the only posses-
...n fact, you do not use apostrophes with any of the pos-

...nouns indicate possession without being used as
..., they may be used as subjects or objects.

...rrow Zan's flashlight because **mine** was lost.

...ere the possessive pronoun *mine* is the subject of its clause.

The Chin house is large, but **yours** is cozy.

In this example, *yours* is the subject of its clause.

▶ **EXAMPLE**   He didn't have any change for a phone call because he had given **his** to the
children begging on the street.

Here the possessive pronoun *his* is a direct object.

I saw Sondra and she going to the movies

Common Sources of Errors in Pronoun Case

When to use Me and I

Compound Constructions

two or more of some kind — Compound subjects and objects often cause problems when they include pronouns. If your sentence includes a compound construction, be sure to use the
correct pronoun case.

▶ **EXAMPLES**

(compound subject)	*object* **Sandra and she** will return the car on Monday.
(compound after linking verb)	That was **my friend and I** whom you saw on the news.
(compound object of a preposition)	They awarded first place trophies to both Dolores and **me**.
(compound direct object)	Julio's boss fired **Mark and him** yesterday.
(compound indirect object)	She had already given **him and me** two chances to make up our minds.

In most cases, you can use a simple test to check whether you have chosen
the right pronoun case when you have a compound construction. Simply remove one of the subjects or objects so that only one pronoun is left. For example, is this sentence correct? *Our host gave **Erin and I** a drink.* Test it by dropping ***Erin and***. *Our host gave **I** a drink.* Now you can see that the *I* should be
me because it is an object (an indirect object). The correct sentence should
read: *Our host gave **Erin and me** a drink.*

1 When to use Me or I ?

■ **PRACTICE** Underline the correct pronoun in the parentheses.

1. My partner and (I me) have just opened a frozen yogurt shop in Buffalo.

2. Our grandmother divided her estate between my sister and (I me).

3. Mr. Calvino wrote letters of recommendation for (she her) and (he him).

4. Bud was not happy that Lou and (he him) had joined the army.

5. Mrs. Cartwright sent Josephine and (they them) to the store.

6. Polyphemus tried to capture Odysseus's men and (he him).

7. For you and (I me), this last year has been a wonderful experience.

8. Orville argued that it was (he him) who had done most of the work on the plane.

9. The library had closed before Jan and (I me) could get there.

10. When Arnold and (we us) first met, the Beatles were still children.

5/14/01

Who and Whom

When to use *who* or *whom* is a mystery to many writers, but you should have no problem with these pronouns if you remember two simple rules.

1. Use the subjective pronoun *who* or *whoever* if it is used as the subject of a verb.

2. Use the objective pronoun *whom* or *whomever* if it is not used as the subject of a verb.

▶ **EXAMPLES** After leaving the airport, I followed the man who had taken my bags. (**Who** is the subject of *had taken*.)

The letter was sent to the person **whom** we had decided to hire. (**Whom** is not the subject of a verb.)

Please give the money to **whoever** needs it. (**Whoever** is the subject of *needs*.)

The man who bought the car left quickly.

The man whom the clerk indentified was arrested

■ **PRACTICE**   Underline the correct pronoun in the parentheses.

1. The actress (who whom) the director chose had not expected to get the part.

2. The couple (who whom) saw the space ship decided to keep it a secret.

3. The puppy was given to the child (who whom) seemed most likely to care for it.

4. The wedding guest talked to (whoever whomever) he could stop.

5. Eliot Ness offered immunity to (whoever whomever) would agree to testify.

Comparisons

When a pronoun is used in a comparison, you often need to supply the implied words in order to know what pronoun case to use. For example, in the sentence *My brother cannot skate as well as I,* the implied words are the verb *can skate: My brother cannot skate as well as I [can skate].*

▶ **EXAMPLE**   The police officer allowed my friend to leave the scene sooner than **me.**

You can tell that *me* is the correct case in this sentence when you supply the implied words:

The police officer allowed my friend to leave the scene sooner than [**she allowed**] me [**to leave**].

■ **PRACTICE**   Underline the correct pronoun in the parentheses.

1. Angie doesn't read the newspaper as often as (I me).

2. The jury obviously believed the other witness more than (he him).

3. Michael Jordan's sister says that she can jump higher than (he him).

4. Even though the husband and wife were both at fault, the children blamed him more than (she her).

as
NO ONE IS CONFUSED AS (I AM)

JOHN IS NOT AS TALL AS (he)

I DID NOT BEAT HER QUICKLY AS ~~He~~
                                  him

5. Count Dracula and the Mummy were certain that no one could frighten
   could
   people as well as (they them).

I DID NOT BEAT HER AS QUICKLY AS HIM

make sure to pick the right word, it makes a difference

I AM TALLER THEN (he)
                  He is

<mark>Appositives</mark>

As you will remember from Chapter Three, an appositive is a word group containing a noun or pronoun that renames another noun or pronoun. When the appositive contains a **pronoun** that does the renaming, be sure that the pronoun is in the same case as the word it renames.

▶ **EXAMPLE**   Some team members—Joe, Frank, and I—were late for practice.
                                    sub

Here *I* is in the subjective case because the appositive *Joe, Frank, and I* renames the word *members,* the subject of the sentence.

▶ **EXAMPLE**   When the show is over, please send your review to the producers, Mark and **her.**

Here *her* is in the objective case because the appositive *Mark and her* renames *producers,* the object of the preposition *to.*

Because the

■ **PRACTICE**   Underline the correct pronoun in the parentheses.

1. Sam told the people at the bar—Norm, Cliff, and (he <u>him</u>)—to leave

   Woody alone.

2. The coach talked to the youngest players, Deborah and (I me).

3. Elena told the driver to stop because the car's passengers, Serena and (she
   her), were beginning to feel sick.

4. The judges gave the best actors, Federico and (she her), an award.
       sub *v*

5. The finalists in the lottery—Tessie, Old Man Warner, and (I me)—did not
       sub

   act very excited.

Positive	comparative	Superlative
big	bigger	biggest
Justred	More Justred	Most Justred :
tall	taler	to lles
good	better	best

■ **PRACTICE**   Underline the correct pronoun form in the parentheses.

1. The scholarship will be given to the student (who whom) has the highest

    grade average and writes the best essay.

2. Cora was afraid that no one was as shy as (she her).   *she was*

3. The company representatives, Mr. Hereford and (I me), will be in Phila-

    delphia on Monday.

4. Do you think that the prince and (she her) will arrive on time?

5. Josh knew he had to apologize to (whoever/whomever) he might have

    insulted.

6. The manager told the troublemakers, Leo and (he him), to leave.

7. Send Jonathan and (she her) down to the mini-market for more potato

    chips and dip.

8. Since Carlotta works harder and longer, our employer pays her more than

    (I me).

9. The baseball star (who whom) the children asked for an autograph told

    them to get lost.

10. Sammy and (she her) argued for hours about who was the better hitter.

my Partener and (I) me have Just opened

For you and (Me) I

Section Two Review

1. The **subjective pronouns** are used in two ways:

   a. As the subjects of sentences

   b. After linking verbs

2. The **objective pronouns** are used in three ways:

   a. As objects of prepositions

   b. As direct objects of action verbs

   c. As indirect objects

3. The **possessive pronouns** are used in two ways:

   a. As adjectives to modify nouns to indicate possession

   b. As subjects and objects

4. Some common sources of errors in pronoun case:

   a. Pronouns in compound constructions

   b. The use of the pronouns *who, whom, whoever,* and *whomever*

   c. Pronouns in comparisons

   d. Pronouns in appositives

Exercise 2A

Underline the correct pronoun form in the parentheses.

1. The medicine had been on the shelf so long that it had lost all of (it's <u>its</u>) potency.

2. In the auditorium near the professor and (he him) sat my wife.

3. The fans gave the team and (she her) a raucous reception.

4. Was it (she her) (who whom) you met by the river?

5. Kelly's new pet rat seems to like Danny more than (she her).

6. Ricardo expected no one except Silvia and (we us) to be at the meeting.

7. The people (who whom) our neighbor invited to his party threw trash all over our front yard last night.

8. Have Sheila and (he him) arrived yet?

9. Mr. Torvald felt sorry for his old dog as he watched it scratch (it's its) fleas.

10. Ms. Cisneros understands the language better than (I me).

11. The final chess match will be between (whoever whomever) finishes first and (whoever whomever) finishes second.

12. Mr. Chekov requested me to tell you and (he him) when the play would begin.

13. The waiters looked impatiently at the last two customers, Diana and (I me).

14. When the gorilla escaped (its it's) enclosure, it approached my daughter and (I me).

15. The three goddesses—Aphrodite, Venus, and (she her)—decided to watch a romantic comedy.

Exercise 2B

Correct any pronoun errors in the following sentences. Some sentences may not contain errors.

1. My older sister has always been a better skier than ~~me~~. *I*

2. Would Theodore Roosevelt and he have negotiated a treaty?

3. Was that her whom called you last night about the meeting?

4. The Sirens' songs were directed at Odysseus and I as the ship sailed by the rocks.

5. The police have asked two people—Ken Howard and him—to act as mediators.

6. The old car in the yard had lost it's engine and tires, so Roger sold the rest of it's parts to friends.

7. The bull charged Juanita and I when we climbed into the pasture.

8. On our trip to Canada, the Nguyens and we traveled with a caravan of people driving motor homes.

9. The farmer who we visited bought a pair of rabbits from my father and I.

10. Travis's fiancee was happy that he could not drive as well as her.

11. Between them and us were a muddy field and a great deal of anxiety.

12. Hillary beat Samuel and them to the top of the hill.

13. It's not an exaggeration to say that the old dog by the fire seemed to be pondering it's destiny.

14. The pizza was given to whomever answered the question correctly.

15. After they had lost the game, Coach Leonard said that the team and her would meet for extra practice every day next week.

Exercise 2C

Correct any errors in pronoun case in the following paragraph.

1. Anyone who is left-handed knows as well as ~~me~~ *I* that being left-handed in a right-handed world can result in any number of awkward and frustrating situations. **2.** One result of being left-handed is having to listen to people whom want to help "correct" the problem. **3.** For instance, my first-grade teacher was determined to turn another "lefty" and I into right-handers. **4.** She would point to the other students and say that they wrote better than us because they held their pencils correctly. **5.** She forced us to practice writing with the "correct" hand for hours—at least until our parents had a talk with the principal and she. **6.** Another result of being left-handed involves the many inconveniences that a left-hander must face. **7.** For example, my sister, whom is also left-handed, and me have both noticed that school classrooms rarely have more than one left-handed desk. **8.** And I have been told by my cousin Earl, another lefty, that his wife and him can rarely find a pair of scissors that will work for a left-handed person. **9.** These types of inconveniences constantly remind the lefties in my family—Earl, my sister, and I—that we are out of place in a right-handed world. **10.** Recently, Earl's wife purchased a new camcorder only to discover that Earl could not work it as easily as her because it was designed to be held and operated with the right hand. **11.** And last month, when my sister visited Las Vegas with some friends for the first time, her friends and her discovered that the handles to all of the slot machines were—where else?—on the right. **12.** Obviously, being left-handed can result in many awkward situations, but I suppose that the other left-handers and me should be grateful. **13.** After all, left-handed people in some past cultures were viewed with suspicion and were sometimes accused of being witches. **14.** We lefties in modern societies certainly have it better than them!

Pronoun Agreement and Reference

when you use the word you= make sure you keep talking to the reader

Pronoun–Antecedent Agreement

Because pronouns stand for or take the place of nouns, it is important that you make it clear in your writing which pronouns stand for which nouns. The noun that the pronoun takes the place of is called the **antecedent**. **Pronoun–antecedent agreement** refers to the idea that a pronoun must match or "agree with" the noun that it stands for in **person** and in **number**.

Person

Person in pronouns refers to the relationship of the speaker (or writer) to the pronoun. There are three persons: **first person, second person,** and **third person.**

1. **First person** pronouns refer to the person speaking or writing:

Singular	Plural
I	we
me	us
my, mine	our, ours

2. **Second person** pronouns refer to the person spoken or written to:

Singular	Plural
you	you
your	your
yours	yours

3. **Third person** pronouns refer to the person or thing spoken or written about:

Singular	Plural
he, she, it	they
him, her, it	them
his, her, hers, its	their, theirs

Because nouns are always in the third person, pronouns that refer to nouns should also be in the third person. Usually this rule poses no problem, but sometimes writers mistakenly shift from third to second person when they are referring to a noun.

when a new student enters. he or she

wrong   *Wrong*

▶ EXAMPLE   When a new **student** first enters the large and crowded registration area, **you** might feel confused and intimidated.

In this sentence, *you* has mistakenly been used to refer to *student*. The mistake occurs because the noun *student* is in the third person, and the pronoun *you* is in the second person. There are two ways to correct the sentence:

   1. You can change the second person pronoun *you* to a third person pronoun.

▶ EXAMPLE *Right*   When a new **student** first enters the large and crowded registration area, **he or she** might feel confused and intimidated.

   2. You can change the noun *student* to the second person pronoun *you*.

▶ EXAMPLE *OK*   When **you** first enter the large and crowded registration area, **you** might feel confused and intimidated.

Here's another incorrect sentence.

▶ EXAMPLE   Most **people** can stay reasonably healthy if **you** watch **your** diet and exercise several times a week.

One way to correct this sentence is to change *you* to *they* and *your* to *their* so that they agree with *people*.

▶ EXAMPLE   Most **people** can stay reasonably healthy if **they** watch **their** diets and exercise several times a week.

■ PRACTICE   Correct any errors in pronoun person in the following sentences. When you correct the pronoun, you also may need to change the verb.

How consistiety

   1. When someone needs to have a cavity filled for the first time, ~~you~~ *he or she* might be nervous.

   2. Most people know the dentist will be careful, yet *they* you can't help but worry when *They* you see all the intimidating equipment in the office.

   3. When patients see the dentist approaching with that long needle, you just *they* want to faint.

   4. When I watched my daughter have her first tooth filled, you *I* could see that she was terrified.

   5. Afterward, she said that the procedure hadn't hurt at all; however, she also *she* said one wouldn't want to have another cavity filled.

then bob Nor the _boys_ Know where their cars are:?

Number

Errors in number are the most common pronoun–antecedent errors. To make pronouns agree with their antecedents in **number,** use singular pronouns to refer to singular nouns and plural pronouns to refer to plural nouns. The following guidelines will help you avoid errors in number.

1. Use pronouns to refer to words joined by *and* unless the words are modified by *each* or *every*.

▶ **EXAMPLE**   General Ulysses S. Grant and General Dwight D. Eisenhower led their armies to victory.

2. Use singular pronouns to refer to the following.

anybody	either	neither	one
anyone	everybody	nobody	somebody
anything	everyone	no one	someone
each	everything	nothing	something

▶ **EXAMPLES**   **Everything** was in **its** place.

Neither of the girls wanted to give up **her** place in line.

One of the fathers was yelling loudly at **his** son throughout the game.

NOTE: In spoken English, the plural pronouns *they, them,* and *their* are often used to refer to the antecedents *everyone* or *everybody*. However, in written English the singular pronoun is still more commonly used.

▶ **EXAMPLE**   **Everybody** at the game cheered for **his** favorite team.

3. In general, use singular pronouns to refer to collective nouns.

▶ **EXAMPLE**   The **troop** of soldiers had almost reached **its** camp when the blizzard started.

4. When antecedents are joined by *or* or *nor,* use a pronoun that agrees with the closer antecedent.

▶ **EXAMPLE**   Neither **Chris** nor **Craig** wanted to spend **his** Saturday mowing the lawn.

NOTE: If one antecedent is singular and one is plural, place the plural antecedent last to avoid awkwardness. If one antecedent is female and one is male, rewrite the sentence to avoid awkwardness.

he team is in danger of loosing it's unbeaten title

ne should never Park his/her car under a tree ful of birs

► **EXAMPLES** (awkward) Either the **members** of the council or the **mayor** will send **his** regrets.

(rewritten) Either the **mayor** or the **members** of the council will send **their** regrets.

(awkward) Either **Mary** or **Ruben** will lend you **his** watch.

(rewritten) You may borrow a watch from either Mary or Ruben.

■ **PRACTICE** Correct any pronoun–antecedent errors in the following sentences. When you correct a pronoun, you may also need to change the verb.

he or she has

1. If an <u>employee wants</u> to get ahead at that company, ~~you have~~ to be very competent and aggressive.

or pepole →

his/her

2. Anyone trying to cross the border was asked for their papers.

Pepole

Pay attention → 3. Sometimes when a person comes home after a long day at work or at

He/she

should feld school, they don't feel like cooking dinner or playing with their children.

dosent   *its*   *his/her*

4. The company that had improved their product the most got an award.

the trainers
their

5. Every dolphin and porpoise at Sea World has refused to respond to its

trainer.

or a
hiss

6. A player from Zimbabwe left their uniform in the locker room.

7. Everyone was laughing at the dog that was trying to catch its tail. ——

He/sh

8. Every time a driver begins a race, you should check all of your gauges.

9. Last night <u>somebody down the street</u> could be heard yelling loudly at

his/her
their dog.

his

10. Either Roberto or Carl needs to see their eye doctor.

when and is used it becomes prural

Sexist Language

In the past it was traditional to use masculine pronouns when referring to singular nouns whose gender could be either masculine or feminine. A good example is the sentence *A **person** should stop delivery of **his** newspaper before **he** leaves on a trip of more than a few days.* Although the noun *person* could be either masculine or feminine, masculine pronouns like *he* or *his* tended to be used in a case like this one.

Because women make up over fifty percent of the English-speaking population, they have been justifiably dissatisfied with this tradition. The problem is that the English language does not contain a singular personal pronoun that can refer to either sex at the same time in the way that the forms of *they* can.

The solutions to this problem can prove awkward. One of the solutions is to use feminine pronouns as freely as masculine ones to refer to singular nouns whose gender could be masculine or feminine. Either of the following sentences using this solution is acceptable.

> A **person** should stop delivery on **her** newspaper before **she** leaves on a trip of more than a few days.

> A **person** should stop delivery on **his** newspaper before **he** leaves on a trip of more than a few days.

Another solution is to change *his* to *his or her* and *he* to *he or she.* Then the sentence would look like this:

> A **person** should stop delivery on **his or her** newspaper before **he or she** leaves on a trip of more than a few days.

As you can see, this solution does not result in a very graceful sentence. An alternative is to use *her/his* and *she/he,* but the result would be about the same. Sometimes a better solution is to change a singular antecedent to a plural one and use the forms of *they,* which can refer to either gender. That would result in a sentence like this:

> **People** should stop delivery of **their** newspapers before **they** leave on a trip of more than a few days.

This sentence is less awkward and just as fair. Finally, in some situations, the masculine pronoun alone will be appropriate, and in others the feminine pronoun alone will be. Here are two such sentences:

> Each of the hockey players threw **his** false teeth into the air after the victory. (The hockey team is known to be all male.)

> The last runner on the relay team passed **her** opponent ten yards before the finish line. (All members of the relay team are female.)

Whatever your solutions to this problem, it is important that you be logical and correct in your pronoun–antecedent agreement in addition to being fair.

Unclear Pronoun Reference

Sometimes, even though a pronoun appears to agree with an antecedent, it is not clear exactly which noun in the sentence is the antecedent. And sometimes a writer will use a pronoun that does not clearly refer to any antecedent at all. The following two points will help you use pronouns correctly.

1. A pronoun should refer to a specific antecedent.

▶ **EXAMPLE**   **Mr. Mellon** told **Larry** that **he** could take a vacation in late August.

In this sentence, *he* could refer to *Mr. Mellon* or to *Larry.* To correct this problem, you can eliminate the pronoun.

▶ **EXAMPLE** *good*   Mr. Mellon told Larry that **Larry** could take his vacation in late August.

Or you can revise the sentence so that the pronoun clearly refers to only one antecedent.

▶ **EXAMPLES** *better*   Mr. Mellon told **Larry** to take **his** vacation in late August.

OR

good   Mr. Mellon told Larry, "Take your vacation in late August."

Here is another example:

▶ **EXAMPLE**   Every time **Patricia** looked at the **cat, she** whined *(wrong)*

In this sentence, the pronoun *she* could refer to *Patricia* or the *cat.* The pronoun reference needs to be clarified.

▶ **EXAMPLES**   **Patricia** whined every time **she** looked at the cat.

OR

The **cat** whined every time Patricia looked at **her.**

■ **PRACTICE**   Revise the following sentences so that each pronoun refers to a specific antecedent.

1. Eileen told her sister that she would be delayed at the airport.

or you

Eileen told her sister, "I will be delayed at the

airport."

2. Every year Odin and Zeus would meet to discuss his problems with the lesser gods.

Every year Odin and Zeus' would meet to

discuss their problems with the lesser gods

3. Whenever Sal called his father, he yelled at him.

whenever

_____

_____

4. Once the doctor had examined the child's injuries and discussed them with the parents, she decided to report them to her supervisors.

_____

_____

5. Michelle put out her cigarette in the ashtray, and then she threw it away.

_____ *the cigarette*

_____

---

2. Pronouns should not refer to implied or unstated antecedents. Be especially careful with the pronouns *this, that, which,* and *it*.

▶ EXAMPLE *wrong*   My baseball coach made us go without dinner if we lost a game; **this** was unfair.   *what*

In this sentence, there is no specific antecedent for the pronoun *this* to refer to. The following sentence clarifies the pronoun reference.

▶ EXAMPLE *good*   My baseball coach made us go without dinner if we lost a game; **this punishment** was unfair.

Sometimes a pronoun refers to a noun that is only implied in the first part of the sentence.

▶ EXAMPLE *wrong*   Mrs. Brovelli is a poet, **which** she does some of every day.

In this sentence, *which* apparently stands for "writing poetry," which is implied in the noun *poet;* however, there is no specific noun for the pronoun *which* to stand for. The faulty pronoun reference can be cleared up in several ways.

▶ EXAMPLES   Mrs. Brovelli is a poet, and **she writes** poetry every day.

Mrs. Brovelli is a poet **who writes** poetry every day.

■   **PRACTICE**   Revise the following sentences so that each pronoun refers to a specific, not an implied or unstated, antecedent. To correct the sentence, you may have to eliminate the pronoun altogether.

1. I do not like basketball, which has always bothered my father.

   My father has always been bothered because

   I do not like basketball.

2. Bertha disliked visiting her in-laws, and this bothered her.

3. Peanut shells were all over the floor, and Marie said that she had eaten them. *The peanut*

4. Dr. Freud daydreamed as he smoked his cigar, which caused him to worry.

5. The last five years have been dry and hot, but this year we have been inundated with rain; that is why I am moving. *◇ rain*

Reflexive and Intensive Pronouns

The reflexive and intensive pronouns are those that end in *self* or *selves*. The singular pronouns end in *self*, and the plural ones end in *selves*.

Singular	*Plural*
myself	ourselves
yourself	yourselves
himself	themselves
herself	
itself	
oneself	

These are the only reflexive and intensive forms. Avoid nonstandard forms like *hisself, ourselfs, theirselves,* or *themselfs.*

The **reflexive pronouns** are used to reflect the action of a verb back to the subject.

▶ **EXAMPLE**   **Amos** gave **himself** a bloody nose when he tried to slap a mosquito.

The **intensive pronouns** emphasize or intensify a noun or another pronoun in the sentence.

▶ **EXAMPLE**   Let's have **Estella Cordova herself** show us how to cross-examine a witness in court.

To help you use intensive and reflexive pronouns correctly, remember these three points.

1. Do not use a reflexive pronoun unless it is reflecting the action of a verb back to a subject.

2. Do not use an intensive pronoun unless the sentence contains a noun or pronoun for it to emphasize or intensify.

3. In general, do not use a reflexive or intensive pronoun where a personal pronoun is called for. For example, reflexive and intensive pronouns are never used as subjects.

▶ **EXAMPLES**   (incorrect)   Tim's mother and **myself** often go shopping together on Saturdays.

(correct)   Tim's mother and **I** often go shopping together on Saturdays.

(incorrect)   The other employees at the restaurant gave Carmen and **myself** large bouquets of flowers on the anniversary of our first year there.

(correct)   The other employees of the restaurant gave Carmen and **me** large bouquets of flowers on the anniversary of our first year there.

■   **PRACTICE**   Correct any errors in the use of reflexive or intensive pronouns in the following sentences.

themselves

1. John and his wife repainted their house all by ~~theirselves~~.

2. After we went swimming, Gill and myself changed.

3. Mr. Barton told the receptionist that Mrs. Barton and hisself had lost their invitations to the party.

4. Ever since that day in the garden, Adam and herself had disagreed about apple leaves as a fashion statement.

5. Because we could not afford a contractor, we built our house by ourself.

■   **PRACTICE**   Correct any errors in pronoun reference or in the use of reflexive and intensive pronouns in the following sentences.

cigarettes

1. I used to smoke two packs a day, but I don't like ~~them~~ anymore.

2. When Vesuvius erupted, Flavius and herself ran fast.

3. My sister had some strange friends in high school; this worried my parents.

4. Michelle thanked her grandmother even though she was not a very polite person.

5. When the movie ended, Chris asked Charlie and myself if we thought Mel Gibson was a convincing Hamlet.

6. Tory wanted to go cycling on Monday, but it was broken.

7. Mr. Holcroft refused to pay the bill for his dinner, which angered the waiter.

8. Lewis and Clark often asked theirself if the trip was worthwhile.

9. Duval accidentally hit the door with his knee and broke it.

10. Because he was feeling depressed, Sam called Edward after dinner.

Section Three Review

1. The **antecedent** is the word a pronoun stands for.

2. A pronoun must agree with its **antecedent** in **person** and in **number**.

3. Use a plural pronoun to refer to antecedents joined by *and*.

4. Use a singular pronoun to refer to an **indefinite pronoun**.

5. Use a singular pronoun to refer to a **collective noun**.

6. When you refer to two antecedents that are joined by *either/or, neither/nor, or, nor,* or *not only/but also,* your pronoun usually should agree with the closer word.

7. Make sure a pronoun refers to a specific antecedent in its sentence or in the previous sentence.

8. Be sure that your pronoun does not refer to an implied or unstated antecedent.

9. A **reflexive pronoun** reflects the action of a verb back to the subject.

10. An **intensive pronoun** emphasizes or intensifies a noun or pronoun in the sentence.

11. Do not use a reflexive or intensive pronoun when a personal pronoun is called for.

Exercise 3A

Underline the correct pronouns in the parentheses.

1. Joann talks about thermonuclear physics all the time, but David doesn't consider (<u>it</u> them) a very interesting topic.

2. Everyone in the office smiled when (he or she they) heard the news about the pay raise.

3. After the class had raised enough money, (it they) went on a field trip.

4. When the team returned to (its their) school, the band was playing.

5. Somebody has left (his or her their) lights on in the parking lot.

6. Daedalus was worried that Icarus and (he himself) would never escape from the Minotaur.

7. When a person is in a situation like that, (she they you) had better be able to act fast.

8. The seagull chose (it's its) target from among the unsuspecting sailors.

9. Although she knew that almost everyone has stress on (his or her their) job, the air traffic controller felt that (her their) stress was more dangerous than most.

10. Each coach at the tournament wanted the members of (his their) team to be good sports.

11. After trying experiment after experiment, the chemists asked (theirselfs themselves) if there weren't a different approach.

12. When a diver goes out into the water (he or she they you) should always have a companion along.

13. The bicycle had a long gash in (it's its) front tire.

14. Anyone who applies to adopt a child knows that (he or she they) must have patience and persistence.

15. If it starts to snow, each camper should return to (her your their) campsite immediately.

Exercise 3B

Correct all errors in pronoun usage in the following sentences. Do nothing if the sentence is correct.

1. When a shopper has looked for an item at several stores in three different malls, ~~you~~ *he or she* can become quite frustrated.

2. The sightseeing group finally arrived back at their bus.

3. Everybody sitting on the steps of the cathedral was wearing a gold earring in their left ear.

4. The class raised the most money for their school.

5. Either the two Doberman pinschers next door or the Labrador retriever down the street barks whenever they hear a car drive by.

6. When a traveler first walks to the edge of the Grand Canyon, you will be amazed by its size and beauty.

7. Our Saint Bernard stands eagerly by the front door whenever it is time for Marie and itself to go for a walk.

8. Todd decided to quit drinking alcohol after he watched *Leaving Las Vegas*, which his friends thought was absurd.

9. Whenever Mr. Ed and myself go for a ride, we have a long conversation.

10. Because they were feeling worried, Denny and Martha called their parents.

11. Two young men wearing pink, spiky hair, earrings, and heavy leather boots rang the doorbell and asked to speak to me; this worried my mother.

12. Whenever someone would volunteer for a chore, Chuck would laugh at them.

13. Marianne knew that Sylvia and herself would have to work hard if they planned to become famous poets.

14. On Sunday Susan stopped smoking because she found out she was pregnant, which pleased her friends.

Exercise 3B

continued

15. Anyone who regularly drives through the Mojave Desert knows that you should always

carry a supply of extra water.

Exercise 3C

In the following paragraph, correct any errors in pronoun agreement or reference or in the use of intensive and reflexive pronouns.

1. If a son found out that his uncle had murdered his father and married his mother and *he* taken his rightful place as king, surely ~~you~~ would not hesitate to seek revenge. **2.** Almost every reader or viewer of *Hamlet*, the world's most famous play, scratches their head over the question of what causes Hamlet to hesitate. **3.** If one tries to oversimplify the cause of Hamlet's hesitation, you will usually end up in an argument with people who adamantly disagree. **4.** For instance, if a writer claims that Hamlet was just a procrastinator, they will be confronted by the Freudians. **5.** The Freudians believe that Hamlet cannot kill his uncle Claudius because he has recently done what he wanted to do. **6.** They will claim that Hamlet had secret desires to do it, too. **7.** Therefore, killing his uncle would be the same as if you killed yourself. **8.** On the other hand, perhaps Hamlet hesitates because he knows you need a good reason to kill your uncle, the king. **9.** Hamlet has to prove that his uncle killed his father, which is difficult. **10.** Another very practical cause exists for Hamlet's hesitation, and its important to keep in mind. **11.** If a person, even a prince, just rushes up to stab a king, they risk being killed themself. **12.** When Hamlet finally decides that Claudius is guilty, he puts off killing him because he is praying. **13.** Any person in Hamlet's place would hesitate if they had all of these problems. **14.** Hamlet interests most readers and viewers because he is just like theirselves.

Sentence Practice: Using Transitions

Writers use certain words and phrases to indicate the relationships among the ideas in their sentences and paragraphs. These words and phrases provide links between ideas, leading a reader from one idea to another smoothly. They show relationships like time, addition, or contrast. Consider this paragraph from Rachel Carson's *Edge of the Sea:*

> **When** the tide is rising the shore is a place of unrest, with the surge leaping high over jutting rocks **and** running in lacy cascades of foam over the landward side of massive boulders. **But** on the ebb it is more peaceful, **for then** the waves do not have behind them the push of the inward pressing tides. There is no particular drama about the turn of the tide, **but presently** a zone of wetness shows on the gray rock slopes, **and** offshore the incoming swells begin to swirl **and** break over hidden ledges. **Soon** the rocks that the high tide had concealed rise into view and glisten with the wetness left on them by the receding water.

Because she is writing about a process, most of Rachel Carson's transitional words indicate a relationship in time (*when, then, presently, soon*). But she also uses transitional words that indicate contrast (*but*), cause (*for*), and addition (*and*). As you can see, she uses these expressions to lead her readers smoothly from one idea to another.

The sentence combining exercises in this chapter are designed to give you practice in using transitional words and phrases to link your ideas. Try to use as many different ones as you can. For your convenience, here is a list of commonly used transitional words and phrases.

- Time: *then, soon, first, second, finally, meanwhile, next, at first, in the beginning*

- Contrast: *yet, but, however, instead, otherwise, on the other hand, on the contrary*

- Addition: *and, also, besides, furthermore, in addition, likewise, moreover, similarly*

- Cause–effect: *for, because, consequently, so, therefore, hence, thus, as a result*

- Example: *for example, for instance, that is, such as*

- Conclusion: *thus, hence, finally, generally, as a result, in conclusion*

look →

■ **PRACTICE**   Add transitions to the following sentences.

1. My car has given me nothing but trouble since I bought it. _____, two

    days after I purchased it, the car stalled in the middle of rush hour traffic.

2. Edna withdrew $10,325 from the First Interstate Bank of Brawley.

    _____, she gave it all to the car dealer.

3. Bryan has started two successful insurance companies. _____, he

    operates many promotional golf tournaments.

4. Homer ate three cans of Spam before he went to bed last night.

    _____, he felt ill this morning.

5. This weekend I should spend at least five hours studying. _____,

    maybe I'll forget everything and go visit some friends.

Sentence Combining Exercises

Combine the following sentences, using transitions as indicated in the directions.

▶ **EXAMPLE** Combine these sentences into two sentences. Use transitions that indicate contrast, example, and addition. Underline your transitions.

   a. Herman knows he needs to lose weight.
   b. He is unable to resist the urge to eat ice cream.
   c. Yesterday he drank a low-fat fiber shake for lunch.
   d. After work he stopped at a 31 Flavors ice cream store.
   e. He ate a large chocolate sundae.

Herman knows he needs to lose weight, <u>but</u> he is unable to resist

the urge to eat ice cream. <u>For example,</u> yesterday he drank a

low-fat fiber shake for lunch, <u>but</u> after work he stopped at a 31

Flavors ice cream store <u>and</u> ate a large chocolate sundae.

look

1. Combine the following sentences into two sentences. Use transitions that show contrast. Underline your transitions.

   a. Mr. Rodriguez enjoyed the television program *Cheers*.
   b. Mr. Rodriguez did not like the way everyone treated Cliff.
   c. Mrs. Rodriguez did not enjoy *Cheers*.
   d. Mrs. Rodriguez did think that Woody was a funny character.

   _____

   _____

   _____

   _____

2. Combine the following sentences into one sentence. Use transitions that indicate cause–effect and addition. Underline your transitions.

   a. The crow has a larger brain than most other birds.
   b. It can learn to recognize when a farmer is merely going about his work.
   c. It can learn to recognize when a farmer has a rifle in hand.
   d. It can learn to recognize when a farmer has plans to shoot it.

   _____

   _____

   _____

Sentence Combining Exercises

continued

3. Combine sentences a and b using a cause–effect transition. Then combine sentences c, d, e, and f. Underline your transitions.

    a. The symbol of barbers is a red and white striped pole.
    b. In the twelfth century barbers had the job of bleeding people who were sick.
    c. The red stripes represent blood.
    d. The white stripes represent bandages.
    e. The gold knob at the end represents a basin.
    f. The barber used the basin to catch blood.

4. Combine the following sentences into two sentences. Use transitions that show time relationships. Underline your transitions.

    a. The earthquake started with a faint rumbling sound.
    b. The vase on the bookshelf began to vibrate.
    c. The mirror on the wall started to rattle.
    d. The entire room started to shake back and forth.

Sentence Combining Exercises

continued

5. Combine the following sentences into one or two sentences, using transitions that show contrast and cause–effect. Underline your transitions.

   a. Michel wanted to attend Pitcairn College.
   b. Pitcairn College is an expensive private college.
   c. Michel got a job delivering the *Los Angeles Times*.
   d. Michel worked nights at the Fox Theater.

   _____

   _____

   _____

   _____

6. Combine the following sentences into three sentences. Use transitions that indicate relationships of time and addition. Underline your transitions.

   a. The bubonic plague starts out as a bacterial disease in rats.
   b. The bubonic plague is known as the Black Death.
   c. Fleas become infected when they bite the rats.
   d. Fleas spread the plague from rat to rat.
   e. Fleas spread the plague from human to human.
   f. Humans spread the plague to each other.
   g. Humans spread the plague when they speak, cough, or sneeze.

   _____

   _____

   _____

   _____

continued

7. Combine the following sentences into three or four sentences, using transitions that show addition. Underline your transitions.

   a. The common shirt has almost twenty parts.
   b. Each part has its own name.
   c. The face of the shirt has a front placket for the buttonholes.
   d. Each sleeve has a placket.
   e. The shirt has a neck band.
   f. The shirt has a shirttail, a breast pocket, and a lapel.
   g. The back has a yoke and sometimes a tailor's loop.

   _____

   _____

   _____

   _____

8. Combine the following sentences into two sentences. Use transitions that indicate relationships of time, contrast, and cause. Underline your transitions.

   a. Scientists believed that dinosaurs became extinct slowly.
   b. The earth's climate changed gradually but dramatically over thousands of years.
   c. Many scientists believe that the dinosaurs disappeared quickly.
   d. Sudden climactic changes occurred.
   e. An asteroid hit the earth.

   _____

   _____

   _____

   _____

Sentence Combining Exercises

continued

9. Combine the following sentences into two sentences. Use transitions that indicate contrast and cause–effect. Underline your transitions.

    a. Today the paper or plastic kite is a popular child's toy.
    b. It was originally designed by the Chinese in 1200 B.C.
    c. It was designed to send coded military messages.
    d. Each kite's unique shape, color, and movements were ideal for sending coded messages.
    e. Only someone who knew the code could decode it.

_____

_____

_____

_____

10. Combine the following sentences into three sentences. Use transitions that indicate example and addition. Underline your transitions.

    a. Hundreds of English words have found their way into other languages.
    b. In the Ukraine, people visit the barber.
    c. They want a *herkot*.
    d. In Spain, people become chilly.
    e. They put on a *sueter*.
    f. One might need to place a phone call in the Netherlands.
    g. He or she asks for the *telefoon*.
    h. In China, one asks for the *te le fung*.

_____

_____

_____

_____

Paragraph Practice:
Explaining Causes and Effects

Writing Assignment

In Chapter Three you wrote an expository paragraph that used examples to support a point expressed in a topic sentence. Such an organization—one that calls for a listing of examples to support an idea—is very common in college papers and tests. Another common assignment is one that asks you to explain the **causes** or the **effects** of something. In an American history class, for example, you might be asked to explain the causes of the South's failure to win the Civil War. Or in a psychology class you might be asked to explain the long-term effects that physical abuse can have on children.

A paper that focuses on causes explains <u>why</u> a certain event might have occurred or why people do what they do. On the other hand, a paper that focuses on effects explains what has <u>resulted</u> or might result from an event, action, or behavior. In this chapter, Exercise 1C explains why the alphabet is so widespread and why its letters are shaped the way they are; Exercise 2C explains the effects that being left-handed has on people; and Exercise 3C explains possible causes of Hamlet's hesitation in Shakespeare's play. Each of these paragraphs states the purpose of the paragraph (to explain causes or effects) in a topic sentence and then presents several specific causes or effects.

Your assignment is to write a paragraph that explains *either* the causes *or* the effects of a topic with which you are personally familiar. Develop your paragraph from one of the suggestions below or from an idea suggested by your instructor.

Reading Assignment

The reading selections in the "Explaining Causes and Effects" section of Chapter Seven illustrate several ways that professional writers consider causes and effects. Read one or more of the selections, as assigned by your instructor, and use the questions that follow them to develop ideas for your own paper.

Prewriting

Prewriting Application: Finding Your Topic

Use prewriting techniques (freewriting, brainstorming, or clustering) to decide which of the following topics interests you the most. Consider *several* topic ideas before making your final choice.

ANALYZING CAUSES

1. Why do you or do you not admire, respect, or trust a particular person?

2. Why are you doing well or poorly in a particular course?

3. Why did your or your parents' marriage or relationship fail, or why is it a success?

4. Why was your childhood or some other period the best or worst time of your life?

5. Why did you move from one place to another?

6. Why did you buy the particular car or other item that you did?

7. Why are you attending a particular college?

8. Why did you make an important decision?

9. Why did a particular experience affect you the way it did?

10. Why will you never go to *that* restaurant, hotel, beach, or lake again?

ANALYZING EFFECTS

1. What were the effects of an important decision that you made?

2. What were the effects of your move to a new place?

3. What were the effects of your being an only child, or an oldest child, or a youngest child, or of growing up in a large family?

4. What are the effects of stress on the way you act, feel, or think?

5. What were the effects on you of a major change in your life—having a child, getting married, changing jobs, experiencing a divorce?

6. What have been the effects of a serious compulsion or addiction to drugs, alcohol, gambling, or overeating on someone you know or on his or her loved ones?

7. What have been the effects of mental, emotional, or physical abuse on you or someone you know?

8. What have been the effects of discrimination or prejudice on you or someone you know? (Discrimination might involve race, gender, age, sexuality, or religion.)

9. What have been the effects on you and/or on your family of working and/or raising a family and attending school at the same time?

10. What have been the effects on you of some major change in your lifestyle or values?

Once you have chosen your topic, keep prewriting to develop the causes or effects that you might include in your paper. Remember to keep your writing focused on *either* causes *or* effects. Don't mix the two together. And don't necessarily settle for the first causes or effects that come to mind. Sometimes the most significant ideas will come only after you have written for a while.

Now write a preliminary topic sentence. It should state both your topic and the central point of the paragraph. Your topic sentence should make it clear whether your paragraph is explaining causes or effects.

Prewriting Application: Working with Topic Sentences

Identify the topic sentences in Exercises 1C (page 208), 2C (page 220), and 3C (page 235). Then identify the topic and the central point in each topic sentence.

Prewriting Application: Evaluating Topic Sentences

Write "No" before each sentence that would not make an effective topic sentence *for this assignment*. Write "Yes" before each sentence that would make an effective one. Identify each effective topic sentence as introducing a paragraph about causes or about effects. Be prepared to explain your answers.

Yes **1.** My father's generosity, sensitivity, and openness have made him into the most important person in my life.

No **2.** I divorced my husband on June 30 of last year.

Yes **3.** Although I loved living in Boulder, Colorado, several events over the past few years helped me decide that it was time to move.

No **4.** Whenever I let myself worry too much about my job, school, or family responsibilities, everyone that I love is affected by my strange behavior.

Yes **5.** My life has changed in many ways since I was young.

No **6.** Many students at our local high school use marijuana, methamphetamines, and even cocaine.

No **7.** Telling my parents that I was gay was one of the biggest mistakes that I ever made.

Yes **8.** Growing up as an only child helped me become an independent, decisive, and responsible person.

No **9.** My new computer, which uses all the latest technology, came loaded with my favorite games and word processing software.

Yes **10.** Attending a college away from home has caused me to become a much better person in a number of ways.

Prewriting Application: Talking to Others

Form a group of three or four people and tell each other what topic you have chosen and whether you plan to discuss causes or effects. Use the following guidelines to discuss your paragraphs.

1. What is the topic of the paragraph? Will the paragraph focus on causes or effects?

2. What causes or effects will be included? Can they be more specific and descriptive? Can they be explained more clearly?

3. What other causes or effects could be included? Are there any less obvious but more interesting ones?

4. Are you convinced? Have enough causes or effects been provided to illustrate the topic idea? Should any of them be explained or described more thoroughly?

5. Which cause or effect should the student's paper open with? Which should it close with?

Writing

Write the first draft of your paragraph, opening with your preliminary topic sentence. As you explain the causes or effects in the body of your paragraph, be as specific and as detailed as you can.

Introduce each new cause or effect with a clear transitional sentence, as discussed in Section Five of Chapter Three. Also, add transitions between sentences to help with clarity, as discussed in the Sentence Practice section of this chapter.

Writing Application: Identifying Transitional Words, Phrases, and Sentences

Examine Exercises 1C (page 208), 2C (page 220), and 3C (page 235). Identify the transitional sentences that introduce each new cause or effect. Then identify any other transitions that serve to connect ideas between sentences.

Our school have becom are in trouble ——— : the written of this antical suggest that we should Reform our Schools, I agree for the following Reasons: (Teacher low pay, the attendes passing program, and teacher/Parent involbment.

Teacher low pay is one way to reform our Schools

attendancer passing program is another reason our school should be reformed. Finally teach/Parent

Rewriting

1. Revise your sentences so that they include specific and concrete details. As often as possible, use actual names of people and places. Refer to specific details whenever possible.

2. Add or revise transitions wherever doing so will help clarify your movement from one idea to another.

3. Improve your preliminary topic sentence so that it more accurately states the central point of your paragraph.

4. Examine your draft for simple sentences that can be combined to make compound, complex, or compound-complex sentences. Watch also for sentences that can be combined using participial phrases, appositives, infinitive phrases, or adjective clauses.

Rewriting Application: Responding to Writing

Read the following paragraph. Then respond to the questions following it.

Changing Careers

asked for tessis ?

Two years ago, after serving for over twenty-five years in the U.S. Navy, I decided that it was time to move on to new and better things, and I have never regretted that decision. One of the most pleasant effects of retiring from the military has been not having to endure any more family separations. While in the navy, I spent most of my career aboard ship and made many six-month deployments or had to stand duty every four or five days when not on deployment. Now that I have more time to spend with my family, I have joined a family bowling league and have time to attend school events that my children are participating in. Another effect of leaving the military is that I am able to get involved with community activities because I know that I won't be moving to another city in two or three years. During one period of my career my family and I lived in San Francisco two years; Norfolk, Virginia, three years; and then San Diego. Now that I don't plan to move within two or three years, I have joined the Parent-Teacher Association at my son's school, become an active member in the local Boy Scout troop, and become a board member of my homeowners' association. Finally, by working fewer hours than I did when I was in the navy, I have the opportunity to go to school. I am able to use the Montgomery

G.I. Bill to supplement my income while in school and obtain a degree in business management. My wife and I agree that we made the right decision to leave the military when I did. The week after I retired, the ship I had been stationed on made an unexpected nine-month deployment to Somalia. I obtained a good civil service job after I retired, and my supervisor allows me to attend school in the mornings and work in the afternoons and weekends.

1. Identify the topic sentence. State its topic and central idea. Is it an effective topic sentence? Can you tell whether the paper will focus on causes or effects?

2. How many causes or effects are mentioned in this paper? Identify them.

3. Identify the transitional sentences that introduce each cause or effect. What other transitions are used between sentences in this paragraph?

4. What parts of each cause or effect could be made still more specific?

5. Consider the organization of the paragraph. Would you change the order of the causes or effects? Explain why or why not.

Rewriting Application: Revising and Editing Your Own Draft

As you revise your draft a final time, look closely at your topic sentence and transitions. Make any improvements that are needed. Consider your causes or effects, too. Do they need to be explained more thoroughly or described in more detail? If your paragraph contains too many brief sentences or too many compound sentences joined by *and*, revise them to use subordinate clauses as well as verbal phrases and appositives.

When editing your paper, check for the following errors:

- Sentence fragments

- Comma splices

- Fused sentences

- Misplaced modifiers

- Dangling modifiers

- Incorrect subject–verb agreement

- Incorrect pronoun case

- Incorrect pronoun–antecedent agreement or pronoun reference

- Misspelled words

Prepare a clean final draft, following the format your instructor has asked for. Before you turn in your final draft, proofread it carefully and make any necessary corrections.

Chapter Four Practice Test

I. Review of Chapters One, Two, and Three

A. Underline all subjects once and complete verbs twice. Place all prepositional phrases in parentheses.

1. Neither the army nor the navy could find the solution to the problem.

2. Georgia started to paint when she saw the deep purple flower on the vine.

3. My father listens to classical music on his car radio, but my mother prefers jazz.

4. Nathan saved his pennies in a special album for that purpose.

5. Granny stared at the cart and then stepped quickly into it.

B. Correct any fragments, fused sentences, or comma splices in the following sentences. Do nothing if the sentence is correct.

6. The boy looked up at the sun then he began to fly.

   _____

   _____

7. Mr. Juarez, knowing that his flight was going to be late.

   _____

   _____

8. On a bench was a beautiful trophy, the prize for the cow chip throwing contest.

   _____

   _____

9. Reading the owner's manual for the new stereo system that he had just bought.

   _____

   _____

Chapter Four Practice Test

continued

10. It rained for a month, consequently, the okra crop was ruined.

_____

_____

C. At the places indicated, add adjective clauses, appositives, infinitive phrases, or participial phrases to the following sentences as directed in the parentheses. Use commas where they are needed.

11. The fish ^ floated upside down in the aquarium. (adjective clause)

_____

_____

12. Andrea bought some mats for her new car ^ because the rainy season was beginning. (appositive)

_____

_____

13. ^ Alexis slapped her knees and rocked back and forth in her chair. (participial phrase)

_____

_____

14. The yards in front and in back were overgrown, so Smerdly hired a gardener ^ . (infinitive)

_____

_____

15. Emma stared at the ants ^ and started to scream. (participial phrase)

_____

_____

Chapter Four Practice Test

continued

D. Correct any dangling or misplaced modifiers in the following sentences. Do nothing if the sentence is correct.

16. Crossing Death Valley, the hikers almost drank ten gallons of water.

_____

_____

17. The package mistakenly went to Toledo that was supposed to go to Tokyo.

_____

_____

18. Drawing for about ten hours, Mr. Trudeau's cartoon was almost finished.

_____

_____

19. The Boy Scout troop brought only two forks on the camping trip.

_____

_____

20. Gathering all the receipts, the tax return was finally ready to be completed.

_____

_____

II. Chapter Four

A. Underline the correct verb form in the parentheses.

21. Every one of the calves (was were) branded by the ranch hands.

22. Mumps (has have) once again become a problem for adults.

23. The most important item on the town council's agenda (concerns concern) mosquitoes.

24. A mother cat with eight kittens (lives live) under my bed.

25. Here (is are) the oven and refrigerator that you ordered.

continued

B. Correct any subject–verb agreement errors in the following sentences. Do nothing if the sentence is correct.

26. A Pakistani man and woman from Chicago has moved into our apartment building.

27. Harley told me that some of the apples in the basket are ripe.

28. Either Kirk or his family are going to pay for the damages.

29. Have Andy or the other actors been practicing their parts?

30. A flock of Canada geese arrive at our lake each spring.

C. Underline the correct pronoun in the parentheses.

31. My Russian pen pal and (I me) have been exchanging letters for over ten years.

32. Our teacher refereed the chess match between Sarafina and (I me).

33. My uncle thought that Ashley was taller than (he him).

34. Cerebella told everyone (who whom) she met about her IQ.

35. At the end of the competition we gave the two fastest skiers—Alberto and (she her)—

    a large trophy.

D. Correct any pronoun errors in the following sentences. Do nothing if the sentence is correct.

36. Mr. Marx asked John Lenin and I to help him write his book.

37. The Edelsteins and we traveled to England and Ireland in 1983.

38. Hal paid more for his computer than me.

39. The stroller had lost one of it's wheels, so Maria and he took turns carrying the baby.

40. Has Annie or her received a postcard from Wyoming yet?

Chapter Four Practice Test

continued

E. Underline the correct pronouns in the parentheses.

41. Practically anyone can change (his or her their) bad habits with determination.

42. The soccer player and her coach worked in the off-season, and (her their) effort

paid off.

43. The family was proud of (its their) home beside the waterfall.

44. Neither the teacher nor the students knew whether (his their) experiment was a

success yet.

45. Although they knew nothing about plumbing, Steve and Marlyle decided to repair the

leak by (theirselves themself themselves themselfs).

F. Correct any pronoun errors in the following sentences. Do nothing if the sentence is correct.

46. When a marathon runner gets to the last few miles, you really have to concentrate to

keep going.

47. Melanie whispered to Charlotte that she would get the job.

48. Benny's father made him smoke a pack before he ate dinner, which made Benny sick.

49. Suzanne and myself wrote the report on exotic snakes and presented it to the

conference.

50. Norma's mother praised her for her courage, but this was too late.

Using Punctuation and Capitalization

When we speak to people face to face, we have a number of signals, aside from the words we choose, to let them know how we feel. Facial expressions—smiles, frowns, grimaces—convey our emotions and attitudes. Tone of voice can tell a listener whether we feel sad or lighthearted or sarcastic about what we are saying. Hand gestures and other body language add further messages to the communication. In fact, experts tell us that these nonverbal communications make up over eighty percent of the messages in a conversation.

When we write in order to communicate with a reader, we must make up for that eighty percent of lost, nonverbal communication by using the writing signals that we know. Some of the most important signals in writing are the punctuation marks. They signal whether we are making a statement or asking a question. They indicate the boundaries of our sentences. They determine much of the rhythm and emotion of our writing.

If you are able to use punctuation effectively, you have a powerful tool to control how your writing affects your readers. If you do not know the basic rules of punctuation, you run the risk of being misunderstood or of confusing your readers. In this chapter we will discuss the essential rules of punctuation, not just so that your writing will be correct but, more important, so that you will be able to express your ideas exactly the way you want them to be expressed.

Using Commas

The comma gives writers more trouble than any of the other punctuation marks. Before printing was developed, commas came into use to tell readers when to put in a slight pause when they were reading aloud. Now, although the placement of the comma does affect the rhythm of sentences, it also conveys many messages that are more important than when to pause. Because the comma is such an important punctuation mark and because it can be troublesome to you if you don't know how to use it correctly, we take it up first. You are already familiar with several of its uses.

Comma usage can be explained by four general rules:

1. **Use commas before coordinating conjunctions that join main clauses to form a compound sentence.**

2. **Use commas between elements in a series.**

3. **Use commas after introductory elements.**

4. **Use commas before and after interrupters.**

Commas in Compound Sentences

1. When you join two main clauses with one of the coordinating conjunctions to form a compound sentence, use a comma before the conjunction.

▶ **EXAMPLES**
I don't know her, **but** I like her already.

The tableware in the restaurant was exquisite, **and** the food was some of the best I have ever tasted.

We had to remove the huge eucalyptus tree, **or** its encroaching roots would have undermined our happy home.

2. When conjunctions join other parts of a sentence, such as two words, two phrases, or two subordinate clauses, do not put commas before the conjunctions.

▶ **EXAMPLE**
Every morning that scoundrel **has** a drink <u>and</u> then thoroughly **beats** his poor dog.

No comma is needed before *and* because it does not join two main clauses. Instead, it joins the verbs *has* and *beats*.

▶ **EXAMPLE**
I decided to visit France because I had never had a chance to see that country <u>and</u> because my travel agent was able to offer me a special discount on the trip.

No comma is needed before *and* because it joins two subordinate clauses, not two main clauses.

■ **PRACTICE** Add commas to the following sentences where necessary.

1. Don Quixote loved Dulcinea ,and he told everyone about her beauty.

2. Bonnie Parker loved Clyde Barrow but all he cared about was robbing banks.

3. Lancelot loved Queen Guinevere but did not have enough sense to keep quiet about it.

4. Marc Antony loved Cleopatra so he spent a good deal of time at her place.

5. Beauty loved the Beast for his beautiful soul and for his luxuriant head of hair.

Commas with Elements in a Series

1. When listing three or more elements (words, phrases, clauses) in a series, separate them by commas. When the last two elements are joined by a coordinating conjunction, a comma before the conjunction is optional.

▶ **EXAMPLES**

(words)   The gazpacho was **cold, spicy, and fresh.**

(phrases)   In the mountains, he had been **thrown by his horse, bitten by a snake, and chased by a bear.**

(clauses)   To rescue the koala, **the firefighters brought a ladder, the police brought a rope, and the mayor brought a speech.**

2. When using two or more adjectives to modify the same noun, separate them with commas if you can put *and* between the adjectives without changing the meaning or if you can easily reverse the order of the adjectives.

▶ **EXAMPLES**

She eagerly stepped into the **comforting, cool water.**

A **stubborn, obnoxious** boll weevil is ruining my cotton patch.

Note that you could easily use *and* between the above adjectives. (The water is *comforting* and *cool;* the boll weevil is *stubborn* and *obnoxious.*) You could also reverse the adjectives (the *cool, comforting water* or the *obnoxious, stubborn* boll weevil).

3. On the other hand, if the adjectives cannot be joined by *and* or are not easily reversed, no comma is necessary.

► **EXAMPLE**   A bureaucrat wearing a **black leather jacket** and a smirk strode into the auditorium.

Notice how awkward the sentence would sound if you placed *and* between the adjectives (*a black and leather jacket*) or if you reversed them (*a leather black jacket*).

■ **PRACTICE**   Insert commas between main clauses joined by a coordinating conjunction and between items in a series.

1. I have always enjoyed Roscoe's sense of humor **,** so I will not be offended if you invite him to your party.

2. An empty can of Coca Cola two Snickers wrappers and half of a peanut butter sandwich were all that remained of Oscar's lunch.

3. Betsy tore a hole in the flag mended it and then added a new star.

4. The elves could be seen traipsing across the untidy overgrown lawn.

5. Selena read the complicated confusing instructions very carefully for she knew that they held the key to the puzzle.

6. Roger covered the lower part of his face with thick hot lather and then he shaved.

7. Tex polished his classic Jaguar twice a week yet never would drive it.

8. Maxwell Smart reached for his secret shoe phone but his shoe had disappeared.

9. Anne flew to Paris toured the Louvre museum ate some escargots bought a beret and left for Switzerland.

10. The frightening unexpected news caused Mr. Toad to experience a serious emotional depression.

Commas with Introductory Elements

When you begin a sentence with certain introductory words, phrases, or clauses, place a comma after the introductory element.

1. Use a comma after the following introductory words and transitional expressions.

Introductory Words		*Transitional Expressions*
next	similarly	on the other hand
first	nevertheless	in a similar manner
second	therefore	in other words
third	indeed	for example
moreover	yes	for instance
however	no	in fact
		in addition
		as a result

► **EXAMPLES**

First, we will strike at the heart of the matter and then pursue other clichés.

For example, let's all stand up and be counted.

2. Use a comma after introductory prepositional phrases of five or more words. However, you may need to use a comma after shorter introductory prepositional phrases if not doing so would cause confusion.

► **EXAMPLES**

After a long and thrilling nap, Buster went looking for a cat to chase.

After dinner we all went for a walk around the lake.

In spring, time seems to catch up with small furry animals.

Without the comma, this last sentence might look as if it begins *In springtime.*

3. Use a comma after all introductory infinitive and participial phrases.

► **EXAMPLES**

Blackened with soot, the little boy toddled out of the smoldering house.

Begging for her forgiveness, Homer assured Hortense that they would never run short of Spam again.

To break in your new car properly, drive at varying speeds for the first one thousand miles.

4. Use a comma after introductory adverb subordinate clauses.

▶ EXAMPLES

Because Umberto played the tuba so well, he was awarded a music scholarship.

As soon as he arrived on shore, Columbus claimed the land for Spain.

Although it was raining furiously, Freida ran six miles anyway.

■ PRACTICE   Insert commas after introductory elements.

1. Next ,you will be telling us the moon is made of cheese.

2. Stuffed with jelly doughnuts and chocolate eclairs Charlie and Meredith felt just a little woozy.

3. Teetering dangerously at the top of the hill the large stone might have rolled down and crushed Sisyphus.

4. When you see her the next time she will have removed that load from her shoulders.

5. In other words you must resign from your position by midnight tomorrow.

6. Pledging his undying devotion Popeye asked Olive Oyl to marry him.

7. As Homer read the instructions Hortense heated up the grease.

8. While standing in line for the concert tickets Linda met a woman who had recently immigrated from Bulgaria.

9. In fact the story about the killer zucchinis was just a hoax.

10. To impress Daisy Jay Gatsby threw his beautiful shirts onto the table.

Commas with Interrupters

Sometimes certain words, phrases, or clauses will interrupt the flow of thought in a sentence to add emphasis or additional information. These interrupters are enclosed by commas.

1. Use commas to set off parenthetical expressions. Common parenthetical expressions include *however, indeed, consequently, as a result, moreover, of course, for example, for instance, that is, in fact, after all, I think,* and *therefore.*

▶ **EXAMPLES**   The answer, **after all,** lay right under his left big toe.

That big blue bird by the feeder is, **I think,** one of those unruly Steller's jays.

She is, **moreover,** a notorious misspeller of the word *deceitful.*

NOTE: Whenever a parenthetical expression introduces a second main clause after a semicolon, the semicolon takes the place of the comma in front of it. (See page 274 for a review of this rule.)

▶ **EXAMPLE**   Yes, you may eat your snails in front of me; **after all,** we are old friends.

■ **PRACTICE**   Use commas to set off any parenthetical elements in the following sentences.

1. Belinda ,in fact ,is the only person I know who does not like chocolate.

2. The San Gabriel Mountains for example rose five inches during the last earthquake.

3. Homer loved Hortense; therefore he agreed to change the corn husks in the mattress.

4. He has a cup of tea I think every time that he has a difficult decision to make.

5. The person who finishes last therefore will not receive any ice cream.

---

2. Use commas to set off nonrestrictive elements. Nonrestrictive elements are modifying words, phrases, or clauses that are not necessary to identify the words they modify. They include adjective subordinate clauses, appositives, and participial phrases.

Adjective Clauses

(See pages 148–149 if you need to review adjective clauses.) If the information in an adjective clause <u>is not necessary to identify the word it modifies</u>, it is called a **nonrestrictive clause**, and it is enclosed in commas.

► **EXAMPLE**   Ms. Erindira Sanchez, **who is president of that company,** began twenty years ago as a secretary.

Because the name of the person is used, the adjective clause is not necessary to identify which woman began twenty years ago as a secretary, so the commas are needed.

However, if her name is not used, the adjective clause is a **restrictive** one <u>because the woman is not already identified</u>. In this case, the commas are not necessary.

► **EXAMPLE**   The woman **who is president of that company** began twenty years ago as a secretary.

The following are additional examples of nonrestrictive clauses.

► **EXAMPLE**   My oldest brother, **who is a park ranger,** showed me his collection of arrowheads.

Because a person can have only one oldest brother, the brother is already identified, and the adjective clause is <u>not needed to identify him</u>, making it nonrestrictive.

► **EXAMPLE**   His home town, **which is somewhere in northeastern Indiana,** wants him to return for its centennial celebration.

A person can have only one home town, so the adjective clause is nonrestrictive.

■ **PRACTICE**   In the following sentences, set off all nonrestrictive clauses with commas.

1. My mother served me my favorite meal**,**which is red beans and rice and corn bread.

2. My oldest daughter who is a painter often uses *Alice in Wonderland* characters in her work.

3. Tranquility Base which was the name of the first lunar landing site was established in 1969.

4. The person who stole your cotton candy has been apprehended by the SWAT team.

5. *The Awakening* which was written by Kate Chopin in 1899 was not widely read until years after her death.

Participial Phrases

(See pages 138–140 if you need to review participial phrases.) Participial phrases that <u>do not contain information necessary to identify the words they modify</u> are nonrestrictive and are therefore set off by commas. Restrictive participial phrases do not require commas.

▶ **EXAMPLE**   (nonrestrictive)   The President, **seeking to be reelected**, traveled throughout the country making speeches and kissing babies.

Because we have only one president, the participial phrase *seeking to be re-elected* is nonrestrictive. It is not necessary to identify who is meant by *President.*

▶ **EXAMPLE**   (restrictive)   The woman **sitting by the door** is a famous surgeon.

Sitting by the door is a restrictive participial phrase because it is necessary to identify which woman is the famous surgeon.

▶ **EXAMPLE**   Foxworth, **discouraged by years of failure**, decided to buy a pet chimpanzee.

Discouraged by years of failure is a nonrestrictive past participial phrase. It is not necessary to identify Foxworth.

■ **PRACTICE**   In the following sentences, set off nonrestrictive participial phrases with commas.

1. Billy Claiborn**,**delighted at the antics of the juggler**,**laughed and laughed.

2. Virginia's toy poodle feeling lost and alone wandered slowly down the street.

3. Leonard Cohen trying not to show his despair kept singing in front of the three beautiful women in black.

4. Roxanne trained always to be polite tried not to giggle at the sight of such a large nose.

5. The concert was about to begin, and Troy hoping to play well closed his eyes in concentration.

Appositives

(See pages 150–151 if you need to review appositives.) Appositives usually contain information <u>not necessary to identify the words they modify</u> and are therefore nonrestrictive. Set them off with commas.

▶ **EXAMPLES**   Natalie's mother, **a lawyer in Boston**, will be coming to visit her soon.

Kleenex, **a household necessity**, was invented as a substitute for bandages during World War I because of a cotton shortage.

Parker took his stamp collection to Mr. Poindexter, **a noted stamp expert**.

■ **PRACTICE**   In the following sentences, set off all nonrestrictive appositives with commas.

1. The Purple Lily, my favorite restaurant, is located just two blocks from my home.

2. Perry's father a retired librarian swore that he never wanted to see another book.

3. Hamlet did not know what to do about his uncle the new king of Denmark.

4. The poodle a popular household pet was first bred in Germany as a hunting dog.

5. Mammoth Mountain one of Bill's favorite places to ski received seven feet of new snow last week.

---

3. <u>Use commas to separate most explanatory words from direct quotations.</u>

▶ **EXAMPLES**   **Mr. Jones asked,** "Where are you going?"

"I will arrive before dinner is over," **he remarked.**

"Tonight's dinner," **he said,** "will be delayed."

NOTE: Do not use commas to separate explanatory words from a partial direct quotation.

▶ **EXAMPLE**   He described the clouds as "ominous, dark, and threatening."

4. <u>Use commas to set off words of direct address.</u> If a writer addresses someone directly in a sentence, the word or words that stand for that person or persons are set off by commas. If the word or words in direct address begin the sentence, they are followed by a comma.

► **EXAMPLES**

And now, **my good friends**, I think it is time to end this conversation.

Mr. Chairman, I rise to a point of order.

I would like to present my proposal, **my esteemed colleagues**.

5. <u>Use commas to set off dates and addresses.</u> If your sentence contains two, three, or more elements of the date or address, use commas to set off these elements. The following sentences contain two or more elements.

► **EXAMPLES**

We visited Disneyland on **Monday, June 5**, in order to avoid the weekend rush.

We visited Disneyland on **Monday, June 5, 1998**, in order to avoid the weekend rush.

Celia has lived at **3225 Oliver Street, San Diego**, for five years.

Celia has lived at **3225 Oliver Street, San Diego, California**, for five years.

Celia has lived at **3225 Oliver Street, San Diego, California 92023**, for five years.

NOTE: The ZIP code is not separated from the state by a comma.

The following sentences contain only one element.

► **EXAMPLES**

We visited Disneyland on **Monday** in order to avoid the weekend rush.

Celia has lived at **3225 Oliver Street** for five years.

■ **PRACTICE**

In the following sentences, use commas to set off words in direct address or dates and addresses that have two or more elements.

1. Jill, did you say your address was 579 Concord Boulevard, Portsmouth, New Hampshire?

2. Alphonse was sure that January 18 1998 would be the day the world ended.

3. Tell me Candi where you were in the fall of 1985.

4. Send this order of trout to Harbor House 2978 South First Street Seattle

Washington by noon tomorrow.

5. Chelsea please close the door to the basement.

■ **PRACTICE**   Use commas to set off parenthetical expressions, nonrestrictive elements, explanatory words for direct quotations, words in direct address, and dates and addresses that have two or more elements.

1. Marvin Blasco, of course, never passes up a chance to indulge in chocolate.

2. Gary stood up in the middle of the meeting and said "Use the force Luke."

3. *Dracula* a novel by Bram Stoker has scared many readers and has been the

subject of many movies.

4. Will you please help me with this job Bartleby?

5. Henry moved into his house next to the volcano on February 5 1999 and

stayed there for two years.

6. Bill was born in a hospital in Knoxville Tennessee in 1943 on a warm

summer evening.

7. Kenneth suddenly remembered his pet iguana forgotten in his car two

hours ago.

8. The Toronto Blue Jays Jordan's favorite baseball team moved into first

place last week.

9. The first part of the rafting trip however is smooth and safe.

10. Andrea give your report to Pam who will read and approve it.

Rules for the Use of the Comma

1. <u>Use a comma before a coordinating conjunction that joins two main clauses.</u>

2. <u>Use commas to separate elements in a series.</u>

   a. Elements in a series may be words, phrases, or clauses.

   b. Two or more adjectives that modify the same noun may need to be separated with commas.

3. <u>Use a comma after an introductory element.</u> Introductory elements include:

   a. Introductory words

   b. Transitional expressions

   c. Prepositional phrases

   d. Verbal phrases

   e. Adverb clauses

4. <u>Use commas to separate interrupters from the rest of the sentence.</u> Interrupters include:

   a. Parenthetical expressions

   b. Nonrestrictive clauses

   c. Nonrestrictive participial phrases

   d. Appositives

   e. Explanatory words for direct quotations

   f. Words in direct address

   g. Dates and addresses with two or more elements

Exercise 1A

Add commas to the following sentences where necessary.

1. Clayborn was wrong about his accusations, and he knew it.

2. Nevertheless he refused to apologize to anyone whom he had falsely accused.

3. Arachna had long thin arms and legs but never considered herself unattractive.

4. The group performed a hip-hop version of "Eleanor Rigby" a Beatles song.

5. In fact he would not let anyone see his copy of *Spam Recipes for the World Traveler.*

6. My dentist who is also a lepidopterist has pictures of butterflies on his office walls.

7. At the end of the tedious boring film the main character smokes a last cigar and mercifully walks away forever.

8. Narcissus staring into the still pond fell in love with his own reflection.

9. Heartened by the audience's enthusiasm Hominy Grits a tissue-and-comb band decided to do an encore.

10. Bruce it is time to start gathering essays for next semester's exam.

11. Because he refused to give up Gordon was able to finish his plate of linguine.

12. On April 1 1992 the presidential candidate held a news conference but his vague evasive answers shed no new light on his views.

13. They were alone for thirty balmy days in a hot air balloon; however all the couple could think of to do was tell knock-knock jokes.

14. Yes I also eagerly await the arrival in Sandspur South Dakota of the first McDonald's.

15. Humphrey Bogart who starred in *Casablanca* never did make the request "Play it again Sam."

Exercise 1B

Add commas to the following sentences where necessary.

1. Once the train was out of sight, Twyla began her long walk home.

2. Many people for example dislike Ernest Hemingway's writing style.

3. Appearing calm and unconcerned about the approaching tornado Dorothy took Toto for a walk.

4. Ants invaded the kitchen and weeds overwhelmed the garden.

5. The new manager of the baseball team frightened by the threats to his life called the police.

6. Vylani was proud of her proficiency at origami the ancient Japanese art of paper folding.

7. Miss Emily did not know who the new mayor was nor did she care what the townspeople had to say about her.

8. To save money for his trip to Apple Valley Carl stole all of his neighbors' Sunday newspapers and then he clipped the coupons from them.

9. Phrona lived in Sioux Falls South Dakota from April 3 1945 to September 12 1999 when she moved to Seattle Washington.

10. Ryan looked at his list of things to do added a few more items to it and then left for the beach.

11. Confused by the noise and bright lights Elmer fell off the stage and into the audience.

12. Lizzie Borden who supposedly killed her mother with an ax was actually acquitted of the crime.

13. Because Sylvester refused to brush his teeth his mother enrolled him in a new self-help group Halitosis Anonymous.

Exercise 1B

continued

14. Mario who recently won the Employee of the Month award was described by a co-worker

as "a lazy good-for-nothing bum."

15. "Does anyone know" asked Steve "who took my answering machine computer and copier?"

Exercise 1C

In the following paragraph, add commas wherever they are needed.

1. Two familiar love stories **,** one a tragedy and one a comedy **,** are actually modern versions of earlier tales. **2.** For example the 1957 musical *West Side Story* and Shakespeare's *Romeo and Juliet* have many similarities. **3.** Both stories involve a conflict between two major groups of people—two gangs the Jets and Sharks from lower Manhattan in *West Side Story* and two families the Montagues and Capulets of Verona in *Romeo and Juliet*. **4.** In *West Side Story* Tony and Maria must hide their love from their friends and in *Romeo and Juliet* the central characters must hide their love from their families. **5.** Although both love affairs have the potential to bring the warring factions together ultimately they fail to do so. **6.** Each story ends in death; however Romeo and Juliet kill themselves but Tony is gunned down by a rival gang member while Maria lives. **7.** Another story Steve Martin's comedy *Roxanne* is based on the nineteenth-century play *Cyrano de Bergerac*. **8.** The central characters of both stories are witty well-spoken men who believe their long noses would prevent the beautiful Roxanne from loving them. **9.** They both are swordsmen (although Steve Martin's sword is a tennis racket) and they both provide the words for a man named Chris (or Christian in the earlier version) to woo Roxanne. **10.** In the Steve Martin version the central character who is played by Steve Martin ultimately wins Roxanne's love but that is not true for all earlier versions of the story. **11.** These two love stories are of course just two of many modern plays films and novels that are based on earlier works of literature.

Other Punctuation Marks

Punctuation would be simple if we could just include a page of punctuation marks at the end of a piece of writing and invite readers to sprinkle them about anywhere they choose. But if you want to be an effective writer, it helps a great deal to know how to use not only those troublesome commas but also all of the other marks of punctuation. In this section, we will take up end punctuation and the other punctuation marks.

The placement of punctuation marks can affect the meaning of a sentence profoundly. Here are a few examples.

In this sentence, the dog recognizes its owner.

▶ EXAMPLE   A clever dog knows **its** master.

In this one, the dog is in charge.

▶ EXAMPLE   A clever dog knows **it's** master.

In this sentence, we find a deliberately rude butler.

▶ EXAMPLE   The butler stood by the door and called the **guests** names as they entered.

In this sentence, he is more mannerly.

▶ EXAMPLE   The butler stood by the door and called the **guests'** names as they entered.

And in this sentence, we find a person who doesn't trust his friends.

▶ EXAMPLE   Everyone **I know** has secret ambitions.

Add two commas, and you change the meaning.

▶ EXAMPLE   Everyone, **I know,** has secret ambitions.

As you can see, punctuation marks are potent tools.

End Punctuation

The Period

1. The period is used at the end of a sentence that makes a statement or gives a command.

▶ EXAMPLES   This rule is probably the easiest of all.

Circle the subject in the above sentence.

2. The period is used with most abbreviations.

▶ **EXAMPLES**   Mr., Mrs., Dr., A.D., Ph.D., U.S., min., sec., tsp., Sgt., Lt.

The Question Mark

1. The question mark is used at the end of sentences that ask questions.

▶ **EXAMPLES**   Where have all the flowers gone?

Is the water hot yet?

2. A question mark is not used at the end of an indirect question.

▶ **EXAMPLES**   (direct question)   Why is Emile going to the dance?

(indirect question)   I wonder why Emile is going to the dance.

The Exclamation Point

1. The exclamation point is used after words, phrases, and short sentences that show strong emotion.

▶ **EXAMPLES**   Rats!

Not on your life!

Watch it, Buster!

Ouch! That hurt!

2. The exclamation point is not often used in college writing. For the most part, the words themselves should express the excitement.

▶ **EXAMPLE**   Chased by a ravenous pack of ocelots, Cedric raced through the forest to his condo, bolted up his stairs, swiftly locked the door, and threw himself, quivering and exhausted, onto his beanbag chair.

■ **PRACTICE**   Use periods, question marks, and exclamation points in the following sentences.

1. I wonder if Gloria will wear her new dress to the fiesta.

2. Have you seen my new car

3. Don't touch me, you fiend

4. Ask Melanie if her back still hurts

5. Why does everyone keep staring at me and laughing

6. How does that movie end

7. Go jump in a lake

8. After her name were the letters M D

9. Has Dr Payne agreed to treat you

10. Smithers asked why the bank had closed early

Internal Punctuation

The Semicolon

1. A semicolon is used to join two main clauses that are not joined by a coordinating conjunction. Sometimes a transitional word or phrase follows the semicolon.

► **EXAMPLES**   Thirteen people saw the incident; each one described it differently.

All tragedies end in death; on the other hand, all comedies end in marriage.

2. A semicolon can be used to join elements in a series when the elements require further internal punctuation.

► **EXAMPLE**   Before making his decision, Elrod consulted his banker, who abused him; his lawyer, who ignored him; his minister, who consoled him; and his mother, who scolded him.

3. Do not use a semicolon to separate two phrases or two subordinate clauses.

► **EXAMPLE**   (incorrect)   I will pay you for the work when you return the tape deck that was stolen from our car; and when you repair the dented left fender.

The Colon

1. A colon is used to join two main clauses when the second clause is an example, an explanation, or a restatement of the first clause.

► **EXAMPLES**   The past fifty years had been a time of turmoil: war, drought, and famine had plagued the small country.

The garden was a delight to all insects: aphids abounded in it, ladybugs exulted in it, and praying mantises cavorted in it.

2. A colon is used when a complete sentence introduces an example, a series, a list, or a direct quotation. Often a colon will come after the words *follows* or *following*.

► **EXAMPLES**   The paper explored the comic elements of three Melville novels: *Moby Dick, Mardi,* and *Pierre.*

The list of complaints included the following items: leaky faucets, peeling wallpaper, and a nauseous green love seat.

3. A colon is generally not used after a verb.

► **EXAMPLES**   (incorrect)   At the store I bought: bread, eggs, and bacon.

(correct)   At the store I bought bread, eggs, and bacon.

■ **PRACTICE**   In the following sentences, add semicolons and colons where necessary.

1. Read the directions **;** then follow them carefully.

2. On his list were the following names Santa Claus, Peter Pan, and Batman.

3. Tessie looked forward to the lottery however, she did not really want

to win.

4. Please pick up these items Spam, garlic, sherry, flour, and salt.

5. Every night Wilbur had the same dream he saw himself flying through the

air in some strange machine.

Quotation Marks

1. Quotation marks are used to enclose direct quotations and dialogue.

► **EXAMPLES**   "When a stupid man is doing something he is ashamed of, he always declares that it is his duty."

—George Bernard Shaw

Woody Allen said, "If my film makes one more person miserable, I've done my job."

2. Quotation marks are not used with indirect quotations.

► **EXAMPLES**   (direct quotation)   Fernando said, "I will be at the airfield before the dawn."

(indirect quotation)   Fernando said that he would be at the airfield before the dawn.

3. <u>Place periods and commas inside quotation marks.</u>

▶ **EXAMPLES**

Flannery O'Connor wrote the short story "A Good Man Is Hard to Find."

"Always forgive your enemies—nothing annoys them so much," quipped Oscar Wilde.

4. <u>Place colons and semicolons outside quotation marks.</u>

▶ **EXAMPLES**

Priscilla was disgusted by the story "The Great Toad Massacre": it was grossly unfair to toads and contained too much gratuitous violence.

Abner felt everyone should read the essay "The Shocking State of Okra Cookery"; he had even had several copies made just in case he found someone who was interested.

5. <u>Place the question mark inside the quotation marks if the quotation is a question. Place the question mark outside the quotation marks if the quotation is not a question but the whole sentence is.</u>

▶ **EXAMPLES**

The poem asks, "What are patterns for?"

Did Mark Twain say, "Never put off until tomorrow what you can do the day after tomorrow"?

6. <u>Place the exclamation point inside the quotation marks if the quotation is an exclamation. Place it outside the quotation marks if the quotation is not an exclamation but the whole sentence is.</u>

▶ **EXAMPLES**

"An earwig in my ointment!" the disgusted pharmacist proclaimed.

Please stop saying "It's time to leave"!

■ **PRACTICE**

Add semicolons, colons, and quotation marks to the following sentences.

1. Francis said, "Paris is the most beautiful city in the world"; however, he had not seen Los Angeles yet.

2. Call me Ishmael are the opening words of what novel?

3. Evanne looked at her teacher and said, Have a good summer then she left the room.

4. Paul kept repeating the following words to himself One if by land, and two if by sea.

5. That last step was quite a surprise, said Peyton Farquhar.

6. Would you like to hear a riddle? asked the Sphinx.

7. Andrew stood up in the middle of the crowd and yelled, Somebody

   save me!

8. Where was Neil Armstrong when he said, That's one small step for a man,

   one giant leap for mankind?

9. Ambrose Bierce said, A bore is someone who talks when you wish him to

   listen.

10. Tina's team must have won she was smiling broadly as she entered the

    locker room.

The Apostrophe

1. <u>Apostrophes are used to form contractions.</u> The apostrophe replaces the
   omitted letter or letters.

I am	I'm	did not	didn't
you are	you're	is not	isn't
it is	it's	were not	weren't
they are	they're	will not	won't
does not	doesn't	cannot	can't

2. <u>Apostrophes are used to form the possessives of nouns and indefinite
   pronouns.</u>

   a. Add 's to form the possessive of all singular nouns and all indefinite
      pronouns.

► **EXAMPLES**

(singular nouns)   The **girl's** hair was shiny.

Charles's car is rolling down the hill.

(indefinite pronouns)   **Everyone's** watch was affected by the giant
magnet.

(compound words)   Mr. Giuliano left on Monday to attend his **son-
in-law's** graduation.

(joint possession)   **Vladimir and Natasha's** wedding was long and
elaborate.

b. Add only an apostrophe to form the possessive of plural nouns that end in *s*. However, add *'s* to form the possessive of plural nouns that do not end in *s*.

▶ **EXAMPLES**

(plural nouns that end in *s*)	The **Joneses'** cabin had been visited by an untidy bear.
	We could hear the three **friends'** conversation all the way down the hall.
(plural nouns that do not end in *s*)	During the storm the parents were concerned about their **children's** safety.

c. Expressions referring to time or money often require an apostrophe.

▶ **EXAMPLES**

Please give me one **dollar's** worth.

Two **weeks'** vacation is simply not enough.

3. Do not use apostrophes with the possessive forms of personal pronouns.

Incorrect	*Correct*
her's	hers
our's	ours
their's	theirs

NOTE: *It's* means "it is." The possessive form of *it* is *its*.

■ **PRACTICE** Add apostrophes (or *'s*) to the following sentences where necessary.

1. I wonder where Frederica's mother is; she doesn't answer her phone.

2. James car was last seen in front of a local liquor store.

3. Did you enjoy Mel Gibsons role in that movie?

4. The policer office was awarded two months salary for bravery in the line of duty.

5. Tinas problem was that she didnt know when to quit.

6. Its time to move the baby cockatiel away from its mother.

7. As he rode in the back of his managers car, the boxer said, "I couldve been a contender!"

8. The editor-in-chiefs poor judgment cost him a months pay.

9. Right in the middle of Billys concert, someones cell phone started to ring.

10. The three finalists hotel bills were paid for by our committee.

■ **PRACTICE**   Write sentences of your own according to the instructions.

1. Write a complete sentence in which you use the possessive form of *men.*

   The men's room is being remodeled.

   _____

2. Write a complete sentence in which you use the possessive form of *Charles.*

   _____

   _____

3. Write a complete sentence in which you use the possessive form of *father-in-law.*

   _____

   _____

4. Write a complete sentence in which you use the possessive form of *people.*

   _____

   _____

5. Write a complete sentence in which you use the possessive form of *Mr. Andrews* and the contraction for *does not.*

   _____

   _____

Section Two Review

1. Use a **period** at the end of sentences that make statements or commands.

2. Use a **period** to indicate most abbreviations.

3. Use a **question mark** at the end of sentences that ask questions.

4. Do not use a **question mark** at the end of an indirect question.

5. Use an **exclamation point** after exclamatory words, phrases, and short sentences.

6. Use the **exclamation point** sparingly in college writing.

7. Use a **semicolon** to join two main clauses that are not joined by a coordinating conjunction.

8. Use a **semicolon** to separate elements in a series when the elements require further internal punctuation.

9. Do not use a **semicolon** to separate two phrases or two subordinate clauses.

10. Use a **colon** to join two main clauses when the second main clause is an example, an explanation, or a restatement.

11. Use a **colon** to introduce an example, a series, a list, or a direct quotation.

12. Do not use a **colon** to introduce a series of items that follows a verb.

13. Use **quotation marks** to enclose direct quotations and dialogue.

14. Do not use **quotation marks** with indirect quotations.

15. Place periods and commas inside **quotation marks.**

16. Place colons and semicolons outside **quotation marks.**

17. If a quotation is a question, place the question mark <u>inside</u> the **quotation marks.** If the quotation is not a question, but the whole sentence is, place the question mark <u>outside</u> the quotation marks.

18. If the quotation is an exclamation, place the exclamation mark <u>inside</u> the **quotation marks.** If the quotation is not an exclamation, but the whole sentence is, place the exclamation point <u>outside</u> the quotation marks.

19. Use **apostrophes** to form contractions.

20. Use **apostrophes** to form the possessives of nouns and indefinite pronouns.

Exercise 2A

Add periods, question marks, exclamation points, semicolons, colons, quotation marks, and apostrophes (or *'s*) to the following sentences as necessary.

1. Watch out!

2. Matthew wondered why so many people were leaving the city

3. Isnt Dad ever coming home asked Telemachus

4. Each of these people was one of Garths heroes Roy Rogers, Hopalong Cassidy, and Gene Autry

5. A tiny sparrow landed on my friends shoulder and pecked at his ear

6. Mark Twain said, Never put off till tomorrow what you can do the day after tomorrow just as well

7. Rodrigo looked at me and asked, Do you know the way to San Jose

8. A tornado warning was posted this morning as a result, we have canceled the race

9. Did Ogden Nash say, Candy is dandy, but liquor is quicker

10. Kay Scarpetta, M D , finished the autopsy at 2:35 P M and headed for home

11. The lion paced rapidly up and down in its cage then it suddenly turned and stared at my youngest daughters cotton candy

12. Boyds mother brought asparagus wine to the reception however, no one would drink it because of its olive green tint

13. Where do you think youre going with my fathers wallet

14. The company commander looked at his troops and yelled, Forward

15. Arlene Mitchell, M D, looked at the X-rays and then asked, Have you been eating paper clips

Exercise 2B

Add periods, question marks, exclamation points, semicolons, colons, quotation marks, apostrophes (or *'s*), and commas to the following sentences where necessary.

1. Deliver this package to the old mansion with all of its windows broken at 203 Pierce Boulevard, Concordia, California.

2. That hurts yelled John when his sister touched his sunburned back.

3. Are you still planning to build a pyramid or have you changed your mind

4. I didnt care for the Smiths appetizers however the soup certainly deserved a round of applause

5. Henry finally admitted that hed taken the last eclair of course none of us were surprised

6. Its like déjà vu all over again said Yogi Berra.

7. Ralph Waldo Emerson said That which we call sin in others is experiment in us however not everyone would agree with Emerson

8. Did Robin ask Marian if she believed the sheriffs accusation

9. Marthas son asked Was Abe really honest

10. What a wonderful view exclaimed Jack as he stood at the top of Mount Everest.

11. Harley Starling stated When I sell my poem Ill acquire the following a black cloak with a scarlet lining a floor-length scarf a beret a mysterious girlfriend and a battered typewriter

12. The minister wondered if anyones attention was on him that morning

13. Where have all the flowers gone asks a well-known folk song.

14. The childrens trip to the park was interrupted when the vans right front tire blew out

15. I dont want to see you again in addition I want you to return the gifts that I gave you

Exercise 2C

In the following paragraph, correct any errors in the use of periods, exclamation points, question marks, semicolons, colons, quotation marks, or apostrophes.

1. Two years ago, I moved from Sunset Shores, a fifty-year-old beach community on the Pacific, to Oak Grove, a newly formed city at the edge of the high desert. **2.** At the time, the two places seemed to be as different as they could be however, over the two years' that I have lived in Oak Grove, many similarities between the two cities have become apparent. **3.** One of the first similarities that I noticed was: the clean, spacious skies of both cities. **4.** Since Sunset Shores sits on the edge of the Pacific, it's skies are always fresh and clear; swept clean by the constant ocean breezes. **5.** From the hill's of Sunset Shores, I have often looked out over the Pacific and said to myself, "The sky and the ocean seem to go on forever". **6.** In Oak Grove the same endless sky and clean breezes are present. **7.** Standing in the middle of the city and looking in any direction; one can see Oak Groves deep blue sky sweeping off to a horizon far in the distance. **8.** In addition, every afternoon warm desert breeze's scrub the atmosphere clean. **9.** "Oak Groves' air", says my neighbor, "seems to sparkle." **10.** Another similarity between the two cities is the residents commitment to each other, both cities have a true small-town atmosphere. **11.** Sunset Shores, although only one of many suburbs of San Diego; has always managed to maintain its' own unique sense of geographic and cultural identity. **12.** Its surrounded by hills on the: north, south, and east; and protected by the ocean to the west, so it's residents quickly get to know each other and take pride in their unique town. **13.** Oak Groves residents feel much the same way. **14.** Like Sunset Shores, Oak Grove is physically separated from neighboring cities', so its residents spend their time with each other; developing a sense of pride in their own community. **15.** I often hear people in Oak Grove say that "they have more friends here than theyve ever had before." **16.** Its undeniable that there are many differences between Sunset Shores and Oak Grove, but Ive come to think: that the similarities far outweigh any differences.

Titles, Capitalization, and Numbers

The rules regarding titles, capitalization, and numbers are not, perhaps, as critical to clear writing as the ones for the punctuation marks discussed in the previous two sections. In fact, you can forget to capitalize at all without losing the meaning of what you are writing. So why should you learn to apply these rules correctly? The answer is simple. You should know how to apply them for the same reason you should know whether it is appropriate to slap a person on the back or to kiss him on both cheeks when you are first introduced. **How people write** says as much about them as **how they act**. Your ability to apply the rules presented in this section, as well as in other sections, identifies you as an educated person.

Titles

1. Underline or place in italics the titles of works that are published separately, such as books, periodicals, and plays.

   - Books: Huckleberry Finn, Webster's Dictionary
   - Plays: Hamlet, Death of a Salesman
   - Pamphlets: How to Paint Your House, Worms for Profit
   - Long musical works: Beethoven's Egmont Overture, Miles Davis's Kind of Blue
   - Long poems: Paradise Lost, Beowulf
   - Periodicals: New York Times, Newsweek
   - Films: Titanic, Psycho
   - Television and radio programs: Friends, Morning Edition
   - Works of art: Rembrandt's Night Watch, Venus de Milo

   ▶ **EXAMPLES**   Hortencia has subscriptions to Newsweek and The New Yorker.

   The Los Angeles Chamber Orchestra played Bach's Brandenburg Concerto Number Five.

2. Use quotation marks to enclose the titles of works that are parts of other works, such as articles, songs, poems, and short stories.

   - Songs: "Honeysuckle Rose," "Yesterday"
   - Poems: "Stopping by Woods on a Snowy Evening," "The Waste Land"

- Articles in periodicals: "Texas Air's New Flak Attack," "Of Planets and the Presidency"
- Short stories: "Paul's Case," "Barn Burning"
- Essays: "A Modest Proposal," "Once More to the Lake"
- Episodes of radio and television programs: "Tolstoy: From Rags to Riches," "Lord Mountbatten: The Last Viceroy"
- Subdivisions of books: "The Pulpit" (Chapter Eight of *Moby Dick*)

▶ **EXAMPLES**
The professor played a recording of Dylan Thomas reading his poem "After the Funeral."

Many writing textbooks include Jonathan Swift's essay "A Modest Proposal."

■ **PRACTICE**
In the following sentences, correct any errors in the use of titles.

1. My mother was sitting in a lawn chair and reading C. S. Lewis's novel <u>Till We Have Faces</u>.

2. Everyday Use is the title of a popular short story by Alice Walker.

3. On the table in the car repair shop were copies of Architectural Digest and Psychology Today magazines.

4. Robert Frost's poem Design features a fat white spider.

5. Two of his favorite movies are Invaders from Mars and Swamp Thing.

Capitalization

1. Capitalize the personal pronoun *I*.

▶ **EXAMPLE**
In fact, I am not sure I like the way you said that.

2. Capitalize the first letter of every sentence.

▶ **EXAMPLE**
The road through the desert was endlessly straight and boring.

3. Capitalize the first letter of each word in a title except for *a, an,* and *the,* coordinating conjunctions, and prepositions.

NOTE: The first letter of the first word and the first letter of the last word of a title are always capitalized.

- Titles of books: <u>Moby Dick</u>, <u>Encyclopaedia Britannica</u>
- Titles of newspapers and magazines: <u>People</u>, <u>Cosmopolitan</u>, <u>Los Angeles Times</u>
- Titles of stories, poems, plays, and films: "The Lady with the Dog," "The Road Not Taken," <u>Othello</u>, <u>Gone with the Wind</u>

4. <u>Capitalize the first letter of all proper nouns and adjectives derived from proper nouns.</u>

- Names and titles of people: Coretta Scott King, Mr. Birch, Mayor Golding, President Roosevelt, Cousin Alice, Aunt Bea
- Names of specific places: Yosemite National Park, Albuquerque, New Mexico, London, England, Saudi Arabia, Rockefeller Center, London Bridge, Elm Street, Venus, the Rio Grande, the Rocky Mountains, the Midwest

NOTE: Do not capitalize the first letter of words that refer to a direction (such as "north," "south," "east," or "west"). Do capitalize these words when they refer to a specific region.

▶   **EXAMPLES**

Texas and Arizona are in the **Southwest.**

The police officer told us to drive **east** along the gravel road and turn **north** at the big pine tree.

- Names of national, ethnic, or racial groups: Indian, Native American, Spanish, Irish, Italian, African American
- Names of groups or organizations: Baptists, Mormons, Democrats, Republicans, American Indian Movement, Boy Scouts of America, Indianapolis Colts, U.S. Post Office
- Names of companies: Ford Motor Company, Montgomery Ward, Coca Cola Bottling Company
- Names of the days of the week and months of the year but not the seasons: Thursday, August, spring
- Names of holidays and historical events: Memorial Day, the Fourth of July, the French Revolution, the Chicago Fire
- Names of <u>specific</u> gods and religious writings: God, Mohammed, Talmud, Bible

5. The names of academic subjects are not capitalized unless they refer to an ethnic or national origin or are the names of specific courses. Examples include mathematics, political science, English, History 105.

■ PRACTICE · Correct any errors in the use of titles or capitalization.

       O   F   S   L A   P

1. On friday, september 2, the los angeles philharmonic will present
    B   S   N   F
Beethoven's symphony number five.

2. e. annie proulx won the pulitzer prize in 1994 for her novel the shipping news.

3. each summer i look forward to catching up on reading my old mad magazines.

4. the beach boys' song the little old lady from pasadena is one of my mom's favorites.

5. when homer had the chance to buy the brooklyn bridge, he called hortense in south dakota with the good news.

6. every year danville sponsors an easter egg hunt on the saturday before easter sunday.

7. a majority of the people in south africa used to feel that they did not participate in their government's decisions.

8. arthur miller's play death of a salesman starred brian dennehy when it was last performed on television.

9. as professor hohman sat in the airliner, a flight attendant offered her copies of time, american pilot, and new yorker magazines.

10. next winter we will rent a cabin in mammoth lakes, california, which is located north of lone pine.

Numbers

The following rules about numbers apply to general writing rather than to technical or scientific writing.

1. <u>Spell out numbers that require no more than two words. Use numerals for numbers that require more than two words.</u>

▶ **EXAMPLES**

Last year it rained on only **eighty-four** days.

In 1986 it rained on more than **120** days.

2. <u>Always spell out a number at the beginning of a sentence.</u>

▶ **EXAMPLE**

Six hundred ninety miles in one day is a long way to drive.

3. <u>In general, use numerals in the following situations:</u>

- Dates: August 9, 2000   30 A.D.

- Sections of books and plays: Chapter 5, page 22
  Act 1, scene 3, lines 30–41

- Addresses: 1756 Grand Avenue
  Hemostat, Idaho 60047

- Decimals, percents, and fractions: 75.8   30%, 30 percent   1/5

- Exact amounts of money: $7.95 $1,300,000

- Scores and statistics: Padres 8 Dodgers 5   a ratio of 6 to 1

- Time of day: 3:05   8:15

NOTE: Round amounts of money that can be expressed in a few words can be written out: *twenty cents, fifty dollars, one hundred dollars.* Also, when the word *o'clock* is used with the time of day, the time of day can be written out: *seven o'clock.*

4. <u>When numbers are compared, are joined by conjunctions, or occur in a series, either consistently use numerals or consistently spell them out.</u>

▶ **EXAMPLE**

For the company picnic we need **twenty-five** pounds of fried chicken, **fifteen** pounds of potato salad, **one hundred twenty-five** cans of soda, **eighty-five** paper plates, **two hundred thirty** napkins, and **eighty-five** sets of plastic utensils.

OR

For the company picnic we need **25** pounds of fried chicken, **15** pounds of potato salad, **125** cans of soda, **85** paper plates, **230** napkins, and **85** sets of plastic utensils.

■   **PRACTICE**   Correct any errors in the use of numbers in the following sentences.

Five thousand
1. ~~5000~~ runners participated in the marathon Saturday.

2. Trains from New York will be arriving at eight o'clock, 8:15, and eight-thirty-two.

3. For the class party, Suzette bought 10 boxes of plastic knives and forks, one hundred forty-five paper plates of various sizes, 55 plastic cups, one hundred ten paper coffee cups, and three hundred fifty paper napkins.

4. Lisette moved to one hundred fifteen Normandy Street on March second, 1999.

5. Mr. Johnson told 5 of his students to read Act One, scene four of the play.

Section Three Review

1. Underline or place in italics the **titles** of works that are published separately, such as books, plays, and films.

2. Use quotation marks to enclose the **titles** of works that are parts of other works, such as songs, poems, and short stories.

3. **Capitalize** the personal pronoun *I*.

4. **Capitalize** the first letter of every sentence.

5. **Capitalize** the first letter of each word in a title except *a, an, the,* coordinating conjunctions, and prepositions.

6. **Capitalize** all proper nouns and adjectives derived from proper nouns.

7. **Do not capitalize** names of academic subjects unless they refer to an ethnic or national origin or are the names of specific courses.

8. Spell out **numbers** that require no more than two words. Use numerals for numbers that require more than two words.

9. Always spell out a **number** at the beginning of a sentence.

10. In general, use **numerals** for dates, sections of books and plays, addresses, decimals, percents, fractions, exact amounts of money, scores, statistics, and time of day.

11. When **numbers** are compared, are joined by conjunctions, or occur in a series, either consistently use numerals or consistently spell them out.

Exercise 3A

The following sentences contain errors in the use of titles, capitalization, and numbers. Correct any errors you find.

1. After the film was released, the theme music from *C*hariots of *F*ire became popular.

2. The song white christmas was first sung by bing crosby in the movie holiday inn.

3. 92 people moved away from fargo, north dakota, during the latest floods.

4. Once the clock read two twenty-five, every student in mojave desert high school was ready to go home.

5. Last night our softball team, which is called comedy of errors, defeated the defending league champs by a score of twenty-five to twenty.

6. When the cambodian tourist saw the 5 mustangs and the fifteen morgan horses, he was quite impressed.

7. My original edition of the novel old yeller was worth more than the three hundred ninety-five dollars that I was offered, so I donated it to the carlsbad public library.

8. While working at ralph's supermarket last night, I stocked 115 boxes of cereal, twelve cases of diapers, 45 bags of potato chips, and two hundred three oranges.

9. Sometimes the powdermilk biscuit company sponsors a portion of the weekly radio program a prairie home companion.

10. One of my favorite selections by the jazz group blurring the edges is called canticle for richard.

11. When the nbc nightly news was over, eudora sat down and read a newsweek magazine essay entitled i am not an economist.

12. According to the magazine world weekly news, eight out of ten people who shop at super-markets buy one of those gossip newspapers like national enquirer.

13. Chloe wrote in her notebook as professor sandoval told the literature 120 class that the turning point in hamlet is in act three.

Exercise 3A

continued

14. Impressionism, a style of painting initiated by claude monet, derives its name from monet's painting entitled impression: sunrise.

15. The essay entitled spam: text and subtext won first place and a prize of 15 ripe avocados in rocco's health 101 class.

Exercise 3B

Compose sentences of your own according to the instructions.

1. Write a sentence that includes the author and title of a book.

   During his vacation, Rafael read Tom Clancy's novel

   Patriot Games.

2. Write a sentence that describes a song you like and the musician who wrote it or performs it.

   _____

   _____

3. Tell what movie you last saw in a theater and how much you paid to see it.

   _____

   _____

4. Write a sentence that tells what school you attend and what classes you are taking.

   _____

   _____

5. Write a sentence that tells the number of people in your family, the number of years you have gone to school, the number of classes you are taking, and the approximate number of students at your school.

   _____

   _____

6. Write a sentence that mentions a magazine you have read lately. If possible, include the title of an article.

   _____

   _____

7. In a sentence, describe your favorite television program.

   _____

   _____

continued

8. Tell where you would go on your ideal vacation. Be specific about the name of the place and its geographical location.

_____

_____

9. Write a sentence that includes your age and address. (Feel free to lie about either one.)

_____

_____

10. Write a sentence that names a musician or musical group that you like and an album, tape, or compact disc that you like.

_____

_____

11. Write a sentence that includes the name of a local newspaper, its approximate circulation, and the average number of pages during the week.

_____

_____

12. Write a sentence that includes a work of art that you know about and the name of the artist. If you need to, make up the name of a work of art and its artist.

_____

_____

13. Write a sentence that includes the score of the last baseball, football, or basketball game you were aware of. If you are not a sports fan, make up a score.

_____

_____

continued

14. Write a sentence that tells what time you get up on Mondays, what time your first class starts, what time you have lunch, and what time you usually have dinner.

_____

_____

Exercise 3C

In the following paragraph, correct any errors in the use of capitalization, numbers, or titles.

1. One of the most striking ways to see how our attitudes toward ~~F~~amily life have changed over the past ~~40~~ *forty* years is to contrast a few ~~F~~amily sitcoms from recent years with those of the past. 2. For instance, the families in I Love Lucy and "Roseanne" portray 2 very different views of wife and mother. 3. Lucy lives in a Middle-Class apartment and is totally dependent on her entertainer husband, Ricky Ricardo. 4. A magazine article entitled Do I Really Love Lucy? describes her as a ditzy and relatively helpless housewife who is constantly getting herself into jams that Ricky has to get her out of. 5. The character of Roseanne, on the other hand, is anything but ditzy and is certainly not helpless. 6. She works as a Lower-Middle-Class waitress, and together she and her husband make about one thousand five hundred dollars a month. 7. "Time" magazine once described her as living life with a constant chip on her shoulder, but it went on to say that 2 redeeming features, her acerbic wit and her love for her family, make her character attractive. 8. 2 other family sitcoms, Father Knows Best and Married . . . with Children, also reflect a change in attitude toward the american family. 9. Led by Jim, a successful Insurance Agent, and Margaret, a 1950s wife and mother who always cleans house in a tasteful dress and high heels, the Andersons of Father Knows Best are portrayed as an ideal american family. 10. Jim and Margaret are patient, loving, well-dressed parents who have an answer to every problem, and their 3 children—Betty ("Princess"), Bud, and Kathy ("Kitten")—are happy and well adjusted. 11. The corresponding family on "Married . . . With Children" is quite different. 12. In fact, the article Life With The Bundys has called the show "anti-family" in its negative portrayal of Family Life. 13. Al Bundy is a lazy and decidedly unsuccessful Salesman of Ladies' Shoes, and his wife, Peg, is portrayed as a sex-starved floozy who shops and eats bonbons. 14. Their daughter, Kelly, who is as obsessed with Sex as her Mother, can barely count to 10, and their cynical son, Bud, is forever trying (unsuccessfully) to score with every girl he meets. 15. Clearly, Family Sitcoms and their portrayals of the american family have changed dramatically over the years.

Sentence Practice: Sentence Variety

Writing is challenging. As we have pointed out a number of times already, writing is a process that requires constant and countless choices. Much head scratching and crossing out go on between the beginning and the end of composing a paragraph. Each sentence can be framed in numerous ways, each version changing—subtly or dramatically—the relationships among the ideas.

Sometimes a short sentence is best. Look at the one that begins this paragraph and the one that begins the paragraph above. At other times you will need longer sentences to get just the right meaning and feeling. Sentence combining exercises give you an opportunity to practice how to express ideas in various ways by encouraging you to move words, phrases, and clauses around to achieve different effects.

When you construct a sentence, you should be aware not only of how it expresses your ideas but also of how it affects the other sentences in the paragraph. Consider the following paragraph as an example. It is the opening paragraph of Rachel Carson's book *The Edge of the Sea*.

The edge of the sea is a strange and beautiful place. All through the long history of the earth it has been an area of unrest where waves have broken heavily against the land, where the tides have pressed forward over the continents, receded, and then returned. For no two successive days is the shoreline precisely the same. Not only do the tides advance and retreat in their eternal rhythms, but the level of the sea itself is never at rest. It rises or falls as the glaciers melt or grow, as the floor of the deep ocean basins shifts under its increasing load of sediments, or as the earth's crust along the continental margins warps up or down in adjustment to strain and tension. Today a little more land may belong to the sea, tomorrow a little less. Always the edge of the sea remains an elusive and indefinable boundary.

As you can see, Rachel Carson opens her paragraph with a short, simple sentence. Then she writes a sentence that is much longer and more complicated because it begins to explain the general ideas in the first one. It even seems to capture the rhythm of the sea against the land. She follows that one with another short, simple sentence. As the paragraph continues, she varies the length and complexity of her sentences according to what she needs to say. Notice how she ends the paragraph with another simple statement that matches her opening sentence.

Sentence Combining Exercises

In the following sentence combining exercises, you will practice writing sentences so that some are short and concise and others are lengthier and more complex.

▶ **EXAMPLE**   Combine the following sentences into three sentences. Experiment with which sounds best.

   a. Sometimes a very simple idea can make a person wealthy.
   b. It was 1873.
   c. A fifteen-year-old boy was uncomfortable in the harsh Maine weather.
   d. He asked his mother to make him a pair of "ear flaps."
   e. All of his neighbors wanted pairs of their own.
   f. His family patented the idea.
   g. They soon became rich.
   h. They called their new product Ear Muffs.

Sometimes a very simple idea can make a person wealthy. In 1873, a fifteen-year-old boy was uncomfortable in the harsh Maine winter, so he asked his mother to make him a pair of "ear flaps." When all of his neighbors wanted pairs of their own, his family patented the idea and soon became rich, calling their new product Ear Muffs.

1. Combine the following sentences into two or three sentences.

   a. It was 1866.
   b. General Placido Vega of Mexico sent four of his men to San Francisco.
   c. They were to buy arms and ammunition.
   d. One man died before they reached San Francisco.
   e. That man was the only one who had the authority to approve any purchase.
   f. The other three men buried the six bags.
   g. The bags were full of gold and heirloom jewelry.
   h. The gold and jewelry were worth $200,000.
   i. They buried the bags in the hills outside of San Bruno.

_____

_____

_____

_____

Sentence Combining Exercises

continued

2. Combine the following sentences into two or three sentences.

   a. There was a shepherd named Diego Moreno.
   b. He saw the men bury the treasure.
   c. The men rode away.
   d. Diego unearthed the six bundles.
   e. He found gold and jewelry.
   f. It was enough to allow him to return to his home.
   g. His home was in Sonora, Mexico.
   h. He would be a rich man.

   _____

   _____

   _____

   _____

3. Combine the following sentences into two sentences.

   a. Diego was on his way home.
   b. He feared he was about to be robbed.
   c. He buried the treasure beneath a tree.
   d. The tree was in the Cahuenga Pass.
   e. The Cahuenga Pass is just north of present-day Hollywood.
   f. Diego rode on to Los Angeles.

   _____

   _____

   _____

   _____

continued

4. Combine the following sentences into three sentences.

    a. In Los Angeles Diego Moreno became ill.
    b. There was a wealthy rancho owner.
    c. He was named Jesus Martinez.
    d. He took Diego into his home.
    e. He cared for Diego.
    f. Diego Moreno was grateful.
    g. Diego told Don Jesus about the treasure.
    h. He promised to share it with Don Jesus.
    i. It was as soon as the promise had left his lips.
    j. Diego went into convulsions and died.

_____

_____

_____

_____

5. Combine the following sentences into three sentences.

    a. Jesus Martinez traveled to the Cahuenga Pass.
    b. His stepson Gumisindo Correa traveled with him.
    c. They went to find the treasure.
    d. They found the tree.
    e. It was the tree Diego Moreno had told them about.
    f. They began to dig beneath the tree.
    g. At that very moment Don Jesus had a seizure and died.
    h. His stepson fled from the area.
    i. He vowed never to return.

_____

_____

_____

_____

Sentence Combining Exercises

continued

6. Combine the following sentences into three sentences.

   a. General Vega's three agents returned to San Bruno Hills.
   b. They intended to retrieve the treasure they had buried.
   c. They discovered it had been stolen.
   d. Two of the men were suspicious of each other.
   e. They began to argue.
   f. They drew their pistols.
   g. They killed each other.
   h. The third agent was murdered a few years later.
   i. He was in a mining dispute in Arizona.

   _____

   _____

   _____

   _____

7. Combine the following sentences into three sentences.

   a. It was 1886.
   b. A Basque shepherd found his dog digging.
   c. It was digging beneath a tree in the Cahuenga Pass.
   d. He looked at where the dog was digging.
   e. He found an old bag.
   f. The bag was full of gold coins and jewelry.
   g. The shepherd believed the treasure was a sign from God.
   h. The sign was to return to his home in Spain.

   _____

   _____

   _____

   _____

continued

8. Combine the following sentences into two sentences.

    a. The shepherd wanted to hide the treasure from robbers.
    b. He sewed the coins and jewelry into the lining of his poncho.
    c. He was wearing the poncho on a dock.
    d. The dock was in Barcelona Harbor.
    e. He lost his balance.
    f. He fell into the water.
    g. He drowned.

_____

_____

_____

_____

9. Combine the following sentences into three sentences.

    a. The rest of the treasure remained hidden.
    b. It was 1892.
    c. It was twenty-six years after the treasure was first buried.
    d. Gumisindo Correa heard the story about the single bag of treasure.
    e. It was the bag of treasure discovered by the Basque shepherd.
    f. Correa knew that six bags had been buried.
    g. He decided to return to the Cahuenga Pass.
    h. He wanted to find the other five bags.

_____

_____

_____

_____

Sentence Combining Exercises

continued

10. Combine the following sentences into two sentences.

    a. It was the day Correa planned to leave Los Angeles for the Cahuenga Pass.

    b. He was killed by an unknown assailant.

    c. To this day, no one has ever discovered the Cahuenga Pass treasure.

    d. It lies beneath some unmarked tree.

    e. The tree is between Hollywood and the San Fernando Valley.

_____

_____

_____

_____

Paragraph Practice:
Comparing and Contrasting

Writing Assignment

Comparing or contrasting two topics is an activity that you participate in nearly every day. When you recognize that two people have much in common, you have observed similarities between them. When you decide to take one route rather than another, you have noticed differences between the two routes. Even something as simple as buying one toothpaste rather than another involves some sort of comparison and contrast. In fact, recognizing similarities and differences affects every part of our lives. How could you know if you were looking at a tree or a bush if you were not able to see their differences as well as their similarities?

Much college writing involves comparing or contrasting two topics. You may be asked to compare (show similarities between) the results of two lab experiments in a biology class or to contrast (show differences between) the religious beliefs of two cultures in an anthropology class. In addition, in many classes you may be asked to write papers or reports or to take essay exams in which you show both the similarities and the differences between two related topics.

Exercises 1C, 2C, and 3C in this chapter are comparison/contrast paragraphs. Exercise 1C compares two modern love stories to two from the past; Exercise 2C compares a beach city to a desert city; and Exercise 3C contrasts two recent family sitcoms with two from the past. Note that each of these paragraphs opens with a topic sentence that points out a similarity or a difference. (Note also that the topic sentence in Exercise 2C is the second sentence, not the first sentence, of the paragraph.)

Reading Assignment

The reading selections in the "Comparing and Contrasting" section of Chapter Seven can help you see how professional writers examine similarities or differences. Read one or more of the selections, as assigned by your instructor, and use the questions that follow them to develop ideas for your own paper.

Prewriting

Prewriting Application: Finding Your Topic

As you read the following topics, remember that the one that looks the easiest may not result in the best paper for you. Use the techniques of freewriting, brainstorming, and/or clustering to develop your reactions to several of these ideas before you choose one of them. Look for the topic idea that interests you the most, the one you have an emotional or personal reaction to.

1. Compare and/or contrast your city or neighborhood with one you used to live in.

2. Compare and/or contrast a place as it is today with the way it was when you were a child.

3. Compare and/or contrast what you expected college to be like before you enrolled in your first class with what you found it to be like later on.

4. If you are returning to school after several years' absence, compare and/or contrast your last school experience with your current one.

5. Compare and/or contrast the characteristics of someone you know with the stereotype of that type of person. For example, if you know an athlete or a police officer, compare and/or contrast that person's actual personality with the stereotype people have of athletes or police officers.

6. Compare and/or contrast your latest vacation or trip with your vision of the ideal vacation or trip.

7. Compare and/or contrast two sports, two athletes, or two teams.

8. Compare and/or contrast the person you are today with the person you were several years ago.

9. Compare and/or contrast any two places, persons, or events that you remember well.

10. If you have a background in two cultures, compare and/or contrast a few specific characteristics of both cultures.

When you have decided on a likely topic, keep prewriting to develop your ideas. Don't worry about the "correctness" of your writing at this point. Just write down as many similarities or differences as you can think of, looking for those that will express your idea the very best.

Once you have decided on the most interesting similarities or differences, write a topic sentence to introduce them.

Prewriting Application: Working with Topic Sentences

Identify the topic sentences in Exercises 1C (page 271), 2C (page 283), and 3C (page 296). Then identify the topic and the central point in each topic sentence. Finally, state whether the topic sentence is introducing a paragraph that will examine similarities or differences.

Prewriting Application: Evaluating Topic Sentences

Write "No" before each sentence that would not make an effective topic sentence *for this assignment*. Write "Yes" before each sentence that would make an effective one and identify it as introducing a paragraph about similarities or differences. Be prepared to explain your answers.

_____ **1.** I had not seen my hometown of Monroe, South Dakota, for over fifteen years, so when I visited it last summer I was amazed at how little it had changed.

_____ **2.** My father and mother love to watch the Kentucky Derby.

_____ **3.** Many holidays that are common to both Mexico and the United States are celebrated in very different ways.

_____ **4.** Our society is much worse in this day and age than it used to be.

_____ **5.** This year's San Diego Padres is a better team than last year's in several key areas.

_____ **6.** *Roxanne*, a 1980s movie starring Steve Martin, contains many similarities to the play *Cyrano de Bergerac*.

_____ **7.** About the only thing that snowboarders and skiers have in common is that they share the same mountain.

_____ **8.** While walking down the Las Vegas Strip last year, I was amazed at how bright and colorful everything was, even at two o'clock in the morning.

_____ **9.** Although both the San Diego Zoo and the Wild Animal Park feature exotic animals, the two places are not at all similar.

_____ **10.** Many things have happened to me in the past few years to make me a more tolerant person.

Prewriting Application: Talking to Others

Form a group of three or four people and discuss the topics you have chosen. Your goal here is to help each other clarify the differences or similarities that you are writing about. Explain your points as clearly as you can. As you listen to the others in your group, use the following questions to help them clarify their ideas.

1. Is the paragraph focusing on similarities or on differences?

2. Exactly what similarities or differences will be examined in the paragraph? Can you list them?

3. Which similarities or differences need to be explained more clearly or fully?

4. Which points are the most significant or most interesting? Why?

5. Which similarity or difference should the paper open with? Which should it close with?

Organizing Similarities and Differences

One of the most effective ways to present your ideas when you compare or contrast two topics is called a **point-by-point** organization. Using this method, you cover one similarity or difference at a time. For example, if you were contrasting snowboarders and skiers, one of the differences might be the general age level of each group. The first part of your paper would then contrast the ages of most snowboarders with the ages of most skiers. Another difference might be the clothing worn by the two groups. So you would next contrast the clothing of snowboarders with the clothing of skiers. You might then contrast the physical activity itself, explaining what snowboarders do on the snow that is different from what skiers do. Whatever points you cover, you take them one at a time, point by point. An outline for this method would look like this:

Point by Point

Topic Sentence: About the only thing that snowboarders and skiers have in common is that they share the same mountain.
   I. Ages
      A. Snowboarders
      B. Skiers
  II. Clothing
      A. Snowboarders
      B. Skiers
 III. Physical Activity
      A. Snowboarders
      B. Skiers
Concluding Sentence

Another method of organization presents the topics **subject by subject**. Using this method, you cover each point of one topic first and then each point of the second topic. Be careful with this organization. Because the points are presented separately rather than together, your paper might end up reading like two separate descriptions rather than like a comparison or contrast of the two topics. To make the comparison or contrast clear, cover the same points in the same order, like this:

Subject by Subject

Topic Sentence: About the only thing that snowboarders and skiers have in common is that they share the same mountain.

    I. Snowboarders
       A. Ages
       B. Clothing
       C. Physical Activity
   II. Skiers
       A. Ages
       B. Clothing
       C. Physical Activity
Concluding Sentence

Prewriting Application: Organization of the Comparison/Contrast Paragraph

Examine Exercise 1C (page 271), Exercise 2C (page 283), and Exercise 3C (page 296). Outline the paragraph in each exercise as shown above.

Writing

Now write the rough draft of your paragraph. Pay particular attention to transitions as you write. If you are using a point-by-point organization, use a clear transitional sentence to introduce each point of comparison or contrast. For subject-by-subject organizations, write a clear transitional sentence as you move from the first subject of your paper to the second. In addition, as you write the second half of a subject-by-subject paper, use transitional words and phrases that refer to the first half of the paper to emphasize the similarities or differences.

Writing Application: Identifying Transitional Words, Phrases, and Sentences

Examine Exercises 1C (page 271), 2C (page 283), and 3C (page 296).

1. Identify the organizational pattern of each as point-by-point or subject-by-subject.

2. Identify transitional sentences that introduce each point of comparison or contrast in a point-by-point paragraph or that move from one subject to another in a subject-by-subject paragraph.

3. In the subject-by-subject paragraph, identify transitions in the second half of the paragraph that emphasize the comparison or contrast by referring to the subject of the first half.

4. Identify any other transitions that serve to connect ideas between sentences.

Rewriting

...ces so they include specific and concrete details. As
...use actual names of people and places, and refer to spe-
...ver possible.

...itions wherever doing so would help clarify movement
...iother.

...ninary topic sentence so that it more accurately states
...your paragraph.

...for sentence variety. If many of your sentences tend to
..., try varying their length and their structure by com-
...g the techniques you have studied in the Sentence
...is text.

... Responding to Writing

Read the following paragraph. Then respond to the questions following it.

Romeo and Juliet—Then and Now

The 1968 movie version of William Shakespeare's play *Romeo and Juliet* contrasts with the updated version of 1996 in a number of ways. First, the 1968 director had the characters battle each other with swords. That is the way they fought back then, but today's youth couldn't really relate to that kind of situation. In the 1996 version the director wanted to show a weapon that the audience had seen on TV shows and in other movies. Swords were replaced with shiny, artistic-looking handguns. Another contrast between the '68 version and the '96 one is the style of costumes. The '68 designers kept the clothing as it would have looked during Shakespeare's time, making the male actors wear puffy-sleeved shirts, tights, and little beanie hats. The women had to endure much worse attire, such as long, heavy dresses. The designers in the updated version knew that today's youth wouldn't sit through a movie about guys wearing tights or women wearing clothes that hid everything. Instead, they had the men wear shirts that were colorful, comfortable, and modern. They also wore basic black and dark blue pants. I felt I could take the characters more seriously in normal clothes than in the old English attire. Although both versions did keep the original words of the play, I am glad that the new version changed the music of the earlier one. For instance, the boring love song "A Time for Us" was replaced by a touching, romantic tune called

"Kissing You." The new music helped me follow the plot a little better. When I watched the old version, there wasn't very much background music at all. I really had to follow what was going on by watching the actors, and even then the movie was hard to follow. In conclusion, I think the director of the '96 version did a wonderful job making *Romeo and Juliet* into a movie that appeals to the young people of today.

1. Identify the topic sentence. State its topic and central idea. Is it an effective topic sentence? Can you tell whether the paper will focus on similarities or differences?

2. Is this a point-by-point or subject-by-subject organization? How many points of contrast are covered in this paper? Identify them.

3. Identify the transitional sentences that introduce each major section of the paragraph. What other transitions are used between sentences?

4. Consider the organization of the paragraph. Would you change the order of the contrasts? Explain why or why not.

5. Consider the sentence variety. What sentences would you combine to improve the paragraph?

Rewriting Application: Revising and Editing Your Own Draft

Look closely at your topic sentence and transitions. Make any improvements that are needed. Consider your points of comparison or contrast. Do they need to be explained more thoroughly or described in more detail? Is the organization of your points clear? Can the reader tell where one point ends and another begins? If your paragraph contains too many brief sentences or too many compound sentences joined by *and*, revise them to improve the sentence variety of your paper. When editing your paper, check your draft for the following errors:

• Sentence fragments, comma splices, and fused sentences

• Misplaced modifiers and dangling modifiers

• Errors in subject–verb agreement

• Errors in pronoun case, pronoun–antecedent agreement, and pronoun reference

• Errors in comma use

• Errors in the use of periods, question marks, exclamation points, colons, semicolons, and quotation marks

• Errors in capitalization, titles, and numbers

• Misspelled words

Prepare a clean final draft, following the format your instructor has asked for. Before you turn in your final draft, proofread it carefully and make any necessary corrections.

Chapter Five Practice Test

I. Review of Chapters Two, Three, and Four

A. Correct any fragments, fused sentences, or comma splices in the following sentences. Do nothing if the sentence is correct.

1. The collie chasing the station wagon.

   _____

   _____

2. Marie did not know what to do about her brother, he kept ending up in jail.

   _____

   _____

3. When she saw the two mountain climbers who had been lost for fourteen days.

   _____

   _____

4. Ignoring the red light, the truck raced through the intersection it nearly hit a pedestrian.

   _____

   _____

5. He has some very strange habits, for example, every Monday he eats pancakes and ice cream for breakfast.

   _____

   _____

B. Correct any dangling or misplaced modifiers in the following sentences. Do nothing if the sentence is correct.

6. To be a successful gardener, thorough nourishment and watering of the soil are necessary.

   _____

   _____

311

Chapter Five Practice Test

continued

7. A young woman with a dachshund smiling from ear to ear approached my cousin.

_____

_____

8. After cleaning everything thoroughly, my job is still not over.

_____

_____

9. It was almost time to drive home, so Amaretto only decided to order a Coke.

_____

_____

10. The toy poodle embarrassed my sister chasing the mail carrier.

_____

_____

C. Correct any subject–verb agreement errors in the following sentences. Do nothing if the sentence is correct.

11. One of the guards were checking to see whether anyone was bringing liquor or drugs into the concert.

12. Do your daughter or the children next door plan to attend the birthday party?

13. The audience have finally stopped clapping, so we can continue with our performance.

14. There is a clown and a masked man waiting to see the dentist.

15. Every computer in both of our labs seem to have been tampered with.

D. Correct any pronoun use errors in the following sentences. Do nothing if the sentence is correct.

16. Everyone who attended the lecture agreed it was the best she had ever heard.

17. Gary crashed his bicycle into the man carrying a bag of groceries, but he was not injured.

Chapter Five Practice Test

continued

18. Between Estevan and I we had enough money to buy a wedding present for Alfredo and her.

19. Amanda wanted to know if the winners of the lottery were Laura and her.

20. Most people who go to see that movie know that you will be crying before it is over.

II. Chapter Five

A. Add commas to the following sentences where necessary. Do nothing if the sentence is correct.

21. Pam would you like to switch offices or are you happy with the one you have?

22. When we went back to Columbus Ohio for our high school reunion we brought our children with us.

23. Ichabod's true love had no idea what she would do with four calling birds three French hens two turtle doves and a partridge in a pear tree.

24. The damp dense fog made it difficult to see but Alexander decided to leave anyway.

25. When July 16 1996 arrived Alex canceled his magazine subscriptions unplugged his television set threw out his chocolate chip cookies and set out on his new life.

26. John ran quickly to the end of the alley and jumped over the fence into a neighbor's back yard.

27. Edna's dog a large English mastiff followed her into the house; however it was not allowed to stay inside.

28. As a matter of fact the movie was wonderful but the dinner afterward was a disaster.

29. For the first few hours of morning the cloudy misty weather threatened to ruin their kite-flying excursion.

30. While visiting Missouri we stopped in Hannibal Mark Twain's hometown.

continued

B. Add periods, exclamation points, question marks, quotation marks, semicolons, colons, and apostrophes (or *'s*) where necessary. Do not add or delete any commas.

31. Did Howard say that he would prefer the clams to the snails

32. Page asked, Where did you find that wonderful cummerbund

33. Oscar knew that he needed to find these items a needle, a spool of thread, and a box of bandages

34. Dizzy shouted, Hey, you bent my trumpet

35. The disoriented mockingbird flew into our living room and crashed against one window then it flew out our back door

36. The engine of Dons car began to overheat suddenly, it burst into flames

37. Desdemona, hide the pillows and handkerchiefs, advised Emilia

38. Barbies legs were longer than Kens, and he knew it

39. Ken asked, How will you be able to fit into your new Barbie car

40. The childrens projects werent completed on time therefore, the schools science show was canceled

C. In the following sentences correct any errors in the use of titles, capitalization, and numbers. Do not add or delete any commas. Do nothing if the sentence is correct.

41. I must have read eudora welty's short story a worn path at least 15 times.

42. On new year's eve, nineteen ninety-nine, Serena published her novel death in life.

43. More than 300 people were standing in line to see the movie mystery men.

44. 785 cars pass through that intersection every thursday.

Chapter Five Practice Test

continued

45. The play kiss me, kate will be performed at the howard brubeck theater at seven forty-five tonight.

46. Every spring Homer switches breakfast cereals from froot loops to frosted flakes.

47. 95 members of the ship's crew pooled their money and gave a remington shotgun to captain queeg when he retired.

48. From the book browning's poetry, professor donaldson chose the poem love among the ruins to discuss with his literature class on tuesday.

49. Mr. Muneton has decided to rent his house on oliver street to 2 sophomores from the nearby college.

50. Did you hear that two point five percent of all people in the midwest do not know what a windchill factor is?

Choosing the Right Words and Spelling Them Correctly

English is a diverse language. It has borrowed words from hundreds of different sources. *Moccasin,* for instance, is Native American in origin; *patio* comes from Spanish; *colonel* and *lieutenant* entered English from Norman French; and *thermonuclear* is both Greek and Latin. All of this diversity makes English a complex and interesting language, but it also makes it quite difficult sometimes.

As you know, we have three words that sound just like *to* and three words that sound just like *there*. In fact, English is full of words that sound alike or that have such similar meanings that they are often mistaken for one another. A careful writer learns to make distinctions among these words.

Failing to make correct word choices or to spell words correctly can cause a number of problems. Most important, you may fail to make your ideas clear, or you may confuse your reader. In addition, you may lose the confidence of your reader if your writing contains misspelled or poorly chosen words. Sometimes, you can even embarrass yourself.

For instance, here is a fellow who wants to meet either a fish or the bottom of a shoe:

▶ **EXAMPLE**   When I went to college, I did not know a **sole.**

This person has writing mixed up with the building trade:

▶ **EXAMPLE**   I began to take my talent for writing for **granite,** but I lacked the ability to organize my thoughts in a coherent **manor.**

And here the early American settlers enjoy a means of transportation that had not yet been invented:

▶ **EXAMPLE**   The pioneers appeared to prefer the open **planes** to the dense forests.

Most misspellings and incorrect word choices, however, are not as humorous or embarrassing as these. Instead, they are simple errors in word choice that are usually caused by carelessness and a lack of attention to detail.

Use Your Dictionary

This chapter will cover errors in word choice and spelling caused by irregular verbs and by words that are commonly confused. It will also present several of the basic "rules" of spelling. However, if you are not sure of a particular spelling (the difference between *effect* and *affect,* for instance), consult your dictionary. A dictionary shows how to spell, pronounce, and use words. A dictionary gives you the definitions of words, shows you the principal parts of verbs, and tells you whether or not a word is appropriate for formal writing. In addition, most dictionaries contain other useful information, such as biographical and geographical data.

Irregular Verbs

Because verbs in the English language change their spelling in a variety of ways to express different verb tenses, spelling them correctly can sometimes be a challenge. To use verbs correctly, you need to know the basic verb forms. These forms are known as the **three principal parts of the verb**: the **present,** the **past,** and the **past participle.**

You use the present to form both the present and future tenses, the past to form the past tense, and the past participle (with *have, has, had*) to form the perfect tenses.

Most verbs, the **regular verbs,** form the past and past participle by adding *d* or *ed* to the present. For example, the three principal parts of *create* are *create* (present), *created* (past), and *created* (past participle). The three principal parts of *talk* are *talk, talked,* and *talked.*

However, about two hundred verbs form the past and past participle in different ways. These verbs are called the **irregular verbs.** They are some of the oldest and most important verbs in English, such as *eat* or *fight* or *buy*—basic human actions. Because these words are so common, you should know their principal parts. Here is a list of the principal parts of most irregular verbs.

Present	Past	Past Participle
am, are, is	was, were	been
beat	beat	beaten
become	became	become
begin	began	begun
bend	bent	bent
bet	bet	bet
bite	bit	bitten
bleed	bled	bled
blow	blew	blown
break	broke	broken
bring	brought	brought
build	built	built
burst	burst	burst
buy	bought	bought
catch	caught	caught
choose	chose	chosen
come	came	come
cost	cost	cost
cut	cut	cut
dig	dug	dug
do, does	did	done

Present	Past	Past Participle
draw	drew	drawn
drink	drank	drunk
drive	drove	driven
eat	ate	eaten
fall	fell	fallen
feed	fed	fed
feel	felt	felt
fight	fought	fought
find	found	found
fly	flew	flown
forget	forgot	forgotten or forgot
freeze	froze	frozen
get	got	got or gotten
give	gave	given
go, goes	went	gone
grow	grew	grown
hang	hung	hung
hang (to execute)	hanged	hanged
have, has	had	had
hear	heard	heard
hide	hid	hidden
hit	hit	hit
hold	held	held
hurt	hurt	hurt
keep	kept	kept
know	knew	known
lay (to place or put)	laid	laid
lead	led	led
leave	left	left
lend	lent	lent
let	let	let
lie (to recline)	lay	lain
light	lit	lit
lose	lost	lost
make	made	made
mean	meant	meant
meet	met	met
pay	paid	paid
prove	proved	proved or proven

Present	*Past*	*Past Participle*
put	put	put
quit	quit	quit
read	read	read
ride	rode	ridden
ring	rang	rung
rise	rose	risen
run	ran	run
say	said	said
see	saw	seen
sell	sold	sold
send	sent	sent
set	set	set
shake	shook	shaken
shine	shone or shined	shone or shined
shoot	shot	shot
show	showed	shown
shrink	shrank	shrunk
shut	shut	shut
sing	sang	sung
sink	sank	sunk
sit	sat	sat
sleep	slept	slept
slide	slid	slid
speak	spoke	spoken
speed	sped	sped
spend	spent	spent
spin	spun	spun
stand	stood	stood
steal	stole	stolen
stick	stuck	stuck
sting	stung	stung
strike	struck	struck
swear	swore	sworn
sweep	swept	swept
swim	swam	swum
swing	swung	swung
take	took	taken

Present	Past	Past Participle
teach	taught	taught
tear	tore	torn
tell	told	told
think	thought	thought
throw	threw	thrown
wake	woke or waked	woken or waked
wear	wore	worn
weave	wove	woven
weep	wept	wept
win	won	won
wind	wound	wound
wring	wrung	wrung
write	wrote	written

Special Problems with Irregular Verbs

Lie–Lay

1. The irregular verb *lie* means "to recline." It never takes a direct object. The principal parts of this verb are *lie, lay,* and *lain.*

▶ **EXAMPLES**   On Saturdays, I **lie** in bed until at least 11:00.

Last Saturday, I **lay** in bed until almost 1:00.

Today, I **have lain** in bed too long.

2. The verb *lay* means "to place or put." It takes a direct object. Its principal parts are *lay, laid,* and *laid.*

▶ **EXAMPLES**   As Paul enters the house, he always **lays** his keys on the table.

Yesterday Paul **laid** his keys on the television set.

After he **had laid** the flowers on the kitchen table, Mr. Best kissed his wife.

Sit–Set

1. The verb *sit* means "to be seated." It never takes a direct object. Its principal parts are *sit, sat,* and *sat.*

▶ **EXAMPLES**   At the movies, Juan usually **sits** in the back row.

Last week Juan **sat** in the middle of the theater.

2. The verb *set* means "to place or put." It takes a direct object. Its principal parts are *set, set,* and *set.*

► EXAMPLES   At night Floyd always **sets** a glass of water by his bed.

Cora **set** her books on the librarian's desk.

Rise–Raise

1. The verb *rise* means "to stand" or "to attain a greater height." It never takes a direct object. Its principal parts are *rise, rose,* and *risen.*

► EXAMPLES   I like it when the sun **rises** over the mountains on a clear day.

All of the people **rose** every time the queen entered the room.

2. The verb *raise* is a regular verb. It means "to elevate." It takes a direct object. Its principal parts are *raise, raised,* and *raised.*

► EXAMPLES   Every morning a Boy Scout **raises** the flag in front of the school.

Christopher always politely **raised** his hand whenever he had a question.

Verbs with *u* in the Past Participle

Because these verbs sound odd, some people tend to use the past form when they should be using the past participle. Here are the ones that are most often confused.

drink	drank	**drunk:**	So far I **have drunk** eight glasses of water today.
swim	swam	**swum:**	Petra **has swum** thirty-five laps today.
shrink	shrank	**shrunk:**	The grocer wondered why his profits **had shrunk.**
sing	sang	**sung:**	Often Carmine **has sung** the National Anthem before hockey games.

■ PRACTICE   Underline the correct verb form in the parentheses.

1. During the hot afternoons, my cat usually (lays <u>lies</u>) on my back porch.

2. When the temperature (rose raised), the snow began to melt.

3. The coach told the team members that they had (swam swum) well in the tournament.

4. As Juan (laid lay) his money down, he asked for a receipt.

5. A pile of newspapers (set sat) on the kitchen table.

6. After the storm, leaves were (lying laying) all over the patio.

7. When I removed my sweater from the dryer, I saw that it had (shrank shrunk).

8. Melinda wondered who had (drank drunk) the can of soda that was (setting sitting) on the table.

9. Because I knew that I (sang sung) poorly, I did not (rise raise) my hand to volunteer.

10. Josef (laid lay) his coat on the chair and looked at Miriam, who (laid, lay) on the couch.

Section One Review

1. The **three principal parts of a verb** are **present, past,** and **past participle.**

2. **Regular verbs** form the past and past participle by adding *d* or *ed* to the present.

3. **Irregular** verbs form the past and past participle in a variety of other ways. See the lists on pages 318–321.

4. Irregular verbs that often cause confusion are *lie/lay, sit/set, rise/raise,* and **verbs with** *u* **in the past participle.**

Exercise 1A

Underline the correct form of the verb in the parentheses.

1. By noon, Frieda had (swam <u>swum</u>) nearly halfway across the lake.

2. At the auto show, Jack (saw seen) the car he wanted.

3. The little boy cried when his Mickey Mouse balloon (busted burst).

4. Goodman Brown's decision (cost costed) him his peace of mind.

5. This morning my cat (lay laid) in the sun for two hours while I cleaned the house.

6. Othello (set sat) down and tried to decide whom to believe.

7. Every morning for the last thirty years Reverend Moody has (rang rung) the church bell at eight o'clock.

8. As the sailor (rose raised) the flag, Roseanne (began begun) to sing.

9. Steve would not admit that he had gained weight; instead, he insisted that his pants had (shrank shrunk).

10. As *Titanic* (began begun) to sink, the band played.

11. After Mr. Oliveros finished his speech, he (lay laid) his glasses on the table.

12. Randy Johnson could not believe that he had not (threw thrown) one strike in twenty pitches.

13. Howard (wringed wrung) out his socks before he (hanged hung) them up.

14. The naked man (set sat) with his chin in his hand for the sculptor.

15. Once the Saint Bernard had (shook shaken) itself dry, it jumped back into the pool.

Exercise 1B

In the blanks, write the correct form of the verb indicated.

1. At the zoo we stared at the rare pandas as they ___*lay*___ in their enclosure. (lie)

2. Steve wondered if he should have _____ the waitress a larger tip. (give)

3. Fortunato _____ and stared at the wall of bricks before him. (sit)

4. Icarus would have _____ farther if he had taken his father's advice. (fly)

5. Has Craig really _____ that entire case of root beer? (drink)

6. The sun had just _____ when the attack began. (rise)

7. Boyd cleaned the carburetor and then _____ it on the work bench. (lay)

8. The doctor asked Moira if she had _____ any water that day. (drink)

9. The witness had _____ the defendant leave the store after the robbery. (see)

10. The mail had _____, but the package was not there. (come)

11. Has the bell for lunch _____ yet? (ring)

12. The crowd _____ to its feet to acknowledge the hero. (rise)

13. Taylor didn't realize he had _____ in the sun for so long. (lie)

14. After Natasha had _____ the English Channel, the Queen gave her a medal. (swim)

15. Because his new shirt had _____ so much, he could no longer wear it. (shrink)

Exercise 1C

Check the following paragraph for correct verb forms. Underline any incorrect verb forms and write the correct forms above them.

1. All those students ~~setting~~ [*sitting*] in classrooms in public colleges and universities cost the taxpayers a lot of money, but maybe there is a way for the students to return the favor. 2. I know that the tuition that I paid at my college was much less than what my education costed the state. 3. One way for students to repay this debt would be for them to perform community service as part of their course work. 4. For instance, students could help if they done work for local charities. 5. Other students could chose to help the environment with recycling efforts. 6. In the past, students have began awareness campaigns on water pollution and conservation. 7. Young people could help old or disabled people who are laying in hospitals or convalescent homes. 8. A friend of mine once went and swum with people who were undergoing rehabilitation for strokes or injuries. 9. Another thing they could do would be to help sit books back on the shelves in local public libraries. 10. What a big help it would be if some college students teached elementary and high school students some of the things they have learned. 11. They could also speak to youngsters who have quitted school to encourage them to return. 12. Even going to visit kids who have went to jail might help alleviate the juvenile delinquency problem. 13. Some students would complain that if they spended much time in this way, there would be no time to study. 14. However, some institutions have gave students credit for community service, and some students have wrote about these experiences in English or social studies classes. 15. As I seen it, a required bit of community service would set well with the taxpayers and make the students more aware of the need for volunteerism.

Commonly Confused Words

Most word choice errors are made either because two words sound alike or look alike or because their meanings are so similar that they are mistakenly used in place of each other. Here are some of the most commonly confused sets of words.

A/an/and

A is used before words that begin with **consonant sounds**. It is an article, a type of **adjective**.

▶ **EXAMPLES**   a porcupine, a bat, a sword, a good boy

An is used before words that begin with **vowel sounds**. It is also an article.

▶ **EXAMPLES**   an apple, an honor, an unusual cloud formation

And is a **coordinating conjunction** used to join words, phrases, or clauses.

▶ **EXAMPLE**   Homer **and** Hortense

Accept/except

Accept means "to take or receive what is offered or given." It is a **verb**.

▶ **EXAMPLE**   Severino gladly **accepted** the reward for the money he had returned.

Except means "excluded" or "but." It is a **preposition**.

▶ **EXAMPLE**   Flowers were in everyone's room **except** Sonia's.

Advice/advise

Advice means "an opinion about what to do or how to handle a situation." It is a **noun**.

▶ **EXAMPLE**   The counselor gave Phillipa **advice** about how to apply for graduate school.

Advise means "to give advice" or "to counsel." It is a **verb**.

▶ **EXAMPLE**   The judge **advised** the defense attorney to control his temper.

Affect/effect

Affect means "to influence" or "to produce a change in." It is a **verb**.

► **EXAMPLE**   The continued destruction of the ozone layer will **affect** future weather patterns drastically.

Effect is "a result" or "something brought about by a cause." It is a **noun**.

► **EXAMPLE**   The decorator liked the **effect** of the newly painted room.

NOTE: *Effect* can be used as a verb when it means "to bring about" or "to cause."

► **EXAMPLE**   The reward **effected** a change in the lion's behavior.

All ready/already

All ready means "everyone or everything is prepared or ready."

► **EXAMPLE**   After a strenuous game of softball, we were **all ready** for a cold root beer.

Already means "by or before a specific or implied time."

► **EXAMPLE**   By the time he had climbed the first flight of stairs, Bob was **already** out of breath.

All right/"alright"

All right means "satisfactory" or "unhurt."

► **EXAMPLE**   After she fell from her horse, Hannah smiled and said she was **all right**.

Alright is a misspelling. Do not use it.

Among/between

Among means "in the company of" or "included with." Use it when discussing <u>three or more</u> things or ideas. It is a **preposition**.

► **EXAMPLE**   **Among** the demands of the workers was drinkable coffee.

Between means "in or through the space that separates two things." Use it only when you are discussing <u>two things or ideas</u>. It is a **preposition**.

► **EXAMPLE**   Betty could not choose **between** Sid and Slim.

Amount/number

Use *amount* to refer to things that are usually not separated, such as milk, oil, salt, or flour.

▶ **EXAMPLE**   The **amount** of sugar the recipe calls for is two cups.

Use *number* to refer to things that are usually separated or counted individually, such as people, books, cats, or apples.

▶ **EXAMPLE**   The large **number** of people in the small room made the air stuffy.

Anxious/eager

Anxious means "apprehensive, uneasy, worried." It is an **adjective**.

▶ **EXAMPLE**   The lawyer was **anxious** about the jury's verdict.

Eager means "keen desire or enthusiasm in pursuit of something." It is also an **adjective**.

▶ **EXAMPLE**   The children were **eager** for summer vacation to begin.

Are/our

Are is a **linking verb** or a **helping verb**.

▶ **EXAMPLES**   We **are** late for dinner.

We **are** leaving soon.

Our is a **possessive pronoun**.

▶ **EXAMPLE**   **Our** dinner was delicious.

Brake/break

Brake is the device that stops or slows a vehicle. It may be used as a **noun** or a **verb**.

▶ **EXAMPLES**   The service station attendant told Molly that her **brakes** were dangerously worn.

Arlo **braked** just in time to avoid going over the cliff.

Break can also be used as a **noun** or a **verb**. As a **verb**, it means "to cause to come apart by force."

► **EXAMPLE**   Every time Humphrey walks through a room, he **breaks** something.

As a noun, *break* means "an interruption of an action or a thing."

► **EXAMPLES**   When there was a **break** in the storm, we continued the game.

The worker fixed the **break** in the water pipe.

Choose/chose

Choose means "select." It is a **present tense verb**.

► **EXAMPLE**   Every Friday afternoon, the children **choose** a movie to watch in the evening.

Chose means "selected." It is the **past tense** of *choose*.

► **EXAMPLE**   Last Friday, the children **chose** The Lion King.

Complement/compliment

A *complement* is "that which completes or brings to perfection." It is a **noun** or a **verb**.

► **EXAMPLES**   The bright yellow tie was a handsome **complement** to Pierre's new suit.

The bright yellow tie **complemented** Pierre's new suit.

A *compliment* is "an expression of praise, respect, or courtesy." It is a **noun** or a **verb**.

► **EXAMPLES**   Whenever Mr. Trujillo receives a **compliment** for his beautiful sculptures, he smiles and blushes.

Whenever his wife **compliments** Mr. Trujillo for his beautiful sculpture, he smiles and blushes.

Conscience/conscious

Conscience is "a knowledge or sense of right and wrong." It is a **noun**.

► **EXAMPLE**   Javier said that his **conscience** kept him from looking at Lucy's paper during the physics examination.

Conscious can mean either "aware" or "awake." It is an **adjective**.

► **EXAMPLE**   As he walked through the dark woods, Frank was **conscious** of the animals all around him.

Disinterested/uninterested

Disinterested means "neutral" or "impartial." It is an **adjective**.

▶ **EXAMPLE**   A judge must remain **disinterested** as he considers a case before him.

Uninterested means "not interested." It is an **adjective**.

▶ **EXAMPLE**   Shirley was profoundly **uninterested** in the subject of the lecture.

■ **PRACTICE**   Underline the correct word in the parentheses.

1. The two sisters were so (anxious <u>eager</u>) to get to Disneyland that they forgot to get (<u>advice</u> advise) about the best attractions.

2. Ishmael's (conscious conscience) did not bother him even though everyone else had died, so he ate (a an) excellent meal.

3. Polly would not (accept except) the idea that the sun could have such a dangerous (affect effect) on her skin.

4. The three witches could not agree (between among) themselves about how to tell Macbeth.

5. The two sides agreed to abide by the opinion of the (disinterested uninterested) mediator.

6. The odor of Homer's cooking did not have a good (effect affect) on his guests.

7. After packing the car, we were (already all ready) to go.

8. Huck wondered whether it would be (all right alright) not to return Jim.

9. Barbara knew that a thick chocolate milkshake would be the perfect (compliment complement) to her lunch of celery and carrot sticks.

10. The Romans had a hard time deciding the (number amount) of men a centurion would lead.

11. (Are Our) station wagon needs a (brake break) job.

12. When Mrs. Dimmesdale needed some sewing (advise advice), she (chose choose) Hester Prynne.

Fewer/less

Use *fewer* to discuss items that can be counted separately, such as trees, automobiles, or pencils. It is an **adjective**.

► **EXAMPLE**   When the cutters had finished, there were many **fewer** trees in the grove.

Use *less* to refer to amounts that are not usually separated, such as water, dirt, sand, or gasoline. It is an **adjective**.

► **EXAMPLE**   Because of the drought, there is **less** water in the lake this year.

Lead/led

As a **noun**, *lead* is a heavy metal or a part of a pencil. As a **verb**, it is the present tense of the verb *to lead,* meaning "to guide" or "to show the way."

► **EXAMPLES**   The diver used weights made of **lead** to keep him from floating to the surface.

Every summer Mr. Archer **leads** his scout troop on a long backpacking trip.

Led is the past or past participle form of the **verb** *to lead.*

► **EXAMPLE**   Last summer, Mr. Archer **led** his scout troop on a backpacking trip.

Loose/lose

Loose means "not confined or restrained, free, unbound." It is an **adjective**.

► **EXAMPLE**   Mr. Castro was chasing a cow that had gotten **loose** and was trampling his garden.

Lose means "to become unable to find" or "to mislay." It is a **verb**.

► **EXAMPLE**   I was afraid I would **lose** my contact lenses if I went swimming with them.

Nauseous/nauseated

If something is *nauseous,* it causes nausea or is sickening or disgusting. *Nauseous* is an adjective.

▶ **EXAMPLE**   A **nauseous** odor filled the room.

To be *nauseated* is to be sick or to feel nausea. *Nauseated* is the past or past participle form of the verb *nauseate* and is often used as an **adjective.**

▶ **EXAMPLE**   The bad news made Aribella feel **nauseated.**

Passed/past

Passed is the past or past participle form of the **verb** *to pass,* which means "to go or move forward, through, or out."

▶ **EXAMPLE**   As I drove to school, I **passed** a serious traffic accident.

Past as an **adjective** means "gone by, ended, over." As a **noun,** it means "the time that has gone by." As a **preposition,** it means "beyond."

▶ **EXAMPLES**   His **past** mistakes will not bar him from further indiscretions.

In the **past,** I have always been in favor of opening doors for women.

Horst waved as he drove **past** Jill's house.

Personal/personnel

Personal means "private" or "individual." It is an **adjective.**

▶ **EXAMPLE**   Helen feels her political ideas are her **personal** business.

Personnel means "persons employed in any work or enterprise." It is a **noun.**

▶ **EXAMPLE**   The sign on the bulletin board directed all **personnel** to report to the auditorium for a meeting.

Precede/proceed

Precede means "to go before." It is a **verb.**

▶ **EXAMPLE**   The Great Depression **preceded** World War II.

Proceed means "to advance or go on." It is a **verb.**

▶ **EXAMPLE**   After a short pause, Mrs. Quintan **proceeded** with her inventory.

Principal/principle

As an **adjective**, *principal* means "first in rank or importance." As a **noun**, it usually means "the head of a school."

▶ **EXAMPLES**   Kevin's **principal** concern was the safety of his children.

At the assembly the **principal** discussed drug abuse with the students and teachers.

A *principle* is a "fundamental truth, law, or doctrine." It is a **noun**.

▶ **EXAMPLE**   One of my **principles** is that you never get something for nothing.

Quit/quite/quiet

Quit means "to stop doing something." It is a **verb**.

▶ **EXAMPLE**   George **quit** smoking a year ago.

Quite means "completely" or "really." It is an **adverb**.

▶ **EXAMPLE**   It was **quite** hot during the whole month of August.

Quiet means "silent." It is usually used as an **adjective**, but it can be used as a **noun**.

▶ **EXAMPLES**   The **quiet** student in the third row rarely said a word.

In the **quiet** of the evening, Hank strummed his guitar.

Than/then

Use *than* to make comparisons. It is a **conjunction**.

▶ **EXAMPLE**   It is cloudier today **than** it was yesterday.

Then means "at that time" or "soon afterward" or "next." It is an **adverb**.

▶ **EXAMPLE**   Audrey mowed the back yard, and **then** she drank a large iced tea.

Their/there/they're

Their is a **possessive pronoun** meaning "belonging to them."

▶ **EXAMPLE**   All of the people in the room suddenly started clinking the ice in **their** drinks.

There is an **adverb** meaning "in that place."

▶ **EXAMPLE**   "Let's park the car **there**," proclaimed Fern.

They're is a contraction for *they are*.

► **EXAMPLE**   "**They're** back," said the little girl ominously.

Threw/through

Threw is the past tense form of the **verb** *to throw*.

► **EXAMPLE**   Hector **threw** the spear with godlike accuracy.

Through is a **preposition** meaning "in one side and out the other side of."

► **EXAMPLE**   The ship sailed **through** the Bermuda Triangle without peril.

To/too/two

To is a **preposition** meaning "in the direction of."

► **EXAMPLE**   Jeremy went **to** his rustic cabin by the babbling brook for a poetic weekend.

Too is an **adverb** meaning "also" or "more than enough."

► **EXAMPLES**   Cecily was at the spree, **too**.

The senator found that the burden of public adulation was **too** heavy.

Two is the number after *one*.

► **EXAMPLE**   Bill has **two** daughters and one cat and too many televisions, so he wants to go to Jeremy's rustic cabin, too.

We're/were/where

We're is a contraction for *we are*.

► **EXAMPLE**   **We're** almost there.

Were is a **linking verb** or a **helping verb** in the past tense.

► **EXAMPLES**   We **were** late for dinner.

Our hosts **were** eating dessert when we arrived.

Where indicates **place**.

► **EXAMPLES**   **Where** is the key to the cellar?

He showed them **where** he had buried the money.

Your/you're

Your is a **possessive pronoun** meaning "belonging to you."

► **EXAMPLE** "**Your** insights have contributed greatly to my sense of well-being," said the toady.

You're is a contraction for *you are.*

► **EXAMPLE** "**You're** just saying that because **you're** so nice," replied the other toady.

■ **PRACTICE** Underline the correct words in the parentheses.

1. The (amount <u>number</u>) of lawyers in the state has become (to <u>too</u> two) high, so (their <u>they're</u> there) having a hard time finding enough work.

2. The Oklahomans noticed that each day brought (less fewer) jobs (than then) the day before.

3. Did you say that your (principal principle) concern is whether (your you're) going to be able to balance your checkbook?

4. As the townspeople (passed past) Emily's house, they noticed a (nauseated nauseous) odor.

5. As we (lead led) the way (threw through) southern Utah, we agreed that we would not (lose loose) the race.

6. Some of the (personal personnel) failed to pass (their they're there) physical exams.

7. The (principal principle) that is more important than any other is to love (your you're) neighbor.

8. Mrs. Turpin saw that there were (to too two) many people in the waiting room, so she kicked (to too two) of them out.

9. The (amount number) of milk in the bottle is (less fewer) (than then) it was an hour ago.

10. Macbeth had to (choose chose) between the (advice advise) of his wife and of his conscience.

11. Because it was (quit quite quiet) late when we got home, we had to be (quit quite quiet) so that we wouldn't wake our parents.

12. Only one person knew (were where we're) the purloined letters (were where we're).

Section Two Review

Be careful when you use the following words:

a/an/and
accept/except
advice/advise
affect/effect
all ready/already
all right/"alright"
among/between
amount/number
anxious/eager
are/our
brake/break
choose/chose
complement/compliment
conscience/conscious
disinterested/uninterested
fewer/less
lead/led
loose/lose
nauseous/nauseated
passed/past
personal/personnel
precede/proceed
principal/principle
quit/quite/quiet
than/then
their/there/they're
threw/through
to/too/two
we're/were/where
your/you're

Exercise 2A

Underline the correct word in the parentheses.

1. First, Leonard consulted an astrologer; (<u>then</u> than) he planned the rest of his life.

2. A (break brake) in the weather allowed Daedalus and Icarus to take off.

3. We (we're were where) (anxious eager) to begin (are our) exciting new jobs as zebra handlers at the zoo.

4. (Among between) the four friends was only five dollars.

5. The hare had a difficult time (accepting excepting) the (principle principal) that slow-but-steady wins the race.

6. Gertrude did not know how the news of her marriage would (affect effect) her son.

7. My (conscience conscious) told me to report my tips on my tax form.

8. Harley knew that to be a good umpire, he must remain (uninterested disinterested) in who won the game.

9. I want to know why (your you're) not eating (your you're) chocolate-covered ants.

10. The (number amount) of empty bottles lying around after the reception was amazing.

11. By the time we reached the beach, the grunion had (already all ready) left.

12. When she saw the painting, my teacher (complimented complemented) me on my use of color.

13. Mr. Oaks was afraid he would (loose lose) his seat if he went to the snack bar.

14. (There They're Their) were four burned spots (were where we're) the Martian craft had stood.

15. Othello loved Desdemona, and she loved him (two to too), but Iago was determined (two to too) destroy that love.

Exercise 2B

Correct any word choice errors in the following sentences.

1. It has been almost *an* ~~a~~ hour since you *accepted* ~~excepted~~ my apology.

2. "Your dead meat," said Homer while eating a Spam sandwich on his brake.

3. I was conscience during the operation, and the doctor was to.

4. Elvis felt alright until his hound dog began to howl to loudly.

5. Sometimes his advise is too personnel.

6. Sergeant Pepper lead the band right threw the rain.

7. When life gets hectic, it is easy to loose sight of your goals.

8. After the Spam and okra and spinach greens, the children where anxious for dessert.

9. As the ball flew over the fence, Mitch knew that he had hit it farther then he ever had before.

10. Barbara's daughter received many complements for the amount of boxes of cookies she had sold.

11. Bored and sleepy, Isaac realized that he was disinterested in hearing any more about the sex life of Japanese beetles.

12. The candidate stuck to his principal not to except money from corporations regulated by the government.

13. Even though she felt nauseous and irritable, Jodi preceded to eat her entire dinner.

14. My brother and sister and I agreed between ourselves that we where responsible for the family's difficulties.

15. Are you conscience of the affect that DDT can have on are environment?

Edit the following paragraph for word use. Underline any incorrect words, and write the correct words above them.

1. Some people do not enjoy any type of competition, but I believe that self-directed competition (that is, competing against one's own <u>personnel</u> [*personal*] standard) can bring many benefits. **2.** For example, self-directed competition has really effected how well I play classical guitar. **3.** When I first started, I could not play the guitar well, so I decided to learn to play at least one piece or perform one technique more effectively then the week before. **4.** As each week past, I "competed" with myself. **5.** Now, only two years later, I have excepted a invitation to perform for are local Chamber of Commerce. **6.** The principal of self-directed competition has also helped me learn to snow ski. **7.** Last year, I went skiing with some neighbors who all ready knew how to ski. **8.** Instead of trying to keep up with them (and maybe brake a leg), I stayed on one slope until I could ski it from top to bottom. **9.** Only than would it be alright for me to try a more difficult slope. **10.** By the end of the ski season, their where less then four slopes (all of them expert runs) that I had not yet skied. **11.** Today I'm anxiously looking forward to next winter. **12.** Finally, self-directed competition has made me a better student. **13.** When I am in class, I could chose to compare myself to other students, but I don't; instead, I just try to improve what I have done. **14.** For instance, when I received a C on my first report in biology, I did not loose my hope for an A in the class. **15.** I knew that threw self-directed competition I could do better, and I did. **16.** By the end of the semester the amount of A's I had received far outweighed my C's, and I did receive a A for the class. **17.** Self-directed competition may not be for everyone, but my advise is that it is a good way to enjoy life while becoming better at what you like to do.

Spelling Rules

Spelling words correctly should be simple. After all, if you can say a word, it would just seem to make sense that you should be able to spell it. Why, then, is accurate spelling such a problem for some people? Well, as anyone who has ever written anything in English knows, one of the problems is that the same sound is spelled different ways in different situations. For instance, the long *e* sound may be spelled *ea,* as in *mean; ee,* as in *seem; ei,* as in *receive; ie,* as in *niece;* or *e-consonant-e,* as in *precede.* On the other hand, many words in English use similar spellings but have totally different pronunciations, as in *rough, bough, though, through,* and *cough.* As if these problems weren't enough, there are times when consonants are doubled (*rob* becomes *robbed*), times when consonants are not doubled (*robe* becomes *robed*), times when a final *e* is dropped (*move* becomes *moving*), and times when the final *e* is not dropped (*move* becomes *movement*). Unfortunately, these are just a few of the variations that occur in the spelling of English words—so perhaps it is understandable that accurate spelling poses a problem for many people.

In this section, you will study various rules of spelling that will help you through specific spelling situations. However, before we examine the specific rules of spelling, consider these points to improve your spelling in any writing activity.

Techniques to Improve Your Spelling

1. <u>Pay attention to your own reactions as you write.</u> If you are not confident of the spelling of a word, assume you have probably misspelled it and use your dictionary to check it.

2. <u>Buy and use a dictionary.</u> Small, inexpensive paperback dictionaries are available in nearly every bookstore or supermarket. Keep one next to you as you write and get used to using it.

3. <u>Don't rely too much on spelling checkers.</u> Although spelling checkers are excellent tools that you should use, don't assume they will solve all of your spelling problems, because they won't. They are particularly useless when you confuse the kinds of words covered in the previous section, such as *their, there,* and *they're.*

4. <u>Pronounce words carefully and accurately.</u> Some misspellings are the result of poor pronunciation. Examine the following misspelled words. Pronounce and spell them correctly. Extend the list with examples of other words you have heard mispronounced.

Incorrect	*Correct*	*Incorrect*	*Correct*
athelete	_____	perfer	_____
discription	_____	perscription	_____
enviroment	_____	probally	_____
heigth	_____	realaty	_____
libary	_____	suprise	_____
nucular	_____	unusal	_____
paticular	_____	usally	_____

5. <u>Use memory tricks.</u> You can memorize the spelling of many words by using some memory techniques.

► **EXAMPLES**

There is a rat in *separate*.

The first ll's are parallel in *parallel*.

Dessert *has two ss's because everyone wants two desserts.*

6. <u>Read more often.</u> The most effective way to become a better speller (and, for that matter, a better writer and thinker) is to read on a regular basis. If you do not read novels, perhaps now is the time to start. Ask your instructor to recommend some good books, newspapers, and magazines.

7. <u>Learn the rules of spelling.</u> The following explanations should help you improve your spelling. However, note that each of these "rules" contains numerous exceptions. You must use a dictionary if you have any doubt about the spelling of a word.

Using *ie* or *ei*

You have probably heard this bit of simple verse:

Use *i* before *e*
Except after *c*
Or when sounded like *ay*
As in *neighbor* or *weigh*.

Although there are exceptions to this rule, it works in most cases.

► **EXAMPLES**

IE	EI (after C)	EI (sounded like Ay)
grief	deceive	sleigh
niece	ceiling	eight
belief	receipt	weigh
achieve	perceive	neighbor

Exceptions:

► **EXAMPLES**

ancient	conscience	foreign	neither	science	stein
caffeine	deity	height	protein	seize	their
codeine	either	leisure	proficient	society	weird

■ **PRACTICE**   Supply the correct *ie/ei* spellings in the following sentences.

1. Erin's n*ie*ce decided to w*ei*gh her new puppy.

2. Thoreau's n__ghbors were rel__ved when Henry finally moved out of town.

3. No one bel__ved me when I said that Paul Bunyan's best fr__nd was a blue ox named Babe.

4. As the fr__ght train passed, shaking the entire house, a large p__ce of plaster fell from the c__ling.

5. According to an anc__nt tradition, the person who rec__ves the black dot will be stoned to death.

Keeping or Changing a Final -y

When you add letters to a word ending in -y, change the *y* to *i* if it is preceded by a consonant. If it is preceded by a vowel, do not change the -y. A major exception: If you are adding *-ing*, never change the *y*.

► **EXAMPLES**

Preceded by a Consonant			Preceded by a Vowel		
study + ed = studied			delay + ed = delayed		
pretty + est = prettiest			buy + er = buyer		
happy + ness = happiness			employ + ment = employment		

Exceptions:

study + ing = studying			say + d = said		
worry + ing = worrying			pay + d = paid		

■   **PRACTICE**   Add the ending in parentheses to each of the following words.

1.	study	(ed)	*studied*
		(es)	*studies*
		(ing)	*studying*
2.	angry	(est)	_____
		(er)	_____
		(ly)	_____
3.	portray	(ed)	_____
		(s)	_____
		(ing)	_____
		(al)	_____
4.	busy	(ness)	_____
		(er)	_____
		(est)	_____
5.	employ	(er)	_____
		(ed)	_____
		(able)	_____

Keeping or Dropping a Silent Final -e

When a word ends in a silent -e, drop the -e when you add an ending that begins with a vowel. Keep the -e when you add an ending that begins with a consonant.

▶ **EXAMPLES**

	Before a Vowel				Before a Consonant	
move	+ ing	= moving		hope	+ less	= hopeless
advise	+ able	= advisable		move	+ ment	= movement
pure	+ ity	= purity		safe	+ ly	= safely

Exceptions:

▶ **EXAMPLES**

courage	+ ous	= courageous		judge	+ ment	= judgment
change	+ able	= changeable		argue	+ ment	= argument
notice	+ able	= noticeable		true	+ ly	= truly

■ **PRACTICE**

Add the ending shown to each word, keeping or dropping the final -e when necessary.

1. require + ment = _requirement_

2. require + ing = _____

3. inspire + ing = _____

4. love + able = _____

5. love + ly = _____

6. manage + ing = _____

7. manage + ment = _____

8. complete + ly = _____

9. judge + ment = _____

10. notice + able = _____

Doubling the Final Consonant

In a single-syllable word that ends in one consonant preceded by one vowel (as in *drop*), double the final consonant when you add an ending that starts with a vowel. If a word has two or more syllables, the same rule applies *only if the emphasis is on the final syllable.*

▶ **EXAMPLES**

One Syllable	Two or More Syllables (emphasis on final syllable)
drop + ing = dropping	expel + ing = expelling
slap + ed = slapped	occur + ence = occurrence
thin + est = thinnest	begin + er = beginner

■ **PRACTICE**   Add the indicated endings to the following words. Double the final consonants where necessary.

1. brag + ing =   *bragging*

2. wild + est =   _____

3. refer + ed =   _____

4. proceed + ing =   _____

5. dim + er =   _____

6. clean + er =   _____

7. commit + ed =   _____

8. forget + able =   _____

9. happen + ing =   _____

10. compel + ed =   _____

Using Prefixes

A **prefix** is one or more syllables added at the start of a word to change its meaning. **Do not change any letters of the root word when you add a prefix to it.** (The **root** is the part of the word that carries its central idea.)

▶ **EXAMPLES**

prefix	+	root	=	new word
im	+	possible	=	impossible
mis	+	spell	=	misspell
il	+	legal	=	illegal
un	+	necessary	=	unnecessary

■ **PRACTICE** Circle the correct spellings.

1. dissappoint   (disappoint)

2. unatural   unnatural

3. dissatisified   disatisfied

4. illegible   ilegible

5. mistrial   misstrial

6. imoral   immoral

7. mispell   misspell

8. ireversible   irreversible

9. ilicit   illicit

10. unethical   unnethical

Forming Plurals

1. Add *-s* to make most nouns plural. Add *-es* if the noun ends in *ch, sh, ss,* or *x*.

► EXAMPLES

Add *-s*		Add *-es*	
street	streets	church	churches
dog	dogs	bush	bushes
problem	problems	hiss	hisses
issue	issues	box	boxes

2. If a noun ends in *o*, add *-s* if the *o* is preceded by a vowel. Add *-es* if it is preceded by a consonant.

► EXAMPLES

Add *-s*				Add *-es*			
stereo	+	s	= stereos	hero	+	es	= heroes
radio	+	s	= radios	potato	+	es	= potatoes

Exceptions: *pianos, sopranos, solos, autos, memos*

3. Some nouns that end in *-f* or *-fe* form the plural by changing the ending to *-ve* before the *s*.

► EXAMPLES

half	+	s	=	halves
wife	+	s	=	wives
leaf	+	s	=	leaves

4. Some words form plurals by changing spelling.

► EXAMPLES

woman	=	women
goose	=	geese
foot	=	feet
child	=	children

5. Many words borrowed from other languages also form plurals by changing spelling.

► EXAMPLES

alumnus	=	alumni
alumna	=	alumnae

analysis	=	analyses
basis	=	bases
medium	=	media
crisis	=	crises
criterion	=	criteria
memorandum	=	memoranda
phenomenon	=	phenomena

■ **PRACTICE** Write the plural forms of the following words.

    1. tax   *taxes*

    2. monkey   _____

    3. echo   _____

    4. knife   _____

    5. match   _____

    6. month   _____

    7. kiss   _____

    8. stereo   _____

    9. candy   _____

   10. phenomenon   _____

Commonly Misspelled Words

Many words that are commonly misspelled do not relate to any particular spelling rule. In such cases, you need to be willing to use a dictionary to check the correct spelling.

■ **PRACTICE** Correct each of the misspelled words below. Use a dictionary when you are unsure of the correct spelling.

1. accross   *across*
2. alot   _____
3. athelete   _____
4. behavor   _____
5. brillient   _____
6. buisness   _____
7. carefuly   _____
8. carreer   _____
9. competion   _____
10. definate   _____
11. desparate   _____
12. develope   _____
13. diffrent   _____
14. dinning   _____
15. discribe   _____
16. dosen't   _____

17. embarass   _____
18. enviroment   _____
19. exagerate   _____
20. Febuary   _____
21. fasinate   _____
22. goverment   _____
23. grammer   _____
24. heigth   _____
25. imediate   _____
26. intrest   _____
27. knowlege   _____
28. mathmatics   _____
29. neccessary   _____
30. ocassion   _____
31. oppinion   _____
32. oportunity   _____

33. orginal _____

34. particlar _____

35. potatoe _____

36. preform _____

37. prehaps _____

38. probally _____

39. ridiclous _____

40. seperate _____

41. simular _____

42. sincerly _____

43. studing _____

44. suprise _____

45. temperture _____

46. Thrusday _____

47. unusal _____

48. writting _____

Section Three Review

1. Using *ie* or *ei*:

   > Use *i* before *e*
   >
   > Except after *c*
   >
   > Or when sounded like *ay*
   >
   > As in *neighbor* or *weigh*.

2. Keeping or Changing a Final *-y*:

   - Change the *-y* to *-i* when the *y* follows a consonant.

   - Do not change the *-y* to *-i* if the *y* follows a vowel. Do not change the *-y* to *-i* if you are adding *-ing*.

3. Keeping or Dropping a Silent Final *-e*:

   - In general, drop the final *-e* before an ending that begins with a vowel.

   - In general, keep the final *-e* before an ending that begins with a consonant.

4. Doubling the Final Consonant:

   - In a one-syllable word, double the final consonant only if a single vowel precedes the final consonant.

   - In a word of more than one syllable, apply the above rule only if the last syllable is accented.

5. Using Prefixes:

   - A prefix is one or more syllables added at the start of a word to change its meaning. Do not change any letters of the root word when you add a prefix to it.

6. Forming Plurals

   - Add *-s* to make most nouns plural. Add *-es* if the noun ends in *ch, sh, ss,* or *x*.

   - If a noun ends in *o*, add *-s* if the *o* is preceded by a vowel. Add *-es* if the *o* is preceded by a consonant.

   - Some nouns that end in *-f* or *-fe* form the plural by changing the ending to *-ve* before the *s*.

   - Some words, especially words borrowed from other languages, form plurals by changing spelling.

7. Using Your Dictionary:

   - Whenever you're in doubt about the spelling of a word, consult your dictionary.

Exercise 3A

Correct any spelling errors in the following sentences by crossing out the incorrectly spelled word and writing the correct spelling above it.

1. After ~~worring~~ *worrying* for five days, Raymundo decided that ~~niether~~ *neither* solution would work.

2. Paco kept a sliegh on his patioe, but it never snowed.

3. Barb and Deborah often dissagree about whether or not a word is mispelled.

4. The police officers sincerly believed the judgement of the court would be not guilty.

5. The weary traveller looked at the sky and finally admitted that he had no idea where he was.

6. Jack's book on the protien deit was stolen.

7. Chelsea payed the annoied clerk sixty-five pennys for the candy bar.

8. Ulysses was hopeing that the innacuracies in his report would not be noticed.

9. Although the flaw in his sweater was not very noticable, Brent decided that he should probally not wear it to the job interview.

10. Bart gave a lecture on his knowlege of the heros of the Old West.

11. When Megan explained how intrested she was in black holes, her instructor refered her to a book by Stephen Hawking.

12. The calfs were desperatly trying to avoid the cowboys.

13. It was a dissappointing ski season because the temperture of the outside air rarely fell below freezing.

14. Mr. Pagan truely beleived that being a Leo made him special.

15. Hector could hardly contain his excitement when he heard about the discovery of a valueable source of clean energy.

Exercise 3B

Correct any spelling errors in the following sentences by crossing out the incorrectly spelled word and writing the correct spelling above it. If a sentence is correct, do nothing to it.

1. The two best ~~sopranoes~~ *sopranos* in the choir ~~discribed~~ *described* the person who had stolen their sheet music.

2. Travis is efficeint at stoping fires from spreading.

3. The new realator said that she prefered to sell commercial propertys.

4. The casheir gave me a reciept for my purchase.

5. Once Dennis had merged safly into the freeway traffic, he knew that he would easyly pass his driver's exam.

6. It was unecessary to remind the monkies that it was time for lunch.

7. Because of the missprint, both attornies filed suit against each other.

8. Mr. Sullivan often terrifys children by preforming strange magic tricks.

9. The mare's skittishness was definately caused by the bites of several large horseflys.

10. Alot of the time I come accross mistakes in my phone bill.

11. Although Issac was quite good at mathmatics, he prefered to spend his time sitting under apple trees.

12. Corbin wanted to develope an intrest in herpetology.

13. Mark had always believed that his niece would achieve her dream of finding an ancient society where neighbors were friendly and never deceived each other.

14. Usally a person will become fasinated when Laura Asply slithers in.

15. Controling his temper, Louis tryed to offer encouragment to his son.

Exercise 3C

Correct any spelling errors in the following sentences by crossing out the incorrectly spelled word and writing the correct spelling above it. If a sentence is correct, do nothing to it.

1. One of the things I would like to see changed ~~imediately~~ *immediately* is movie theaters, especially the noisy ~~enviroment~~ *environment*, the overpriced refreshments, and the ~~vilent~~ *violent*, indecent movies. **2.** People definately pay a good price to see a film, so they should at least be asured of a quite atmosfere to see it in. **3.** I am not exagerating when I say that hardly a time goes by when I am not anoyed by people talking or babys crying in the theater. **4.** My oppinion is that parents should not be aloud to bring their babys to the theater. **5.** They should be stoped at the door if neccessary or not sold tikets. **6.** Prehaps theaters should build specal soundproof rooms for parints with children, and they could pay extra because they are saving the cost of a babysitter. **7.** Anyway, I would be sincerly embarassed for my young children to see alot of the movies being shown now. **8.** Everbody complains about the refreshments, which are way to expinsive. **9.** I often have payed more for popcorn, candy bars, and soft drinks than I have for addmision. **10.** If theaters are going to charge that much, than they should alow us to bring in are own food from outside. **11.** If they're were more competion for refreshments, they would probally lower their prices. **12.** There is not room hear for me to put into writting what I think about the qualuty of the diffrent items they sell. **13.** It is not just the babies' crys or the poor food that bothers me; I don't like alot of the movies that they show. **14.** It is a common complant that movies are to vilent and sexualy explicit. **15.** I no our goverment dosen't want to get into the business of censoring films, but something should be done in the intrest of decensy. **16.** Films are an important source of entertanment, so something should be done about improving the atmosfere and the kinds of films being shown in our theaters.

Sentence Practice:
Effective and Meaningful Sentences

These final sentence combining exercises are presented without specific directions. There will be a number of possible combinations for each group. Experiment to discover the most effective way to combine the sentences, supplying transitional words where necessary. You may also want to change the order in which the ideas are presented.

Sentence Combining Exercises

▶ **EXAMPLE**

a. The first marathon was run in 1896.
b. It was run at the Olympic Games in Athens, Greece.
c. The marathon was founded to honor the Greek soldier Pheidippides.
d. He is supposed to have run from the town of Marathon to Athens in 409 B.C.
e. The distance is 22 miles, 1470 yards.
f. He ran to bring the news of the victory of the Greeks over the Persians.
g. In 1924 the distance was standardized to 26 miles, 385 yards.

The first marathon was run at the Olympic Games in Athens, Greece, in 1896. The marathon was founded to honor the Greek soldier Pheidippides, who, in 409 B.C., is supposed to have run from the town of Marathon to Athens, a distance of 22 miles, 1470 yards, to bring the news of the victory of the Greeks over the Persians. In 1924 the distance was standardized to 26 miles, 385 yards.

1. Combine the following sentences.

a. We get the expression "grin like a Cheshire cat" from a cheese.
b. The cheese was sold in Cheshire County, Ireland.
c. The cheese was molded in the shape of a cat.
d. The cat had a very broad grin.

_____

_____

_____

_____

_____

Sentence Combining Exercises

continued

2. Combine the following sentences.

    a. The word *acre* comes from the Anglo-Saxon language.
    b. It originally meant the amount of land plowable in a day.
    c. The measurement of an acre was codified in the fourteenth century.
    d. Before then the actual size of an acre would vary.
    e. Its size would depend on the quality of the land being plowed.
    f. It would also depend on the animals used.

_____

_____

_____

_____

_____

3. Combine the following sentences.

    a. The Canada Biting Fly Center made the report.
    b. It reported that a fly lands upside down on a ceiling.
    c. It lands by raising its forelegs above its head.
    d. They make contact with the ceiling.
    e. The fly brings its second and hind legs forward.
    f. It brings these legs up to the ceiling.
    g. The fly thus performs a flip in midair.
    h. It lands upside down on the ceiling.

_____

_____

_____

_____

_____

Sentence Combining Exercises

continued

4. Combine the following sentences.

   a. The word *fore* is yelled by golfers to warn of an errant golf shot.
   b. It originated in the English military.
   c. Troops used to fire in lines.
   d. The command "'ware before" would warn the front lines.
   e. They needed to kneel so the back lines wouldn't blow their heads off.
   f. *Fore* is simply a shortened version of "'ware before."

   _____

   _____

   _____

   _____

5. Combine the following sentences.

   a. Alexander Graham Bell invented the telephone.
   b. He tried to get financial backing for his invention.
   c. He was arrested.
   d. He was charged with attempting to obtain money under false pretenses.
   e. A local newspaper reported the arrest.
   f. It called him a fraud.
   g. It also called him an unscrupulous trickster.

   _____

   _____

   _____

   _____

continued

6. Combine the following sentences.

    a. Early Dutch settlers in America made popular a treat.
    b. It was called "oily cakes" or "fried cakes."
    c. These treats were often served as balls of dough.
    d. The dough was sweetened.
    e. The dough was fried in fat.
    f. These treats came to be called "doughnuts."

_____

_____

_____

_____

7. Combine the following sentences.

    a. No one really knows who invented the doughnut "hole."
    b. One gentleman is sometimes credited with doing so.
    c. His name was Hanson Gregory.
    d. He was a sea captain.
    e. Supposedly, he was eating a fried cake one night.
    f. Stormy weather arose.
    g. He needed both hands to steer his ship.
    h. He rammed the cake over a nearby wooden spoke.
    i. Later, he gave an order to his cook.
    j. He wanted all of his fried cakes to have holes in them.

_____

_____

_____

_____

_____

continued

8. Combine the following sentences.

    a. The people in beer commercials are almost always men.
    b. They are never overweight.
    c. They are never drunk.
    d. They are never belligerent.
    e. They are always neatly dressed.
    f. They are almost always engaged in "manly" occupations.
    g. Sometimes they are famous retired sports figures.
    h. They are never alone.
    i. They are usually surrounded by pals.
    j. Do beer commercials represent reality?

_____

_____

_____

_____

9. Combine the following sentences.

    a. The tradition of growing lawns has existed for centuries.
    b. The Chinese grew lawns five thousand years ago.
    c. The Mayans and the Aztecs also seem to have grown lawns.
    d. In the Middle Ages monarchs surrounded their castles with lawns.
    e. In colonial America the lawn soon came to be a status symbol.
    f. Dr. John Falk works for the Smithsonian Institution.
    g. He believes that our love of lawns reveals a preference.
    h. The preference is genetically encoded.
    i. The preference is for a savannah-like terrain.

_____

_____

_____

_____

Sentence Combining Exercises

continued

10. Combine the following sentences.

    a. It was 1847.
    b. Dr. Semmelweiss discovered something about a doctor's unwashed hands.
    c. They could transmit a fatal infection.
    d. The infection was transmitted to women who were giving birth.
    e. He suggested that physicians should wash their hands before entering the maternity ward.
    f. His fellow doctors were outraged.
    g. They banned him from the hospital where he made the discovery.
    h. Fifty years passed before his advice was taken.
    i. Thousands of new mothers died needlessly each year.

_____

_____

_____

_____

_____

Paragraph Practice: Expressing an Opinion

Writing Assignment

You have now written a narrative and a descriptive paragraph (in Chapters One and Two) and several expository paragraphs (in Chapters Three, Four, and Five). Your final writing assignment will be an **opinion paragraph** (also called an "argumentative" paragraph). As in earlier chapters, Exercises 1C, 2C, and 3C in this chapter have been designed as models of the paragraph you will now write. Exercise 1C argues that college students should be required to perform community service; Exercise 2C expresses the opinion that "self-directed" competition can bring many benefits; and Exercise 3C claims that movie theaters need to be improved.

Note that each of these paragraphs includes a topic sentence that expresses an opinion. Each of the above paragraphs expresses an opinion that is supported by details and examples drawn from the writer's personal experience. Notice, for example, that the paragraph in Exercise 2C presents three reasons to show that today's movie theaters need to be improved. Those three reasons discuss the noise, the refreshments, and the movies themselves, and each of them is drawn from the personal experience of the writer. Your assignment is to write a paragraph in which you express an opinion that you support with examples and details drawn from your own experiences or observations.

Reading Assignment

The reading selections in the "Expressing an Opinion" section of Chapter Seven can help you see how professional writers express and support their arguments. Read one or more of the selections, as assigned by your instructor, and use the questions that follow them to develop ideas for your own paper.

Prewriting

Prewriting Application: Finding Your Topic

Use prewriting techniques to develop your thoughts about one of the following topics or a topic suggested by your instructor. Before you choose a topic, prewrite to develop a list of possible reasons and examples that you can use to support your opinion. Don't choose a topic if you do not have examples with which you can support it.

1. Choose a proverb and show why it may not always be good advice. Consider these:

   Don't count your chickens before they hatch.

   The early bird gets the worm.

   Look before you leap.

   If at first you don't succeed, try, try again.

   If you can't beat 'em, join 'em.

   Money can't buy happiness.

2. Support an opinion about the condition of your neighborhood, your college campus, your home, or some other place with which you are familiar.

3. Some people compete in nearly everything they do, whether it be participating in sports, working on the job, or studying in college classes. Other people find competition distracting and even offensive. Write a paragraph in which you support your opinion about competition.

4. Do you eat in fast-food restaurants? Write a paragraph in which you support your opinion about eating in such places.

5. Should parents spank children? Write a paper in which you support your opinion for or against such discipline.

6. Should high school students work at part-time jobs while going to school? Write a paper in which you support an opinion for or against their doing so.

7. Do you know couples who live together without marrying? Write a paper in which you support an opinion for or against such an arrangement.

8. Is peer pressure really a very serious problem for people today? Write a paper in which you support an opinion about the seriousness of peer pressure.

9. Is racism, sexism, homophobia, or religious intolerance still a common problem in our society? Write a paper in which you support your opinion one way or the other.

10. Do general education requirements benefit college students? Write a paper in which you support your opinion about such classes.

Prewriting Application: Working with Topic Sentences

Identify the topic sentences in Exercises 1C (page 327), 2C (page 342), and 3C (page 357). What are the topic and the central point in each topic sentence?

Prewriting Application: Evaluating Topic Sentences

Write "No" before each sentence that would not make an effective topic sentence *for this assignment*. Write "Yes" before each sentence that would make an effective one. Identify the opinion expressed by each effective topic sentence Be prepared to explain your answers.

_____ **1.** The intersection of Whitewoc
most dangerous traffic spots

_____ **2.** Sometimes the old proverl
again" is the worst advice th

_____ **3.** Racism has existed in our country for h.

_____ **4.** My father and mother are not married and never ha

_____ **5.** Not everyone needs to be married to have a strong relationship and a happy family.

_____ **6.** Almost every young teenager could benefit from participating in competitive sports.

_____ **7.** Many high school students today work at part-time jobs.

_____ **8.** Body piercing can be a healthy, safe expression of one's individuality.

_____ **9.** There are several good reasons why a person should never drink carbonated soft drinks.

_____ **10.** Most people's family values are going straight downhill.

Prewriting Application: Talking to Others

Form a group of three or four people and discuss the topics you have chosen. Your goal here is to help each other clarify your opinions and determine if you have enough evidence to support it. Explain why you hold your opinion and what specific reasons and examples you will use to support it. As you listen to the others in your group, use the following questions to help them clarify their ideas.

1. Can the opinion be reasonably supported in a brief paper? Is its topic too general or broad?

2. What specific examples will the writer provide as support? Are they convincing?

3. What is the weakest reason or example? Why? Should it be made stronger or completely replaced?

4. Which reasons or examples are the strongest? Why?

5. Which reason or example should the paper open with? Which should it close with?

Writing

Write the rough draft of your paragraph. Open it with a topic sentence that clearly states your opinion. Then support your opinion with several reasons that are illustrated with personal examples and details.

Introduce each new reason with a clear transitional sentence. Add transitions between sentences where they might be needed for clarity. Write a concluding sentence that reemphasizes the central point of your paragraph.

Writing Application: Identifying Transitional Words, Phrases, and Sentences

Examine Exercises 1C (page 327), 2C (page 342), and 3C (page 357). Identify the transitional sentences that introduce each new reason offered in support of your opinion. Then identify any other transitions that serve to connect ideas between sentences.

Rewriting

1. Revise your sentences so they include specific and concrete details. As much as possible, use actual names of people and places and refer to specific details whenever possible.

2. Add or revise transitions wherever doing so would help clarify movement from one idea to another.

3. Improve your preliminary topic sentence so that it more accurately states the central point of your paragraph.

4. Examine your draft for sentence variety. If many of your sentences tend to be of the same length, try varying their length and their structure by combining sentences using the techniques you have studied in the Sentence Practice sections of this text.

Rewriting Application: Responding to Writing

Read the following paragraph. Then respond to the questions following it.

School Sports

Many of my relatives believe that playing sports in high school and college is a waste of time and energy, but I disagree. I believe that school sports can help a person stay out of trouble and can lead to bigger and better things. I know, for instance, that sports can help young people who are heading for trouble with the law. I have a close friend who grew up in a very hostile environment. His parents abused him, and he belonged to gangs ever since he was very young. He had been in and out of juvenile court several times when he discovered something special about himself. He discovered that he is a good athlete. He began to excel at baseball and football. He developed a love for both sports. After playing football at Escondido High School, he earned a full scholarship to the University of Nevada. Playing sports can also help people emotionally. For example, sports have helped me learn to control my anger. I am a very emotional person, and when I get angry I just want to hit someone—hard. Whenever I feel like that, I get out on the football field and get physical. By the end of a hard practice, I'm ready to go back and live my life. Football helps me when I'm stressed out or depressed, too. I can always count on my teammates to bring me back up when I'm down. Furthermore, playing sports encourages students to stay in school and motivates them to do well. I'm the kind of person who hates school, but through sports I have learned that the road to success includes an education. There have been many times when I have wanted to drop out of school, but always holding me back is my love for the game of football. I know that football is not always going to be there for me, but school sports have changed my life and have affected the lives of many others as well.

1. Identify the topic sentence. State its topic and central idea. Does it express a definite opinion?

2. How many supporting points are presented in this paper? Identify them.

3. Identify the transitional sentences that introduce each major supporting point. What other transitions are used between sentences?

4. Consider the organization of the paragraph. Would you change the order of the supporting material? Explain why or why not.

5. Consider the sentence variety. What sentences would you combine to improve the paragraph?

Rewriting Application: Revising and Editing Your Own Draft

Look closely at your topic sentence and transitions. Make any improvements that are needed. Consider your supporting points. Do they need to be explained more thoroughly or described in more detail? Is the organization of your points clear? Can the reader tell where one point ends and another begins? If your paragraph contains too many brief sentences or too many compound sentences joined by *and*, revise them to improve the sentence variety of your paper.

When editing your paper, check your draft for the following errors:

• Sentence fragments, comma splices, and fused sentences

• Misplaced modifiers and dangling modifiers

• Errors in subject–verb agreement

• Errors in pronoun case, pronoun–antecedent agreement, or pronoun reference

• Errors in comma use

• Errors in the use of periods, question marks, exclamation points, colons, semicolons, and quotation marks

• Errors in capitalization, titles, and numbers

• Errors in the use of irregular verbs or in word choice

• Misspelled words

Now prepare a clean final draft, following the format your instructor has asked for. Before you turn in your final draft, proofread it carefully and make any necessary corrections.

Chapter Six Practice Test

I. Review of Chapters Three, Four, and Five

A. Correct any misplaced or dangling modifiers. Do nothing if the sentence is correct.

  1. Hanging from a limb halfway up the tree, my heart was beating rapidly.

  _____

  _____

  2. Sumi almost swam thirty laps in her workout this morning.

  _____

  _____

  3. Anton lent the money to his friend that he was saving for his trip to Russia.

  _____

  _____

  4. The dog with the man with long ears and a bushy tail was barking at everything that came by.

  _____

  _____

  5. The tightrope walker lost his balance and fell into the pool of sharks bothered by memories of his unhappy childhood.

  _____

  _____

B. Correct any subject–verb agreement or pronoun use errors in the following sentences. Do nothing if the sentence is correct.

  6. Gymnastics as run by our school's coaches was a quality experience.

  7. Amy yelled down to her sister that she should be ready in about an hour.

  8. Everyone in Crete except the king and queen were happy to see the men fly away.

continued

9. Our grandparents bought Willy and I new computers when we left for college.

10. When travelers want to visit a scenic, clean, and friendly place, you should consider Lucerne, Switzerland.

C. Add commas to the following sentences where necessary.

11. Yes the new library will be ready by September but all of the books may not have arrived by then.

12. Zorro walked into the store and ordered a bullwhip a mask a sword and a mustang.

13. Nicole wanted to live in Seattle Washington; however there were no jobs for sand sculptors available.

14. When the weather becomes hot and dry Sachiko goes to her favorite place her cabin in the Rockies.

D. Add periods, question marks, exclamation points, quotation marks, semicolons, colons, and apostrophes (or 's) where necessary, and correct any mistakes in the use of capitalization, titles, and numbers. Do not add or delete any commas.

15. When we looked into my brothers car, we found copies of these magazines newsweek, time, sports illustrated, and soap opera digest

16. After the lights came on, Tomás asked, Is that all?

17. The police officer inquired, Did you know your license had expired

18. 5 people who were selling candy came to my house at 590 hershey street, mars, pennsylvania, one day in autumn.

19. On monday many citizens are going to the school board meeting to argue about the boards decision to ban the novel huckleberry finn.

20. In yesterdays paper there were 3 articles on pet care; the title of one was how to be kind to your iguana.

Chapter Six Practice Test

II. Chapter Six

A. In the blanks, write in the correct forms of the verbs indicated.

21. It was so hot that I must have _____ two gallons of water by noon. (drink)

22. Dotra's skin was so red that I thought she must have _____ in the sun for hours. (lie)

23. Leo was surprised because he had never _____ five miles before. (swim)

24. Pooh had _____ for hours trying to escape the bees. (run)

25. Since last week, the water level has _____ at least fifteen feet. (rise)

B. Correct any verb form errors in the following sentences. Do nothing if the sentence is correct.

26. After work yesterday, I just lay around the house all day.

27. By the time they lay their eggs, the salmon have swam for many miles up the river.

28. Whenever I make a fire, my dog lays in front of it.

29. Sven must have drank ten cups of coffee last night.

30. On Saturdays my mother has always brung lemon icebox pie for dessert.

C. Underline the correct word in the parentheses.

31. Katie was pleased with the (complements compliments) she received for her latest painting.

32. Cal's father was having a difficult time (accepting excepting) his excuse for the dent in the car.

33. Richard's daughter Avia was (anxious eager) to go to Sea World.

34. The high decibel level at the concert (affected effected) my ability to talk with my date.

35. Whenever Wayne is faced with a moral dilemma, he tries to remember the (principles principals) that his father taught him.

D. Correct any incorrect word choices in the following sentences. Do nothing if the sentence is correct.

36. The soldiers were nervous, but they were already for the battle.

37. I'm usually more in the mood for Spam then the other members of my family.

38. We wanted to throw Mr. Perro a bone, but he was disinterested.

39. It was all right with the students if their final examinations contained fewer questions than their midterm examinations.

40. The judge did not want the question to effect the jurors, so he disallowed it.

E. Underline the correctly spelled word in parentheses.

41. When we (received recieved) the strange package, we wondered if it contained our missing (library libary) books.

42. In Fergal's class, we were (studing studying) the (potato potatoe) blight.

43. Jethro and Abner were not really (disatisifed dissatisfied) with (their thier) low grades, but they did not tell us that.

44. Thoren (prefered preferred) the more immediate danger, but he was still (completely completly) discouraged.

45. Grendel was not very (paticular particular) about whom he fought, but he realized he was in trouble when Beowulf (seized siezed) his arm.

F. Correct any spelling errors in the following sentences by crossing out the incorrectly spelled word and writing the correct spelling above it.

46. When Corpulo wieghed himself this morning, he cryed with happiness.

47. Shawna's poor handwritting is practically ilegible.

continued

48. When Shaun's date discribed what he had done last night, he was embarassed.

49. The young doctor was quite suprised when she realized that her patient was a well-known goverment official.

50. Ahab listened to the arguements of Starbuck and the crew and then admited that all he cared about was the white whale.

Readings for Writers

We hope the reading selections in this chapter will interest you as well as stimulate you to think about the ideas they present. In these selections you will find stories of youthful recklessness and insecurities, reflections on how we should live our lives, and arguments about current issues. If you read these selections thoughtfully, you will find many ideas for topics of your own.

The reading selections are divided into groups of three, with each group illustrating one type of writing assignment from Chapters 1 through 6. Read these selections carefully, as you would any college reading assignment. To get the most out of each selection, use the following guidelines.

Strategies for Successful Reading

Establish Your Expectations

- *Before* you read, take a moment to think. Consider the title of the selection. Does it raise any questions in your mind? Does it suggest a topic or point that you should look for as you read? Consider any background information that accompanies the reading selection. What does it suggest about the author or the reading material?

- Thinking about these questions should take only a minute or two, but these few minutes are important. They will help you understand more of what you read because you are starting your reading with a focused, active attitude.

First Reading: Underline or Highlight as You Read

- With a pen, pencil, or highlighter in hand, read the material from start to finish, slowly and carefully. During the first reading, you're trying to get an overall sense of the main idea of the selection. Don't try to take notes yet. Instead, just underline or highlight whatever sentences seem important to you. If a sentence seems to state a significant idea, mark it. If an example or fact is particularly striking, mark it, too. If you come across words that you do not recognize, circle or mark them.

Second Reading: Make Notes in the Margins

- Re-read the sentences you have underlined or highlighted. In just a few words, write your thoughts or reactions to what you have marked. If you disagree with an idea, say so in the margin. If you don't understand something, write a question mark next to it. Some of the passages you have underlined won't seem important to you anymore. So skip them.

- Completing this step will help you understand what you have read much better than if you merely read the selection through once. You might also begin to recognize both the main idea of the reading selection and the organization of its supporting material.

Find the Central and Supporting Ideas

- Each of the writing assignments in *Inside Writing* asks you to focus on one central idea. Really, everything you write or read has some sort of central idea—even a shopping list. (Its central idea would be "Buy these things!") As you read each of the following selections, watch for the idea it develops. Sometimes the central idea will be stated clearly and obviously. Other times you will need to figure it out without the writer stating it directly. In either case, write out the central idea *in your own words*. Try to express it in only one or two sentences.

- If the central idea expresses an opinion or requires explanation, the reading selection will also include supporting ideas. Identify the supporting ideas, either by marking them in the margin of the selection or by writing them out on a separate sheet of paper.

Respond to the Reading Material

- Your reaction to what you have read is important. Depending on the nature of the reading selection, you may find yourself identifying with the writer, beginning to look at an idea you had never examined before, or disagreeing with the writer altogether. If you have questions or objections or new ideas as or after you read, write them down before you have moved on to other reading material.

Sample Reading Selection

Kill Your Television

James A. Herrick

James Herrick, an associate professor of communications at Hope College in Holland, Michigan, wrote the following selection for the Scripps Howard News Service in 1994. In it he presents five reasons why he does not watch television.

Vocabulary Check

dilemma (2)	uncompensated (6)	noxious (11)
garnering (5)	vacuous (11)	inadvertently (12)

People sometimes ask why I, a professor of communication, do not have a television in my home. When I try to explain this apparent inconsistency, the usual response is something like: "I admire that decision, but I don't think it would work for me." **1**

A dilemma
It wastes time but
we are still
attracted to it.

Television presents a dilemma: Many of us find that it does not represent a productive or enriching use of time, but we nevertheless find it attractive as a source of entertainment and information. **2**

So how can a thoroughly modern American choose to get rid of the tube without committing cultural suicide? **3**

Eliminating television from your life can be a perfectly reasonable decision. Here are some of my reasons for taking the cultural path less traveled. **4**

1ˢᵗ reason to stop—
Objects to the
commercial system
(What does he
mean here?)

First, I object to the system that drives television. Commercial television in America today must be understood, not principally as a medium for delivering entertainment and information, but as an enormous industry centered on garnering viewers of commercials. Entertainment and information are bait in television's great fishing expedition for audiences. And television seeks audiences for only one reason—to sell those audiences to advertisers. Commercials are the point of *commercial* television, and programming is a means of securing attention to those commercials. **5**

When I watch television, I am investing uncompensated time as a "commercials viewer"—my time is being sold to an advertiser by a network.

No, thanks. I've got better things to do.

(Second,) television viewing is a gigantic waste of time. The typical American family has the television on for five or six hours each day, and in many households it's on considerably longer than that. The only other activities to which most of us devote that much time are work and sleep. Our reward for that investment of time is a meager one—a heavily edited view of world events through "news" programming and the shallow comedies and tragedies of prime time. Given the choice, I would rather spend that time reading, taking a walk, talking with a friend. Which brings me to my (third point.)

*2ⁿᵈ—a gigantic
waste of time
5–6 hours/day!
little reward*

Television robs relationships of time. Relationships among friends and family members take time to develop—quantity time. Marriages, for example, are nurtured on communication, and this communication takes time—lots of time, regular time. Television steals the time it takes to build and enjoy real-life relationships, which are a lot more satisfying than sitcoms.

*3ʳᵈ—robs
relationships
of time

True!*

Doesn't time spent watching television together build relationships? No. Television does not usually encourage communication, either while people are watching it or afterward. I am an advocate of conversation, and thus an opponent of television.

(Fourth,) let's face it: Television programming is mostly vacuous, noxious or both. Need I elaborate? Does television programming typically set a high standard for personal conduct? Does it ask me to think hard about what I ought to value, and why? Does it provide insights into the intricate issues that face any citizen of this increasingly complex and diverse society?

*4ᵗʰ—the shows
are lousy*

Television seldom does any of these things. And even when it inadvertently does accomplish a worthwhile goal, there are any number of surer paths to these ends. Most of us need more, not less, incentive to live humanely, think broadly, and engage relationships emphatically.

(My final) reason for turning off the tube is that involvement with it is often based on an unexamined concept of entertainment. Television is usually justified as a means of entertaining ourselves, of relaxing from

*5ᵗʰ—an unexamined
concept of
entertainment*

the demands of work. But many of us have accepted uncritically the Hollywood notion of entertainment as "amusement without boundaries," whether those boundaries are of time or subject matter. I am not arguing against the fatigued duo of sex and violence. Rather, I am asking: How much time should go to entertaining myself, and which activities are really relaxing? Maybe I'm missing something here, but I don't find television viewing relaxing at all.

Is TV really relaxing?

Finding better sources of entertainment, information and relaxation is not difficult. People freed from the tube find a lot of imaginative and satisfying ways to fill newly discovered time.

14

There are better things to do.

Each of us has precious little time to use as we wish. Why should so much of that time go to television?

15

Narrating an Event

Salvation

Langston Hughes

Langston Hughes is a distinguished twentieth-century American writer. An African American who is best known for his poetry, he also wrote stories, novels, essays, an autobiography, and plays. The following selection, drawn from his autobiography, tells of a crisis early in his life.

Vocabulary Check

revival (1)   rounder (6)

dire (3)   knickerbockered (11)

I was saved from sin when I was going on thirteen. But not really saved.   1
It happened like this. There was a big revival at my Auntie Reed's church. Every night for weeks there had been much preaching, singing, praying, and shouting, and some very hardened sinners had been brought to Christ, and the membership of the church had grown by leaps and bounds. Then just before the revival ended, they had a special meeting for children, "to bring the young lambs to the fold." My aunt spoke of it for days ahead. That night I was escorted to the front row and placed on the mourners' bench with all the other young sinners, who had not yet been brought to Jesus.

My aunt told me that when you were saved you saw a light, and   2
something happened to you inside! And Jesus came into your life! And God was with you from then on! She said you could see and hear and feel Jesus in your soul. I believed her. I had heard a great many old people say the same thing and it seemed to me they ought to know. So I sat there calmly in the hot, crowded church, waiting for Jesus to come to me.

The preacher preached a wonderful rhythmical sermon, all moans   3
and shouts and lonely cries and dire pictures of hell, and then he sang a song about the ninety and nine safe in the fold, but one little lamb was left out in the cold. Then he said: "Won't you come? Won't you come to Jesus? Young lambs, won't you come?" And he held out his arms to all of us young sinners there on the mourners' bench. And the little girls cried. And some of them jumped up and went to Jesus right away. But most of us just sat there.

A great many old people came and knelt around us and prayed, old 4
women with jet-black faces and braided hair, old men with work-
gnarled hands. And the church sang a song about the lower lights are
burning, some poor sinners to be saved. And the whole building rocked
with prayer and song.

Still I kept waiting to *see* Jesus. 5

Finally all the young people had gone to the altar and were saved, 6
but one boy and me. He was a rounder's son named Westley. Westley
and I were surrounded by sisters and deacons praying. It was very hot
in the church, and getting late now. Finally Westley said to me in a
whisper: "God damn! I'm tired o' sitting here. Let's get up and be
saved." So he got up and was saved.

Then I was left all alone on the mourners' bench. My aunt came 7
and knelt at my knees and cried, while prayers and songs swirled all
around me in the little church. The whole congregation prayed for me
alone, in a mighty wail of moans and voices. And I kept waiting
serenely for Jesus, waiting, waiting—but he didn't come. I wanted to
see him, but nothing happened to me. Nothing! I wanted something to
happen to me, but nothing happened.

I heard the songs and the minister saying: "Why don't you come? 8
My dear child, why don't you come to Jesus? Jesus is waiting for you.
He wants you. Why don't you come? Sister Reed, what is this child's
name?"

"Langston," my aunt sobbed. 9

"Langston, why don't you come? Why don't you come and be 10
saved? Oh, Lamb of God! Why don't you come?"

Now it was really getting late. I began to be ashamed of myself, 11
holding everything up so long. I began to wonder what God thought
about Westley who certainly hadn't seen Jesus either, but who was now
sitting proudly on the platform, swinging his knickerbockered legs and
grinning down at me, surrounded by deacons and old women on their
knees praying. God had not struck Westley dead for taking his name in
vain or for lying in the temple. So I decided that maybe to save further
trouble, I'd better lie, too, and say that Jesus had come, and get up and
be saved.

So I got up. 12

Suddenly the whole room broke into a sea of shouting, as they saw   13
me rise. Waves of rejoicing swept the place. Women leaped in the air.
My aunt threw her arms around me. The minister took me by the hand
and led me to the platform.

When things quieted down, in a hushed silence, punctuated by a   14
few ecstatic "Amens," all the new young lambs were blessed in the
name of God. Then joyous singing filled the room.

That night, for the last time in my life but one—for I was a big boy   15
twelve years old—I cried, in bed alone, and couldn't stop. I buried my
head under the quilts, but my aunt heard me. She woke up and told my
uncle I was crying because the Holy Ghost had come into my life, and
because I had seen Jesus. But I was really crying because I couldn't bear
to tell her that I had lied, that I had deceived everybody in the church,
that I hadn't seen Jesus, and that now I didn't believe there was a Jesus
any more, since he didn't come to help me.

QUESTIONS FOR DISCUSSION

1. What did the young Hughes expect would happen to him in the church?
   Why did he expect what he did?

2. Narratives often build in tension until they reach a turning point, after
   which everything is different, both in the story and in the narrator's life.
   Identify what you believe to be the turning point in this story, and explain
   why you think it is.

3. Why is Hughes crying at the end of the story? How has he changed? Do
   you consider the change that has occurred significant? Why or why not?

SUGGESTIONS FOR WRITING

1. In the middle of this event, Hughes is surrounded by people, all of them
   praying for him and calling out for him to step forward. Have you ever
   felt the kind of pressure he might be feeling? Have you ever done something you regretted or made some unfortunate decision because of pressure from other people? Write about such a situation, explaining what
   happened and why.

2. Many people have experienced some event that changed the way they
   think about life, other people, or themselves. If you have experienced such
   an event, write a paper telling what happened and in what way you
   changed.

The Dare

Roger Hoffman

In the seventh grade, Roger Hoffman was a "fussed-over smart boy" who needed to "dirty up" his act if he wanted acceptance. Then came the "dare." Although we may have responded differently, Hoffman's narrative reminds us that everyone—adults and children alike—must decide how to respond to the pressures and challenges of life.

Vocabulary Check

shard (1)   implicit (4)
cronies (2)   ambiguous (4)

The secret to diving under a moving freight train and rolling out of the other side with all your parts attached lies in picking the right spot between the tracks to hit with your back. Ideally, you want soft dirt or pea gravel, clear of glass shards and railroad spikes that could cause you instinctively, and fatally, to sit up. Today, at thirty-eight, I couldn't be threatened or baited enough to attempt that dive. But as a seventh grader struggling to make the cut in a tough Atlanta grammar school, all it took was a dare. **1**

I coasted through my first years of school as a fussed-over smart kid, the teacher's pet who finished his work first and then strutted around the room tutoring other students. By the seventh grade, I had more A's than friends. Even my old cronies, Dwayne and O. T., made it clear I'd never be one of the guys in junior high if I didn't dirty up my act. They challenged me to break the rules, and I did. The I-dare-you's escalated: shoplifting, sugaring teachers' gas tanks, dropping lighted matches into public mailboxes. Each guerrilla act won me the approval I never got for just being smart. **2**

Walking home by the railroad tracks after school, we started playing chicken with oncoming trains. O. T., who was failing that year, always won. One afternoon he charged a boxcar from the side, stopping just short of throwing himself between the wheels. I was stunned. After the train disappeared, we debated whether someone could dive under a moving car, stay put for a10-count, then scramble out the other side. I thought it could be done and said so. O. T. immediately stepped in front of me and smiled. Not by me, I added quickly, I certainly didn't mean **3** that I could do it. "A smart guy like you," he said, his smile evaporating, "you could figure it out easy." And then, squeezing each word for effect, "I...DARE...you." I'd just turned twelve. The monkey clawing my back was Teacher's Pet. And I'd been dared.

As an adult, I've been on both ends of life's implicit business and social I-dare-you's, although adults don't use those words. We provoke with body language, tone of voice, ambiguous phrases. I dare you to: argue with the boss, tell Fred what you think of him, send the wine back. Only rarely are the risks physical. How we respond to dares when we are young may have something to do with which of the truly hazardous male inner dares—attacking mountains, tempting bulls at Pamplona—we embrace or ignore as men.

For two weeks, I scouted trains and tracks. I studied moving boxcars close up, memorizing how they squatted on their axles, never getting used to the squeal or the way the air felt hot from the sides. I created an imaginary, friendly train and ran next to it. I mastered a shallow, head-first dive with a simple half-twist. I'd land on my back, count to ten, imagine wheels and, locking both hands on the rail to my left, heave myself over and out. Even under pure sky, though, I had to fight to keep my eyes open and my shoulders between the rails.

The next Saturday, O. T., Dwayne and three eighth graders met me below the hill that backed up to the lumberyard. The track followed a slow bend there and opened to a straight, slightly uphill climb for a solid third of a mile. My run started two hundred yards after the bend. The train would have its tongue hanging out.

The other boys huddled off to one side, a circle on another planet, and watched quietly as I double-knotted my shoelaces. My hands trembled. O. T. broke the circle and came over to me. He kept his hands hidden in the pockets of his jacket. We looked at each other. BB's of sweat appeared beneath his nose. I stuffed my wallet in one of his pockets, rubbing it against his knuckles on the way in, and slid my house key, wired to a red-and-white fishing bobber, into the other. We backed away from each other, and he turned and ran to join the four already climbing up the hill.

I watched them all the way to the top. They clustered together as if   8
I were taking their picture. Their silhouette resembled a round shoul-
dered tombstone. They waved down to me, and I dropped them from
my mind and sat down on the rail. Immediately, I jumped back. The
steel was vibrating.

The train sounded like a cow going short of breath. I pulled my   9
shirttail out and looked down at my spot, then up the incline of track
ahead of me. Suddenly the air went hot, and the engine was by me. I
hadn't pictured it moving that fast. A man's bare head leaned out and
stared at me. I waved to him with my left hand and turned into the
train, burying my face into the incredible noise. When I looked up, the
head was gone.

I started running alongside the boxcars. Quickly, I found their pace,   10
held it, and then eased off, concentrating on each thick wheel that cut
past me. I slowed another notch. Over my shoulder, I picked my car as
it came off the bend, locking in the image of the white mountain goat
painted on its side. I waited, leaned forward like the anchor in a 440-
relay, wishing the baton up the track behind me. Then the big goat fired
by me, and I was flying and then tucking my shoulder as I dipped under
the train.

A heavy blanket of red dust settled over me. I felt bolted to the   11
earth. Sheet-metal bellies thundered and shook above my face. Count to
ten, a voice said, watch the axles and look to your left for daylight. But
I couldn't count, and I couldn't find left if my life depended on it, which
it did. The colors overhead went from brown to red to black to red
again. Finally, I ripped my hands free, forced them to the rail, and, in
one convulsive jerk, threw myself into the blue light.

I lay there face down until there was no more noise, and I could feel   12
the sun against the back of my neck. I sat up. The last ribbon of train
was slipping away in the distance. Across the tracks, O. T. was leading a
cavalry charge down the hill, five very small, galloping boys, their fists
whirling above them. I pulled my knees to my chest. My corduroy
pants puckered wet across my thighs. I didn't care.

QUESTIONS FOR DISCUSSION

1. Why does the young Hoffman accept the dare? As you explain his motivation, refer to specific statements from the narrative to back up your ideas.

2. In what way can the young boy's actions be said to parallel our actions as adults? What paragraph makes that connection? Do you find the connection convincing?

3. How does the boy feel by the end of the story? How can you tell? How does the adult Hoffman, who tells the story, feel about the event? How can you tell?

SUGGESTIONS FOR WRITING

1. Roger Hoffman's narrative gives us an idea of what a person might do to be accepted by his peers. Write a paper in which you tell about such an event that happened to you. How you felt at the time of the event as well as how you feel now should be clear by the end of the story.

2. Hoffman suggests that adults are faced with "I-dare-you's" also, although they are not as obviously expressed as those from our childhood. Write a paper that tells the story of your response to such an adult "dare," describing what you did and why.

As They Say, Drugs Kill

Laura Rowley

Laura Rowley graduated from the University of Illinois in 1987, where she was the city editor of the *Daily Illini*. Since then she has worked at the *United Nations Chronicle* in New York City and as a freelance writer. The following selection was first published in *Newsweek on Campus* in 1987.

Vocabulary Check

cardiac arrest (2)	chorus (16)	randomly (29)
ambivalence (2)	gnashing (21)	speculated (29)
stupefied (3)	irreverent (26)	

The fastest way to end a party is to have someone die in the middle of it.   1

At a party last fall I watched a 22-year-old die of cardiac arrest after he had used drugs. It was a painful, undignified way to die. And I would like to think that anyone who shared the experience would feel his or her ambivalence about substance abuse dissolving.   2

This victim won't be singled out like Len Bias as a bitter example for "troubled youth." He was just another ordinary guy celebrating with friends at a private house party, the kind where they roll in the keg first thing in the morning and get stupefied while watching the football games on cable all afternoon. The living room was littered with beer cans from last night's party—along with dirty socks and the stuffing from the secondhand couch.   3

And there were drugs, as at so many other college parties. The drug of choice this evening was psilocybin, hallucinogenic mushrooms. If you're cool you call them " 'shrooms."   4

This wasn't a crowd huddled in the corner of a darkened room with a single red bulb, shooting needles in their arms. People played darts, made jokes, passed around a joint and listened to the Grateful Dead on the stereo.   5

Suddenly, a thin, tall, brown-haired young man began to gasp. His eyes rolled back in his head, and he hit the floor face first with a crash. Someone laughed, not appreciating the violence of his fall, thinking the afternoon's festivities had finally caught up with another guest. The   6 laugh lasted only a second, as the brown-haired guest began to convulse and choke. The sound of the stereo and laughter evaporated. Bystanders shouted frantic suggestions:

"It's an epileptic fit, put something in his mouth!"   7

"Roll him over on his stomach!"   8

"Call an ambulance; God, somebody breathe into his mouth."   9

A girl kneeling next to him began to sob his name, and he seemed   10
to moan.

"Wait, he's semicoherent." Four people grabbed for the telephone,   11
to find no dial tone, and ran to use a neighbor's. One slammed the dead
phone against the wall in frustration—and miraculously produced a
dial tone.

But the body was now motionless on the kitchen floor. "He has a   12
pulse, he has a pulse."

"But he's not breathing!"   13

"Well, get away—give him some f——ing air!" The three or four   14
guests gathered around his body unbuttoned his shirt.

"Wait—is he OK? Should I call the damn ambulance?"   15

A chorus of frightened voices shouted, "Yes, yes!"   16

"Come on, come on, breathe again. Breathe!"   17

Over muffled sobs came a sudden grating, desperate breath that   18
passed through bloody lips and echoed through the kitchen and living
room.

"He's had this reaction before—when he did acid at a concert last   19
spring. But he recovered in 15 seconds...," one friend confided.

The rest of the guests looked uncomfortably at the floor or paced   20
purposelessly around the room. One or two whispered, "Oh, my God,"
over and over, like a prayer. A friend stood next to me, eyes fixed on the
kitchen floor. He mumbled, just audibly, "I've seen this before. My dad
died of a heart attack. He had the same look...." I touched his shoulder and leaned against a wall, repeating reassurances to myself. People
don't die at parties. People don't die at parties.

Eventually, no more horrible, gnashing sounds tore their way from   21
the victim's lungs. I pushed my hands deep in my jeans pockets wondering how much it costs to pump a stomach and how someone could be

so careless if he had had this reaction with another drug. What would he tell his parents about the hospital bill?

Two uniformed paramedics finally arrived, lifted him onto a stretcher and quickly rolled him out. His face was grayish blue, his mouth hung open, rimmed with blood, and his eyes were rolled back with a yellowish color on the rims. 22

The paramedics could be seen moving rhythmically forward and back through the small windows of the ambulance, whose lights threw a red wash over the stunned watchers on the porch. The paramedics' hands were massaging his chest when someone said, "Did you tell them he took psilocybin? Did you tell them?" 23

"No, I…" 24

"My God, so tell them—do you want him to die?" Two people ran to tell the paramedics the student had eaten mushrooms five minutes before the attack. 25

It seemed irreverent to talk as the ambulance pulled away. My friend, who still saw his father's image, muttered, "That guy's dead." I put my arms around him half to comfort him, half to stop him from saying things I couldn't believe. 26

The next day, when I called someone who lived in the house, I found that my friend was right. 27

My hands began to shake and my eyes filled with tears for someone I didn't know. Weeks later the pain has dulled, but I still can't unravel the knot of emotion that has moved from my stomach to my head. When I told one friend what happened, she shook her head and spoke of the stupidity of filling your body with chemical substances. People who would do drugs after seeing that didn't value their lives too highly, she said. 28

But others refused to read any universal lessons from the incident. Many of those I spoke to about the event considered him the victim of a freak accident, randomly struck down by drugs as a pedestrian might be hit by a speeding taxi. They speculated that the student must have had special physical problems; what happened to him could not happen to them. 29

Couldn't it? Now when I hear people discussing drugs I'm haunted   30
by the image of him lying on the floor, his body straining to rid itself of
substances he chose to take. Painful, undignified, unnecessary—like a
wartime casualty. But in war, at least, lessons are supposed to be
learned, so that old mistakes are not repeated. If this death cannot
make people think and change, that will be an even greater tragedy.

QUESTIONS FOR DISCUSSION

1. Len Bias was a talented young basketball player who died of a drug over-
   dose after signing with the Boston Celtics. Why does Rowley insist that the
   victim in her article is different from Bias, that he's "just another ordinary
   guy"?

2. Consider the effect of the opening paragraph. How did it affect you? Why
   did Rowley start a new paragraph with the second sentence?

3. Rowley suggests many reactions to the young man's death both as it happens and after, both from those present and from those who later heard
   about it. Identify the different reactions. Why does Rowley present so
   many?

SUGGESTIONS FOR WRITING

1. Narrative writing is often used to persuade readers to take or avoid action.
   Sometimes stories like the one Rowley tells us can engage a reader's emotions and convince him or her of a point more effectively than any argument. Describe one event from your own experience or observation that
   you hope will move some readers to change their behaviors. Consider an
   event that depicts some reality about drinking alcohol, smoking cigarettes,
   driving recklessly, or some other similar behavior.

2. Narrate an event that taught you some truth about life, such as the need
   for honesty in relationships, the importance of taking personal responsibility for one's actions, or the harm caused by stereotyping people.

Describing a Place

Tinker Creek

Annie Dillard

Born in Pittsburgh in 1945, Annie Dillard has established a name for herself as a poet, essayist, and literary critic. Before she was thirty, she won a Pulitzer Prize for *Pilgrim at Tinker Creek*, which chronicles her scientific, spiritual, and philosophical reflections while living in the Roanoke Valley of Virginia. In this selection from *Pilgrim at Tinker Creek,* Dillard takes us from a windless summer evening on the bank of a creek to a vision of "stars, deep stars giving way to deeper stars, deeper stars bowing to deepest stars at the crown of an infinite core."

Vocabulary Check

stalk (1)	unfathomable (2)	axis (4)
carp (1)	delta (2)	tarantella (4)
muskrat (1)	latitude (4)	

Where Tinker Creek flows under the sycamore log bridge to the tear-shaped island, it is slow and shallow, fringed thinly in cattail marsh. At this spot an astonishing bloom of life supports vast breeding populations of insects, fish, reptiles, birds, and mammals. On windless summer evenings I stalk along the creek bank or straddle the sycamore log in absolute stillness, watching for muskrats. The night I stayed too late I was hunched on the log staring spellbound at spreading, reflected stains of lilac on the water. A cloud in the sky suddenly lighted as if turned on by a switch; its reflection just as suddenly materialized on the water upstream, flat and floating, so that I couldn't see the creek bottom, or life in the water under the cloud. Downstream, away from the cloud on the water, water turtles smooth as beans were gliding down with the current in a series of easy, weightless push-offs, as men bound on the moon. I didn't know whether to trace the progress of one turtle I was sure of, risking sticking my face in one of the bridge's spider webs made invisible by the gathering dark, or take a chance on seeing the carp, or scan the mudbank in hope of seeing a muskrat, or follow the last of the swallows who caught at my heart and trailed it after them like stream-

1

ers as they appeared from directly below, under the log, flying upstream with their tails forked, so fast.

But shadows spread, and deepened, and stayed. After thousands of years we're still strangers to darkness, fearful aliens in an enemy camp with our arms crossed over our chests. I stirred. A land turtle on the bank, startled, hissed the air from its lungs and withdrew into its shell. An uneasy pink here, an unfathomable blue there, gave great suggestion of lurking beings. Things were going on. I couldn't see whether that sere rustle I heard was a distant rattlesnake, slit-eyed, or a nearby sparrow kicking in the dry flood debris slung at the foot of a willow. Tremendous action roiled the water everywhere I looked, big action, inexplicable. A tremor welled up beside a gaping muskrat burrow in the bank and I caught my breath, but no muskrat appeared. The ripples continued to fan upstream with a steady, powerful thrust. Night was knitting over my face an eyeless mask, and I still sat transfixed. A distant airplane, a delta wing out of nightmare, made a gliding shadow on the creek's bottom that looked like a stingray cruising upstream. At once a black fin slit the pink cloud on the water, shearing it in two. The two halves merged together and seemed to dissolve before my eyes. Darkness pooled in the cleft of the creek and rose, as water collects in a well. Untamed, dreaming lights flickered over the sky. I saw hints of hulking underwater shadows, two pale splashes out of the water, and round ripples rolling close together from a blackened center. 2

At last I stared upstream where only the deepest violet remained of the cloud, a cloud so high its underbelly still glowed feeble color reflected from a hidden sky lighted in turn by a sun halfway to China. And out of that violet, a sudden enormous black body arced over the water. I saw only a cylindrical sleekness. Head and tail, if there was a head and tail, were both submerged in cloud. I saw only one ebony fling, a headlong dive to darkness; then the waters closed, and the lights went out. 3

I walked home in a shivering daze, up hill and down. Later I lay open-mouthed in bed, my arms flung wide at my sides to steady the whirling darkness. At this latitude I'm spinning 836 miles an hour round the earth's axis; I often fancy I feel my sweeping fall as a break- 4 neck arc like the dive of dolphins, and the hollow rushing of wind raises hair on my neck, and the side of my face. In orbit around the sun I'm moving 64,800 miles an hour. The solar system as a whole, like a merry-go-round unhinged, spins, bobs, and blinks at the speed of 43,200 miles an hour along a course set east of Hercules. Someone has piped, and we are dancing a tarantella until the sweat pours. I open my eyes and I see dark, muscled forms curl out of water, with flapping gills and flattened eyes. I close my eyes and I see stars, deep stars giving way to deeper stars, deeper stars bowing to deepest stars at the crown of an infinite cone.

QUESTIONS FOR DISCUSSION

1. How does Dillard respond to the scene? What seems to be her central impression, her emotional reaction? Point out any sentences that help you determine her reaction.

2. "After thousands of years we're still strangers, fearful aliens in an enemy camp with our arms crossed over our chests." What does Dillard mean? What prompts her to make such a statement?

3. Consider paragraph 4. In what way are Dillard's thoughts about the spinning earth connected to her observations of Tinker Creek?

SUGGESTIONS FOR WRITING

1. Consider any natural setting with which you are familiar and about which you have a strong feeling. Choose a specific place, one you remember well. If you can, revisit the place, paying particular attention to the specific sights, sounds, smells that are there. Write a paper that conveys your central impression of the place as you describe it.

2. Tinker Creek causes Annie Dillard to reflect on her place in the universe full of stars as well as in a world of "dark, muscled forms...with flapping gills and flattened eyes." Has any place ever caused you to reflect on who you are or *why* you are? Write a paper describing such a place in detail and the effect it had on you.

Loving Las Vegas

Dan DeLuca

Dan DeLuca first visited Las Vegas in 1997. He says the city was "a monument to Mammon. It was incredible, mind-blowing." This selection, which first appeared in the *Philadelphia Inquirer* in 1997, describes the city as "a Disneyland for adults." As you read it, consider what DeLuca means when he writes, "But for all its orchestrated unreality, Las Vegas is very much American."

Vocabulary Check

mecca (7)	metamorphosis (19)	inhibition (24)
swashbuckling (7)	decadence (21)	nostalgic (24)
replicate (8)	doldrums (22)	cliché (34)
trilogy (10)	conjures (24)	surreality (34)

In *Mars Attacks,* the aliens went there to blow Jack Nicholson—and his UFO-themed casino—to smithereens.   1

In *Showgirls,* Elizabeth Berkley went there to become a professional dancer, and got sidetracked into lap-dancing.   2

In *Honeymoon in Vegas,* Nicolas Cage went to the Mojave Desert's neon oasis to get married. In *Leaving Las Vegas,* he returned to drink himself to death. And in *Con Air,* out next month, he's back, crashlanding a transport plane in the middle of the Strip.   3

Irish rockers U2 descended on Sin City last month to launch their flashy, state-of-the-art "Popmart" tour, which hits Philadelphia on June 7 and 8.   4

And in September, Tupac Shakur went to the largest hotel in the world, Vegas' 5,005-room MGM Grand, for a Mike Tyson fight, and, hours later, was hit with a fatal barrage of gunfire while riding to Suge Knight's hip-hop nightclub.   5

Las Vegas isn't only the fastest-growing city in the nation: It's where American pop culture has gone to play out the end of the century.   6

The gambling mecca in the middle of nowhere has grown bigger than visionary mobster Bugsy Siegel could have imagined when he opened the Flamingo Hotel in 1946. With casinos from the Luxor (a black glass pyramid bigger than the Great Pyramid in Egypt) and New York-New York (with its quarterscale replica of the Manhattan sky-   7 line), to the swashbuckling Treasure Island and rock-and-roll Hard Rock, Vegas retains its reputation as a Disneyland for adults.

But Vegas doesn't just replicate the culture. In the '90's, it has *become* culture, its influence reaching coast to coast and beyond.   8

The first in a national chain of Vegas-themed eateries will open in Times Square next year. (Developers hope to follow with a Philadelphia location in '99.) Filmmakers use the city as a metaphor for sex, greed and the American dream of making the big score. Casinos are turning up on riverboats and Indian reservations nationwide. Strip clubs like Delilah's Den have gone mainstream. And a new generation has embraced the martini-swilling lounge culture epitomized by swingin' Vegas icons Frank Sinatra, Dean Martin and Sammy Davis Jr.   9

"It's the place where the action is," says Michael Ventura, a long-time Las Vegas resident whose latest novel, *The Death of Frank Sinatra,* is the first of a Vegas trilogy. "What other symbol do we have that says 'America, 1997'? Not New York City. Not the Grand Canyon. It's Vegas."   10

What Nevadans insist on calling "gaming" is still what makes Vegas run: Twenty-nine million visitors dropped $5.5 billion gambling there last year. The industry is at the core of an economy that each month attracts 3,000 new residents to the town whose Spanish name translates as "the meadows."   11

(Despite a growing number of visitors, gambling revenue on the Strip was actually down slightly in 1996. Insiders attribute the drop to the family vacationers the city began cultivating a few years back and predict that the department of tourism will soon return to its senses.)   12

But since the Hard Rock Hotel and Casino opened in 1995, Las Vegas—once equated with the fat Elvis and has-been pop artists—has gone hip. The image of Elvis has been unofficially banned from the Strip, and bands such as No Doubt, Live and Marilyn Manson have all played the Joint, the Hard Rock's concert venue.   13

U2's decision to open its intentionally sleazy Popmart spectacular in Vegas made perfect sense. "I slept under a pyramid, looked outside my window and saw the New York skyline," Bono said from the stage of Sam Boyd Stadium. "This is the only town on the planet where nobody's going to notice a 40-foot lemon [on stage]."   14

Camera crews are crawling all over the town. Twenty-nine feature   **15**
films were at least partially shot in Vegas last year, according to Bob
Hirsch, director of the Nevada Motion Picture Division. Never mind
the music videos and TV shows and commercials.

In the last three months alone, the city has starred in Chevy Chase's   **16**
Vegas Vacation and the Matthew Perry-Salma Hayek romantic comedy
Fools Rush In, and had a featured role in Mike Myers' hipster comedy
Austin Powers. After *Con Air* in June, its next big part will come in the
film adaptation of Hunter Thompson's hallucinogenic memoir *Fear and
Loathing in Las Vegas,* which begins shooting in July with Johnny
Depp playing the gonzo journalist.

"We reinvent ourselves every six months, so there's always some-   **17**
thing new for people to shoot" says Hirsch. "Next week, we're shooting a commercial for a chewing gum company in Finland and another
with a company that makes stoves in Brazil."

"Vegas has become a required course in pop-cultural literacy," says   **18**
Hirsch. "It's a place that you're supposed to go."

Steve Saeta, associate producer of *Fools Rush In*—one of the few   **19**
flicks to acknowledge, in Hayek's Mexican American character, the existence of Vegas' swelling minority population—agrees that the city's
constant metamorphosis is a draw.

"There are scenes we shot a year ago we couldn't get today," says   **20**
Saeta, who was an assistant director on Robert Urich's *Vega$* TV series
in the '70s. Plus, he says, Vegas has "a collection of landmarks as iden-
tifiable as the Eiffel Tower. The bigger and the gaudier the better."

In last year's Gen X lounge movie *Swingers,* director Doug Liman   **21**
sends two of his Los Angeleno characters to Vegas in quest of deca-
dence.

"One of the guys hasn't been out of his apartment for six months,"   **22**
says Liman. "And there's only one cure for those kind of doldrums:
Vegas."

But Vegas is more than a locale, Liman says. It's a state of mind.   **23**

"One of the things Vegas represents is the Rat Pack, and all the   **24**
emotions and images the Rat Pack conjures up," says the director. It's
about a lack of inhibition, and time "when smoking wasn't bad for you
and drinking wasn't bad for you and it was fine to whistle at a woman.

The characters in the movie have a nostalgic view of what dating was like in the '50s, before the age of the answering machine."

Kitschy appreciation of the finger-snappin' Vegas of old is what defines the Cocktail Nation, represented by new bands such as Combustible Edison and Love Jones, and cheesy '60s artists like Esquivel and Martin Denny.

"The MTV generation is looking back at people like Tony Bennett and Frank Sinatra and thinking, 'Wow, that's really cool,'" says James Austin, producer of the Rhino Records anthology *Jackpot! The Las Vegas Story,* which includes Wayne Newton, Engelbert Humperdinck and Liberace. "Vegas used to have a real stigma attached to it, but now they look at the glitz and glitter as being fun."

Las Vegas native Susan Berman, who coproduced a four-hour documentary on the city for the Arts & Entertainment channel, is the daughter of Davie Berman, a Bugsy Siegel lieutenant who ran the Flamingo after Siegel's death. She says she isn't surprised by Vegas' growth spurt. (In addition to the recently opened $460 million New York-New York, Vegas impresario Steve Wynn is building the $1.25 billion Italianate Bellagio, and there are Paris- and Venice-themed casinos under construction.)

"It's a town of second chances," says Berman, who's developing a Vegas-based TV series with the producers of *Baywatch*. "Fantasy never quits," not even—or perhaps, especially—when the economy falls on hard times.

But for all its orchestrated unreality, Las Vegas is very much American.

"People act as if it's this weird place where you go that doesn't have anything to do with America," says David Shields, author of the pop-culture memoir *Remote*. "But it's America multiplied—all concentrated on a 10-mile-by-10-mile plot of land in the desert. Good and bad, vital and comical...Las Vegas is like a pornographic movie of the American imagination."

"Las Vegas is the Rorschach test of popular culture," says Andrew Raines, chairman of Creative Cafes, the Los Angeles company that, in the next five years, plans to open twenty-five Vegas! restaurants in the United States and abroad. "It's the place where people take the idea of what fun and pleasure should be and create it.

"One of the exportable elements of American culture, besides music   32
and movies, is Las Vegas," says Raines, whose cafes will feature showgirls, marquee lounge entertainment and a "safe" gaming area where
people can wage without losing money. "As the world becomes homog-
enized and American culture becomes dominant, people want to come
to Mecca. Vegas is one of the key icons, and people want to see it. I'm
taking it around the world."

So even as the rest of the country goes lap-dancing and considers le-   33
galizing gambling, by remaking itself bigger and more outrageous than
ever, Vegas has managed to preserve its unique identity.

"The cliché is that America has caught up to Vegas—that all the   34
things that used to be considered criminal aren't anymore," says Ventura. "But Vegas is still a place where you can go and be bad legally.
And everywhere you go, there's a level of surreality that only means
Vegas."

QUESTIONS FOR DISCUSSION

1. What central impression of Las Vegas does this article convey? Point out
   any sentences in the selection that suggest its central impression to you.

2. Explain what David Shields means in paragraph 30 when he says that Las
   Vegas is "America multiplied." Do you agree with him? Why or why not?

3. Consider the opening paragraphs of this selection. What details does
   DeLuca include? What effect do they have on the central impression of the
   essay?

SUGGESTIONS FOR WRITING

1. Have you ever visited a place that seemed to stand as a symbol for or to
   represent some aspect of the United States or its culture? Write a paper that
   describes such a place in detail, making it clear what that place represented
   to you.

2. DeLuca describes Vegas as a "Disneyland for adults." Write a paper in
   which you use specific and concrete details to convey your impression of
   any similar place you have ever visited. You might consider any amusement
   park or tourist attraction you have visited.

In the Land of Coke-Cola

William Least Heat-Moon

William Least Heat-Moon is the pen name of William Trogdon, who traveled the off-roads of the United States in his van, Ghost Dancing. In 1986 these travels formed the basis of his best-selling work *Blue Highways*, a book named after his encounters on the secondary roads of America, those marked in blue on highway maps. "In the Land of Coke-Cola" presents one such encounter in a rural Georgia restaurant.

Vocabulary Check

artesian (1)	herbicide (2)	tepid (2)
coppice (1)	nematicide (2)	conglomerate (4)
tallow (2)	fumigant (2)	husbandry (6)
fungicide (2)	dehydrated (2)	chert (9)

In the land of "Coke-Cola" it was hot and dry. The artesian water was finished. Along route 72, an hour west of Ninety-Six, I tried not to look for a spring; I knew I wouldn't find one, but I kept looking. The Savannah River, dammed to an unnatural wideness, lay below, wet and cool. I'd come into Georgia. The sun seemed to press on the roadway, and inside the truck, hot light bounced off chrome, flickering like a torch. Then I saw what I was trying not look for: in a coppice, a long-handled pump.

I stopped and took my bottles to the well. A small sign: WATER UNSAFE FOR DRINKING. I drooped like warm tallow. What fungicide, herbicide, nematicide, fumigant, or growth regulant—potions that rebuilt Southern agriculture—had seeped into the ground water? In the old movie Westerns there is commonly a scene where a dehydrated man, crossing the barren waste, at last comes to a water hole; he lies flat to drink the tepid stuff. Just as lips touch water, he sees on the other side a steer skull. I drove off thirsty but feeling a part of mythic history.

The thirst subsided when hunger took over. I hadn't eaten since morning. Sunset arrived west of Oglesby, and the air cooled. Then a road sign:

SWAMP GUINEA'S FISH LODGE

ALL YOU CAN EAT!

An arrow pointed down a county highway. I would gorge myself. A record would be set. They'd ask me to leave. An embarrassment to all.

The road through the orange earth of north Georgia passed an old, three-story house with a thin black child hanging out of every window like an illustration for "The Old Woman Who Lived in a Shoe"; on into hills and finally to Swamp Guinea's, a conglomerate of plywood and two-by-fours laid over with the smell of damp pine woods. **4**

Inside, wherever an oddity or natural phenomenon could hang, one hung: stuffed rump of a deer, snowshoe, flintlock, hornet's nest. The place looked as if a Boy Scout Troop had decorated it. Thirty or so people, black and white, sat around tables almost foundering under piled platters of food. I took a seat by the reproduction of a seventeenth-century woodcut depicting some Rabelaisian banquet at the groaning board. **5**

The diners were mostly Oglethorpe County red-shirt farmers. In Georgia tones they talked about their husbandry in terms of rain and nitrogen and hope. An immense woman with a glossy picture of a hooked bass leaping the front of her shirt said, "I'm gonna be sick from how much I've ate." **6**

I was watching everyone else and didn't see the waitress standing quietly by. Her voice was deep and soft like water moving in a cavern. I ordered the $4.50 special. In a few minutes she wheeled up a cart and began offloading dinner: ham and eggs, fried catfish, fried perch fingerlings, fried shrimp, chunks of barbecued beef, fried chicken, French fries, hush puppies, a broad bowl of cole slaw, another of lemon, a quart of ice tea, a quart of ice, and an entire loaf of factory-wrapped white bread. The table was covered. **7**

"Call me if y'all want any more." She wasn't joking. I quenched the thirst and then—slowly—went to the eating. I had to stand to reach plates across the table, but I intended to do the supper in. It was all Southern fried and good, except the Southern-style sweetened ice tea; still I took care of a quart of it. As I ate, making up for meals lost, the Old-Woman-in-the-Shoe house flashed before me, lightning in darkness. I had no moral right to eat so much. But I did. Headline: STOMACH PUMP FAILS TO REVIVE TRAVELER. **8**

The loaf of bread lay unopened when I finally abandoned the meal. At the register, I paid a man who looked as if he'd been chipped out of Georgia chert. The Swamp Guinea. I asked about the name. He spoke **9** of himself in the third person like the Wizard of Oz. "The Swamp Guinea only tells regulars."

"I'd be one, Mr. Guinea, if I didn't live in Missouri."   10

"Y'all from the North? Here, I got somethin' for you." He went to   11
the office and returned with a 45 rpm record. "It's my daughter singin'.
A little promotion we did. Take it along." Later, I heard a husky north
Georgia voice let go a down-home lyric rendering of Swamp Guinea's
menu:

> *That's all you can eat*
> *For a dollar fifty,*
> *Hey! The barbecue's nifty!*

And so on through the fried chicken and potatoes.

As I left, the Swamp Guinea, a former antique dealer whose name   12
was Rudell Burroughs, said, "The nickname don't mean anything. Just
made it up. Tried to figure a good one so we can franchise someday."

The frogs, high and low, shrilled and bellowed from the trees and   13
ponds. It was cool going into Athens, a city suffering from a nasty case
of the sprawls. On the University of Georgia campus, I tried to walk
down Swamp Guinea's supper. Everywhere couples entwined like
moonflower vines, each waiting for the blossom that opens only once.

QUESTIONS FOR DISCUSSION

1. Can you visualize the Swamp Guinea's Fish Lodge? List the details you re-member and discuss what about them makes them memorable to you.

2. Why does Least Heat-Moon say the place "looked as if a Boy Scout troop had decorated it"? What is he responding to?

3. How many of the five senses are called into play in this selection? List all those you can find.

SUGGESTIONS FOR WRITING

1. Have you ever visited an out-of-the-way café, store, gas station, or any other place far off the main road? Describe it as thoroughly as you can, us-ing specific and concrete details to convey your central impression of it.

2. The patrons in the Swamp Guinea's lodge, the waitress, and the Swamp Guinea himself can all be considered "details" that contribute to Least Heat-Moon's reaction to this place. Have you ever visited such a place, a place where the people themselves contribute to its unique atmosphere? If you have, describe it, using specific and concrete details to convey your central impression of it.

Using Examples

My Way!

Margo Kaufman

Margo Kaufman has published essays in *Newsweek, USA Today, Cosmopolitan,* and *The Village Voice.* The following selection, taken from her first book *1-800-Am-I-Nuts* (1993), illustrates a personality type that we all participate in from time to time. See if you recognize yourself among the many examples she provides.

Vocabulary Check

atrophy (2)	scoffs (6)	hyperventilating (15)
compulsively (4)	compromised (7)	laissez-faire (16)

Is it my imagination, or is this the age of the control freak? I'm standing in front of the triceps machine at my gym. I've just set the weights, and I'm about to begin my exercise when a lightly muscled bully in turquoise spandex interrupts her chest presses to bark at me. "I'm using that," she growls as she leaps up from her slant board, darts over to the triceps machine, and resets the weights. 1

I'm tempted to point out that, while she may have been planning to use the machine, she was, in fact, on the opposite side of the room. And that her muscles won't atrophy if she waits for me to finish. Instead, I go to work on my biceps. Life's too short to fight over a Nautilus machine. Of course, *I'm* not a control freak. 2

Control freaks will fight over anything: a parking space, the room temperature, the last pair of marked-down Maude Frizon pumps, even whether you should barbecue with the top on or off the Weber kettle. Nothing is too insignificant. Everything has to be just so. 3

Just so *they* like it. "These people compulsively have to have their own way," says Los Angeles psychologist Gary Emery. "Their egos are based on being right," Emery says, "on proving they're the boss." (And it isn't enough for the control freak to win. Others have to lose.) 4

"Control freaks are overconcerned with the means, rather than the end," Emergy says. "So it's more important that the string beans are the right kind than it is to just enjoy the meal." 5

"What do you mean just enjoy the meal?" scoffs my friend Marc. 6
"There's a right way to do things and then there's everything else." It
goes without saying that he, and only he, has access to that Big Right
Way in the Sky. And that Marc lives alone.

"I really hate to be in any situation where my control over what I'm 7
doing is compromised," he admits. "Like if somebody says, 'I'll handle
the cooking and you can shuck the corn or slice the zucchini,' I tell
them to do it without me."

A control freak's kitchen can be his or her castle. "Let me show you 8
the right way to make rice," said my husband the first time I made the
mistake of fixing dinner. By the time Duke had sharpened the knives,
rechopped the vegetables into two-inch squares, and chided me for using the wrong size pan, I had decided to surrender all control of the
stove. (For the record, this wasn't a big sacrifice. I don't like to cook.)

"It's easier in a marriage when you both don't care about the same 9
things," says Milton Wolpin, a psychology professor at the University
of Southern California. "Otherwise, everything would be a battle."

And every automobile would be a battleground. There's nothing 10
worse than having two control freaks in the same car. "I prefer to
drive," my friend Claire says. "But no sooner do I pull out of the driveway than Fred starts telling me what to do. He thinks that I'm an idiot
behind the wheel and that I make a lot of stupid mistakes."

She doesn't think he drives any better. "I think he goes really, really 11
fast, and I'm sure that someday he's going to kill us both," she says.
"And I complain about it constantly. But it's still a little easier for me to
take a back seat. I'd rather get to pick him apart than get picked on."

My friend Katie would withstand the abuse. "I like to control every- 12
thing," she says. "From where we're going to eat to what we're going to
eat to what movie we're going to see, what time we're going to see it,
where we're going to see it, where we're going to park. Everything!"

But you can't control everything. So much life is beyond our control. 13
And to me, that's what makes it interesting. But not to Katie. "I don't like
having my fate in someone else's hands," she says firmly. "If I take
charge, I know that whatever it is will get done and it will get done well."

I shuffle my feet guiltily. Not too long ago I invited Katie and a 14
bunch of friends out to dinner to celebrate my birthday. It was a control

freak's nightmare. Not only did I pick the restaurant and arrange to pick up the check, but Duke also called in advance and ordered an elaborate Chinese banquet. I thought Katie was going to lose her mind.

"What did you order? I have to know," she cried, seizing a menu. 15 "I'm a vegetarian. There are things I won't eat." Duke assured her that he had accounted for everybody's taste. Still, Katie didn't stop hyperventilating until the food arrived. "I was very pleasantly surprised," she confesses. "And I would trust Duke again."

"I'm sure there are areas where you're the control freak," says Professor Wolpin, "areas where you're more concerned about things than your husband." *Me?* The champion of laissez-faire? "You get very upset if you find something visible to the naked eye on the kitchen counter," Duke reminds me. "And you think you know much better than me what the right shirt for me to wear is." 16

But I'm just particular. I'm not a control freak. 17

"A control freak is just someone who cares about something more than you do," Wolpin says. 18

So what's wrong with being a control freak? 19

QUESTIONS FOR DISCUSSION

1. Consider the opening two paragraphs. Why does Kaufman present an example there rather than wait until later? What effect does the opening example have on the reader?

2. What does psychologist Gary Emery mean when he says, "Control freaks are overconcerned with the means, rather than the end"?

3. How many separate examples does Kaufman present in this essay? Identify them and discuss why they are or are not effective.

SUGGESTIONS FOR WRITING

1. "Control freaks" all have one personality trait in common—the need to be in control—although they may exhibit that need in different ways. Identify another personality trait that many people have in common, and write a paper in which you illustrate it with examples of your own.

2. Kaufman writes, "But you can't control everything. So much of life is beyond our control." What do you think of that observation? Is it a philosophy that you live by, or do you prefer to maintain control of life? Write a paper in which you use examples to illustrate the kind of person you are.

Gender Benders

Jack Rosenthal

Chicken soup and beef soup—which is feminine and which is masculine? Jack Rosenthal suggests that most Americans will answer similarly and that our answers reveal much about some deeply embedded values in our culture. The following selection appeared in the Sunday *Magazine* section of the *New York Times* in 1986.

Vocabulary Check

unanimity (1)	consensus (8)	inherently (14)
superficial (1)	agile (9)	purging (15)
overwrought (2)	embedded (12)	

Chicken soup and beef soup. Which is masculine and which is feminine? In English, neither chicken nor beef nor soup has formal gender. Yet most people find the question easy to answer: chicken soup is feminine and beef soup is masculine, and that unanimity demonstrates how vast is the task of stamping out sexist words. That effort, while constructive, remains superficial, deep within language lurks the powerful force of Hidden Gender.

Many languages use formal gender to categorize nouns and pronouns as masculine, feminine, and neuter. There's not much logic in these categories. "In German," Mark Twain once wrote, "a young lady has no sex, while a turnip has. Think what overwrought reverence that shows for the turnip and what callous disrespect for the girl." A Spanish butterfly is aptly feminine: *la mariposa*. A French butterfly is masculine, but at least the word sounds delicate: *le papillon*. A Germany butterfly is, as an old linguistic's joke observes, masculine and it sounds it: *der Schmetterling*.

Beyond formal gender, societies observe a ceremonial gender. A nation is a "she." So is a ship, an invention, an engine. Think of "Star Trek": one can just hear Scotty down in the engine room calling Captain Kirk: "I canna' get her into warp drive, Capt'n!"

Women's liberation has brought a new turn toward neutering language—using firefighter instead of fireman and generalizing with "they" instead of "he." This process, generally positive, can be carried to extremes. When someone once denounced *yeoman* as sexist and urged *yeoperson* instead, the *Times* groaned in an editorial, fearing the ulti-

1

2

3

4

mate absurdity—*woperson*. Nonsense, several letter writers promptly responded. The ultimate absurdity, they observed, would be *woperdaughter.*

Hidden Gender, compared with such questions of surface gender, rolls beneath the language like the tide. The chicken soup/beef soup question is just one illustration. Consider some variations on the idea, which began as a children's game and has been elaborated by Roger W. Shuy and other sociologists at Georgetown University.   5

Which of the following is masculine and which is feminine: 6

Ford and Chevrolet

Chocolate and vanilla

Salt and pepper

Pink and purple

From English speakers, the answers usually come back the same, regardless of age, race, class, region—or sex. Some people see no gender at all in any of the terms. But those who do usually say that Ford, chocolate, pepper and purple are masculine.   7

The consensus is not limited to these pairs. You can get the same predictability by making up other combinations—coffee and tea, shoes and boots, skis and skates, plane and train.   8

Why does almost everybody label chicken soup feminine? One obvious explanation is that beef connotes cattle—big, solid, stolid animals. Chickens are small, frail, agile. Why does almost everybody label Chevrolet feminine? Perhaps for reasons of sound. Ford ends in a tough, blunt consonant, almost as masculine-sounding as a *Mack truck*. By comparison, Chevro-lay seems graceful and flexible.   9

Why do so many people label vanilla feminine? Sound is probably part of it, but so also is color and character. Chocolate, being darker and with a more pronounced taste, is masculine in this pairing. Likewise for pepper and purple.   10

Consider the attributes associated with masculine: solid, blunt, more pronounced, and those associated with feminine: frail, graceful, light. They do not arise from the words themselves but from the pairings. What the game exposes is that Hidden Gender is relative.   11

In assigning gender to one word or the other, we expose attributes so deeply embedded in our culture that most of us, male or female, ma-   12 cho or feminist, share them. We turn values into gender and gender into communication.

Try playing the game with single words instead of pairs. When you   13
ask people the gender of fork, you'll get blank looks. Hidden Gender
only shows up when people are asked to give relative importance to
two words.

Which is masculine and which is feminine: knife or fork? Usually,   14
the answer is that fork is feminine. But why? There's nothing inherently
feminine about the word fork. The answer is obvious when you try a
different pair. Which is masculine and which is feminine: fork or
spoon?

Purging language of sexist terms is worth doing for its own sake,   15
but the superficiality of the effort should also be recognized. Whether
one refers to ocean liners or God as "she" is a cosmetic matter. Hidden
Gender endures, and the only way to alter it is to alter the culture on
which it feeds.

QUESTIONS FOR DISCUSSION

1. "Hidden Gender, compared with such questions of surface gender, rolls beneath the language like the tide." What distinction is Rosenthal making between hidden and surface gender? Explain your understanding of hidden
gender.

2. Rosenthal says that a fork is considered feminine when paired with a knife
but not when paired with a spoon. Why is that? Explain Rosenthal's point
in this example.

3. What is Rosenthal's attitude toward sexist language? Does he think we
should change words to eliminate such language? Does he think such
changes would make much of a difference? Refer to sentences in the essay
to support your response.

SUGGESTIONS FOR WRITING

1. Rosenthal focuses on language to reveal the hidden gender attitudes of our
culture. Can you think of another area of life that reveals cultural attitudes
toward women or men? Write a paper that uses detailed examples to illustrate those attitudes.

2. Rosenthal suggests that some attitudes are "so deeply embedded in our culture that most of us...share them." What attitudes other than gender assumptions might most of us share? The desire to succeed? The need to be
independent? Fear of failure? The importance of hard work? Use examples
to illustrate one trait that you think is embedded in our culture.

She's Your Basic L.O.L. in N.A.D.

Perri Klass

Perri Klass is a pediatrician, a mother of three children, and a writer of fiction as well as nonfiction. She has published essays, short stories, and novels. In the following selection she uses examples to illustrate her reactions to the language of medicine during her first three months working as a medical student in a hospital.

Vocabulary Check

jargon (2)	perennial (7)	pompous (15)
primeval (2)	syndromes (9)	locutions (15)

"Mrs. Tolstoy is your basic L.O.L. in N.A.D., admitted for a soft rule-out M.I.," the intern announces. I scribble that on my patient list. In other words Mrs. Tolstoy is a Little Old Lady in No Apparent Distress who is in the hospital to make sure she hasn't had a heart attack (rule out a myocardial infarction). And we think it's unlikely that she has had a heart attack (a *soft* rule-out).

1

If I learned nothing else during my first three months of working in the hospital as a medical student, I learned endless jargon and abbreviations. I started out in a state of primeval innocence, in which I didn't even know that "s̄ C.P., S.O.B., N/V" meant "without chest pain, shortness of breath, or nausea and vomiting." By the end I took the abbreviations so for granted that I would complain to my mother the English Professor, "And can you believe I had to put down three NG tubes last night?"

2

"You'll have to tell me what an NG tube is if you want me to sympathize properly," my mother said. NG, nasogastric—isn't it obvious?

3

I picked up not only the specific expressions but also the patterns of speech and the grammatical conventions; for example, you never say that a patient's blood pressure fell or that his cardiac enzymes rose. Instead, the patient is always the subject of the verb: "He dropped his pressure." "He bumped his enzymes." This sort of construction probably reflects that profound irritation of the intern when the nurses come in the middle of the night to say that Mr. Dickinson has disturbingly low blood pressure. "Oh, he's gonna hurt me bad tonight," the intern may say, inevitably angry at Mr. Dickinson for dropping his pressure and creating a problem.

4

When chemotherapy fails to cure Mrs. Bacon's cancer, what we say   5
is, "Mrs. Bacon failed chemotherapy."

"Well, we've already had one hit today, and we're up next, but at   6
least we've got mostly stable players on our team." This means that our
team (group of doctors and medical students) has already gotten one
new admission today, and it is our turn again, so we'll get whoever is
next admitted in emergency, but at least most of the patients we already
have are fairly stable, that is, unlikely to drop their pressures or in any
other way get suddenly sicker and hurt us bad. Baseball metaphor is
pervasive: a no-hitter is a night without any new admissions. A player is
always a patient—a nitrate player is a patient on nitrates, a unit player
is a patient in the intensive-care unit and so on, until you reach the terminal player.

It is interesting to consider what it means to be winning, or doing   7
well, in this perennial baseball game. When the intern hangs up the
phone and announces, "I got a hit," that is not cause for congratula-
tions. The team is not scoring points; rather, it is getting hit, being bom-
barded with new patients. The object of the game from the point of
view of the doctors, considering the players for whom they are already
responsible, is to get as few new hits as possible.

These special languages contribute to a sense of closeness and pro-   8
fessional spirit among people who are under a great deal of stress. As a
medical student, it was exciting for me to discover that I'd finally
cracked the code, that I could understand what doctors said and wrote
and could use the same formulations myself. Some people seem to become enamored of the jargon for its own sake, perhaps because they
are so deeply thrilled with the idea of medicine, with the idea of themselves as doctors.

I knew a medical student who was referred to by the interns on the   9
team as Mr. Eponym because he was so infatuated with eponymous terminology, the more obscure the better. He never said "capillary pulsa-
tion" if he could say "Quincke's pulses." He would lovingly tell over
the multinamed syndromes—Wolff-Parkinson-White, Lown-Ganong-
Levine, Henoch-Schonlein—until the temptation to suggest Schleswig-
Holstein or Stevenson-Kefauver or Baskin-Robbins became irresistible
to his less reverent colleagues.

And there is the jargon that you don't ever want to hear yourself us-   **10**
ing. You know that your training is changing you, but there are certain
changes you think would be going a little too far.

The resident was describing a man with devastating terminal pan-   **11**
creatic cancer. "Basically he's C.T.D.," the resident concluded. I reminded myself that I had resolved not to be shy about asking when I
didn't understand things, "C.T.D.?" I asked timidly.

The resident smirked at me. "Circling The Drain."   **12**

The images are vivid and terrible. "What happened to Mrs.   **13**
Melville?"

"Oh, she boxed last night." To box is to die, of course.   **14**

Then there are the more pompous locutions that can make the be-   **15**
ginning medical student nervous about the effects of medical training. A
friend of mine was told by his resident, "A pregnant woman with
sickle-cell represents a failure of genetic counseling."

Mr. Eponym, who tried hard to talk like the doctors, once ex-   **16**
plained to me, "An infant is basically a brainstem preparation." A
brainstem preparation, as used in neurological research, is an animal
whose higher brain functions have been destroyed so that only the most
primitive reflexes remain, like the sucking reflex, the startle reflex, and
the rooting reflex.

The more extreme forms aside, one most important function of   **17**
medical jargon is to help doctors maintain some distance from their patients. By reformulating a patient's pain and problems into a language
that the patient doesn't even speak, I suppose we are in some sense taking those pains and problems under our jurisdiction and also reducing
their emotional impact. This linguistic separation between doctors and
patients allows conversations to go on at the bedside that are unintelli-
gible to the patient. "Naturally, we're worried about adreno-C.A.," the
intern can say to the medical student, and lung cancer need never be
mentioned.

I learned a new language this past summer. At times it thrills me to   **18**
hear myself using it. It enables me to understand my colleagues, to communicate effectively in the hospital. Yet I am uncomfortably aware that
I will never again notice the peculiarities and even atrocities of medical
language as keenly as I did this summer. There may be specific expres-

sions I manage to avoid, but even as I remark them, promising myself I will never use them, I find that this language is becoming my professional speech. It no longer sounds strange in my ears—or coming from my mouth. And I am afraid that as with any new language, to use it properly you must absorb not only the vocabulary but also the structure, the logic, the attitudes. At first you may notice these new alien assumptions every time you put together a sentence, but with time and increased fluency you stop being aware of them at all. And as you lose that awareness, for better or for worse, you move closer and closer to being a doctor instead of just talking like one.

QUESTIONS FOR DISCUSSION

1. Jargon is language unique to a specific profession. What is Klass's reaction to the medical jargon she discusses in this essay? Does she have one overall reaction or several different reactions? Refer to specific statements that reveal her attitude.

2. What is your reaction to the terminology in this selection? Do you find it offensive? Understandable? Dehumanizing? Humorous?

3. Klass writes, "And I am afraid that as with any new language, to use it properly you must absorb not only the vocabulary but also the structure, the logic, the attitudes." What does she mean by this statement? Why should she fear absorbing this new vocabulary?

SUGGESTIONS FOR WRITING

1. Klass discovers a new way of talking and thinking while working as a medical student. Consider your own experiences in new situations. Have you ever found yourself in a new environment, one that changed the way you thought, talked, or acted? Perhaps your first year as a college student introduced you to new ways of thinking or acting. Maybe a new job affected you the same way, or a new group of friends. Write a paper in which you use examples to illustrate how you changed for the better or the worse in a new environment.

2. Like doctors, many groups have their own unique ways of speaking that identify members of that group and exclude others. Write a paper examining the language of a group to which you belong. Give examples of that language, explaining not only what it means but also its purpose. Do certain terms create a bond among the speakers? Do they suggest an attitude toward others? Explain the purpose of each example as clearly as you can.

Explaining Causes and Effects

Black Men and Public Space

Brent Staples

Brent Staples comes from Chester, Pennsylvania, a poor and sometimes violent industrial city. After receiving his B.A. from Widener University in Chester and his Ph.D. in psychology from the University of Chicago, he wrote for the *Chicago Sun Times* and the *New York Times*. The following essay was first published in *Harper's* in 1986. In it he examines one of his recurrent themes—the reality of being a black male in contemporary America.

Vocabulary Check

discreet (1)	foyer (2)	bravado (7)
unwieldy (2)	errant (2)	labyrinthine (8)
quarry (2)	warrenlike (5)	skittish (11)
dicey (2)	lethality (6)	constitutionals (12)

My first victim was a woman—white, well-dressed, probably in her early twenties. I came upon her late one evening on a deserted street in Hyde Park, a relatively affluent neighborhood in an otherwise mean, impoverished section of Chicago. As I swung onto the avenue behind her, there seemed to be a discreet, uninflammatory distance between us. Not so. She cast back a worried glance. To her, the youngish black man—a broad 6 feet 2 inches with a beard and billowing hair, both hands shoved into the pockets of a bulky military jacket—seemed menacingly close. After a few more quick glimpses, she picked up her pace and was soon running in earnest. Within seconds she disappeared into a cross street.

That was more than a decade ago. I was 22 years old, a graduate student newly arrived at the University of Chicago. It was in the echo of that terrified woman's footfalls that I first began to know the unwieldy inheritance I'd come into—the ability to alter public space in ugly ways. It was clear that she thought herself the quarry of a mugger, a rapist, or worse. Suffering a bout of insomnia, however, I was stalking sleep, not defenseless wayfarers. As a softy who is scarcely able to take a knife to a raw chicken—let alone hold one to a person's throat—I was sur-

1

2

prised, embarrassed, and dismayed all at once. Her flight made me feel like an accomplice in tyranny. It also made it clear that I was indistinguishable from the muggers who occasionally seeped into the area from the surrounding ghetto. That first encounter, and those that followed, signified that a vast, unnerving gulf lay between nighttime pedestrians—particularly women—and me. And I soon gathered that being perceived as dangerous is a hazard in itself. I only needed to turn a corner into a dicey situation, or crowd some frightened, armed person in a foyer somewhere, or make an errant move after being pulled over by a policeman. Where fear and weapons meet—and they often do in urban America—there is always the possibility of death.

In that first year, my first away from my hometown, I was to become thoroughly familiar with the language of fear. At dark, shadowy intersections, I could cross in front of a car stopped at a traffic light and elicit the *thunk, thunk, thunk, thunk* of the driver—black, white, male, or female—hammering down the door locks. On less traveled streets after dark, I grew accustomed to but never comfortable with people crossing to the other side of the street rather than pass me. Then there were the standard unpleasantries with policemen, doormen, bouncers, cabdrivers, and others whose business it is to screen out troublesome individuals *before* there is any nastiness.

I moved to New York nearly two years ago and I have remained an avid night walker. In central Manhattan, the near-constant crowd cover minimizes tense one-on-one street encounters. Elsewhere—in SoHo, for example, where sidewalks are narrow and tightly spaced buildings shut out the sky—things can get very taut indeed.

After dark, on the warrenlike streets of Brooklyn where I live, I often see women who fear the worst from me. They seem to have set their faces on neutral, and with their purse straps strung across their chests bandolier-style, they forge ahead as through bracing themselves against being tackled. I understand, of course, that the danger they perceive is not a hallucination. Women are particularly vulnerable to street violence, and young black males are drastically overrepresented among the perpetrators of that violence. Yet these truths are no solace against the kind of alienation that comes of being ever the suspect, a fearsome entity with whom pedestrians avoid making eye contact.

It is not altogether clear to me how I reached the ripe old age of 22   6
without being conscious of the lethality nighttime pedestrians attributed
to me. Perhaps it was because in Chester, Pennsylvania, the small, angry
industrial town where I came of age in the 1960s, I was scarcely noticeable against a backdrop of gang warfare, street knifings, and murders. I
grew up one of the good boys, had perhaps a half-dozen fistfights. In
retrospect, my shyness of combat has clear sources.

As a boy, I saw countless tough guys locked away; I have since   7
buried several, too. They were babies, really—a teenage cousin, a
brother of 22, a childhood friend in his mid-twenties—all gone down in
episodes of bravado played out in the streets. I came to doubt the
virtues of intimidation early on. I chose, perhaps unconsciously, to remain a shadow—timid, but a survivor.

The fearsomeness mistakenly attributed to me in public places often   8
has a perilous flavor. The most frightening of these confusions occurred
in the late 1970s and early 1980s, when I worked as a journalist in
Chicago. One day, rushing into the office of a magazine I was writing
for with a deadline story in hand, I was mistaken for a burglar. The office manager called security and, with an ad hoc posse, pursued me
through the labyrinthine halls, nearly to my editor's door. I had no way
of proving who I was. I could only move briskly toward the company
of someone who knew me.

Another time I was on assignment for a local paper and killing time   9
before an interview. I entered a jewelry store on the city's affluent Near
North Side. The proprietor excused herself and returned with an enormous red Doberman pinscher straining at the end of a leash. She stood,
the dog extended toward me, silent to my questions, her eyes bulging
nearly out of her head. I took a cursory look around, nodded, and bade
her good night.

Relatively speaking, however, I never fared as badly as another   10
black male journalist. He went to nearby Waukegan, Illinois, a couple
of summers ago to work on a story about a murderer who was born
there. Mistaking the reporter for the killer, police officers hauled him
from his car at gunpoint and but for his press credentials would probably have tried to book him. Such episodes are not uncommon. Black
men trade tales like this all the time.

Over the years, I learned to smother the rage I felt at so often being   11
taken for a criminal. Not to do so would surely have led to madness. I
now take precautions to make myself less threatening. I move about
with care, particularly late in the evening. I give a wide berth to nervous
people on subway platforms during the wee hours, particularly when I
have exchanged business clothes for jeans. If I happen to be entering a
building behind some people who appear skittish, I may walk by, letting
them clear the lobby before I return, so as not to seem to be following
them. I have been calm and extremely congenial on those rare occasions
when I've been pulled over by the police.

And on late-evening constitutionals I employ what has proved to   12
be an excellent tension-reducing measure: I whistle melodies from
Beethoven and Vivaldi and the more popular classical composers. Even
steely New Yorkers hunching toward nighttime destinations seem to relax, and occasionally they even join in the tune. Virtually everybody
seems to sense that a mugger wouldn't be warbling bright, sunny selections from Vivaldi's *Four Seasons*. It is my equivalent of the cowbell
that hikers wear when they know they are in bear country.

QUESTIONS FOR DISCUSSION

1. Why does Staples refer to the woman described in the first paragraph as his
   first "victim"? What is the "unwieldy inheritance" he refers to in paragraph 2?

2. Why is Staples treated with suspicion and fear in his encounters? Examine
   the various examples he provides and explain what causes those reactions.

3. What seems to be the central idea of this selection? Use your own words to
   state its point.

SUGGESTIONS FOR WRITING

1. Have you ever been stereotyped because of your age, race, gender, appearance, ethnicity, or religion—or for any other reason? If you have, write a
   paper explaining how that stereotype affected the way people reacted to
   you or treated you.

2. What situations cause you to modify your normal appearance or behavior?
   Write a paper explaining what causes you to act differently from your
   "normal" self.

I Refuse to Live in Fear

Diana Bletter

Diana Bletter was born in New York in 1957. Since graduating from Cornell University in 1978, she has published articles in many periodicals, including *Newsday* and the *International Herald Tribune*. With her friend Samia Zina, whom she mentions in this selection, she helped organize Dove of Peace, a group of friends composed of Arab and Jewish women. The following selection was first published in *Mademoiselle* in 1996.

Vocabulary Check

imploded (6)	reflexive (9)	prophetic (13)
tranquil (7)	vanquished (12)	paranoid (15)

For most of my life, I thought a shoe box was just a shoe box. Until the afternoon I discovered that it could also be considered a lethal weapon. 1

This is what happened: I had gone shopping for shoes—one of my favorite pastimes—in the small Mediterranean town of Nahariyya in northern Israel, where I've lived for the last five years. I sat down on a bench to change into my new purchase. I was so busy admiring my feet that I left the shoe box (with my old shoes) on the bench. Fifteen minutes later, I suddenly remembered it and turned back. When I approached the street, I saw crowds of people, barricades and at least five policemen. 2

"What happened?" I asked. 3

"Everyone's been evacuated. Someone reported a suspicious object on a bench down the street." 4

"Oh, no!" I shouted. "My shoes!" 5

Had I arrived even a few seconds later, a special bomb squad—complete with robot—would have imploded my shoe box to deactivate what could have been a bomb hidden inside. The policeman shook his finger at me. "This is the Middle East!" he said angrily. "You can't be careless like that!" 6

Reality Bites, Hard

Moving to Israel from America's tranquil suburbia has taught me about living with the threat of terrorism, something we Americans—after the bomb at Atlanta's Olympic Games and the explosion of TWA Flight 7

800—are finally being forced to think about on our own turf. The brutal fact of a terrorist attack is that it shatters the innocent peace of our days, the happy logic of our lives. It inalterably changes the way we live.

I can no longer daydream as I walk down a street—now I know **8**
that, to stay alive, I have to remain aware of who and what surrounds me. As my fiancé always tells me, "Your eyes are your best friends!" and I use them to keep track of emergency exits, the closest windows, the nearest heavy object that could be used in self-defense.

I used to be a reflexive litter-grabber—in my hometown, I never hes- **9**
itated to pick up a coffee cup from the sidewalk and toss it in a nearby garbage can. In Israel, I've learned not to touch litter and to stay away from garbage cans—on several occasions, bombs have been placed in them. If I see a knapsack, shopping bag or—yes—a shoe box left unattended, I now do three things: One, ask passersby if they forgot the package; two, get away from it as fast as I can; and three, report it to the police.

Necessary Inconveniences

Living in a country where terrorism is always a possibility means that **10**
at every entrance to a public place, guards search every bag. I forgot this the first time I walked into Nahariyya's lone department store; a guard stopped me to look through my pocketbook. "How could I have shoplifted?" I asked. "I haven't set foot in the store." Then I remembered that in America, people worry about what someone might sneak *out* of a store; in Israel, people worry about weapons or bombs someone might sneak *in* to a store.

The first few days after a terrorist attack seem very quiet. Since all **11**
of Israel is only the size of New Jersey, everybody usually knows someone who was hurt or killed. The nation slips into mourning: People avoid going out, attending parties, sitting in cafés.

Gradually, though, daily life returns to normal. Israelis (and now, **12**
Americans) have to prove again and again to potential terrorists that we're not giving in to our fears. If we voluntarily restrict our movements and our lives, terrorists have vanquished us.

During the latest hostilities in Lebanon (whose border is about 13 seven miles from Nahariyya), Samia Zina, my dear friend—and a Muslim Arab—dreamed about me, one of those vivid dreams that seems prophetic when you wake. She dreamed that the fighting had forced her to flee her home, and that I'd hidden her and her children in my house (and I certainly would have, had the nightmare been a reality). The next day, Samia popped by to tell me her dream and to give me the two stuffed chickens she'd been moved to cook for me.

"Thank you," I said, astonished by the food and the dream. "But I 14 know you would have hidden me, too."

Terrorists attempt to divide people by fear, but in our community 15 they've brought so-called enemies together: Even Arabs and Jews watch out for each other in public places, knowing that terrorists target everyone. By resisting the temptation to become paranoid and isolated, by sticking up for one another, we remain undefeated.

QUESTIONS FOR DISCUSSION

1. Explain the significance of the forgotten shoe box. What result of terrorism does it illustrate for Bletter?

2. In what other ways has terrorism affected Bletter and the culture in which she lives?

3. Why does Bletter tell us the story of Samia Zina and her dream? What point does this story illustrate?

SUGGESTIONS FOR WRITING

1. Terrorism may not be an immediate concern for most Americans, but fear of some kind certainly affects us all at different times. And in spite of that fear, we need to act; we need to go on with our lives. Write a paper identifying situations that cause you fear and explain how you cope with such situations.

2. Bletter examines some of the effects of terrorism on the people of the Middle East. Write a paper that examines the effects of some other behavior or situation on you or on people you know. Consider, for example, the effects of illness, poverty, crime, alcoholism or drug addiction, or some other related situation.

Why We Crave Horror Movies

Stephen King

Stephen King is one of the best-known writers of horror fiction in the United States. Many of his successful novels have been produced as equally successful movies, including *The Shining* (1976), *Firestarter* (1980), *Pet Sematary* (1983), *Misery* (1987), and *The Stand* (1990). In the following selection, King examines the sources of the American public's fascination with horror movies.

Vocabulary Check

innately (4)	status quo (9)	morbidity (12)
reactionary (4)	coveted (10)	subterranean (12)
voyeur (6)	remonstrance (10)	
penchant (7)	anarchistic (11)	

I think that we're all mentally ill; those of us outside the asylums only hide it a little better—and maybe not all that much better, after all. We've all known people who talk to themselves, people who sometimes squinch their faces into horrible grimaces when they believe no one is watching, people who have some hysterical fear—of snakes, the dark, the tight place, the long drop... and, of course, those final worms and grubs that are waiting so patiently underground.

When we pay our four or five bucks and seat ourselves at tenth-row center in a theater showing a horror movie, we are daring the night-mare.

Why? Some of the reasons are simple and obvious. To show that we can, that we are not afraid, that we can ride this roller coaster. Which is not to say that a really good horror movie may not surprise a scream out of us at some point, the way we may scream when the roller coaster twists through a complete 360 or plows through a lake at the bottom of the drop. And horror movies, like roller coasters, have always been the special province of the young; by the time one turns 40 or 50, one's appetite for double twists or 360-degree loops may be considerably depleted.

We also go to reestablish our feelings of essential normality; the hor-ror movie is innately conservative, even reactionary. Freda Jackson as the horrible melting woman in *Die, Monster, Die!* confirms for us that no matter how far we may be removed from the beauty of a Robert Redford or a Diana Ross, we are still light-years from true ugliness.

And we go to have fun. 5

Ah, but this is where the ground starts to slope away, isn't it? Because this is a very peculiar sort of fun, indeed. The fun comes from seeing others menaced—sometimes killed. One critic has suggested that if pro football has become the voyeur's version of combat, then the horror film has become the modern version of the public lynching. 6

It is true that the mythic, "fairy-tale" horror film intends to take away the shades of gray.... It urges us to put away our more civilized and adult penchant for analysis and to become children again, seeing things in pure blacks and whites. It may be that horror movies provide psychic relief on this level because this invitation to lapse into simplicity, irrationality, and even outright madness is extended so rarely. We are told we may allow our emotions a free rein...or no rein at all. 7

If we are all insane, then sanity becomes a matter of degree. If your insanity leads you to carve up women, like Jack the Ripper or the Cleveland Torso Murderer, we clap you away in the funny farm (but neither of those two amateur-night surgeons was ever caught, heh-heh-heh); if, on the other hand, your insanity leads you only to talk to yourself when you're under stress or to pick your nose on your morning bus, then you are left alone to go about your business...though it is doubtful that you will ever be invited to the best parties. 8

The potential lyncher is in almost all of us (excluding saints, past and present; but then, most saints have been crazy in their own ways), and every now and then, he has to be let loose to scream and roll around in the grass. Our emotions and our fears form their own body, and we recognize that it demands its own exercise to maintain proper muscle tone. Certain of these emotional muscles are accepted—even exalted—in civilized society; they are, of course, the emotions that tend to maintain the status quo of civilization itself. Love, friendship, loyalty, kindness—these are all the emotions that we applaud, emotions that have been immortalized in the couplets of Hallmark cards and in the verses (I don't dare call it poetry) of Leonard Nimoy. 9

When we exhibit these emotions, society showers us with positive reinforcement; we learn this even before we get out of diapers. When, as children, we hug our rotten little puke of a sister and give her a kiss, 10 all the aunts and uncles smile and twit and cry, "Isn't he the sweetest little thing?" Such coveted treats as chocolate-covered graham crackers often follow. But if we deliberately slam the rotten little puke of a sister's fingers in the door, sanctions follow—angry remonstrance from parents, aunts and uncles; instead of a chocolate-covered graham cracker, a spanking.

But anticivilization emotions don't go away, and they demand periodic exercise. We have such "sick" jokes as, "What's the difference between a truckload of bowling balls and a truckload of dead babies?" (You can't unload a truckload of bowling balls with a pitchfork...a joke, by the way, that I heard originally from a ten-year-old.) Such a joke may surprise a laugh or a grin out of us even as we recoil, a possibility that confirms the thesis: If we share a brotherhood of man, then we also share an insanity of man. None of which is intended as a defense of either the sick joke or insanity, but merely as an explanation of why the best horror films, like the best fairy tales, manage to be reactionary, anarchistic, and revolutionary all at the same time.   11

The mythic horror movie, like the sick joke, has a dirty job to do. It deliberately appeals to all that is worst in us. It is morbidity unchained, our most base instincts let free, our nastiest fantasies realized..., and it all happens, fittingly enough, in the dark. For those reasons, good liberals often shy away from horror films. For myself, I like to see the most aggressive of them—*Dawn of the Dead,* for instance—as lifting a trap door in the civilized forebrain and throwing a basket of raw meat to the hungry alligators swimming around in the subterranean river beneath.   12

Why bother? Because it keeps them from getting out, man. It keeps them down there and me up here. It was Lennon and McCartney who said that all you need is love, and I would agree with that.   13

As long as you keep the gators fed.   14

QUESTIONS FOR DISCUSSION

1. King suggests several reasons why we crave horror movies in the first five paragraphs of his essay. What are those reasons?

2. Starting with paragraph 6 and continuing through the rest of the selection, King examines another reason we watch horror movies. Explain what that reason is.

3. Why does King recount the sick joke about dead babies? According to him, how do many people react to such sick jokes, and what does that reaction have to do with why we crave horror movies?

SUGGESTIONS FOR WRITING

1. If we watch horror movies because they allow us to release our violent, "anticivilization" emotions, why do we watch other types of movies, such as romantic comedies, science fiction, or thrillers? For that matter, why do we watch soap operas on television, or MTV, or police dramas? Choose one type of movie or television show and explain what causes people to watch it.

2. Consider the attraction of other aspects of our culture. Why are fast-food restaurants so popular? What is the attraction of rap music (or any other kind of music)? Why is skateboarding popular? Why do so many high school students dress in baggy, loose clothing? Explain what causes any one of these or similar topics.

Comparing and Contrasting

Americanization Is Tough on Macho

Rose del Castillo Guilbault

Rose del Castillo Guilbault, the recipient of numerous awards in journalism, has written stories for newspapers, periodicals, radio, and television. In 1991 she was appointed to President George Bush's Advisory Commission on Educational Excellence for Hispanic Students. The following essay first appeared in 1989 in the *San Francisco Chronicle*. In it the author examines differing expectations of what it means to be *macho* in American and Hispanic cultures.

Vocabulary Check

connotations (2)	recalcitrant (10)	patriarchal (15)
disdain (4)	stoically (10)	chauvinistic (16)
quintessential (7)	menial (11)	semantics (16)
ambiguities (10)	indulgent (11)	prototype (16)

What is *macho?* That depends which side of the border you come from. 1

Although it's not unusual for words and expressions to lose their 2 subtlety in translation, the negative connotations of *macho* in this country are troublesome to Hispanics.

Take the newspaper descriptions of alleged mass murderer Ramon 3 Salcido. That an insensitive, insanely jealous, hard-drinking, violent Latin male is referred to as *macho* makes Hispanics cringe.

"*Es muy macho,*" the women in my family nod approvingly, de- 4 scribing a man they respect. But in the United States, when women say, "He's so macho," it's with disdain.

The Hispanic *macho* is manly, responsible, hardworking, a man in 5 charge, a patriarch. A man who expresses strength through silence. What the Yiddish language would call a *mensch*.

The American *macho* is a chauvinist, a brute, uncouth, selfish, loud, 6 abrasive, capable of inflicting pain, and sexually promiscuous.

Quintessential *macho* models in this country are Sylvester Stallone, 7 Arnold Schwarzenegger, and Charles Bronson. In their movies, they exude toughness, independence, masculinity. But a closer look reveals their machismo is really violence masquerading as courage, sullenness disguised as silence, and irresponsibility camouflaged as independence.

If the Hispanic ideal of *macho* were translated to American screen   8
roles, they might be Jimmy Stewart, Sean Connery, and Laurence
Olivier.

In Spanish, *macho* ennobles Latin males. In English, it devalues   9
them. This pattern seems consistent with the conflicts ethnic minority
males experience in this country. Typically the cultural traits other societies value don't translate as desirable characteristics in America.

I watched my own father struggle with these cultural ambiguities.   10
He worked on a farm for twenty years. He laid down miles of irrigation
pipe, carefully plowed long, neat rows in fields, hacked away at recalci-
trant weeds and drove tractors through whirlpools of dust. He stoically
worked twenty-hour days during harvest season, accepting the long
hours as part of agricultural work. When the boss complained or up-
braided him for minor mistakes, he kept quiet, even when it was obvious the boss had erred.

He handled the most menial tasks with pride. At home he was a   11
good provider, helped out my mother's family in Mexico without com-
plaint, and was indulgent with me. Arguments between my mother and
him generally had to do with money, or with his stubborn reluctance to
share his troubles. He tried to work them out in his own silence. He
didn't want to trouble my mother—of course that backfired, because
the imagined is always worse than the reality.

Americans regarded my father as decidedly un-*macho*. His charac-   12
ter was interpreted as nonassertive, his loyalty nonambition, and his
quietness ignorance. I once overheard the boss's son blame him for
plowing crooked rows in a field. My father merely smiled at the lie,
knowing the boy had done it, but didn't refute it, confident his good
work was well known. But the boss instead ridiculed him for being
"stupid" and letting a kid get away with a lie. Seeing my embarrassment, my father dismissed the incident, saying, "They're the dumb
ones. Imagine, me fighting with a kid."

I tried not to look at him with American eyes because sometimes   13
the reflection hurt.

Listening to my aunts' clucks of approval, my vision focused on the   14
qualities America overlooked. "He's such a hard worker. So serious, so
responsible." My aunts would secretly compliment my mother. The un-

spoken comparison was that he was not like some of their husbands, who drank and womanized. My uncles represented the darker side of *macho*.

In a patriarchal society, few challenge their roles. If men drink, it's 15 because it's the manly thing to do. If they gamble, it's because it's how men relax. And if they fool around, well, it's because a man simply can't hold back so much man! My aunts didn't exactly meekly sit back, but they put up with these transgressions because Mexican society dictated this was their lot in life.

In the United States, I believe it was the feminist movement of the 16 early seventies that changed *macho*'s meaning. Perhaps my generation of Latin women was in part responsible. I recall Chicanos complaining about the chauvinistic nature of Latin men and the notion they wanted their women barefoot, pregnant and in the kitchen. The generalization that Latin men embodied chauvinistic traits led to this interesting twist of semantics. Suddenly a word that represented something positive in one culture became a negative prototype in another.

The problem with the use of *macho* today is that it's become an ac- 17 cepted stereotype of the Latin male. And like all stereotypes, it distorts truth.

The impact of language in our society is undeniable. And the misuse 18 of *macho* hints at a deeper cultural misunderstanding that extends beyond mere word definitions.

QUESTIONS FOR DISCUSSION

1. What do you mean when you describe someone as *macho*? Do you see it as a desirable or undesirable trait? Does your usage match up with the author's explanation of what it means in the United States?

2. Guilbault mentions Sylvester Stallone, Arnold Schwarzenegger, and Charles Bronson as examples of American macho, and she contrasts them with Jimmy Stewart, Sean Connery, and Laurence Olivier. How do the first three meet her definition of the word? Do you agree with her evaluation of them? What examples of other movie actors or of personalities in other fields can you give?

3. What point is the author making in her description of her father in paragraphs 10–15? To whom does she compare her father?

SUGGESTIONS FOR WRITING

1. Guilbault writes, "Typically the cultural traits other societies value don't translate as desirable characteristics in America." This statement expresses a truth about differences between groups within one society as well as between entire societies. Characteristics valued within one group or society are not valued in another. Write a paper in which you contrast the reactions of two different groups of people to the same behaviors, customs, or attitudes.

2. Guilbault writes that today the word *macho* suggests a stereotype and that all stereotypes distort truth. Write a paper in which you examine how one stereotype with which you are familiar distorts the truth. Contrast what that stereotype suggests with examples of real people. For instance, what is the stereotype of a police officer or of a young person dressed all in black, baggy clothing? Contrast the stereotypical characteristics associated with such people with real people you know.

The Just-Right Wife

Ellen Goodman

Ellen Goodman has worked as a nationally syndicated columnist and as assistant editor of the *Boston Globe*. She has published many collections of her popular newspaper columns and in 1980 won the Pulitzer Prize for Distinguished Commentary. In the following selection she considers the desire of the American male for the "just-right" wife.

Vocabulary Check

maliciously (8)   Neanderthal (10)

drudge (10)   siphon (12)

The upper-middle-class men of Arabia are looking for just the right kind of wife. Arabia's merchant class, reports the Associated Press, finds the women of Libya too backward, and the women of Lebanon too forward, and have therefore gone shopping for brides in Egypt.   1

Egyptian women are being married off at the rate of thirty a day—an astonishing increase, according to the Egyptian marriage bureau. It doesn't know whether to be pleased or alarmed at the popularity of its women. According to one recent Saudi Arabian groom, the Egyptian women are "just right."   2

"The Egyptian woman is the happy medium," says Aly Abdul el-Korrary of his bride, Wafaa Ibrahiv (the happy medium herself was not questioned). "She is not too inhibited as they are in conservative Moslem societies, and not too liberal like many Lebanese."   3

Is this beginning to sound familiar? Well, the upper-middle-class, middle-aged, merchant-professional-class man of America also wants a "happy medium" wife. He is confused. He, too, has a problem and he would like us to be more understanding.   4

If it is no longer chic for a sheik to marry a veiled woman, it is somehow no longer "modern" for a successful member of the liberal establishment to be married to what he used to call a "housewife" and what he now hears called a "household drudge."   5

As his father once wanted a wife who had at least started college, now he would like a wife who has a mind, and even a job, of her own. The younger men in his office these days wear their wives' occupations on their sleeves. He thinks he, too, would like a wife—especially for so-   6 cial occasions—whose status would be his status symbol. A lady lawyer would be nice.

These men, you understand, now say (at least in private to younger working women in their office) that they are bored with women who "don't do anything." No matter how much some of them conspired in keeping them at home Back Then, many are now saying, in the best Moslem style, "I divorce thee." They are replacing them with more up-to-date models. A Ph.D. candidate would be nice.

The upper-middle-class, middle-aged man of today wants a wife who won't make him feel guilty. He doesn't want to worry if she's happy. He doesn't want to hear her complain about her dusty American history degree. He doesn't want to know if she's crying at the psychiatrist's office. He most definitely doesn't want to be blamed. He wants her to fulfill herself already! He doesn't mean that maliciously.

On the other hand, Lord knows, he doesn't want a wife who is too forward. The Saudi Arabian merchant believes that the Egyptian woman adapts more easily to his moods and needs. The American merchant also wants a woman who adapts herself to his moods and needs—his need for an independent woman and a traditional wife.

He doesn't want to live with a "household drudge," but it would be nice to have an orderly home and well-scrubbed children. Certainly he wouldn't want a wife who got high on folding socks—he is not a Neanderthal—but it would be nice if she arranged for these things to get done. Without talking about marriage contracts.

He wants a wife who agreed that "marriage is a matter of give and take, not a business deal and 50–50 chores." It would help if she had just enough conflict herself (for not being her mother) to feel more than half the guilt for a full ashtray.

Of course, he sincerely would like her to be involved in her own work and life. But on the other hand, he doesn't want it to siphon away her energy for him. He needs to be taken care of, nurtured. He would like her to enjoy her job, but be ready to move for his, if necessary (after, of course, a long discussion in which he feels awful about asking and she ends up comforting him and packing).

He wants a wife who is a sexually responsive and satisfied woman, 13
and he would even be pleased if she initiated sex with him. Sometimes.
Not too often, however, because then he would get anxious.

He is confused, but he does, in all sincerity (status symbols aside), 14
want a happy marriage to a happy wife. A happy medium. He is not
sure exactly what he means, but he, too, would like a wife who is "just
right."

The difference is that when the upper-middle-class, middle-aged 15
man of Arabia wants his wife he goes out and buys one. His American
"brother" can only offer himself as the prize.

QUESTIONS FOR DISCUSSION

1. What does Goodman see as the characteristics of an American "just-right" wife? Identify places in the selection where she provides those characteristics.

2. What is Goodman's attitude toward the American man who wants such a wife? How do you determine her attitude? Point out places in the selection that reveal what she thinks.

3. In what way does this selection reveal comparison/contrast techniques? Identify what is compared or contrasted with what in this selection.

SUGGESTIONS FOR WRITING

1. Many of us hold unreasonable expectations of other people, whether those people are parents, brothers or sisters, students, or teachers. We want other people to act in a way that will make us comfortable. Write a paper in which you contrast the unreasonable expectations we place on one type of person with the reality of what it might be reasonable to expect.

2. Goodman reveals many characteristics of the "just-right" wife. Is there also a "just-right" husband? Choose three characteristics of the "just-right" wife and compare and/or contrast them with characteristics of the "just-right" husband.

Columbus and the Moon

Tom Wolfe

Tom Wolfe is the author of *The Right Stuff*, a popular book about the U.S. space program that was made into a movie. A journalist and writer of social criticism, Wolfe here compares the voyages of Columbus with the explorations of the National Aeronautics and Space Administration (NASA).

Vocabulary Check

feasible (2)	appropriations (5)	lurid (7)
quest (5)	ignominy (6)	albeit (9)

The National Aeronautics and Space Administration's moon landing 10 years ago today was a Government project, but then so was Columbus's voyage to America in 1492. The Government, in Columbus's case, was the Spanish Court of Ferdinand and Isabella. Spain was engaged in a sea race with Portugal in much the same way that the United States would be caught up in a space race with the Soviet Union four and a half centuries later.   1

The race in 1492 was to create the first shipping lane to Asia. The Portuguese expeditions had always sailed east, around the southern tip of Africa. Columbus decided to head due west, across open ocean, a scheme that was feasible only thanks to a recent invention—the magnetic ship's compass. Until then ships had stayed close to the great land masses even for the longest voyages. Likewise, it was only thanks to an invention of the 1940's and early 1950's, the high-speed electronic computer, that NASA would even consider propelling astronauts out of the Earth's orbit and toward the moon.   2

Both NASA and Columbus made not one but a series of voyages. NASA landed men on six different parts of the moon. Columbus made four voyages to different parts of what he remained convinced was the east coast of Asia. As a result both NASA and Columbus had to keep coming back to the Government with their hands out, pleading for refinancing. In each case the reply of the Government became, after a few years: "This is all very impressive, but what earthly good is it to anyone back home?"   3

Columbus was reduced to making the most desperate claims. When he first reached land in 1492 at San Salvador, off Cuba, he ex-   4 pected to find gold, or at least spices. The Arawak Indians were awed by the strangers and their ships, which they believed had descended from the sky, and they presented them with their most prized possessions, live parrots and balls of cotton. Columbus soon set them digging for gold, which didn't exist. So he brought back reports of fabulous riches in the form of manpower; which is to say, slaves. He was not speaking of the Arawaks, however. With the exception of criminals and prisoners of war, he was supposed to civilize all natives and convert them to Christianity. He was talking about the Carib Indians, who were cannibals and therefore qualified as criminals. The Caribs would fight down to the last unbroken bone rather than endure captivity, and few ever survived the voyages back to Spain. By the end of Columbus's second voyage, in 1496, the Government was becoming testy. A great deal of wealth was going into voyages to Asia, and very little was coming back. Columbus made his men swear to return to Spain saying that they had not only reached the Asian mainland, they had heard Japanese spoken.

Likewise by the early 1970's, it was clear that the moon was in economic terms pretty much what it looked like from Earth, a gray rock. NASA, in the quest for appropriations, was reduced to publicizing the "spinoffs" of the space program. These included Teflon-coated frying pans, a ballpoint pen that would write in a weightless environment, and a computerized biosensor system that would enable doctors to treat heart patients without making house calls. On the whole, not a giant step for mankind.

In 1493, after his first voyage, Columbus had ridden through Barcelona at the side of King Ferdinand in the position once occupied by Ferdinand's late son, Juan. By 1500, the bad-mouthing of Columbus had reached the point where he was put in chains at the conclusion of his third voyage and returned to Spain in disgrace. NASA suffered no such ignominy, of course, but by July 20, 1974, the fifth anniversary of the landing of Apollo 11, things were grim enough. The public had become gloriously bored by space exploration. The fifth anniversary celebration consisted mainly of about 200 souls, mostly NASA people, sitting on folding chairs underneath a camp meeting canopy on the marble prairie outside the old Smithsonian Air Museum in Washington listening to speeches by Neil Armstrong, Michael Collins, and Buzz Aldrin and watching the caloric waves ripple.

Extraordinary rumors had begun to circulate about the astronauts. 7 The most lurid said that trips to the moon, and even into earth orbit, had so traumatized the men, they had fallen victim to religious and spiritualist manias or plain madness. (Of the total 73 astronauts chosen, one, Aldrin, is known to have suffered from depression, rooted, as his own memoir makes clear, in matters that had nothing to do with space flight. Two teamed up in an evangelical organization, and one set up a foundation for the scientific study of psychic phenomena—interests the three of them had developed long before they flew in space.) The NASA budget, meanwhile, had been reduced to the light-bill level.

Columbus died in 1509, nearly broke and stripped of most of his 8 honors as Spain's Admiral of the Ocean, a title he preferred. It was only later that history began to look upon him not as an adventurer who had tried and failed to bring home gold—but as a man with a supernatural sense of destiny, whose true glory was his willingness to plunge into the unknown, including the remotest parts of the universe he could hope to reach.

NASA still lives, albeit in reduced circumstances, and whether or 9 not history will treat NASA like the admiral is hard to say.

The idea that the exploration of the rest of the universe is its own 10 reward is not very popular, and NASA is forced to keep talking about things such as bigger communications satellites that will enable live television transmission of European soccer games at a fraction of the current cost. Such notions as "building a bridge to the stars for mankind" do not light up the sky today—but may yet.

QUESTIONS FOR DISCUSSION

1. What are some of the similarities between Columbus's voyages and NASA's space program that Wolfe identifies?

2. What seems to be Wolfe's purpose in drawing these comparisons? That is, what seems to be his central point? Do any particular sentences refer to it?

3. What point is Wolfe making in paragraph 5 when he refers to NASA's publicizing the "spinoffs" of the space program? To which part of Columbus's career is Wolfe comparing the "spinoffs"?

SUGGESTIONS FOR WRITING

1. Write a paper in which you explain the similarities or differences between two people of different ages. For example, compare or contrast your attitude toward one of the following topics with the attitude of one of your parents (or one of your children—or a brother or sister): marriage, work, sexuality, religion, money, happiness, drug or alcohol use, smoking, or other such topics.

2. Wolfe examines the similarities between two major periods of exploration in the history of the western world. Write a paper in which you discuss similarities or differences in the history of *yourself*. In other words, compare or contrast the person you are today with the person you were five or ten years ago.

Expressing an Opinion

Let Gays Marry

Andrew Sullivan

Andrew Sullivan holds a B.A. from Oxford University and a Ph.D. from Harvard. He has worked as the senior editor for the *New Republic* and is the author of *Virtually Normal: An Argument about Homosexuality* (1995). In the following selection, he presents his case for why gays should be allowed to marry. His essay originally appeared in *Newsweek* (1996).

Vocabulary Check

deem (1)	sanctioning (6)	monogamy (7)
subvert (2)	polygamy (6)	fidelity (7)

"A state cannot deem a class of persons a stranger to its laws," declared the Supreme Court last week. It was a monumental statement. Gay men and lesbians, the conservative court said, are no longer strangers in America. They are citizens, entitled, like everyone else, to equal protection—no special rights, but simple equality. 1

For the first time in Supreme Court history, gay men and women were seen not as some powerful lobby trying to subvert America, but as the people we truly are—the sons and daughters of countless mothers and fathers, with all the weaknesses and strengths and hopes of everybody else. And what we seek is not some special place in America but merely to be a full and equal part of America, to give back to our society without being forced to lie or hide or live as second-class citizens. 2

That is why marriage is so central to our hopes. People ask us why we want the right to marry, but the answer is obvious. It's the same reason anyone wants the right to marry. At some point in our lives, some of us are lucky enough to meet the person we truly love. And we want to commit to that person in front of family and country for the rest of our lives. It's the most simple, the most natural, the most human instinct in the world. How could anyone seek to oppose that? 3

Yes, at first blush, it seems like a radical proposal, but, when you think about it some more, it's actually the opposite. Throughout American history, to be sure, marriage has been between a man and a woman, 4 and in many ways our society is built upon that institution. But none of that need change in the slightest. After all, no one is seeking to take away anybody's right to marry, and no one is seeking to force any church to change any doctrine in any way. Particular religious arguments against same-sex marriage are rightly debated within the churches and faiths themselves. That is not the issue here: There is a separation between church and state in this country. We are only asking that when the government gives out *civil* marriage licenses, those of us who are gay should be treated like anybody else.

Of course, some argue that marriage is *by definition* between a man 5 and a woman. But for centuries, marriage was *by definition* a contract in which the wife was her husband's legal property. And we changed that. For centuries, marriage was *by definition* between two people of the same race. And we changed that. We changed these things because we recognized that human dignity is the same whether you are a man or a woman, black or white. And no one has any more of a choice to be gay than to be black or white or male or female.

Some say that marriage is only about raising children, but we let 6 childless heterosexual couples be married (Bob and Elizabeth Dole, Pat and Shelley Buchanan, for instance). Why should gay couples be treated differently? Others fear that there is no logical difference between allowing same-sex marriage and sanctioning polygamy and other horrors. But the issue whether to sanction multiple spouses (gay or straight) is completely separate from whether, in the existing institution between two unrelated adults, the government should discriminate between its citizens.

This is, in fact, if only Bill Bennett could see it, a deeply conserva- 7 tive cause. It seeks to change no one else's rights or marriages in any way. It seeks merely to promote monogamy, fidelity, and the disciplines of family life among people who have long been cast to the margins of society. And what could be a more conservative project than that? Why indeed would any conservative seek to oppose those very family values for gay people that he or she supports for everybody else? Except, of course, to make gay men and lesbians strangers in their own country, to forbid them ever to come home.

QUESTIONS FOR DISCUSSION

1. What distinction does Sullivan make between civil marriage licenses and marriages within a church? Why is such a distinction important to his argument?

2. How does Sullivan try to answer the argument that "marriage is *by definition* between a man and a woman"?

3. In what way is allowing marriage between gay people "a deeply conservative cause" (paragraph 7)?

SUGGESTIONS FOR WRITING

1. Write a paper supporting or objecting to gay marriages. Consider using the reasons Sullivan has presented, either supporting or refuting them with ideas of your own.

2. Who should marry whom has often been an issue in our society. Should men and women of different races marry? Should people of different religions marry? What about people from different educational, social, or economic backgrounds? Should people of widely differing ages marry? Write a paper in which you choose one such topic and express your opinion, supporting it with detailed examples of real people.

The Media's Image of Arabs

Jack C. Shaheen

In the following selection, Jack Shaheen asks us to consider the damage done by the media's persistently negative portrayal of Arab Americans. He makes it clear that all such stereotypes "blur our vision and corrupt the imagination." This selection first appeared in *Newsweek* in 1988.

Vocabulary Check

stereotype (1)	cliché (2)	whipping boy (7)
caricatures (1)	humane (5)	swarthy (8)

America's bogeyman is the Arab. Until the nightly news brought us TV pictures of Palestinian boys being punched and beaten, almost all portraits of Arabs seen in America were dangerously threatening. Arabs were either billionaires or bombers—rarely victims. They were hardly ever seen as ordinary people practicing law, driving taxis, singing lullabies or healing the sick. Though TV news may portray them more sympathetically now, the absence of positive media images nurtures suspicion and stereotype. As an Arab-American, I have found that ugly caricatures have had an enduring impact on my family.

I was sheltered from prejudicial portraits at first. My parents came from Lebanon in the 1920s; they met and married in America. Our home in the steel city of Clairton, Pa., was a center for ethnic sharing— black, white, Jew and gentile. There was only one major source of media images then, at the State movie theater where I was lucky enough to get a part-time job as an usher. But in the late 1940s, Westerns and war movies were popular, not Middle Eastern dramas. Memories of World War II were fresh, and the screen heavies were the Japanese and the Germans. True to the cliché of the times, the only good Indian was a dead Indian. But when I mimicked or mocked the bad guys, my mother cautioned me. She explained that stereotypes blur our vision and corrupt the imagination. "Have compassion for all people, Jackie," she said. "This way, you'll learn to experience the joy of accepting people as they are, and not as they appear in films. Stereotypes hurt."

Mother was right. I can remember the Saturday afternoon when my son, Michael, who was seven, and my daughter Michele, six, suddenly called out: "Daddy, Daddy, they've got some bad Arabs on TV." They

1

2

3

were watching that great American morality play, TV wrestling. Akbar the Great, who liked to hear the cracking of bones, and Abdullah the Butcher, a dirty fighter who liked to inflict pain, were pinning their foes with "camel locks." From that day on, I knew I had to try to neutralize the media caricatures.

It hasn't been easy. With my children, I have watch animated heroes **4**
Heckle and Jeckle pull the rug from under "Ali Boo-Boo, the Desert Rat," and Laverne and Shirley stop "Sheik Ha-Mean-Ie" from conquering "the U.S. and the world." I have read comic books like the "Fantastic Four" and "G.I. Combat" whose characters have sketched Arabs as "lowlifes" and "human hyenas." Negative stereotypes were everywhere. A dictionary informed my youngsters that an Arab is a "vagabond, drifter, hobo and vagrant." Whatever happened, my wife wondered, to Aladdin's good genie?

To a child, the world is simple: good versus evil. But my children **5**
and others with Arab roots grew up without ever having seen a humane Arab on the silver screen, someone to pattern their lives after. Is it easier for a camel to go through the eye of a needle than for a screen Arab to appear as a genuine human being?

Hollywood producers must have an instant Ali Baba kit that con- **6**
tains scimitars, veils, sunglasses and such Arab clothing as *chadors* and *kufiyahs*. In the mythical "Ay-rabland," oil wells, tents, mosques, goats and shepherds prevail. Between the sand dunes, the camera focuses on a mock-up of a palace from "Arabian Nights"—or a military air base. Recent movies suggest that Americans are at war with Arabs, forgetting the fact that out of 21 Arab nations, America is friendly with 19 of them. And in "Wanted Dead or Alive," a movie that starred Gene Simmons, the leader of the rock group Kiss, the war comes home when an Arab terrorist comes to the United States dressed as a rabbi and, among other things, conspires with Arab-Americans to poison the people of Los Angeles. The movie was released last year.

The Arab remains American culture's favorite whipping boy. In his **7**
memoirs, Terrel Bell, Ronald Reagan's first secretary of education, writes about an "apparent bias among mid-level, right-wing staffers at the White House" who dismissed Arabs as "sand niggers." Sadly, the

racial slurs continue. At a recent teacher's conference, I met a woman from Sioux Falls, S.D., who told me about the persistence of discrimination. She was in the process of adopting a baby when an agency staffer warned her that the infant had a problem. When she asked whether the child was mentally ill, or physically handicapped, there was silence. Finally, the worker said: "The baby is Jordanian."

To me, the Arab demon of today is much like the Jewish demon of yesterday. We deplore the false portrait of Jews as a swarthy menace. Yet a similar portrait has been accepted and transferred to another group of Semites—the Arabs. Print and broadcast journalists have started to challenge this stereotype. They are now revealing more humane images of Palestinian Arabs, a people who traditionally suffered from the myth that Palestinian equals terrorist. Others could follow that lead and retire the stereotypical Arab to media Valhalla. 8

It would be a step in the right direction if movie and TV producers developed characters modeled after real-life Arab-Americans. We could then see a White House correspondent like Helen Thomas, whose father came from Lebanon, in "The Golden Girls," a heart surgeon patterned after Dr. Michael DeBakey on "St. Elsewhere," or a Syrian-American playing tournament chess like Yasser Seirawan, the Seattle grandmaster. 9

Politicians, too, should speak out against the cardboard caricatures. They should refer to Arabs as friends, not just as moderates. And religious leaders could state that Islam like Christianity and Judaism maintains that all mankind is one family in the care of God. When all imagemakers rightfully begin to treat Arabs and all other minorities with respect and dignity, we may begin to unlearn our prejudices. 10

QUESTIONS FOR DISCUSSION

1. What does Shaheen mean when he writes that "the Arab demon of today is much like the Jewish demon of yesterday"?

2. What examples does Shaheen use to support his contention that "America's bogeyman is the Arab"? Do you find his examples convincing? Why or why not?

3. Why does Shaheen tell us what his mother said when he "mimicked or mocked the bad guys" (paragraph 2)?

SUGGESTIONS FOR WRITING

1. Consider the media's handling of other ethnic and racial groups—blacks, Hispanics, Native Americans, Chinese, Italians, or any other group. Write a paper expressing an opinion about how one such group is portrayed by the media and support your opinion with specific examples.

2. Do the media portray any other group of people in an unfair way? Consider the media's portrayal of homemakers, women with careers outside the home, homosexuals, athletes, husbands, or any other group. Write a paper expressing your opinion regarding the media's portrayal of one such group and support your opinion with specific examples.

In Defense of Splitting Up

Barbara Ehrenreich

Is it too easy to divorce today? Do divorces damage the children involved? Should divorce laws be made more restrictive? Barbara Ehrenreich, a respected author, lecturer, and social commentator, considers these questions in the following essay, first published in *Time* magazine (1996). Ehrenreich has published many articles and reviews in the *New York Times Magazine, Esquire,* the *Atlantic Monthly,* the *New Republic,* and *Harper's.*

Vocabulary Check

rhetoric (2)	slanders (5)	prenuptial (8)
offbeat (2)	per se (5)	ideologically (10)
deprecating (3)	stigmatized (6)	
control group (3)	rancorous (7)	

No one seems much concerned about children when the subject is welfare or Medicaid cuts, but mention divorce, and tears flow for their tender psyches. Legislators in half a dozen states are planning to restrict divorce on the grounds that it may cause teen suicide, an inability to "form lasting attachments" and possibly also the piercing of nipples and noses. 1

But if divorce itself hasn't reduced America's youth to emotional cripples, then the efforts to restrict it undoubtedly will. First, there's the effect all this antidivorce rhetoric is bound to have on the children of people already divorced—and we're not talking about some offbeat minority. At least 37% of American children live with divorced parents, and these children already face enough tricky interpersonal situations without having to cope with the public perception that they're damaged goods. 2

Fortunately for the future of the republic, the alleged psyche-scarring effects of divorce have been grossly exaggerated. The most frequently cited study, by California therapist Judith Wallerstein, found that 41% of the children of divorced couples are "doing poorly, worried, underachieving, deprecating and often angry" years after their parents' divorce. But this study has been faulted for including only 60 couples, two-thirds of whom were deemed to lack "adequate psychological functioning" even before they split, and all of whom were self-selected 3 seekers of family therapy. Futhermore, there was no control group of, say, miserable couples who stayed together.

As for some of the wilder claims, such as "teen suicide has tripled as divorces have tripled"; well, roller-blading has probably tripled in the same time period too, and that's hardly a reason to ban in-line skates.

In fact, the current antidivorce rhetoric slanders millions of perfectly wonderful, high-functioning young people, my own children and most of their friends included. Studies that attempt to distinguish between the effects of divorce and those of the income decline so often experienced by divorced mothers have found no lasting psychological damage attributable to divorce per se. Check out a typical college dorm, and you'll find people enthusiastically achieving and forming attachments until late into the night. Ask about family, and you'll hear about Mom and Dad...and Stepmom and Stepdad.

The real problems for kids will begin when the antidivorce movement starts getting its way. For one thing, the more militant among its members want to "re-stigmatize" divorce with the cultural equivalent of a scarlet *D*. Sadly though, divorce is already stigmatized in ways that are harmful to children. Studies show that teachers consistently interpret children's behavior more negatively when they are told that the children are from "broken" homes—and, as we know, teachers' expectations have an effect on children's performance. If the idea is to help the children of divorce, then the goal should be to *de*-stigmatize divorce among all who interact with them—teachers, neighbors, playmates.

Then there are the likely effects on children of the proposed restrictions themselves. Antidivorce legislators want to repeal no-fault divorce laws and return to the system in which one parent has to prove the other guilty of adultery, addiction or worse. True, the divorce rate rose after the introduction of no-fault divorce in the late '60s and '70s. But the divorce rate was already rising at a healthy clip *before* that, so there's no guarantee that the repeal of no-fault laws will reduce the divorce rate now. In fact, one certain effect will be to generate more divorces of the rancorous, potentially child-harming variety. If you think "Mommy and Daddy aren't getting along" sounds a little too blithe, would you rather "Daddy (or Mommy) has been sleeping around"?

Not that divorce is an enviable experience for any of the parties in- **8**
volved. But just as there are bad marriages, there are, as sociologist
Constance Ahrons agrees, "good divorces," in which both parents
maintain their financial and emotional responsibility for the kids.
Maybe the reformers should concentrate on improving the *quality* of
divorces—by, for example, requiring prenuptial agreements specifying
how the children will be cared for in the event of a split.

The antidivorce movement's interest in the emotional status of chil- **9**
dren would be more convincing if it were linked to some concern for their
physical survival. The most destructive feature of divorce, many experts
argue, is the poverty that typically ensues when the children are left with a
low-earning mother, and the way out of this would be to toughen child-
support collection and strengthen the safety net of supportive services for
low-income families—including childcare, Medicaid and welfare.

Too difficult? Too costly? Too ideologically distasteful compared **10**
with denouncing divorce and, by implication, the divorced and their
children? Perhaps. But sometimes grownups have to do difficult and
costly things, whether they feel like doing them or not. For the sake of
the children, that is.

QUESTIONS FOR DISCUSSION

1. Ehrenreich says that antidivorce legislators want to repeal no-fault divorce laws (paragraph 7). What are no-fault divorce laws, and what does Ehrenreich fear will happen if they are repealed?

2. What point is Ehrenreich making when she says that roller-blading has probably tripled in the same time period that divorce has tripled (paragraph 4)?

3. Rather than make getting a divorce more difficult, what does Ehrenreich suggest should be done?

SUGGESTIONS FOR WRITING

1. Ehrenreich writes that "the alleged psyche-scarring effects of divorce [on children] have been grossly exaggerated." Do you think divorce damages children or not? Write a paper in which you support your opinion with specific examples of real people drawn from your experiences or observations.

2. Do you think divorce should be restricted? Should it be more difficult to divorce than it now is? Support your opinion with specific examples of real people drawn from your experiences or observations.

Practice Final Examination

I. Chapter One

A. Underline all subjects once and all verbs twice.

   1. Will you be visiting Washington, D.C., this summer?

   2. The detective and the officer examined the crime scene.

   3. The jazz concert was scheduled for noon, but the band was delayed by the snow storm.

   4. Icarus followed the bees to their hive because he wanted some wax.

   5. Into the dark cave walked the anthropologist and his students.

B. In the space provided, indicate whether the underlined word is a noun (N), pronoun (Pro), verb (V), adjective (Adj), adverb (Adv), preposition (Prep), or conjunction (Conj).

   _____ **6.** The astronaut <u>seldom</u> wished upon a star.

   _____ **7.** The <u>mysterious</u> black sedan turned the corner and sped off into the night.

   _____ **8.** Beowulf respected the dragon, <u>yet</u> he also feared him.

   _____ **9.** Calculators have <u>become</u> smaller and cheaper.

   _____**10.** <u>Into</u> the center of the ring danced Ali.

C. In the following sentences, place all prepositional phrases in parentheses.

   11. One of these days his whole empire will collapse around him.

   12. During the summer Fergal often walks Rory after dinner.

   13. "Sock it to me" was a popular phrase in the sixties.

   14. Through the storm flew the jet from the aircraft carrier.

   15. Jeremy wrapped the present that he had bought for his grandmother and then hid it under his bed.

continued
II. Chapter Two

A. Correct all fragments, comma splices, and fused sentences. If the sentence is correct, do nothing to it.

16. To be in style wherever he went.

_____

_____

17. The salesman opened his eelskin briefcase, out fell three eels.

_____

_____

18. Biking with his friends through Germany, Oswald discovered strudel.

_____

_____

19. The leopard crossed the road slowly then it stopped and stared when it saw the armadillo.

_____

_____

20. Pablo walked through the famous museum he saw not one of his paintings.

_____

_____

21. Because you promised never to wear your Elvis Presley T-shirt again.

_____

_____

continued

22. Geraldo was just walking along minding his own business, the Frisbee came out of nowhere.

_____

_____

23. Charlie Parker's nickname was "Bird" it was short for "Yardbird."

_____

_____

24. Keep doing the same thing.

_____

_____

25. Staring at all the new computers for sale and wishing that he had enough money to buy a new one.

_____

_____

B. Compose simple, compound, complex, and compound-complex sentences according to the instructions.

26. Write a simple sentence that contains a prepositional phrase.

_____

_____

27. Write a compound sentence. Use a coordinating conjunction that indicates a contrast to join the clauses. Use appropriate punctuation.

_____

_____

continued

28. Write a compound sentence. Use a transitional word or phrase to join the clauses. Use appropriate punctuation.

_____

_____

29. Write a complex sentence that begins with a subordinate clause. Use appropriate punctuation.

_____

_____

30. Write a compound-complex sentence. Use a transitional word or phrase to join the main clauses. Use appropriate punctuation.

_____

_____

III. Chapter Three

A. Correct any misplaced or dangling modifiers in the following sentences. If the sentence is correct, do nothing to it.

31. Running up the hill, Darren's side began to ache.

_____

_____

32. Ian brought his dog to the veterinarian that had worms.

_____

_____

33. Hoping for a scholarship, Enrico's daughter wrote a long letter to the dean.

_____

_____

continued

34. Uvaldo almost sat for three hours waiting for the bus.

_____

_____

35. Delighted at the sudden turn of events, a celebration at a fancy restaurant was scheduled.

_____

_____

36. The other team stayed in the bus with measles.

_____

_____

37. Yesterday I only ran two miles instead of my usual five.

_____

_____

38. Scared by the police car, Alfredo's foot moved to the brake.

_____

_____

39. Mrs. Robinson brought a fruitcake to the party that was soaked in rum.

_____

_____

40. Looking hungrily at the dog food, I could see that the collie had not eaten in a long time.

_____

_____

Practice Final Examination

continued

B. Add phrases or clauses to the following sentences according to the instructions. Be sure to punctuate carefully.

41. Add a verbal phrase. Use the verb *scare*.

The old woman dialed the emergency number 911.

_____

_____

42. Add an adjective clause.

The road was closed by the summer storm.

_____

_____

43. Add a present participial phrase to the beginning of this sentence. Use the verb *hope*.

Franco bought Teresa a large bouquet of forget-me-nots.

_____

_____

44. Add an appositive phrase to one of the names in the sentence.

Xena handed her sword to Hercules.

_____

_____

45. Add an infinitive verbal phrase to this sentence. Use the verb *plant*.

At the nursery in Murrieta, Lenny bought two rose bushes and a cottonwood tree.

_____

_____

continued
IV. Chapter Four

A. Correct any subject–verb agreement errors in the following sentences by crossing out the incorrect verb form and writing in the correct form above it. If the sentence is correct, do nothing to it.

46. Every teacher in both schools have an advanced degree.

47. That flock of birds fly south to west Texas each October.

48. Does the dogs or the bear have a better chance in the fight?

49. A bowl of split pea soup with a few crackers make a good lunch.

50. Each of the contestants on the show want to win the million dollars.

51. Two years of a foreign language are required for most majors at my college.

52. Bowls of ice cream or pieces of pie are offered for dessert.

53. Anyone who has children are aware that yelling at them is not the most effective strategy.

54. A book with interesting characters mean more to me than one with an exciting plot.

55. The committee have decided to approve the latest building proposal.

B. Correct any pronoun use errors in the following sentences by crossing out the incorrect pronoun and writing in the correct one above it. In some cases you may have to rewrite part of the sentence. If the sentence is correct, do nothing to it.

56. The man next door and myself put up a fence between our houses.

57. If a jogger develops sore knees, you should try another exercise.

58. Between Hannah and she, they won every race.

59. Rosaline spoke to Babs about her new photos for the calendar.

60. At the theater someone had left their purse in the seat next to mine.

61. The new electronics company gave all of their employees ten shares of stock so that they would feel a part of the company.

62. When he saw the bear, Davy Crockett knew that his friend and hisself were in trouble.

Practice Final Examination

63. Gordon's parents took away his car for six months because he got one D on his report card; this seemed a bit excessive to me.

64. Us parents started to worry when the bus from camp was late.

65. Before the party started, Fred sent Meredith and her to the drugstore for more film.

V. Chapter Five

A. Add commas to the following sentences where necessary. If the sentence is correct, do nothing to it.

66. No I do not like Spam and I do not like turnips.

67. On April 12 1861 the Confederates fired on Fort Sumter and began the Civil War.

68. The candidates agreed to a debate about taxes the environment campaign finance reform and abortion.

69. On the scratched wet floor mops were piled around like pick-up sticks.

70. Some of the bunnies for example had white tails.

71. Owen went skiing at Aspen when he had a slight head cold and was nursing a sore ankle.

72. The climb to the top was a steep difficult one but it was worth the trip because of the view.

73. When you go swimming in that black lagoon you should of course watch for the monster.

74. Next the boxer in the red trunks stumbled and then the other boxer kicked him.

75. Confused by all of the noise Sigmund tried to cover his ears and then he began to call for his mother.

B. Correct any errors in the use of periods, exclamation points, question marks, semicolons, colons, quotation marks, or apostrophes (or 's) in the following sentences. If the sentence is correct, do nothing to it. Do not add or delete any commas.

76. Chicken Little asked, Is the sky really falling

77. It was my mothers favorite dish when I was a child she was a good cook, too, answered Rebecca

continued

78. When did the patriot say, Give me liberty or give me death

79. Mr Nguyen dropped a hammer on his toe, and then he shouted, Ouch

80. Among the things the police didnt find were the following the weapon, the body, and

the perpetrator

C. Correct any errors in the use of capitalization, titles, or numbers in the following sentences. If the sentence is correct, do nothing to it.

81. In today's los angeles times, I read an article called insurance industry's clout cracks.

82. There have been 4 forest fires in yellowstone national park in the last few years.

83. James thurber wrote a very funny short story called the catbird seat.

84. One of the main stories in last week's time magazine was titled election 2000.

85. Last semester in cinema 101 class, we watched the movie roxanne and then read the

play cyrano de bergerac.

VI. Chapter Six

A. In the following sentences correct any errors in the use of irregular verbs by crossing out the incorrect forms and writing in the correct ones above. If the sentence is correct, do nothing to it.

86. The wallet laid next to the water that had froze in the gutter.

87. Esmeralda spinned around, set down, and confessed the whole thing to me.

88. Last night Billy drunk his medicine before lying down.

89. I would have swam a few more laps if I had not ran into the side of the pool with my

head.

90. Lady Godiva carefully folded and lay her clothes on a chair before she begun her ride.

B. Correct any errors in word choice in the following sentences by crossing out any incorrect words and writing the correct words above. If the sentence is correct, do nothing to it.

91. The man would not except the idea that ten cups of coffee a day would have a negative

affect on his health.

continued

92. I was sure you're plane was going to arrive to late for us to make our connecting flight.

93. After eating too much at Thanksgiving dinner, I felt nauseous and was afraid I might loose my dinner.

94. The food was alright, but there could have been less ants at our potluck.

95. Michael and Karen asked me for advise when some neighbors complained about there barking dogs.

C. Correct any spelling errors in the following sentences by crossing out the incorrect spellings and writing the correct spellings above them.

96. The story discribes an ocurence that took place at Owl Creek Bridge.

97. Clem beleived he was an honest person, but he still slipped two of his host's dinner knifes into the pocket of his jacket.

98. Marvel truely thought he had not mispelled penicillin.

99. Both good judgement and skill are needed for a person to drive safely in extremely low tempertures.

100. The suspect admitted niether a crime nor a lie.

Moving from Paragraph to Essay

In Chapters Three, Four, Five and Six of this text, you are asked to write paragraphs that use several points to explain or support their topic sentences. As you write these paragraphs, you will notice that they tend to be a bit long. In fact, you may feel they are *too* long, that they could easily be divided into several paragraphs that make up one essay.

Of course, your reaction is quite accurate. In fact, most college writing consists of essays composed of several paragraphs. The very word *paragraph* comes from two Greek words that indicate that one paragraph is meant to be written with other paragraphs. *Para* means "beside," and *graphos* means "writing," so a paragraph is writing that is meant to be written with other paragraphs.

Many paragraphs in this text could be changed into brief essays with just a little work. In fact, notice how easily the paragraph from Exercise 2C in Chapter Four (reproduced on the next page) can be written as an essay composed of five separate paragraphs.

Original Paragraph

Topic sentence

First support
Example

Anyone who is left-handed knows as well as I that being left-handed in a right-handed world can result in any number of awkward and frustrating situations. <u>One result of being left-handed is having to listen to people who want to help "correct" the problem.</u> For instance, my first grade teacher was determined to turn another "lefty" and me into right-handers. She would point to the other students and say that they wrote better than we because they held their pencils correctly. She forced us to practice writing with the "correct" hand for hours—at least until our parents had a talk with the principal and her.

Second support
Examples

<u>Another result of being left-handed involves the many inconveniences that a left-hander must face.</u> For example, my sister, who is also left-handed, and I have both noticed that school classrooms rarely have more than one left-handed desk. And I have been told by my cousin Earl, another lefty, that his wife and he can rarely find a pair of scissors that will work for a left-handed person.

Third support
Examples

<u>These types of inconveniences constantly remind the lefties in my family—Earl, my sister, and me—that we are out of place in a right-handed world.</u> Recently, Earl's wife purchased a new camcorder only to discover that Earl could not work it as easily as she because it was designed to be held and operated with the right hand. And last month, when my sister visited Las Vegas with some friends for the first time, her friends and she discovered that the handles to all of the slot machines were—where else?—on the right.

Conclusion

<u>Obviously, being left-handed can result in many awkward situations, but I suppose that the other left-handers and I should be grateful. After all, left-handed people in some past cultures were viewed with suspicion and were sometimes accused of being witches. We lefties in modern societies certainly have it better than they!</u>

Essay Form

Introduction
Thesis statement

Anyone who is left-handed knows as well as I that being left-handed in a right-handed world can result in any number of awkward and frustrating situations.

Topic sentence of
first body
paragraph
Example

<u>One result of being left-handed is having to listen to people who want to help "correct" the problem.</u> For instance, my first grade teacher was determined to turn another "lefty" and me into right-handers. She would point to the other students and say that they wrote better than we because they held their pencils correctly. She forced us to practice writing with the "correct" hand for hours—at least until our parents had a talk with the principal and her.

Topic sentence of
second body
paragraph
Examples

<u>Another result of being left-handed involves the many inconveniences that a left-hander must face.</u> For example, my sister, who is also left-handed, and I have both noticed that school classrooms rarely have more than one left-handed desk. And I have been told by my cousin Earl, another lefty, that his wife and he can rarely find a pair of scissors that will work for a left-handed person.

Topic sentence of
third body
paragraph
Example

These types of inconveniences constantly remind the lefties in my family—Earl, my sister, and me—that we are out of place in a right-handed world. Recently, Earl's wife purchased a new camcorder only to discover that Earl could not work it as easily as she because it was designed to be held and operated with the right hand. And last month, when my sister visited Las Vegas with some friends for the first time, her friend and she discovered that the handles to all of the slot machines were—where else?—on the right.

Conclusion

Obviously, being left-handed can result in many awkward situations, but I suppose that the other left-handers and I should be grateful. After all, left-handed people in some past cultures were viewed with suspicion and were sometimes accused of being witches. We lefties in modern societies certainly have it better than they!

As you can see, the original paragraph can be divided into an essay with three major sections: the introduction, the body, and the conclusion. Let's consider each of these sections.

The Introduction

Notice that the topic sentence from the original paragraph is now in a separate introductory paragraph. Because the sentence now introduces an entire *essay*, not just one paragraph, it is called the **thesis statement** of the essay. The thesis statement of an essay is the sentence that states the topic and the central point of the essay.

> **thesis statement**
> The thesis statement of an essay is the sentence that states the topic and the central point of the essay.

Of course, you can write an introduction that is more than one sentence long. When you do write a longer introduction, you should usually keep the thesis statement as the last sentence. Here is one way you could expand the introduction to the above essay:

Thesis statement

Recently my younger brother broke his right arm, and since then he has done nothing but complain about how difficult it is to have to use his left hand for everyday tasks. However, as a "lefty," I don't feel very sorry for him, for I have to live that way all the time. **Anyone who is left-handed knows as well as I that being left-handed in a right-handed world can result in any number of awkward and frustrating situations.**

The Body

The body of the above essay consists of three paragraphs. Each paragraph has its own **topic sentence** (which has been underlined). As you already know, a topic sentence states the topic and the central point of a paragraph. In an essay, it also explains or supports the thesis. Of course, each topic sentence is followed by other sentences, often examples, that explain or support it. You can visualize the structure of an essay this way:

First paragraph:

Introduction and thesis statement

Second paragraph:

First topic sentence to support thesis
Examples to support topic sentence

Third paragraph:

Second topic sentence to support thesis
Examples to support topic sentence

Fourth paragraph:

Third topic sentence to support thesis
Examples to support topic sentence

Fifth paragraph:

Conclusion

■ **PRACTICE**   Answer the following questions about the essay on pages xx–xx.

1. In the first *body* paragraph, how many examples are presented to support

   the topic sentence? _____ What are the examples?

   _____

   _____

2. In the second *body* paragraph, how many examples are presented to

   support the topic sentence? _____ What are the examples?

   _____

   _____

3. In the third *body* paragraph, how many examples are presented to support

the topic sentence? _____ What are the examples?

_____

_____

The Conclusion

The conclusion of an essay often rewords the thesis statement, but it does not usually repeat it word for word.

Thesis statement   Anyone who is left-handed knows as well as I that being left-handed in a right-handed world can result in any number of awkward and frustrating situations.

Conclusion   Obviously, being left-handed can result in many awkward situations, but I suppose that the other left-handers and I should be grateful. After all, left-handed people in some past cultures were viewed with suspicion and were sometimes accused of being witches. We lefties in modern societies certainly have it better than they!

■   **PRACTICE**   The following paragraph appeared as Exercise 1C in Chapter Five. Read it, and then answer the questions after it.

1. Two familiar love stories, one a tragedy and one a comedy, are actually modern versions of earlier tales. **2.** For example, the 1957 musical *West Side Story* and Shakespeare's *Romeo and Juliet* have many similarities. **3.** Both stories involve a conflict between two major groups of people—two gangs, the Jets and Sharks from lower Manhattan in *West Side Story,* and two families, the Montagues and Capulets of Verona in *Romeo and Juliet.* **4.** In *West Side Story* Tony and Maria must hide their love from their friends, and in *Romeo and Juliet* the central characters must hide their love from their families. **5.** Although both love affairs have the potential of bringing the warring factions together, ultimately they fail to do so. **6.** Each story ends in death; however, Romeo and Juliet kill themselves, while Tony is gunned down by a rival gang member and Maria lives. **7.** Another story, Steve Martin's comedy *Roxanne,* is based on the nineteenth-century play *Cyrano de Bergerac.* **8.** The central characters of both stories are witty, well-spoken men who believe their long noses would prevent the beautiful Roxanne from loving them. **9.** They both are swordsmen (although Steve Martin's sword is a tennis racket), and they both provide the words for a man named Chris (or Christian in the earlier version) to woo Roxanne. **10.** In the Steve Martin version, the central character, who is played by Steve Martin, ultimately wins Roxanne's love, but that is not true for all earlier versions of the story. **11.** These two love stories are, of course, just two of many modern plays, films, and novels that are based on earlier works of literature.

1. Divide the paragraph into an essay with an introduction, three body paragraphs, and a conclusion. Then indicate which sentences you included in:

   a. the introduction _____

   b. the first body paragraph _____

   c. the second body paragraph _____

   d. the third body paragraph _____

   e. the conclusion _____

2. Which sentence in the introduction is the thesis statement?

   _____

3. Which sentence in each body paragraph is the topic sentence?

   _____

■ **PRACTICE** The following paragraph appeared as Exercise 2C in Chapter Six. Read it, and then answer the questions after it.

1. Some people do not enjoy any type of competition, but I believe that self-directed competition (that is, competing against one's own personal standard) can bring many benefits. 2. For example, self-directed competition has really affected how well I play classical guitar. 3. When I first started, I could not play the guitar well, so I decided to learn to play at least one piece or perform one technique more effectively than the week before. 4. As each week passed, I "competed" with myself. 5. Now, only two years later, I have accepted an invitation to perform for our local Chamber of Commerce. 6. The principle of self-directed competition has also helped me learn to snow ski. 7. Last year, I went skiing with some neighbors who already knew how to ski. 8. Instead of trying to keep up with them (and maybe break a leg), I stayed on one slope until I could ski it from top to bottom. 9. Only then would it be all right for me to try a more difficult slope. 10. By the end of the ski season, there were fewer than four slopes (all of them expert runs) that I had not yet skied. 11. Today I'm eagerly looking forward to next winter. 12. Finally, self-directed competition has made me a better student. 13. When I am in class, I could choose to compare myself to other students, but I don't; instead, I just try to improve what I have done. 14. For instance, when I received a C on my first report in biology, I did not lose my hope for an A in the class. 15. I knew that through self-directed competition I could do better, and I did. 16. By the end of the semester the number of A's I had received far outweighed my C's, and I did receive an A for the class. 17. Self-directed competition may not be for everyone, but my advice is that it is a good way to enjoy life while becoming better at what you like to do.

1. Divide the paragraph into an essay with an introduction, three body paragraphs, and a conclusion. Then indicate which sentences you included in:

   a. the introduction _____

   b. the first body paragraph _____

   c. the second body paragraph _____

   d. the third body paragraph _____

   e. the conclusion _____

2. Which sentence in the introduction is the thesis statement?

   _____

   _____

3. Which sentence in each body paragraph is the topic sentence?

   _____

   _____

Assignment

Write an essay using one of the writing assignments from Section Five, Chapter Six. Your essay should have an introduction that includes a **thesis statement**. It should also have at least three body paragraphs, each one with a clear **topic sentence**. Within each paragraph, give **examples** to support the topic sentence. The essay should end with a concluding paragraph that rewords your thesis.
   Remember that writing is a process.

1. Before you write the first draft of your paper, spend time prewriting to develop as many possible topics for your body paragraphs as you can think of.

2. After you have seven, eight, or nine possible paragraph topics, choose the three or four that interest you the most.

3. Now prewrite to discover as many examples as you can to include in each paragraph.

4. Once you have your paragraph topics and examples, write the first draft of your paper. As you write, be prepared to discover more examples that may be even more effective than the ones you have already thought of.

5. As you write your first draft, do not worry much about spelling, grammar, and punctuation.

6. When your first draft is complete, write it again. Try to make your thesis statement and your topic sentences as clear as possible. Try to add more descriptive details to your examples. Add more examples to any paragraphs that might need them.

7. Now edit your paper. Correct any spelling, grammar, or punctuation errors that you might find. Watch particularly for errors that you know you regularly make.

8. Prepare a clean final draft, following the format your instructor has asked for.

Answers to Practices

Chapter One

Page 3:

2. Hester, letter, dress
3. Alice, Queen, loser
4. Scots, Nessie, warmth, affection
5. questions, Leda, swan, importance

Page 4:

2. Aeneas, crew, Carthage, apology, note
3. Homer, lips, thought, plate, Spam
4. Gulliver, site, *Yahoo!,* computer
5. governments, freedom, press
6. depression, sense, meaninglessness, king
7. hypocrites, people, impression
8. philosophy, life, ideas, acceptance, willingness
9. United States, Christmas, December, traditions, trees, lights, gifts
10. Darby, thought, enemy

Pages 5–6:

2. nouns: cyclops, men, sheep
   pronouns: Nobody
3. nouns: Homer, Spam, cheese, plate, grits
   pronouns: himself, me
4. nouns: pig, house
   pronouns: What, his
5. nouns: Hortense, saddles, mother
   pronouns: one, it, her
6. nouns: Pinocchio, nose
   pronouns: that, something, everyone, his
7. nouns: General Burnside, way, hair
   pronouns: they, he, his
8. nouns: children, penny, Mr. Scrooge
   pronouns: Each
9. nouns: time, day
   pronouns: This, their
10. nouns: host, Super Bowl
    pronouns: Everyone, whom, him

Page 6:

Answers will vary. Here are some possible ones.
2. The <u>host</u> might persuade <u>her</u> to play <u>a song.</u>
3. <u>Everyone</u> in the <u>audience</u> applauded for the <u>singer</u> on the <u>stage.</u>
4. <u>Who</u> told <u>our class</u> about the <u>fight</u>?
5. After <u>John</u> cooked <u>their</u> <u>dinner,</u> <u>he</u> asked <u>his</u> <u>girlfriend</u> to watch the <u>television</u> with <u>him.</u>

Page 7:

2. disappeared
3. play
4. raised
5. sang

Page 8:

2. is
3. seemed
4. tastes
5. am

Page 9:

2. verb: laughed
   tense: past
3. verb: will visit
   tense: future
4. verb: stared
   tense: past
5. verb: likes
   tense: present

Page 11:

2. HV
3. HV
4. MV
5. HV
6. MV

7. HV
8. MV
9. MV
10. HV

Pages 11–12:

A.

2. HV: have
   MV: lost
3. HV: will
   MV: change

4. HV: Does
   MV: want
5. HV: could have
   MV: given

B. Answers will vary. Here are some possible ones.

7. The ostrich <u>walked</u> to the fence and <u>looked</u> at the tub of water.
8. The glass <u>fell</u> to the floor and <u>broke</u> into hundreds of small pieces.

9. A spider <u>was</u> slowly <u>crawling</u> along the wall behind my sister.
10. One <u>should</u> never <u>place</u> his or her head in a lion's mouth when it <u>is</u> hungry.

Page 13:

2. HV: would
   MV: move
   Verbal: leaning
3. HV: had
   MV: prepared
   Verbal: To please

4. HV: did
   MV: see
   Verbal: swimming
5. HV: asked
   Verbal: waiting

Page 13:

2. HV: had
   MV: tried
   Verbal: to understand
3. HV: Did
   MV: enjoy
4. HV: has
   MV: decided
   Verbal: to become
5. HV: has been
   MV: spotted
   Verbal: going
6. MV: refused
   Verbal: to keep

7. HV: must have
   MV: irritated
8. HV: could
   MV: force
   Verbals: Trembling, to forget
9. HV: had
   MV: refused
   Verbal: to print
10. HV: Has
   MV: painted

Page 14:

2. S: Cleopatra
   MV: desires
3. S: Marc Antony
   HV: has
   MV: advised

4. S: asp
   HV: does
   MV: make
5. S: Hortense
   MV: was

Page 15:

2. S: game
   HV: had
   MV: ended
3. S: night
   HV: will
   MV: prevent

4. S: umbrella
   HV: would
   MV: open
5. S: fans
   MV: grabbed

Page 16:

2. S: wind, rain
   MV: were
3. S: Dorothy, Toto
   MV: opened, stared
4. S: Montagues
   MV: hated
   S: McCoys
   MV: despised

5. S: guide
   MV: arrived
   S: Homer, Hortense
   MV: toured

Page 17:

2. S: pile
   MV: was
3. S: he
   HV: Is
   MV: waiting

4. S: unicorns
   HV: are
   MV: hiding
5. S: You (understood)
   MV: Close

Pages 17–18:

2. subject: Usher
   verb: could have repaired
3. subject: Don Quixote
   verb: will forget
4. subject: uncle
   verb: had wanted
5. subject: Wynton
   verb: does want
6. subject: knight
   verb: could remove

7. subject: you (understood)
   verb: ask
8. subject: groundhog
   verb: did see
   subject: spring
   verb: is
9. subject: recipe
   verb: is
10. subject: Hellcat
    verbs: dove, destroyed

Pages 18–19:

Answers will vary. Here are some possible ones.

2. <u>Frances</u> <u>stretched</u> and <u>began</u> to run.
3. <u>She</u> <u>was</u> <u>running</u> along the river.
4. <u>Are</u> <u>you</u> happy?
5. <u>Check</u> for errors.
6. There <u>is</u> the <u>Spam</u>.

7. The <u>aardvark</u> and the <u>marmot</u> <u>ate</u>
   and then <u>danced.</u>
8. <u>Tom</u> <u>had</u> <u>eaten</u> after <u>he</u> <u>arrived</u>.
9. <u>We</u> <u>can</u> <u>run</u>, or <u>we</u> <u>can</u> <u>walk</u>.
10. <u>Faldo</u> <u>could</u> <u>win</u> because <u>he</u> <u>was</u> ready.

Page 26:

2. *Cold* and *rainy* modify *day*.

3. *Steadily* and *reluctantly* modify *walked*.

4. *Powerful* and *eager* modify *goddess*.

5. *Two* modifies *customers,* and *angrily* modifies *argued*.

Page 27:

A.

2. The April dance will be held on Saturday night.

3. Five gray pelicans glided above the busy beach.

4. After their morning paper had been stolen for the third time, Sharon and her husband decided to cancel their subscription.

5. Next October Homer will spend his vacation time in his redecorated barn making a new Spam costume for the Halloween party.

B. Answers will vary. Here are some possible ones.

7. Snow fell from the _{dark} sky and covered our _{front} lawn.

8. Lamont found some _{expensive} items for his collection in the _{antiques} store.

9. The _{snowplow} operator looked at the street full of _{stalled} cars.

10. The _{rising} water flowed over the sandbags and into the _{small} town.

Page 29:

A.

2. When the hare finally awoke, the tortoise had already crossed the finish line.

3. Puff the Magic Dragon usually lived by the sea, but sometimes he missed his home in the mountains.

4. The boxer slowly rose from the canvas and carefully adjusted his teeth.

5. Aeneas sadly remembered his lately departed friend, Dido.

B. Answers will vary. Here are some possible ones.

7. Esteban toured many cities in Europe and _{especially} studied the old cathedrals.

8. Medusa _{carefully} combed her hair before she jumped into the carriage.

9. Anna _{often} visits her father on Sundays.

10. Hortense _{lovingly} gazed into Homer's bloodshot eyes.

Pages 35–36:

A.

2. subject: rhinoceros
verb: charged
subject: he
verb: jumped
conjunction: so

3. subject: Homer
verb: burned
subject: Hortense
verb: admired
conjunctions: or, yet

4. subject: musicians
verb: could play
subject: audience
verb: did seem
conjunction: but

5. subject: weather
verb: has been
subject: we
verb: could hike
conjunction: yet, so

B.

7. but *or* yet

8. and

9. for

10. so

Page 37:

2. because of, near

3. during, by

4. through, without

5. behind, at

Pages 38–39:

A.

2. Prep   Obj
of the first female journalists
Prep   Obj
in the United States

3. Prep Obj
for weeks
Prep Obj
with him

4. Prep   Obj
in the Potomac River
Prep   Obj
of this habit

5. Prep   Obj
to the riverbank
Prep   Obj
into the cold water

6. Prep   Obj
near the shore
Prep   Obj
on his clothes

7. Prep   Obj
toward the bank
Prep   Obj
for an interview

8. Prep   Obj
In spite of his pleas
Prep Obj
to her

9. Prep   Obj
in the water
Prep   Obj
by the determined reporter

10. Prep   Obj
After this incident
Prep   Obj
of Anne Royale's close friends

Page 48:

1. The dalmatian watched the firefighters.
2. The **faithful** dalmatian watched the firefighters.
3. The faithful dalmatian **near the fire hydrant** watched the firefighters.
4. The faithful dalmatian near the fire hydrant **eagerly** watched the firefighters.
5. The faithful dalmatian near the fire hydrant eagerly watched the firefighters **on the truck.**

Chapter Two

Pages 71–72:

2. MC
3. MC
4. N
5. SC
6. MC

7. SC
8. MC
9. SC
10. N

Page 72:

2. PP
3. PP
4. PP
5. SC
6. SC

7. PP
8. PP
9. SC
10. PP

Pages 72–73:

2. (When) Fergal and Rory entered the room, everyone stood.

3. Before the end of the movie, half of the audience had walked out.

4. Good things happen to people (who) are generous.

5. (If) the new software arrives, we will search the Internet.

6. On New Year's Eve, the station showed folk dances (that) were performed around the world.

7. The clock broke after one year (because) it was poorly made to begin with.

8. The teacher looked at the student (whose) poem she was reading.

9. Mr. Rojas decided not to leave the house (until) he had eaten dinner.

10. The officer looked at the house (where) the hostages were held.

Page 74:

2. (Whenever) Calista sees a doughnut shop, she heads the other way.

3. The snow chains fell off (because) they had not been fastened correctly.

4. Admiral Nelson and Captain Aubrey always stand straight (when) the sea battle is raging around them.

5. Clyde Merdly waited (until) Homer had eaten the Spam cordon bleu.

Page 74:

Answers will vary. Here are possible ones.

2. The train could not make it across the mountain because the snow was so deep.
3. When he saw his enemy, King Richard asked for a horse.
4. Because she was expecting a call from her daughter, Sherri checked her answering machine.
5. When Homer and Hortense had finished their dinner, they asked for the leftovers to take home to their dog.

Page 75:

2. Called Pardner, it is especially for people (who) like western movies.

3. It has a snack bar (that) sells beans and jerky.

4. The films, (which) are always westerns, feature stars like John Wayne, Clint Eastwood, Roy Rogers,

   and Gene Autrey.

5. The street (where) the theater is located is next to the stockyards.

Page 76:

Answers will vary. Here are some possible ones.

2. The girl made her yo-yo do many tricks that entertained the audience.
3. Ms. Than, who lives next door, wore a new coat.
4. Euphegenia showed us a picture of her house, which had just been painted.
5. A major battle of World War I took place at Gallipoli, which is near ancient Troy.

Pages 76–77:

2. Desdemona looked for the handkerchief that she had given to her husband. (Adj)
3. One man pretended to bump into the tourist accidentally while the other man picked his pocket. (Adv)
4. Tran stayed in his seat until the lights came on. (Adv)
5. Darby, my Australian shepherd, liked the man who tossed popcorn to her. (Adj)

Page 77:

Answers will vary. Here are some possible ones.

2. The game that Waldo liked was called Flunk. (Adj)
3. When the game started, each player enrolled in college and tried to fail. (Adv)
4. For instance, Waldo, who knew all about failing, stayed out late and didn't show up for classes. (Adj)
5. As the game progressed, other players didn't study and never looked at their books. (Adv)

Pages 84–85:

Answers will vary. Here are some possible ones.

2. A large crocodile waddled into the kitchen.
3. Here are the keys to Ed's heart.
4. On a Sunday Jerald made his decision.
5. Onto the sidewalk fell a deck of cards.

Pages 86–89:

Answers will vary. Here are some possible ones.

2. Portia almost lost the case; however, she saved a pound of flesh.
3. Her future husband was relieved; therefore, he asked her to join him at a restaurant.
4. They were not in the mood for meat, yet they did share a pound of shrimp.
5. The long conflict with Shylock had tired them; therefore, they went straight home from the restaurant.

Page 87:

2. simple:	S: He	V: was stationed, flew	
3. compound:	S: mountains	V: were	
	S: flights	V: were	
4. compound:	S: mountains	V: were	
	S: pilots	V: were called	
5. simple:	S: Flying	V: was	
6. simple:	S: Captain Bush	V: befriended	
7. compound:	S: mongoose	V: had made	
	S: Captain Bush	V: let	
8. compound:	S: mother	V: would send	
	S: he	V: would share	
9. simple:	S: mongoose	V: had	
10. compound:	S: mongoose	V: will kill	
	S: hut	V: was	

Pages 88–89:

Answers will vary. Here are some possible ones.

2. When you arrive, we will go to the zoo.
3. The girl who lives across the street is a champion skateboarder.
4. After he tasted the okra, he ran from the room.
5. We fired the person who cooked the okra.

Page 90:

Answers will vary. Here are some possible ones.

2. I like the person who cuts my hair; he always gives me tips on the stock market.
3. I like the man who cuts my hair; however, he sometimes cuts my hair too short.
4. If we get paid today, we can buy some new clothes, or we can have the stove repaired.
5. My sister who lives in Seattle writes me often, but my sister in Phoenix never writes.

Page 91:

2. simple:	S: story	V: concerns
3. complex:	S: King Minos	V: ordered
	S: who	V: were
4. simple:	S: Theseus	V: accompanied
5. compound:	S: Ariadne	V: was
	S: she	V: fell
6. simple:	S: Ariadne	V: gave
7. compound-complex:	S: Theseus	V: took
	S: he	V: unraveled
	S: he	V: went
8. compound-complex:	S: He	V: would use
	S: he	V: wanted
	S: he	V: would follow
9. compound:	S: Theseus	V: followed
	S: he	V: found
10. complex:	S: he	V: reached
	S: he	V: killed, led

Pages 101–102:

Answers will vary. Here are some possible ones.

2. *fragment:* The bridge in London that fell down.

possible correction: Shakespeare saw the bridge in London that fell down.

3. *fragment:* When Mr. Nguyen found his missing textbook. Hoping the bookstore would take it back.

possible correction: When Mr. Nguyen found his missing textbook, he returned it to the bookstore hoping it would take it back.

4. *fragment:* Because of the hatter's madness.

possible correction: The party was canceled because of the hatter's madness.

5. *fragment:* After Roberto had tried several times to start his car.

possible correction: After Roberto had tried several times to start his car, he called for a tow truck.

6. *fragment:* Probably because they were afraid of him.

possible correction: Gulliver found himself tied down by some little people, probably because they were afraid of him.

7. *fragment:* Yelling for it to wait for him.

possible correction: The bus pulled away from the curb as Adrian raced down the sidewalk after it, yelling for it to wait for him.

8. *fragment:* After he explained how big the fish was.

possible correction: After he explained how big the fish was, the poor little fellow's nose began to grow.

9. *fragment:* To buy the car after saving enough money for a down payment.

possible correction: I couldn't wait to buy the car after saving enough money for a down payment.

10. *fragment:* while rowing across the Styx River.

possible correction: While rowing across the Styx River, Charon forgot everything.

Pages 105–106:

Answers may vary. Here are some possible ones.

2. F   Homer picked up the cow chip and smelled it; then he rejected it.

3. C

4. CS   One day Snow White went off to work in the mine; therefore the dwarves had to clean the house and cook supper.

5. F Each morning Eustace works on his novel. He sits down at his typewriter and writes for two hours.

6. CS The doorbell rang five times; eventually, someone began to bang on the door.

7. F Melvin ate two packages of potato chips a day; even though he knew they were not good for him, he kept on eating them.

8. C

9. F Dr. Frankenstein searched all night; he knew that he would find the body that he needed.

10. CS The Count went to the Bloodmobile. He often had plenty of extra blood to donate.

Chapter Three

Pages 139–140:

2. In the water, Achilles saw his (mother) holding him by one heel.

3. Turning the corner, the (ant) saw a dead aardvark.

4. Dancing across the stage, (Bill) gave his best performance ever.

5. Taught by Aristotle, (Alexander the Great) was a wise ruler most of the time.

6. The (man) injured in the accident was taken to the hospital.

7. Blaise wanted to meet the (woman) giving the lecture on South Africa.

8. Hurt by her remark, (Chris) slowly turned red.

9. Looking through an old locker in the attic, (Kent) found his high school letter sweater.

10. The (harpoon) sharpened on Monday was in the white whale on Tuesday.

Page 141:

2. Beating around the bush, (Polonius) practiced circumlocution.

3. Most of the shoppers were (glad) to buy the Girl Scout cookies from Tomasita.

4. Bored by the tedious speech, the (people) in the audience drifted away.

5. Sherise finally bought a pink and purple (tapestry) to hang in her living room.

6. Sarafina looked for an (outfit) to wear to the graduation.

7. Racing to the end of the rainbow, (Alicia) searched for the pot of gold.

8. Delighted by the success of his music, (Carlos Santana) accepted his award.

9. Staring directly into the camera, the presidential (candidate) gave his best imitation of a sincere smile.

10. Madame Lafarge had a very good (reason) to storm the Bastille.

Pages 149–150:

2. Jason Groves told me about (Gregor Mendel) who discovered the basic laws of genetics.

3. None of the (operators) who answered the phone could speak Lithuanian.

4. (Camelot), which was the center of King Arthur's realm, was usually crowded with (knights) who wanted to become members of the Round Table.

5. Caesarean section is a surgical procedure named after (Julius Caesar) who was supposedly born by that method.

6. The (probe) that was supposed to land on Mars never did send back any signals.

7. The reporter called the actress to find out a (time) when he could interview her.

8. (Mark Twain) who wrote *The Adventures of Huckleberry Finn* took his name from a river measurement.

9. The prize went to the (runner) who came in second because the (one) who came in first was disqualified.

10. Heather grew up in (San Diego) where she spent her summers sailing and surfing.

Pages 150–151:

2. (Mammoth Mountain,) a ski resort in California, did not get much snow this year.

3. Homer and Hortense will be married at the Spam (factory,) the place of their first date.

4. For the reception, Hortense has prepared Spam (artichoke,) a favorite dish of Homer's.

5. (E-bay,) a popular online auction site, allows people to buy and sell almost anything that one might think of.

6. My (neighbor,) one of the rudest persons I have ever met, did not know how to respond when Jonathon called him a yahoo.

7. (A Christmas Carol,) by Charles Dickens, tells the story of (Ebenezer Scrooge,) a rich but ungrateful man.

8. Athlete card (collecting,) once a hobby for boys, has become a popular hobby for people of both sexes and all ages.

9. (Mica,) Jenna's friend from Argentina, will visit her this summer.

10. Shirley Jackson, who wrote *The Haunting of Hill House,* also wrote ("The Lottery,") an unsettling story about a gruesome tradition in a small town.

Pages 151–152:

Answers will vary. Here are some possible ones.
2. The pyrotechnics that we set off started a small fire.
3. The siren woke up the firefighters, and they slid down the pole, which was in the middle of the station.
4. Ichabod Crane, a brave man, listened fearfully to the story about the strange rider.

5. Antigone, a hard-headed young woman, knew her mother would not be hanging around for long.

6. The postal carrier, who was new to the neighborhood, stared at the fierce dog.

7. The people who lived in the building had been evacuated and were watching from a nearby store.

8. One member of the audience stood up on her chair and then kicked the usher who had insulted her.

9. One of the police officers helped the young boy find his mother and father, who were in a restaurant next door.

10. Nero watched the fire, and his dog, a dalmatian, listened to the fiddling.

Page 161:

2. The band leader told her <u>loudly</u> to play her tuba.
   The band leader told her to play her tuba loudly.

3. Correct.

4. The customer who barged into the office <u>angrily</u> demanded to speak to the manager.
   The customer who angrily barged into the office demanded to speak to the manager.

5. After she had <u>almost</u> driven two hundred miles, Hilary was ready to stop.
   After she had driven almost two hundred miles, Hilary was ready to stop.

6. The soldier <u>nearly</u> carried her friend for ten miles before she could find help.
   The soldier carried her friend for nearly ten miles before she could find help.

7. Even though Alejandro had sat before his computer all day, he had <u>merely</u> written three pages.
   Even though Alejandro had sat before his computer all day, he had written merely three pages.

8. My doctor told me <u>frequently</u> to get some exercise.
   My doctor frequently told me to get some exercise.

9. Billie Bob was disappointed at the county fair because his prize pig <u>only</u> received a second-place ribbon.
   Billie Bob was disappointed at the county fair because his prize pig received only a second-place ribbon.

10. Merilee <u>nearly</u> slept twenty hours the night after she ran the marathon.
    Merilee slept nearly twenty hours the night after she ran the marathon.

Pages 163–164:

2. The boy showed the book to his mother <u>that he had found in the thrift shop</u>.
   The boy showed the book that he had found in the thrift shop to his mother.

3. Chuck avoided his teammates <u>worried about the argument he had just had with his wife</u>.
   Worried about the argument he had just had with his wife, Chuck avoided his teammates.

4. The ten-year-old boy showed the bug to his grandmother <u>that had bitten him on his toe</u>.
   The ten-year-old boy showed the bug that had bitten him on his toe to his grandmother.

5. A thirsty vampire stared at the boy <u>with sharp fangs</u>.
   A thirsty vampire with sharp fangs stared at the boy.

6. Arthur sold a house to his brother <u>that had leaky plumbing</u>.
   Arthur sold a house that had leaky plumbing to his brother.

7. Basil caught some fish for his mother <u>with worms</u>.
   Basil used worms to catch some fish for his mother.

8. I gave some treats to the dog near that little boy <u>that sat up, begged, and rolled over</u>.
   I gave some treats to the dog that sat up, begged, and rolled over near that little boy.

9. The monkeys in the cage looked out at the people <u>hanging from limbs by their tails</u>.
   In the cage, the monkeys hanging from limbs by their tails looked out at the people.

10. Mr. Wolfe showed the pig to his grandmother <u>that he had boiled for dinner</u>.
    Mr. Wolfe showed his grandmother the pig that he had boiled for dinner.

Page 165:

2. D

3. C

4. D

5. C

Pages 167–168:

2. <u>Strolling through the museum</u>, the paintings were enjoyed by Darby until she had to leave for lunch.
As Darby strolled through the museum, she enjoyed the paintings until she had to leave for lunch. (Other correct answers are possible.)

3. <u>After running on a hot day</u>, a long soak in the tub is enjoyable.
After running on a hot day, June enjoys a long soak in the tub. (Other correct answers are possible.)

4. Correct.

5. <u>Shouting profanities</u>, Lear's will was changed last night.
Shouting profanities, Lear changed his will last night. (Other correct answers are possible.)

6. <u>Talking nervously to the police officer</u>, Tomas's nose began to itch.
As Tomas talked nervously to the police officer, his nose began to itch. (Other correct answers are possible.)

7. <u>To watch the solar eclipse</u>, sunglasses will protect your eyes.
To watch the solar eclipse, you need sunglasses to protect your eyes. (Other correct answers are possible.)

8. <u>Looking at the horizon</u>, the sun could be seen reflected on the sea.
Looking at the horizon, we saw the sun reflected on the sea. (Other correct answers are possible.)

9. <u>Disgusted by his behavior</u>, an apology was written by Sid.
Disgusted by his behavior, Sid wrote an apology. (Other correct answers are possible.)

10. <u>To become accurate</u>, much practice with the longbow is needed.
To become accurate with the longbow, you need to practice every day. (Other correct answers are possible.)

Chapter Four

Pages 198–199:

2. The **doors were** unlocked.

3. Every Halloween, my **daughter operates** a neighborhood haunted house.

4. A **student** in my class **brings** coffee each morning.

5. The cottonwood **trees** in my backyard **provide** shade in the summer.

Pages 200–201:

2. My new stereo with six speakers (<u>has</u> have) arrived.
   ^S

3. Each mother and child (<u>hopes</u> hope) to be chosen to appear in the movie.
   ^S ^S

4. Courtesy and timely service (<u>improve</u> improves) customer satisfaction.
   ^S ^S

5. Most of the rose bushes in the planter (was <u>were</u>) dying.
   ^S

6. From the beginning of the game, each of the players (<u>was</u> were) playing with enthusiasm.
   ^S

7. Everyone in the church pews (seem <u>seems</u>) to be having a good time.
   ^S

8. The murder of a king and the appearance of his ghost (<u>create</u> creates) interest from the first scene of the play.
   ^S ^S

9. None of the oil from the car (have <u>has</u>) dripped onto your driveway.
   ^S

10. The Potomac, in addition to other famous American rivers, (<u>is</u> are) to be discussed in the program.
    ^S

Page 202:

      S

2. A team of marine scientists (<u>has</u> have) discovered a white whale.

              S

3. Jason is one of the employees who (deserves <u>deserve</u>) a raise.

      S   S

4. Either my roommate or some bold mice (was <u>were</u>) involved in the theft of my Nutrageous bar.

      S   S

5. My daughter in Idaho or my two sisters in Maine (sends <u>send</u>) me some extra money every month.

         S

6. In that society a jury of one's peers (<u>makes</u> make) the decision.

            S

7. The only one of the cars that (<u>interests</u> interest) me so far is the Mazda.

      S   S

8. (<u>Has</u> Have) Mr. Ed or Private Francis said anything to you?

      S

9. The team that makes the most points (<u>loses</u> lose) in that game.

          S

10. Marcela saw one of the actors who (was <u>were</u>) being considered for the part in the film.

Pages 203–204:

      S

2. Five ounces of gold (<u>weighs</u> weigh) the same as the same amount of dirt.

      S

3. Charles's best idea yesterday (<u>was</u> were) pizza for breakfast.

         S

4. Carlos has found that gymnastics (<u>helps</u> help) him get into shape for the season.

      S

5. (<u>Has</u> Have) the measles recently become a problem in your neighborhood?

      S

6. Six thousand feet of bare wall (<u>inspires</u> inspire) the muralist.

      S

7. (<u>Does</u> Do) James always work so efficiently and serenely?

         S

8. There (flies <u>fly</u>) the last geese to leave our lake for the winter.

      S

9. The main problem of this neighborhood (<u>is</u> are) the planes flying over every half hour.

      S

10. Here (<u>lies</u> lie) the last slice of one gigantic pizza.

Page 211:

2. obj		7. sub	
3. sub		8. obj	
4. obj		9. sub	
5. obj		10. obj	
6. sub			

Page 213:

2. me

3. her, him

4. he

5. them

6. him

7. me

8. he

9. I

10. we

Page 214:

2. who

3. who

4. whomever

5. whoever

Pages 214–215:

2. him

3. he

4. her

5. they

Page 215:

2. me

3. she

4. her

5. I

Page 216:

2. she

3. I

4. she

5. whomever

6. him

7. her

8. me

9. whom

10. she

Page 222:

2. Most people know the dentist will be careful, yet **they** can't help but worry when **they** see all the intimidating equipment in the office.

3. When patients see the dentist approaching with that long needle, **they** just want to faint.

4. When I watched my daughter have her first tooth filled, **I** could see that she was terrified.

5. Afterward, she said that the procedure hadn't hurt at all; however, she also said **she** wouldn't want to have another cavity filled.

Page 224:

2. Anyone trying to cross the border was asked for **his** or **her** papers.

3. Sometimes when a person comes home after a long day at work or at school, **he or she** (doesn't) feel like cooking or playing with **his or her** children.

4. The company that improved **its** product the most received an award.

5. correct.

6. A player from Zimbabwe left **her** (or **his**) uniform in the locker room.

7. correct

8. Every time drivers begin a race, **they** should check **their** gauges.

9. Last night somebody down the street could be heard yelling loudly at **her** [*or* his] dog.

10. Either Roberto or Carl needs to see **his** eye doctor.

Pages 226–227:

Answers will vary. Here are some possible ones.

2. Every year Odin and Zeus would meet to discuss Odin's problems with the lesser gods.

3. Whenever Sal called his father, his father yelled at him.

4. Once the doctor had examined the child's injuries and discussed them with the parents, she decided to report the injuries to her supervisors.

5. Michelle put out her cigarette in the ashtray, and then she threw the cigarette away.

Page 228:

Answers will vary. Here are some possible ones.

2. It bothered Bertha that she disliked visiting her in-laws. (Other correct answers are possible.)

3. Peanut shells were all over the floor, and Marie said that she had eaten the peanuts.

4. Dr. Freud's daydream worried him as he smoked his cigar. (Other correct answers are possible.)

5. The last five years have been dry and hot, but this year we have been inundated with rain; I cannot stand such extreme weather changes, so I am moving.

Page 230:

2. After we went swimming, Gill and **I** changed.

3. Mr. Barton told the receptionist that Mrs. Barton and **he** had lost their invitations to the party.

4. Ever since that day in the garden, Adam and **she** had disagreed about apple leaves as a fashion statement.

5. Because we could not afford a contractor, we built our house by **ourselves**.

Page 230:

2. When Vesuvius erupted, Flavius and **she** ran fast.

3. My mother and father worried because my sister had some strange friends when she was in high school. (Other correct answers are possible.)

4. Michelle thanked her grandmother even though **her grandmother** was not a very polite person. (Other correct answers are possible.)

5. When the movie ended, Chris asked Charlie and **me** if we thought Mel Gibson was a convincing Hamlet.

6. Tory wanted to go cycling on Monday, but **his** bicycle was broken.

7. The waiter was angry when Mr. Holcroft refused to pay the bill for his dinner. (Other correct answers are possible.)

8. Lewis and Clark often asked **themselves** if the trip was worthwhile.

9. Duval broke his knee when he accidentally hit the door. (Other correct answers are possible.)

10. Because **Sam** was feeling depressed, he called Edward after dinner.

Chapter Five

Page 257:

2. Bonnie Parker loved Clyde Barrow, but all he cared about was robbing banks.

3. Lancelot loved Queen Guinevere but did not have enough sense to keep quiet about it.

4. Marc Antony loved Cleopatra, so he spent a good deal of time at her place.

5. Beauty loved the Beast for his beautiful soul and for his luxuriant head of hair.

Page 258:

2. An empty can of Coca Cola, two Snickers wrappers, and half of a peanut butter sandwich were all that remained of Oscar's lunch.
3. Betsy tore a hole in the flag, mended it, and then added a new star.
4. The elves could be seen traipsing across the untidy, overgrown lawn.
5. Selena read the complicated, confusing instructions very carefully, for she knew that they held the key to the puzzle.
6. Roger covered the lower part of his face with thick, hot lather, and then he shaved.
7. Correct
8. Maxwell Smart reached for his secret shoe phone, but his shoe had disappeared.
9. Anne flew to Paris, toured the Louvre museum, ate some escargots, bought a beret, and left for Switzerland.
10. The frightening, unexpected news caused Mr. Toad to experience a serious emotional depression.

Page 260:

2. Stuffed with jelly doughnuts and chocolate eclairs, Charlie and Meredith felt just a little woozy.
3. Teetering dangerously at the top of the hill, the large stone might have rolled down and crushed Sisyphus.
4. When you see her the next time, she will have removed that load from her shoulders.
5. In other words, you must resign from your position by midnight tomorrow.
6. Pledging his undying devotion, Popeye asked Olive Oyl to marry him.
7. As Homer read the instructions, Hortense heated up the grease.
8. While standing in line for the concert tickets, Linda met a woman who had recently immigrated from Bulgaria.
9. In fact, the story about the killer zucchinis was just a hoax.
10. To impress Daisy, Jay Gatsby threw his beautiful shirts onto the table.

Page 261:

2. The San Gabriel Mountains, for example, rose five inches during the last earthquake.
3. Homer loved Hortense; therefore, he agreed to change the corn husks in the mattress.
4. He has a cup of tea, I think, every time that he has a difficult decision to make.
5. The person who finishes last, therefore, will not receive any ice cream.

Pages 262–263:

2. My oldest daughter, who is a painter, often uses *Alice in Wonderland* characters in her work.
3. Tranquility Base, which was the name of the first lunar landing site, was established in 1969.
4. Correct
5. *The Awakening,* which was written by Kate Chopin in 1899, was not widely read until years after her death.

Page 263:

2. Virginia's toy poodle, feeling lost and alone, wandered slowly down the street.
3. Leonard Cohen, trying not to show his despair, kept singing in front of the three beautiful women in black.
4. Roxanne, trained always to be polite, tried not to giggle at the sight of such a large nose.
5. The concert was about to begin, and Troy, hoping to play well, closed his eyes in concentration.

Page 264:

2. Perry's father, a retired librarian, swore that he never wanted to see another book.
3. Hamlet did not know what to do about his uncle, the new king of Denmark.
4. The poodle, a popular household pet, was first bred in Germany as a hunting dog.
5. Mammoth Mountain, one of Bill's favorite places to ski, received seven feet of new snow last week.

Pages 265–266:

2. Alphonse was sure that January 18, 1998, would be the day the world ended.
3. Tell me, Candi, where you were in the fall of 1985.
4. Send this order of trout to Harbor House, 2978 South First Street, Seattle, Washington, by noon tomorrow.
5. Chelsea, please close the door to the basement.

Page 266:

2. Gary stood up in the middle of the meeting and said, "Use the force, Luke."
3. *Dracula,* a novel by Bram Stoker, has scared many readers and has been the subject of many movies.
4. Will you please help me with this job, Bartleby?
5. Henry moved into his house next to the volcano on February 5, 1999, and stayed there for two years.
6. Bill was born in a hospital in Knoxville, Tennessee, in 1943 on a warm summer evening.
7. Kenneth suddenly remembered his pet iguana, forgotten in his car two hours ago.
8. The Toronto Blue Jays, Jordan's favorite baseball team, moved into first place last week.
9. The first part of the rafting trip, however, is smooth and safe.
10. Andrea, give your report to Pam, who will read and approve it.

Pages 273–274:

2. Have you seen my new car?
3. Don't touch me, you fiend!
4. Ask Melanie if her back still hurts.
5. Why does everyone keep staring at me and laughing?
6. How does that movie end?
7. Go jump in a lake!
8. After her name were the letters M.D.
9. Has Dr. Payne agreed to treat you?
10. Smithers asked why the bank had closed early.

Page 275:

2. On his list were the following names: Santa Claus, Peter Pan, and Batman.
3. Tessie looked forward to the lottery; however, she did not really want to win.
4. Please pick up these items: Spam, garlic, sherry, flour, and salt.
5. Every night Wilbur had the same dream: he saw himself flying through the air in some strange machine.

Pages 276–277:

2. "Call me Ishmael" are the opening words of what novel?

3. Evanne looked at her teacher and said, "Have a good summer"; then she left the room.

4. Paul kept repeating the following words to himself: "One if by land, and two if by sea."

5. "That last step was quite a surprise," said Peyton Farquhar.

6. "Would you like to hear a riddle?" asked the Sphinx.

7. Andrew stood up in the middle of the crowd and yelled, "Somebody save me!"

8. Where was Neil Armstrong when he said, "That's one small step for a man, one giant leap for mankind"?

9. Ambrose Bierce said, "A bore is someone who talks when you wish him to listen."

10. Tina's team must have won: she was smiling broadly as she entered the locker room.

Pages 278–279:

2. James's car was last seen in front of a local liquor store.

3. Did you enjoy Mel Gibson's role in that movie?

4. The police officer was awarded two months' salary for bravery in the line of duty.

5. Tina's problem was that she didn't know when to quit.

6. It's time to move the baby cockatiel away from its mother.

7. As he rode in the back of his manager's car, the boxer said, "I could've been a contender!"

8. The editor-in-chief's poor judgment cost him a month's pay.

9. Right in the middle of Billy's concert, someone's cell phone started to ring.

10. The three finalists' hotel bills were paid for by our committee.

Page 279:

Answers will vary. Here are some possible ones.

2. Charles's favorite team lost five games in a row.

3. My father-in-law's table saw is ten years old.

4. Some people's houses were destroyed in the flood.

5. Mr. Andrews's car doesn't look like it needs a paint job.

Page 285:

2. "Everyday Use" is the title of a popular short story by Alice Walker.

3. On the table in the car repair shop were copies of <u>Architectural Digest</u> and <u>Psychology Today</u> magazines.

4. Robert Frost's poem "Design" features a fat white spider.

5. Two of his favorite movies are <u>Invaders from Mars</u> and <u>Swamp Thing</u>.

Page 287:

2. E. Annie Proulx won the Pulitzer Prize in 1994 for her novel <u>The Shipping News</u>.

3. Each summer **I** look forward to catching up on reading my old <u>Mad</u> magazines.

4. The Beach Boys' song "The Little Old Lady from Pasadena" is one of my mom's favorites.

5. When Homer had the chance to buy the Brooklyn Bridge, he called Hortense in South Dakota with the good news.

6. Every year Danville sponsors an Easter egg hunt on the Saturday before Easter Sunday.

7. A majority of the people in South Africa used to <u>feel that they did not</u> participate in their government's decisions.

8. Arthur Miller's play <u>Death of a Salesman</u> starred Brian Dennehy when it was last performed on television.

9. As Professor Hohman sat in the airliner, a flight attendant offered her copies of <u>Time, American Pilot,</u> and <u>New Yorker</u> magazines.

10. Next winter we will rent a cabin in Mammoth Lakes, California, which is located north of Lone Pine.

Page 289:

2. Trains from New York will be arriving at **8:00, 8:15,** and **8:32.**

3. For the class party, Suzette bought **10** boxes of plastic knives and forks, **145** paper plates of various sizes, **55** plastic cups, **110** paper coffee cups, and **350** paper napkins.

4. Lisette moved to **115** Normandy Street on March **2, 1999.**

5. Mr. Johnson told **five** of his students to read Act **1,** scene **4** of the play.

Chapter Six

Pages 322–323:

2. rose

3. swum

4. laid

5. sat

6. lying

7. shrunk

8. drunk, sitting

9. sang, raise

10. laid, lay

Pages 332–333:

2. conscience, an

3. accept, effect

4. among

5. disinterested

6. effect

7. all ready

8. all right

9. complement

10. number

11. Our, brake

12. advice, chose

Pages 337–338:

2. fewer, than

3. principal, you're

4. passed, nauseous

5. led, through, lose

6. personnel, their

7. principle, your

8. too, two

9. amount, less, than

10. choose, advice

11. quite, quiet

12. where, were

Page 345:

2. neighbors, relieved
3. believed, friend

4. freight, piece, ceiling
5. ancient, receives

Pages 346

2. angriest, angrier, angrily
3. portrayed, portrays, portraying, portrayal

4. business, busier, busiest
5. employer, employed, employable

Page 347

2. requiring
3. inspiring
4. lovable
5. lovely
6. managing

7. management
8. completely
9. judgment
10. noticeable

Page 348

2. wildest
3. referred
4. proceeding
5. dimmer
6. cleaner

7. committed
8. forgettable
9. happening
10. compelled

Page 349

2. unnatural
3. dissatisfied
4. illegible
5. mistrial
6. immoral

7. misspell
8. irreversible
9. illicit
10. unethical

Page 351

2. monkeys
3. echoes
4. knives
5. matches
6. months

7. kisses
8. stereos
9. candies
10. phenomena

Pages 352–353:

2. a lot
3. athlete
4. behavior
5. brilliant
6. business
7. carefully
8. career
9. competition
10. definite
11. desperate
12. develop
13. different
14. dining
15. describe
16. doesn't
17. embarrass
18. environment
19. exaggerate
20. February
21. fascinate
22. government
23. grammar
24. height
25. immediate

26. interest
27. knowledge
28. mathematics
29. necessary
30. occasion
31. opinion
32. opportunity
33. original
34. particular
35. potato
36. perform
37. perhaps
38. probably
39. ridiculous
40. separate
41. similar
42. sincerely
43. studying
44. surprise
45. temperature
46. Thursday
47. unusual
48. writing

Credits for Readings, Chapter 7

Index